Keeping the Faith

Keeping the Faith

Ordinary People, Extraordinary Lives

a memoir

WAYNE FLYNT

The University of Alabama Press • Tuscaloosa

Copyright © 2011
The University of Alabama Press
Tuscaloosa, Alabama 35487-0380
All rights reserved
Manufactured in the United States of America

Typeface: Minion

∞

The paper on which this book is printed meets the
minimum requirements of American National Standard
for Information Sciences—Permanence of Paper for
Printed Library Materials, ANSI Z39.48-1984.

Library of Congress Cataloging-in-Publication Data
Flynt, Wayne, 1940–
Keeping the faith : ordinary people, extraordinary lives,
a memoir / Wayne Flynt.
p. cm.
Includes bibliographical references.
ISBN 978-0-8173-1754-6 (cloth : alk. paper)
ISBN 978-0-8173-8596-5 (electronic)
1. Flynt, Wayne, 1940– 2. Historians—Alabama—
Biography. 3. College teachers—Alabama—Auburn—
Biography. 4. Alabama—Historiography. 5. Alabama—
Social conditions. 6. Alabama—Politics and government.
7. Education, Higher—Aims and objectives—United
States. 8. Educational change—United States. 9. Auburn
University—Faculty—Biography. I. Title.
E175.5.F59A3 2011
976.1′063—dc22

For all the Flynts, Roddams, Moores, Owens, Nunnellys, Dosses, Duncans, and Cadenheads who have their own stories to tell, and especially for David, Kelly, Sean, Shannon, Dallas, Harper, and Ambrose Flynt, who will both re-ceive these stories and add their own to the treasure of the ages.

Contents

Illustrations

Keeping the Faith

• one •

Ancestors, Real and Imagined

I was born on the fourth of October 1940 at Rayburn's Clinic in Pontotoc, Mississippi, weighing a robust eight and a half pounds. Some cultures put great stock in numerology, believing that dates and numbers affect or even determine destiny. I'm not sure dates are determinative, but I do believe they are important.

The year of my birth divided two of the most important epochs in human history. The Great Depression lay on the back side. The front end would feature the deadliest war in history. Perhaps if my parents had known what was coming, they would have taken the advice of the kindly physician who had warned mother not to have any more children after a daughter was stillborn. The cataclysm of the Great Depression should have been enough for a couple barely out of their teens who knew deprivation firsthand. They also knew war had already erupted in Asia and Europe. My parents' choice to bring new life into the world anyway gave firm evidence of their indomitable spirit and confidence in the future.

Many couples were not so bold. Children born between 1930 and 1945 represent one of the smallest demographic niches in the twentieth century. In addition to smashing the economy, the Depression seemed to have destroyed all hope in the future. As a consequence, my tiny cohort of the population lived our lives in the crease between two optimistic generations, largely ignored by advertisers and purveyors of popular culture. If the generation that followed ours was the baby boomers, ours should have been called the "baby busters." The Big Band music that we loved gave way to rock-and-roll. Movies, clothes, cars, even popular religion, moved in strange and, to us at least, problematical new directions.

Looking into the rearview mirror of history was sobering to me. A Pontotoc County minister wrote President Franklin Roosevelt to describe conditions in his rural parish five years before I was born. Pontotoc County, he wrote, was a land of small farmers, 80 percent of them tenants and nearly all of them in debt. Most received less than seventy-five dollars a year for their cotton after paying off loans. "We as a people have pride," he concluded, "and the landlords have tried to care for the tenants." Though farmers fed families from their fields, they had no money for clothes, medical care, or emergencies. Drought had cut their cotton production by half, and they were desperate. Barely had my parents moved to this forlorn place than they welcomed me into the world.

Mom had complete confidence in Dr. Rayburn and his clinic. But after a difficult delivery, when he announced that she had a "fine baby boy," she could only manage strength enough to inquire whether or not I was pretty. (Would any physician tell a new mother her baby was ugly?) Photographic evidence contradicted his tactful reply. She did not get to hold me because she was sick with malaria. Dad had to write birth announcements while Mother spent a week recovering in the hospital.

Economic necessity required Dad to return to his sales route, and Mom, after a week's visit by her mother, was left alone with me. The only material evidence of the change in their lives was a photograph of me, wearing a hand-made apron, being held by my father and then by my mother beside his Standard Coffee truck.

Flynt-Owens Ancestors

For people so poor, mythic ancestors constituted a treasured legacy. To my father, Flynts were embedded in the history of Great Britain like veins of quartz are embedded in rock. Flint, a Norse word for fine-grained, hard gray rock that when struck produces sparks and shatters into sharp cutting edges, is not only an accurate geological description but also a fine psychological depiction of the people who bore the name. They tended to be hot-headed, their honor easily offended, and their response violent to sharp blows. Much of what I learned about the early Flynts involved their participation in violence of various kinds, beginning with the Hundred Years War between England and France. In 1415,

Mom, Dad, and me (at three months old), photographed separately beside Dad's Standard Coffee Truck, their only means of transportation, in Pontotoc, Mississippi, December 1940. They had no local friends to take a picture of both of them holding me, so they took turns with the camera. Flynt family photo.

the year of the great medieval Battle of Agincourt, King Henry V's army contained an archer named Thomas Flynt.

The largest concentration of Flynts (and also the home of my maternal Roddam ancestors) was an area along the English-Scottish border referred to in British history simply as "the Borders." Prolonged and terrible violence raged through the area of Lancashire and Yorkshire on the English side as well as across the border in Scotland for three hundred years after 1300. This terrain furnished the killing fields for the Wars of the Roses as Yorkists and Lancastrians contested control of England. These counties also straddled the invasion routes along the North Sea through which marauding Scot and English armies tried to control the island. Violence finally became so endemic that the border folk made war on themselves, raping, murdering, and robbing their own people as well as invaders. Called "reivers," the plunderers ranged from the English Midlands as far north as Ayton, turning the terrain into a vast battlefield for three centuries. These wars bred a race of hard, tough people whose blood feuds, desire for revenge, robbery, and mayhem became the norm among every social class from agricultural laborers to gentleman farmers to true nobility. Unemployed professional soldiers, guerrilla forces, professional cattle thieves, and gangsters (the term "blackmail" originated here) organized a kind of rogue state

Thomas, the first recorded Flynt to come to North America, arrived in Jamestown, Virginia, on the ship *Diana,* in 1618. Family tradition traces Thomas's origins to Ayton, Scotland, at the northern edge of the Borders. Ayton is still a lovely village on the North Sea some forty miles east of Edinburgh, with a single traffic light. When fog and mist roll in from the ocean, they obscure details of the town as surely as genealogy confuses the origins of my family. What brought Thomas to Jamestown is uncertain. It was most likely the prospect of riches, although persistent family lore also connects him to scandal (some ecclesiastics accused his priest-father of watering down communion wine and selling the surplus). He partnered with Sir George Northby of Yorkshire to ferry poor Englishmen to Jamestown in his tiny ships, *Diana* and *Temperance,* in return for grants of land, fifty acres per settler. By the late 1620s, Thomas owned a thousand-acre plantation near what is now Hampton, Virginia, and served in the House of Burgesses.

Gradually, some of the Virginia Flynts moved south to Wake County, North Carolina, and from there to Monroe County in central Georgia. By the Civil War my great-great-grandfather John Flynt owned a thirty-two-room mansion at High Falls on the Flint River, farmed a small plantation with ten slaves, and furnished seven sons to the Confederate Army.

My grandfather Julius Homer Flynt entered the world in 1868 amid widespread devastation, closed schools, and Reconstruction violence. Education was a luxury the family could not afford, so he reached adulthood unable to read or write. The death of his father and squabbling among his siblings sent him on his way to Alabama, where he finally settled in Calhoun County. He found work in an iron foundry on Cane Creek, which emptied into the Coosa River near Ohatchee. It was while working there that he met the woman who would become his wife, Annie Phoebe Owens.

Ten years his junior, Annie was the tenth child of Thomas and Reastria Adeline (Addie) Nunnelly Owens. Addie died in childbirth when my grandmother was born, and Thomas soon remarried and fathered eight additional children. My aunt Lillie Mae, the Flynt family storyteller, referred to Annie as "the last Owens in the first batch," as if they were biscuits hot out of the oven. The eighteen Owens children grew up at Greensport in a large house on the Coosa River, where their father tenant farmed and operated a river ferry.

Privacy was beyond the provision of so large a family, so when Granddad courted Annie, he did so in the presence of many of her siblings. When he finally transported her away in a borrowed buggy to their humble wedding, her parents and siblings lined the porch to wave their best wishes. As he turned a curve in the road that carried them beyond the prying eyes of his future in-laws, Homer leaned over to kiss his fiancée. Annie, startled by his presumption, slapped him "good and hard." As Lillie Mae explained, "Why he just thought he had it made." The new couple settled into the routine of sharecropping, moving on average every 2.4 years until finally settling in the tiny hamlet of Shady Glen.

Moore/Roddam Ancestors

Felix (Pop Fee to his grandchildren) Maxwell Moore, my maternal grandfather, came from a modest family of obscure ancestry. His father died young, leaving his mother, Amanda, to manage a farm of fifteen acres with her young sons. Like the Flynts, they lived in a two-room cabin with an open breezeway or "dog trot" connecting the rooms. Life was hard for most everyone in Alabama, but it was especially challenging for a widow with seven small boys on a hardscrabble farm. Fee was the most academic of the seven, finishing high school between farm seasons and odd jobs. He was a prodigious reader and champion worker of crossword puzzles. After graduation, he taught school while commuting to nearby Howard College, a Baptist school in the Birmingham suburb of East Lake, where he completed a degree in education in 1924. Certified as a teacher, he followed that profession for fifteen years.

Like so many southern men of his class and time, Granddad drank too much, which cost him his teaching career. Reports of his drinking circulated in the Clay community where he was school principal. He confirmed the rumors by showing up drunk for a school trustee meeting. They fired him on the spot, though he tried to preserve his dignity by telling them: "I'm damned glad you fired me because I was about to quit anyway."

That firing ended his fixed occupation and propelled him into a series of short term jobs: carpenter; filling station attendant; rural mail carrier; Pinson's

postmaster; vegetable salesman at the Birmingham farmer's market; WPA camp
guard; elevator operator; owner of a country store on the corner of Sweeny
Hollow Road and the Pinson–Center Point highway. He was also politically
astute and a fiercely partisan Democrat who loved Franklin Roosevelt. Among
his many friends he counted New Deal congressman George Huddleston of
Birmingham and a fellow member of Pinson Baptist Church, who used his office as county commissioner to obtain a Depression-era job for Pop Fee operating an elevator at the Jefferson County courthouse.

Though Mom was embarrassed by his local reputation as a drunk, she also
recognized the degree of difficulty that his life entailed and his service to the
Pinson community. He and other men hauled rocks from Turkey Creek to
build their house, the Baptist church, and Pinson elementary school. He was
baptized in the creek next to the Baptist church.

I remember Pop Fee as proprietor of Moore's Store, built in 1938 after mother
married and left home. He sold his rock house on Highway 79 in the late 1930s
for $7,000, enough to buy land at the crossroads intersection and construct a
two-story building with service station/store on the bottom floor and living
space in the upper. Glass display cases seduced children with a dozen varieties
of candy. A large section of tree attached to legs provided a block on which he
cut meat. A stove toward the middle of the store invited men to sit on apple
crates and upturned wooden Coca-Cola cases to talk while devouring Vienna
sausages, sardines, and crackers. I remember my wonder at the stylish way
Granddad rolled cigarettes with one hand, opening the tobacco pouch with
his teeth, pouring some of the contents into his paper, rolling it, and licking
the edge of the paper to seal it.

Beneath the counter that housed his tall metal cash register, Pop Fee stored
row upon row of small account books in shoe boxes, each book with a family
name written on the spine. Inside the books he recorded credit accounts, sometimes paid when farmers made their cotton crops in the fall, but often left un-
paid when crops failed and tenant farmers moved off into the night, debts forgotten as quickly as the names of the communities they abandoned. Granddad
was known for his easy credit and sympathetic ear for a tale of woe, which is
the reason he never made much money. He operated the store seven days a
week, with Sunday mornings the gathering time for white male customers to
sit on boxes beside the stove and ruminate about politics and sports while their
womenfolk and children attended church.

At age thirty-five, Pop Fee married eighteen-year-old Shirley Belle (Bell
in some records) Roddam. In Mom's opinion, the further back in history you

went, the better the Roddams got. They claimed pretentious origins, which may have contributed to their animosity toward my grandfather. Their ancestral home was a castle in the village of Roddam, located in Northumberland County, England, in the shadow of the Cheviot Hills that formed the border between England and Scotland. Part of the contested English Borders, the area was the wild and lawless equivalent of the land south of Ayton, Scotland, from which the Flynts came.

The Roddams made unwise choices both in politics and religion. Sir John Roddam died in the Battle of Towton, the bloodiest ever fought on English soil, fighting a losing cause for the House of Lancaster against the House of York. Late in the following century, Robert Roddam was persecuted for his "papist" beliefs. The family's Catholicism in a country trending Protestant, the triumph of the House of York in the Wars of the Roses, and the general mayhem and anarchy of these centuries triggered a Roddam exodus to America. Matthew Roddam became the first of his family to move to the New World, settling in the Roman Catholic colony of Maryland a few decades after Thomas Flynt arrived in Jamestown.

Other Roddams landed in Charleston, South Carolina, toward the end of the eighteenth century from whence they made their way to Mobile, Walker County, and Pinson, Alabama. Like the Flynts, Roddams furnished many soldiers to the Confederacy. By the 1890s they had settled on Sweeny Hollow Road in Pinson.

My maternal great-grandfather John (Papa John as he was known unaffectionately by my mother and her siblings) was a hot-tempered scoundrel. He made his living buying, selling, and trading cattle, and spilled his own seed as promiscuously as the bulls he sold. Papa John married Sarah Elizabeth Self in 1894 but was no more faithful to her than he was to his three succeeding wives (or perhaps four). Sarah bore him seven children, one of whom was my grandmother Shirley. Sarah's sister came to help with the pregnancy and wound up pregnant herself by her brother-in-law. Her child was the first of at least three "outside" children, as the family referred to them, but there may have been more. Papa John may or may not have married his longtime mistress Carrie J. Spraul, a married and successful businesswoman.

Shirley Belle Roddam Moore (Mama Moore to the grandchildren) was as tough as Pop Fee was gentle. The closest she came to being a dainty southern belle was at birth when she was given that distinction as a middle name. Perhaps with such a sentimental, alcoholic husband, she had no choice. But her family prepped her well in the ways of a harsh world even before she mar-

"Papa" John Roddam, my maternal grandfather, and his obviously adoring mistress Carrie Spraul. Flynt family photo.

ried. Just to survive as a female member of the Roddam family required that a woman be strong as iron. And she was. Homer Roddam murdered a man at a honky-tonk. Roddy Roddam (whose motto mother described as better to "make a dishonest dollar than an honest one") owned an auto junk yard that allegedly fronted for stolen cars. He was killed by a Birmingham police officer after threatening to take influential people to jail with him if convicted of auto theft. James H. (Jim) Roddam served jail time for shooting a man and later stole a safe from a whiskey store. He and his sons supposedly operated an auto theft ring as well.

My favorite Roddam story involved Mama Moore's 1949 Chevrolet, which she proudly purchased late in life after learning to drive. Late one night as she was reading a magazine, she heard her car engine start. By the time she opened the door, the thief was driving off. She believed until she died at age eighty that one of her Roddam cousins had stolen her car. And when she used her insurance money to buy a blue and white Buick, she chained the car to the store to prevent repetition of the crime.

Then, of course, there was her philandering, adulterous father, Papa John. Once he loaned Pop Fee money to buy vegetables from farmers in order to sell them at the county market. Instead, Granddad got drunk and either spent the money on whiskey or was robbed (alternative versions of the story). Pop Fee was sitting in a chair when he admitted losing the money. Papa John flew into a rage and began beating my drunken grandfather while his children screamed. Mom, only nine or ten at the time, tried to restrain Papa John, but he pushed her down. Granddad's face was swollen and lacerated from the beating. "I just hated him," Mom told me, the only time I ever heard her use those words about a person. She neither forgot nor forgave. When Papa John died, Mama Moore called her to relate details of the funeral. Mom refused to attend.

Mama Moore's life was not easy either. A school dropout after eighth grade, she supplemented family income by sewing clothes for women in the Pinson community and making her daughters' dresses. (During the Depression, she sewed them from flour and feed sacks.) At night she worked at a bakery; during the day she ran a boarding house. Later she worked in the family's store. In her leisure time, she would crochet, embroider, play her pump organ, and read (mainly "pulps" such as *True Story, Modern Romance,* and *True Detective* magazines).

Two years after her marriage she bore the first of five children. Curt, her second child, became mother's lifelong project. He protected her when they were children, and she reciprocated when they were grown. A skilled carpenter and contractor, Curt left a legacy of finely constructed houses and businesses across Pinson. He was, like his father, an honest, decent man with a drinking problem. He fought his own special demons, not always successfully. Once while attending Pinson school, Curt (already a muscular athlete) whipped a fellow student. The boy had made the mistake common to fifth graders of teasing a child with problems. Curt was a mediocre student with a speech impediment. Finally, he had suffered enough verbal abuse and turned on his tormentor. After school when Mom heard about the fight, she searched frantically for her brother to see if he was hurt. She was horrified to find him tied to the flagpole in front of the school. She ran home crying and told her mother what had happened. The two of them raced to the school where Mama Moore confronted the principal. She questioned his judgment and denounced his punishment. How dare he punish a boy for fighting when the child was the victim of endless harassment and teasing. And to tie him to a flagpole in front of the entire community only multiplied his humiliation. "If you ever touch my child again," Mama Moore raged, "I'll beat the hell out of you." No one who knew her doubted for a moment that she would have carried out her threat.

Curt's three oldest children—Patricia (Pat), Arthur Curtis (Arthur), and Jack Alfred (Toot, born December 7, 1941; it was Curt who delivered the message to Mom that he had a new son and that Pearl Harbor had been attacked) — became three of my closest companions.

The birth of Ina, Mom's little sister, was a source of pure delight for my mother. The adorable baby with blond, curly hair was like a doll to her three-year-old sister, and they remained close, lifelong friends. During the Second World War, Ina married the boy next door, Leo Hagood. Their four children (Jan, Joan, Leo, and Rex), together with Curt's three oldest children, became the surrogate friends largely absent from my life because of our nomadic wanderings.

The distance from Ayton and Towton to Shady Glen and Pinson was enormous, both in miles and psychic shock. The optimism of migration, increasing prosperity, and social status before the Civil War gave way to social disintegration, declining fortunes, and debilitating poverty by the 1930s. In ways I did not understand at the time, all these family stories made a permanent impression on me as a boy growing up. I would spend much of my fifty-year career as a historian trying to reconstruct the lives of southern poor whites, to narrate the travails of their lives, and to win for them a respectful hearing. Paralleling my professional career, my avocation and divine calling involved various crusades on behalf of justice for the poor, both black and white. As my own family saga revealed, their story was complex.

Dad

My father was a perfect storm of a man. It always seemed appropriate to me that he was born on April 9, 1917, three days after the United States declared war on Germany. James Homer Flynt Jr. carried the DNA of his ancestors. He instinctively gave off sparks when struck. And life struck him early and often. Dad was opinionated, hot-tempered, emotional, occasionally profane, prideful, and possessed a sense of family honor that often got him into trouble.

Dad was also generous, friendly, never met a stranger, loved to talk, possessed an incredible memory (he recalled his exact salary in every job he had, and there were lots of them), told the best stories, got over his fits of temper as quickly as he became angry, and possessed an encyclopedic collection of one-sentence aphorisms.

In his early years, his temper led to fights. In his middle years he excused his tantrums as a result of the chronic pain of his childhood osteomyelitis. But his siblings, who did not share his pain, did share his temper. When in a rage, Dad was not to be trifled with. What he often said about his brothers was equally true of him: "He would just as soon hit you as look at you." Though he was not "bad to drink," as we say in the South, when he drank, he was bad. Not bad only in the sense that his temper could get the best of him even quicker than usual, but bad in that he became silly and embarrassing. The morning after, he was morose and withdrawn.

Despite his foibles and flaws, he was a wonderful father: protective, loving, generous, industrious, smart, a superb salesman, absolutely loyal to his family. The seventeenth-century poet George Herbert could have had Dad in mind when he wrote that "one father is more than a hundred schoolmasters."

Dad was powerfully influenced by family, beginning with his parents and extending to his siblings. Technically speaking, his name was misleading. He was not really J. H. Flynt Jr. He had the same initials as his father but a different first name. Granddad's J stood for Julius; Dad's J was for James. Both were known as "Homer" most of their lives. That two men so crippled by lack of formal education should have borne the name of an eighth-century-BC Greek epic poet/historian struck me as either shameless chutzpah, classic American aspiration, or serious misidentification. Poetry was not their gift.

After Granddad married Annie Phoebe Owens on August 4, 1901, they began the new century committed to the biblical injunction to replenish the earth. Granddad left foundry for farm, and Annie recorded the births of their eight children on the first page of their family Bible in simple, imprecise handwriting. My dad, the eighth child, was born on April 9, 1917.

Physically, they were not a matched set. Granddad was tall, standing six-feet-five in an age of short men. Raw-boned and burned brown by the sun, he was awkward and clumsy except around farm implements and livestock. Annie (when Granddad was angry with her, he called her Phoebe) was a short, strong, chubby woman with a cherubic face. Like her husband and children, she worked hard in the fields, hoeing, chopping, and picking cotton. Despite her nearly continuous pregnancies, she never missed working a cotton season. She would carry the youngest baby to the field, deposit it under a shade tree with the oldest daughter, and take her place in the long rows of cotton.

It's a good thing her husband was cuddly and loving because she was not.

My paternal grandparents, aunts, and uncles. *First row (l–r):* Annie Phoebe Owens Flynt, Julius Homer Flynt; *second row (l–r):* Ann, Ora, and the family historian, Lillie Mae; *back row (l–r):* Jake, Boyd, Claude, Walter, and my father, James Homer Flynt. Flynt family photo.

Nor was she demonstrative except to Dad, whose illness made him a special case. She ignored housekeeping for fishing in Cane Creek, sewing, making white oak cotton baskets or chair bottoms, wandering in the woods with her children, throwing sticks to knock down English walnuts and hickory nuts. She would cut down cedar trees from which she whittled wooden plates and goblets, and she made wooden toys for the children. As Lillie Mae explained, "She could sit and whittle and let her house go. Now you never would do all of this if you were in the house cleaning 'cause you can find [something to do] in the house all the time. The house didn't bother her."

The world in which Dad grew up was pastoral but far from idyllic. It consisted roughly of twenty square miles, from Alexandria in the northeast quadrant of Calhoun County to Ohatchee in the northwest, with the southern boundary stretching from Oxford to Eastaboga. The Coosa River flowing south from Gadsden constituted the western edge of the Flynt domain; the White Plains valley and beyond that the Talladega National Forest, its eastern extremity. Calhoun County in the foothills of the Appalachian mountains was a place of alluring beauty and abject poverty.

The name Shady Glen imperfectly described the primary location of Dad's childhood. It was a secluded valley at the base of Gooseneck Mountain, so called for a long bend in the Coosa River that bent like a goose's neck. Its geographical isolation was broken by two roads that intersected the valley. The main east-west road ran from Anniston to Macon's Quarter on the Coosa River; the principal north-south road stretched from Greensport-Ohatchee to Eastaboga on the Birmingham highway. Once a year Granddad paid a tax of six dollars or eight days of labor to maintain the dirt roads.

Where the roads intersected in the community of Shady Glen, a three-teacher elementary school containing grades one through eight (by the time Dad began school, it met for seven months, beginning after cotton picking in October) occupied one corner and a church another. The preacher also frequently served as principal or teacher at the school.

The Bell place near Shady Glen, which Dad most vividly remembered and where he lived from age ten until he left home at nineteen, consisted of several hundred acres, although his family conducted intensive cotton cultivation only on about twenty. A breezeway in their dog trot house divided twenty-foot square rooms, each with eighteen-foot ceilings. The breezeway provided tolerable coolness in summer when the wind blew but froze them during wintertime.

Charles Bell, president of Commercial National Bank (his son Charlie Jr. would intersect our lives later as pastor of Parker Memorial Baptist Church in Anniston) was a kindly Christian banker who befriended my grandfather and treated him decently throughout their sharecropper-landlord relationship. When Granddad initially refused to sharecrop for Bell because the farm contained no water, the banker had a well dug. Every spring Granddad would drive a wagon into Anniston and negotiate a loan for seed and fertilizer based on nothing more than a handshake. Every fall he returned to the bank to pay his loan in full.

With most of his sons gone by the 1930s and Homer a worn-out farmer of nearly seventy, Dad and his brother Walter, together with their sister Ann, labored hard in the fields. They produced twelve to fifteen bales of cotton a year by the mid-1930s (a maximum annual income of $300 to $375 to support themselves and their parents). After they borrowed money for seed and fertilizer from the bank, they could afford no more than 100 to 150 pounds of fertilizer, far less than they needed. After paying their fertilizer bill, there was precious little left for coffee, sugar, and other necessary foodstuffs, much less for clothes and shoes. But even this meager existence was a step up from what they had known before. At the other places where they had sharecropped, the owner had taken one-third of the cotton and one-fourth of the corn they grew.

Most anything could interrupt the rhythm of rural life: a visit, journey, tornado, flood, fire, injury, or illness. For Dad, the most important interruption took the form of an ax blade. A glancing blow while chopping firewood left no more than a small gash usually healed with kerosene to kill the germs, my grandmother's favorite remedy for cuts in a world where boys grew up mostly barefoot. She followed that with a poultice of red clay and vinegar to draw out the soreness. Most times the home remedies worked. This time they did not.

Dad was twelve and the year was 1929. It was a bad year for America. It was an even worse year for my father.

Osteomyelitis is an infection of bone marrow caused by a bacterium. The infection quite literally kills the bone by destroying the blood that circulates through tiny passages. Drainage from the bone never stopped, and slivers of dead bone as much as an inch and a half long would sometimes break off and migrate through his skin to the surface. Any hit or bruise could reactivate the disease. At first doctors did not diagnose the condition correctly. When they did, there was no cure short of amputation. Not until the advent of sulfa drugs and penicillin during the 1940s was there a regimen to treat osteomyelitis.

Meanwhile, Dad suffered horribly. His mother would sit up all night, singing to him and applying towels so hot they blistered her hands. When the hot compresses did not ease the pain, she had no recourse save promises. When he recovered, she told him, she would save her egg money and buy him a little red wagon and a bulldog, and they would go to Missouri. Dad lost the entire fifth grade and most of the sixth to osteomyelitis. He walked on crutches for a year and a half. For the next fourteen years, his legs drained and excreted bone.

Disaster befell the entire community in the autumn of Dad's injury. Falling agricultural prices, bank failures, and the stock market panic brought the tinsel economy of the 1920s crashing down. As we talked one day a half century later, Lillie Mae captured the legacy of those years that the locusts claimed:

"I . . . know that the life that we had to live, the hardships that we had to en-
dure, and the nothingness that we had to work with helped to strengthen those
feelings that we have even now, of being conservative with every little thing. I
throw nothing away nor destroy anything that's edible nor allow . . . the children to be wasteful. But I know without having a background of that type . . .
you wouldn't know these things and wouldn't know how to manage or how to
make ends meet. . . . I think experience is the best teacher in the world. And as
I grew up, it was strictly hard."

Dad learned the same lessons though he expressed them less poetically. He
never threw anything away. Not rolls of string or nails or scrap lumber. Not
surplus roofing material, carpet remnants, or worn out tires. If he ever owned
it, he still had it when he died, stored in a long, concrete block building once
occupied by chickens. Who knows, he often reminded me, when you might
need that very thing.

By the time I finished hours of interviews with him, Dad had reinvented the
Great Depression. His family was poor, true enough, but so was everyone in
Shady Glen. Life was hard, but it had always been hard. It was also simple and
elemental. Families were strong and close. His father was a respected community leader despite his poverty and lack of education. By the 1970s, in a world
characterized by disintegrating families, dissatisfaction with life, disloyal employees and company contempt for them, child delinquency, confusion about
moral absolutes, and inadequate public schools, Dad's narrative of the Depression had subtly changed, and the worst of times began to seem like the best of
times.

As Dad's osteomyelitis slowly improved, he returned to school, far behind
his classmates but determined to catch up. In 4-H Club he learned to grow
peanuts in order to diversify farm income. His father implemented the experi-
ment to good effect. Dad was a bright, quick learner who enjoyed school until
an incident midway through eleventh grade ended his formal education. He
had already purchased his 1938 senior ring at Ohatchee High School when he
and his best friend, Hoyt McCulloughs, flirted with two giggling girls who sat
across the aisle from them. Dad's feet were in the aisle as usual because it was
difficult to cram his lanky six-foot frame into the desk he shared with McCulloughs. When his biology teacher entered the room to cacophonous noise and
tripped over Dad's feet, she ordered him out of the room and into the hall until
class ended. He didn't like history, his next class, anyway, so instead he went
outside to sit on the school steps. The next day his teacher would not let him
into the classroom until he apologized to the students. He refused, explaining

I conducted many oral history recording sessions about my dad's family life during the Great Depression. His stories were the genesis of my book *Poor but Proud*. Courtesy Sean Flynt.

that the class didn't order him out of the room. He had offended her and he had apologized to her, but he had not offended them. She sent him to the principal's office, where he was expelled. He left that day and did not return until half a century later when he was invited back to an Ohatchee alumni reunion. Thus he joined his four brothers as a school dropout. Dad pretended that he felt no hurt from the expulsion. But he wore that Ohatchee senior ring until the inscription "Class of 1938" was worn away.

It seemed a good time to leave Shady Glen for new surroundings. He and his brother Walt packed their meager belongings into their 1929 roadster on February 6, 1937, and headed to Pinson. They lived with their sister Lillie Mae Beason and her husband, Ferris, on a twenty-five-acre farm on the Old Bradford Road just off Highway 79, which ran through Pinson from Birmingham to Huntsville.

Five days a week between February and April, the two brothers rode with their brother-in-law to his job at Virginia Bridge Steel Company. They stood outside the factory gates in the numbing cold, snow, and rain with two hundred to three hundred other men hoping to be among the three or four chosen by the foreman about 9:00 a.m. Day after day they were rejected, boarded a streetcar, rode to the end of the line at Eighty-fifth Street, then hitched a ride back to Pinson, only to start over again the next morning. One morning, when trees began to display their springtime foliage, the foreman called out their names. They were put to work fitting steel girders and trusses for water gates on Tennessee Valley Authority dams. Dad caught red hot rivets in a cone-shaped container as they were thrown to him for insertion into the girders. He began working for 27 cents an hour ($14.99 a week), which seemed like a fortune compared to his income on the farm.

At first the plant was nonunion, but the Congress of Industrial Organizations (CIO) soon changed that. Dad never cared much for unions, but he joined anyway and stood a picket line with his brother during a bloody strike. Virginia Bridge hired dirt-poor farmers from Blount County as strike-breakers, bringing them to work on trucks escorted by sheriff's deputies. One day as Dad warmed himself before a roaring fire in a big drum on the picket line, he saw many picketers he did not recognize.

When the 4:00 p.m. shift ended, the factory gates swung open, disgorging the trucks led by their police escorts. Dad and Walt noticed the unidentified picketers move quickly into cars and fall in behind the convoy. The curious Flynt brothers followed. As soon as the trucks crossed the Jefferson County line on Highway 75 bound for Oneonta, the sheriff's cars turned back. When they left, a carload of men (later identified as United Mine Workers) sped by the trucks and stopped diagonally across the road, blocking the trucks. Other cars blocked retreat from behind. Men spilled out of cars, armed with baseball bats and ax handles, the prelude to what Dad described as "the damnedest fight I ever saw." Dad and Walt watched in horror from the safety of a hillside, their loyalties torn between the desperate, poor, dirt farmers, like themselves only months earlier, and their desire for higher wages and better working conditions at the plant.

The sight of so many bloodied men was sickening. And the frequent strikes, lockouts, and layoffs convinced Dad that this was no life for him. Besides, he was sick of living with his sister and brother-in-law. Furthermore, he had met the girl of his dreams.

Mae Ellis Moore was a tall, slender seventeen-year-old with eyes as blue as the sky. She was, to quote Dad, "as cute as a pup under a red wagon." She and her sister Ina made a habit of sitting on the front porch of their house beside Highway 79 after school each day, waving at boys who passed by on the way home from factory shifts in Birmingham. By then the brothers had sold their

1929 roadster and paid $753 for a snappy-looking 85-horsepower four-door Ford, which they alternated driving on weekend dates.

Though mother's sister Ina had originally flirted with Dad, and Mom had preferred Walt, all four switched preferences after their first double date. Walt and Ina dated only a few times, but Dad fell in love almost from the moment he and Mom were formally introduced at a revival at Pinson Baptist Church, which both Mae Ellis and Lillie Mae's family attended.

My maternal grandmother opposed all her children's marriages, so as soon as Mom reached the age of eighteen and graduated high school, she and Dad eloped. He was laid off at Virginia Bridge several months after his marriage, so he had plenty of spare time (with the assistance of his brothers) to build a house on five acres of land he bought below the crest of Oak Mountain south of Birmingham.

Complications arose when Mom became pregnant and was unhappy in their rural isolation. She had to carry water from a neighbor's well because they had none. Dad's long shifts on the other side of Birmingham left her alone most of the day in an area so primitive that she said they were "just like wild cats in the woods." As time approached for the birth, she insisted that they move closer to her doctor in Tarrant City.

When my sister was stillborn, strangled in her umbilical cord, Dad put his land on Highway 280 up for sale. He and his brothers dismantled the house and moved it near Anniston on Buttermilk Road for their parents. It was the only house they ever owned and the place where they would die.

Dad, who had decided the cyclical steel industry held no long-term future, took a job selling burial insurance. He had found his calling. Over the years, Dad developed a full-fledged philosophy of salesmanship. Although he had brief sales training in each job and several weeks of management training by Swift and Company, he always sold according to his instincts.

Dad's most elemental sales principle was simple, "There is more in managing than in making." The aphorism had a double meaning. Managing money is more important than making it. And the salesman matters more than the product. Like the legendary Willy Loman in Arthur Miller's play *Death of a Salesman,* Dad believed that he could sell anything. Unlike Willy, Dad *could* sell anything. Miller's play was perhaps the greatest tragedy ever written about an ordinary man and the universal need to leave a "thumbprint somewhere on the world," a need for a common person's immortality through memory. Dad left his thumbprint large and clear on almost everyone he met.

"Back in those days when I started selling," he once confided to me, "you had to sell. You didn't just take orders." The key to selling was persuading a customer to try your product. Prompt, attentive service and fair treatment by the salesman were imperative. Dad didn't wait for stores to inventory his products. He determined when they were nearly out and reordered for them. "If a customer didn't like you," he recounted, "he might handle your product, but he would make your life hard."

Storytelling was his stock and trade. He preferred to wait until a customer was alone, when he could fully develop his craft. Dad's repertoire of stories, jokes, and aphorisms originated on the farm at Shady Glen and gained new components through the years. Blessed with nearly total recall his whole life, he also had a talent for mimicry and a flawless sense of timing. And he never forgot a punch line. Most of his stories had some connection to the Depression era common to almost all his small town customers.

He was also renowned for his aphorisms (I called them "Dadisms"). Buck Cherry, who was "wild as a Texas jack-rabbit," became his best friend in Birmingham. At six feet five inches tall, Cherry drank as well as he danced and fought. Astride his motorcycle, Buck would meet Dad at honky-tonks, where he entertained patrons with energetic buck dancing and knock-down fights. One night an argument began over who was the better man. The entire clientele followed the two combatants to a bluff overlooking the falls on Turkey Creek where Cherry won the exchange of blows. The men then shook hands and cleaned the blood off their bodies in the creek. Cherry gave his opponent a clean shirt and they parted friends. Dad explained that "Old Buck Cherry would get up and leave food on the table to fight."

Other aphorisms covered nearly every occasion. When speaking of thrifty people, Dad described them as "tight as bark on a tree." Or "Old Roy was tight. He'd skin a dang flea for his hide and tallow." Describing a female cousin who talked too much, Dad told me: "She could talk the horns off a billy-goat." People he did not like were "lower than a suck-egg dog." When they got their comeuppance, it "broke them from sucking eggs." A good putdown inspired Dad to exclaim, "I wouldn't slam a door in the man's face that hard." Speaking of the best syrup maker in Shady Glen, he said, "When Old Man Ben Lloyd made sorghum syrup, it was so clear you could read a newspaper through it." "Back in the Depression," Dad once reminisced, "a quarter was big as a wagon wheel."

After a brief stint in 1939 selling burial insurance, Dad went to work for Standard Coffee Company and moved to Pontotoc, Mississippi. Having seldom been outside the borders of Alabama, he had misgivings about the move

Dad in Pinson, 1936, seated on a motorcycle behind his best friend, Buck Cherry, who was renowned for his drinking and fighting. Flynt family photo.

to Pontotoc, a tiny county seat of a few thousand people. The move in February 1940 brought him to a poor white farm area in the clay hills near Tupelo that had experienced three consecutive years of drought and crop failure. Furthermore, Standard Coffee sold a two-pound-twelve-ounce bag of coffee for a dollar. Housewives could buy a pound of Eight O'Clock coffee at the A&P for fifteen cents. The challenge was daunting. But as Dad explained, "that was what made a good salesman, to be successful under them conditions."

When they moved from Bessemer to Pontotoc, Mom quit her job in a dime store to prepare for my birth. They rented a two-room apartment in a fine brick home on the Tupelo highway. Dad described Mrs. Robinson, the widow who owned the house, as part of the "silk stocking" society of Pontotoc (which must have been pretty small in 1940). When Dad had a bad month and was sent a caged goose as a booby prize, Mrs. Robinson "like to run me off. Made us move almost, because that goose . . . would holler just like a mule braying and she finally told me I was either gonna have to get rid of the goose or move, one or the other."

Most of the week Dad was on the road in his company van, which was their only source of transportation. He would spend two nights in New Albany, Mississippi, at the far end of his route, and other nights closer to Pontotoc. On weekends he was home and tried to park his van in inconspicuous places so as not to alert neighbors that his landlady had taken in boarders due to her declining fortunes. I was born in October, and Dad vowed to relocate his family to Alabama. In thirteen weeks, he had doubled sales on the Pontotoc route, so when he requested a transfer, company officials were eager to accommodate him.

During the winter of 1941, Dad took a route from Birmingham south to Alabaster in Shelby County. But he became furious when he discovered that other salesmen made nearly twice what he made and quit. Always ambitious for a higher salary, he went to work for Brown Service Insurance Company early in 1942 selling burial insurance. He more than tripled his salary, making sixty dollars a week plus commissions. Brown Service sent him to Sheffield on the Tennessee River, where cheap TVA power and booming war industries had brought prosperity. His job involved house-to-house solicitation and weekly collection of small payments from working-class whites and blacks anxious to secure a decent burial. The frugal young couple managed to save $4,200 in a little more than a year, enough to pay cash for a $3,600 house they wanted to buy. Then, suddenly, his osteomyelitis returned.

Unfortunately, the burial insurance salesman had no health insurance. Dad went to John Sherrell, an orthopedic surgeon in Birmingham who warned that he could lose both legs. The urgency of the diagnosis sent the confident, fun-loving salesman into a tailspin. He quit his job, moved Mom and me into his parents' house on Buttermilk Road, and prepared for the fight of his life.

Mom found work as a clerk at Anniston Ordnance Depot, and Dad embarked on a series of operations (the first on his twenty-sixth birthday) that would determine whether or not his legs would have to be amputated. His nerves shattered both by anxiety and pain, Dad, for the only time in his life, drew into a shell. Mom would sometimes hear him sobbing in the bathroom. When she tried to comfort him, he worried how his wife and toddler would survive if he lost his legs.

But he didn't. Despite long, ugly scars on both legs and lifelong pain from recurring bouts of osteomyelitis, sulfa drugs controlled the infection, and he was able to return to work in seven months. The money they had saved, together with a loan from Mom's parents, paid his hospital bills. Dr. Sherrell accepted monthly payments for his charges. Dad returned to work for Brown Service in Gadsden, as poor as when he and Mom had married five years earlier.

Mom and Dad in 1943 at a pivotal point in their marriage. Dad faced surgery and the possible loss of both legs. Mom had to go to work at the Anniston Ordnance Depot and learn how to drive a car. Flynt family photo.

On his insurance route, he encountered resistance from a new source. Many women with husbands in the military questioned why a healthy-looking young salesman was not overseas. The explanation that he had a bone disease convinced no one in 1943, when the army was drafting every man in sight, able-bodied or not. Explaining to Mom that he could no longer tolerate constant challenges to his manhood and patriotism, he volunteered for the army and took his physical. Army doctors took one look at the scars on his legs and declared him 4-F. Mom, at home by herself with a three-year-old and no money, breathed a sigh of relief.

Despairing of door-to-door sales given the response to his lack of military service, Dad quit his insurance job and went to work for Sunshine Biscuit Company, selling crackers and cookies to grocery stores. He never sold door-to-door again. He worked in Anniston until the war ended and a returning soldier reclaimed his sales route. Dad transferred to Gadsden, then to Atlanta. From Atlanta the company transferred him back to Anniston, then to Birmingham, back to Anniston and to Atlanta again.

While he was in Atlanta, Dad learned his mother was terminally ill with tuberculosis. Desperate to return to Anniston, he quit Sunshine Biscuit and went to work for Swift and Company meatpackers, the premier U.S. fresh and canned meat supplier. He sold meat to restaurants and grocery stores until

Despite Dad's obsessive work ethic, we were great pals. In this 1943 photo, I was a proud miniature soldier. Dad, dapperly dressed as always, had returned from leg surgery to renew his career as an insurance salesman. Behind us is a paddle-wheel steamboat on the Coosa River near where we lived outside Gadsden. Flynt family photo.

Annie died in 1949 and Granddad two years later. Then he transferred to Atlanta again, moving into marketing at the district office. A yearlong stay in Augusta ended with another district marketing assignment, traveling out of Atlanta and covering most of Florida. That tour of duty was horrendous, bringing him home a few hours on the weekend before he drove off like a bat out of hell in his unair-conditioned Swift car without a radio for a ten- to fifteen-hour drive on two-lane roads to some destination in Florida.

Threatening to quit resulted in his first stint in management. The district manager sent him to New York state for management training. Dad did not like New York, and when the company later offered him a lucrative job at the national headquarters in Chicago, he responded that the only way he would work at national headquarters was if they moved it south of the Mason-Dixon line.

His first manager's job was in Dothan, Alabama, and from the beginning he was a natural. Mathematically gifted (he did all but the most complex computations in his head), hard working, a seasoned salesman, shrewd bargainer, and harsh critic when occasion demanded, he got the job done. Within months, the unit, which had been losing money, turned a profit. Dad never looked back.

Having found the ideal trouble-shooter manager, Swift sent him to a series of units that were losing money—Anniston; Hattiesburg, Mississippi; Anniston again; Tallahassee, Florida; Opelika, Alabama; Birmingham, where he retired. He never failed to turn a profit, though some places took longer than others.

Retirement did not suit him, and he was soon performing management miracles for a GAF roofing warehouse in Birmingham. He built a house on Flynt Lane in Pinson, and he and Mother moved for the thirty-fourth time in their sixty-year marriage. After retiring from retirement several times, he became content, buying and selling land, cars, and commercial property, as well as building and managing a small strip mall.

Even when modestly well-off financially, Dad chafed at the way some people viewed him: his lack of an original birth certificate and a high school diploma; his sometimes mismatched clothes; the chicken house near his Pinson home; his lack of proper table manners. Wanting desperately to join the middle class and having achieved that status, he never quite fit in. And he always resented that.

When we moved to Anniston while I was in high school, Dad bought a house as far up Tenth Street Mountain on the preferred eastern side of town as we could afford (albeit a simple frame house on the northeast side of Tenth Street rather than a mansion on the southeast end of the mountain). He could be persuaded to vote Republican, but only by the hardest. His heart was with populist Democrats like Senators John Sparkman and Lister Hill. He had trouble voting for George Wallace though he generally agreed with Wallace on racial issues, because Wallace was from aristocratic Barbour County, and Dad refused to vote for anyone from the Black Belt.

Dad was part of perhaps the last generation of American workers who felt strong loyalty to the companies that employed them because the companies seemed to reciprocate that loyalty. That was particularly true of Swift, for whom he worked more than three decades. He took no guff off his bosses, told them exactly what he thought, often threatened to quit, and could not understand why they didn't fire him. The reason was simple. They recognized him as a great salesman as well as a good and decent man. One day Dad told me that he had received instructions forbidding the hiring of salesmen without at least a high school diploma and two years of college. It was a sad irony. He had employed many college graduates as salesmen and considered them generally inferior to less-educated salesmen in work ethic, personal discipline, punctuality, and company loyalty. In short, he could no longer hire people like himself.

After Dad died, I received many letters from people who knew him. Nearly all mentioned his storytelling, homespun charm, friendliness, and generosity. One younger Flynt relative wrote me about a half dollar that Dad had pressed into his hand with a handshake when he was a boy. Dad knew how much he needed the money but wanted to spare him the embarrassment of publicly acknowledging the gift. It was an act of kindness typical of my impulsive father, who never forgot where he came from.

Mom

If Dad was the perfect storm in my life, Mom was the safe harbor. At least that is the way they played their roles until near the end of their lives when each became more like the other, Dad gentler and more restrained, Mom fiery and more combative.

In her early years, Mae Ellis Moore Flynt was easygoing, nurturing, independent, and quiet. (It was a good thing that was her inclination because Dad never gave her an opportunity to be anything else.) Whereas Dad was quick to anger and just as quick to forget, Mom held a grudge for days or even weeks. She was an overly protective mother of an only surviving child. And she doted on me.

Emotionally, my parents reversed traditional gender roles. Just as Dad was quick to anger and to feel remorse, he was easy to move to tears, impulsive purchases, and acts of generosity. When he died, Mother shed not a tear, at least not in the presence of others. When she lay dying in the hospital, I wept as I told her there was no hope and she could let go of her fierce determination to fight and live. She did not shed a tear even in the presence of my despair. Her pale blue eyes reflected resolution, acceptance, and sadness, nothing more. Not fear. Not regret. Only steely resolve to have it over and done with. That was her way, attributable I suspect more to life experiences than DNA. She wept often enough early in life to exhaust her supply of tears. Later on she revealed only stoic acceptance.

Mom was born in, grew up in, and in a psychological sense never left Pinson, a small community about ten miles northeast of Birmingham. Originally called Hagood's Crossroads, it was one of Jefferson County's oldest settlements (in fact it officially predated by one day Jefferson County's creation in 1819).

Due mainly to her father's profligacy, Mom grew up poor. When she had her tonsils removed, she and her mother walked several miles to catch a bus to Hillman Charity Hospital, then after the tonsillectomy rode the bus back to Pinson and walked home. That episode was only the beginning of her medical problems. She contracted both scarlet and rheumatic fever, which damaged her heart and caused fainting spells throughout her life until surgeons at University Hospital replaced her aortic valve on April 9 (my father's birthday and his finest present ever), 1985.

Not all early memories were traumatic, and on balance, she experienced a

Mom and Dad just after their marriage in 1938 in front of his 1935 Willis. Flynt family photo.

happy childhood. As in most small southern towns before the Second World War, the rhythm of Pinson's life was determined by the axis of home, church, and school.

At home, Mom and her siblings, together with the Hagood children next door, would create imaginary worlds of wonder and explore real worlds of nature. Mom's imaginary world consisted largely of books provided by the county book mobile because their only family supply consisted of Pop Fee's Woodmen of the World collection. The book mobile stopped at the intersection in front of their house twice a month. The children checked out the maximum number of books allowed.

Turkey Creek was only a mile away. The first stop for them was the Blue Hole, formed when pounding water from spring rains washed sediment away from a huge rock protruding into the creek bed, creating a pool deep enough for swimming and fishing. Farther down the creek a sharp drop in terrain carved a sloping falls that allowed them to slide all the way down into a deep pool below. The legs of their clothes lasted longer than the seats, which took a beating on the rocky slide.

Poverty affected the family in a variety of ways. One day a stray mutt arrived at their house and stayed for two years. Ring became the children's common possession, although Curt, being the eldest, laid claim to him. During the hardest days of the Depression, a family acquaintance took a fancy to Ring and offered Curt five dollars for the dog. The sum was huge and the family desperate. Torn between his love for the dog and his family's deprivation, Curt made a choice no child should have to make. The children could not bear the pain of Ring's departure, so they went inside to weep for the only pet they would have. Mom remembered the event well enough that as an adult she was never without a dog to love.

Baptist, Methodist, and Presbyterian churches formed another axis of the Pinson community, and Mom's neighborhood had ties to all three. The Hagoods preferred Methodism, and when Ina married Leo Hagood to unite the families, she raised her children in that church. Marvin's Chapel cemetery on a hill behind the church constituted the ecumenical resting place for my maternal uncles, aunts, grandparents, sister, and parents. In time, I will commit my remains to that beautiful Appalachian hillside as well.

Mama Moore attended the rock Presbyterian church next to the school when she went at all. The children attended the Baptist church with Pop Fee, and the Baptist faith took better on Mom than the others. She was baptized in Turkey Creek like her father before her. It was in the church that she made life-long friendships, including the two teenagers, Louise Miller and Marguerite Morris, who would witness her marriage. And it was at a revival there that she first met Dad.

Pinson elementary school was the final anchor of the community that Mom knew and loved. Built on the foundation of rocks her father and other men had carried from Turkey Creek and cemented together, the school was the metaphorical binding that held Pinson together. The teachers were talented in the way teachers must be if they aim to truly educate the young: they inspired, loved, tried to understand, and on occasion even made allowance for their young charges. Sometimes they made mistakes, as in the case of the thoughtless principal who tied Curt to a flagpole. Mostly, though, they loved and inspired. Half a century later Mom still remembered the names of nearly all her teachers. In sixth grade they chose her to be student librarian because she earned good grades and was such a prodigious reader.

After completing elementary school, Mom caught the bus each day to Jefferson County High School in Tarrant City, which served the entire eastern section of the county. She excelled there as well and perhaps would have found a way to attend college in the fall of 1938 despite a new recession had it not been for all those idle hours spent with Ina on the front porch waving at boys returning home from work.

Before meeting Dad, she had dated two other boys. L. C. Stricklin was a tall, thin, guitar-picking country singer who performed at local dances. He lived up Sweeny Hollow Road; more importantly he owned a car. Pop Fee did not, so Mom was tied to buses or boys with cars. Stricklin fell in love with Mom and Pop Fee's homemade ice cream at about the same time. Mom only fell in love with L.C.'s car. Among the flaws she found in Stricklin was his inattentiveness; he would stop for gas and buy himself a cold drink without asking if she wanted one. L.C. proposed marriage. Mom refused. L.C. threatened to kill himself. Mom refused again. He got over her.

She also dated Jimmy Thomas from Chalkville, a boy she liked better and who owned a nicer car. Shorter than Stricklin and better looking, he rated high as a boyfriend until she met Dad.

Dad was older and more mature than her other beaus; he was a newly arrived stranger in town; he was tall and handsome with curly hair; and he owned a half interest in a smart-looking new car. Their romance blossomed, and the week following her high school graduation, they eloped. Actually "elope" is a more impressive sounding event than actually occurred. Mom had neither engagement ring nor wedding band for two years because Dad couldn't afford them. They had to run away to marry because Mama Moore wanted her children to stay home and live with her. Mom and Dad left ostensibly on a date, picked up her two best friends, drove to the Baptist parsonage, and persuaded Rev. J. J. Sandlin to marry them. Mom explained to him that she was eighteen and intended to marry whether or not he performed the ceremony, and she was old enough that Mama Moore could not annul the marriage. Sandlin offended Dad by misspelling his name "Flint" on the marriage certificate. Mom insisted that Dad return her home after the ceremony lest she be late for curfew. She promised to tell her mother that she had married the next morning. Instead, she immediately blurted out the news to Ina, and her fifteen-year-old sister ran out of the room crying. Ina told Johnny, who joined in the weeping. That alerted Mama Moore, who had a fit and insisted that Pop Fee do something. He maintained his calm, assuring his oldest daughter that he accepted the marriage but making her promise to complete college some day.

Within months Mom was pregnant. Certain that the fetus was a girl, she named her Shirley Denise after her mother. The pregnancy seemed normal, the baby active until the last week, when she went strangely still. Mom's doctor stayed with her the night Denise was stillborn. The kindly physician embalmed my sister in their bathroom, a funeral preparation they could not otherwise afford. Dad was stoical and moved on. Mom was distraught and inconsolable. She began to obsess about the newborn baby of their next-door neighbor in Tarrant City. The parents would sometimes leave the baby for a few minutes in a crib outside in the sunshine. Mom explained: "We would drive by there, and I would have this urge to go get that baby. My arms were so empty."

Mom's doctor warned her that she might die if she had another baby. She was too desperate to listen or to care. By the time Dad moved to Pontotoc, she was pregnant again. It was a hard pregnancy. She had to wear a brace during the last months before I was born, and she also contracted malaria. She signed a form at the clinic providing that if there were a medical crisis during the delivery, the doctor must save the baby and let her die. Happily my birth was uneventful.

With Dad gone for days at a time, Mom—unable to nurse me because of malaria, without a car, friends, or family, living in a strange town for only a few months—felt abandoned and desolate. Fortunately, Mrs. Robinson, the maternal and jolly landlady, chose to invest her time in me. She rocked me, sang to me, fed me, and reassured mother that everything would be fine. Dad hired a kindly black woman with a cow who brought them fresh milk and helped with washing, cleaning, and cooking until Mom recovered. (This was the only time she would ever have someone to help her.) A problem arose when the woman tried to hang my diapers on the clothesline, which alerted nosy neighbors that Mrs. Robinson had to take in boarders. She solved that dilemma by buying Mom a wooden rack on which to dry diapers inside the house.

Mom rejoiced when Dad made up his mind to wipe the dust of Mississippi off his feet and return to Alabama. Never had a place looked so fine to them. Back in Birmingham she was reunited with her family and Dad with his brother and sister. And he soon launched his new career selling burial insurance. A brief, profitable, residence in Sheffield seemed to establish them firmly in the lower middle class when disaster struck again in the reemergence of his osteomyelitis.

His impending surgery and their move to Anniston changed her life as much as his. She returned to living in the house that had been moved from Highway 280 and reconstructed near Anniston. She shared the house with her husband's parents and her two-year-old toddler and began searching for a job. The ominous possibility that Dad's legs might have to be amputated added urgency to her job hunt. But she had few marketable skills and did not even know how to drive a car.

Fortunately for her, a booming 1943 wartime economy absorbed all applicants, even women without job experience or driver's licenses. She got a job as a filing clerk at Anniston Ordnance Depot just west of town. Unable to drive her car through the security check because she had no driver's license, Mom would drive Dad's 1941 Chevrolet three miles into Anniston, park the car, and hitch a ride with a woman who worked with her at the depot.

As for so many other women, Mom's wartime employment was both a constant challenge and an empowering adventure. During breaks she listened to 1940s Big Band music. At work she filed and refiled documents, refiling them because she had too little work to do. She also memorized every file so she could locate it immediately. Afraid she would lose her job if Colonel Aspenal, her boss, saw her resting, she would busily file all morning, then at lunch remove all the documents and start over again in the afternoon. The kindly colonel worried that she was working too hard and offered to hire another woman to help her process the massive stack of documents that accumulated so quickly on her desk. Mom only barely dissuaded him.

When Mom returned from work each day, she yearned to spend time with me, but that was often impossible. By then I had worn out my grandparents and there was still work to do. Mom drew water from the well, washed clothes on a rub board, then cooked. By the end of each day, she was so tired that she fell into bed exhausted. Occasionally, she would faint, a symptom, she was to learn later, of the heart problems that would dog her throughout her life.

Mom began working at the depot in March and quit four months later when Dad was able to return to work. For many women, leaving a well-paying wartime job to return to housework and family chores was a disappointment. For Mom, it was an unmitigated joy. We could spend all our time together.

Furthermore, Mom thrived on housework. She and her sister Ina were the neatest and most meticulous housekeepers I ever knew. They raised mopping floors every day to the level of a domestic sacrament. If any germ escaped their cascade of Clorox, it must have created a new super species.

Mom was not adventurous either in her diet or her cooking, which was just fine with Dad and me. We were meat (mainly beef, especially after Dad went to work for Swift and Company) and potato people. Pork was fine as well; chicken was infrequently served, and fish (other than salmon croquets) not at all. Mom's seasoned green beans were legendary, as were her coconut pies. Making homemade bread was not her gift. Beyond cornbread, we relied mainly on store-bought rolls. Dad often surprised her by bringing visiting central office personnel home for lunch, and she never disappointed him no matter how little notice he gave. When he could, he came home for lunch, tribute both to her no-frills grub and their fondness for each other.

Mom also became one of the nation's leading authorities on moving. She

Mom at age twenty-four (in 1944) in Gadsden after she had quit her job at the Anniston Ordnance Depot in order to stay home with me. Courtesy H. and W. Studio,
Gadsden, Alabama.

certainly had enough experience. With a move on average every two years during their sixty-year marriage, she could organize them (because Dad usually
had been sent ahead to begin work and returned only on weekends) with incredible precision. Once my wife and I drove across Birmingham several days
after a move to help her unpack only to discover that she already had all boxes
unloaded; her gallery of family photographs (mainly of me) nailed to walls;
china, pots, pans, and towels all stored; and every item in her salt and pepper
shaker collection properly displayed.

Although home and family dominated her life, church came close behind.
Wherever we landed in our peripatetic wanderings, Mom always headed us to

the nearest Baptist church. When I was a primary student of only five or six, she began teaching Sunday school because I didn't like being separated from her. She continued teaching Bible stories to little children until she entered college decades later.

Those two decisions—teaching children the Bible and entering college—were sequential and related. After years of teaching Sunday school, Mom decided that in order to be the best teacher possible, she needed to know more psychology. She telephoned me one evening while I was in graduate school to ask what I thought about her entering college. "That's wonderful, Mom. What a great idea," I replied enthusiastically. "Do you think I could pass the work?" she inquired anxiously. "Of course you can," I replied confidently. "But it's been so long since I was in school, and children know so much more," she worried. "Perhaps so, Mom, but they are eighteen years old, away from home for the first time, going through puberty, and their hearts and heads aren't into learning."

Thus reassured, she became a special student at the University of Southern Mississippi, taking courses in art, music, and child psychology. At the end of a revelatory first semester, a wise counselor refused to allow her to take additional courses on the smorgasbord plan. From then on, she had to enter a degree program, requiring courses in English, history, mathematics, and lots of other subjects that terrified her. I urged her just to give university a chance. If she decided to quit later, there could be no shame in that. Luckily, she enrolled in a large auditorium history course taught by a kindly historian, John Gonzalez. He took a liking to this older woman working so hard and encouraged her constantly. He was the only professor from Southern Mississippi whose name she remembered, but he wrought the transformation in her life that teachers hope they make but are seldom sure of. She came to believe in her ability because he believed in her. As she explained later to me, "I can't quit college now because I enjoy it so much."

By the time Dad was transferred to Birmingham in 1963, she was a confident coed ready to enroll at Howard College, her father's alma mater, to fulfill her promise to him when she married. An education major like her father, she also relished courses in religion, history, child psychology, and art. Smaller classes at Howard compensated for fewer older, nontraditional students than at Southern Mississippi.

Her senior year at Howard (1965–66) was my first year on the faculty, and I would often see her hurrying between classes, bobby socks beneath her Oxfords and book bag slung on her shoulder. "Hi, Mom!" I once shouted across the quadrangle filled with youthful students who thought I was too young to be a teacher and she too old to be a student. The next time we were together, she scolded: "Don't do that again! It was so embarrassing." The last semester of her senior year my mother made all As, not her first time on the dean's list but her most satisfying.

After practice-teaching in Mountain Brook, she began her first regular teaching job in February 1967 in Center Point near her Pinson home. One school followed another as Dad moved ever higher into management. During her eleven years teaching fourth grade in Pinson, she taught hundreds of students social studies and reading, many of them grandchildren of her classmates from the 1930s. She particularly loved Alabama history. She had the children build Indian houses and play Native American games. She brought in quilters from the Pinson community to teach their craft. She even persuaded a dairy to furnish fresh milk and showed each child how to churn butter. When they studied cotton gins in the fall, she asked a local farmer to demonstrate how a gin worked and let children try to separate cotton from bolls.

She was a meticulously fair teacher. On one occasion, an influential city resident told my mother that she was going to take her son with her on a three-day holiday. Mom explained that she had a right to do that, but the child would miss important work and the absence was unexcused. When the mother returned and demanded that Mom excuse the absence, she refused. The woman took her case to the principal, who supported his teacher.

Pinson's racial integration had just begun when Mom arrived back there in the early 1970s. Most whites did not approve, and even mother had reservations. A group of older black children from Airport Heights neighborhood arrived to a sullen reception and initial unhappiness. Then Mom's empathy meter began to register properly, and she applied all those Sunday school lessons and child psychology courses to the microcosmic problem of troubled children in a racially divided school. Her first revelation was that every child needs to be good at something. She made a point of arranging a footrace among her students one day at recess because she had an African American boy who could barely read but could run like a deer. His victory turned him into a class hero and a more determined student. One by one, she surmounted first her own racial assumptions and then the barriers imposed by her community. As black children increasingly clung to her for encouragement and affirmation, she reciprocated with patience and love. She slowly gained their confidence while they gained her respect.

That sometimes made life more difficult. During the mid-1970s a white fourth grader blurted out that his father and other members of the Ku Klux

Klan were going to burn a cross in her yard because Dad was president of the Pinson Civitan Club, which had refused the Klan use of its building for a meeting. Mom explained that the president of such an organization didn't make such decisions; members voted, though Dad agreed with the decision to deny use of the building. The boy apparently explained democracy sufficiently well to his father that the Klan moved the cross-burning from my parent's front yard to Triangle Park in Pinson.

Black students were not the only fourth graders to benefit from her love and wisdom. At Mom's funeral in 2008, a middle-aged woman told me that her mother had died the summer before she began fourth grade. She felt wretched and abandoned. Mom perceived her pain and spent the year trying to be a surrogate mother, showering her with affection. That year had made all the difference in her life, she explained tearfully. Though she had not seen my mother in more than twenty years, she came that day to offer one last "thank you."

Dad was not certain this new persona was a good thing. He welcomed Mom's added income. (She began teaching in 1967 for $2,800 a year; when heart problems forced her retirement after eighteen years, she made a whopping $15,102. When I later became a critic of obscene salaries paid Alabama and Auburn head football coaches, it was because I compared her teacher's pension of $144.32 a month to their sumptuous lifestyles and golden parachutes and doubted whether their contributions to the future of children matched my mother's.) But beyond her added income, there was the matter of her changing racial ideology. More troubling even than that was her growing independence.

Dad was a loving, faithful spouse. But he could also be abusive. Once (only once, because she warned him that she would leave him if he ever hit her again) he slapped her during one of his temper tantrums. Often he simply took her for granted, froze her out of conversations because he believed she had little to contribute, or contradicted her version of events. She accepted all this because she had no job or professional skills and she had a child to raise. But with me grown and gone and her in college, their relationship began to change.

At first the change was subtle. Dad was proud of her collegiate success but used his wit to remind her of her limitations. When she told him that she was studying the new mathematics (her math was as suspect as his was certain), he answered from behind the newspaper that she needed to learn the old math before she changed to the new. Undeterred, she proudly responded that in the new math she could change base systems and demonstrate that two plus two did not equal four. He rejoined that such a conclusion sounded pretty much like her old math to him.

In social settings Mom talked more, sometimes contradicted his version of events, seemed increasingly confident, and developed interests and professional competency quite apart from him. He only half joked that he had "sent her to college and she hadn't stopped talking since." Until college she was "just someone to cook the meals and wash the clothes," she once told me. Now she was an economic asset and a challenge to his authority. When he planned a new investment or business deal, the purchase of a house or car, or even a move, she expected to be consulted. When he called to chew me out for allowing a black friend to sleep in their house while attending a basketball tournament when they were away on a trip, Mom wrote me to apologize for his call and his sentiment. She frequently moved into another bedroom and refused to speak to him when he flew into a rage.

Rose Gibbs, a heroine in Nanci Kincaid's novel *Balls,* advised her fictional daughter, Dixie, that "being smart can be a real detriment to a woman unless she knows how to go about it tactfully." Mom went about being smart as tactfully as she could, but it was not always tactful enough for Dad.

After Dad died in 1998, I worried whether or not Mom could master all his financial dealings, insurance forms, recordkeeping, and bank accounts. I need not have worried. It was hard work for her, but she labored until she mastered everything. She never wasted money, and though she was less a risk-taker than Dad, she managed just fine.

I once visited her when she was eighty-six and had a plumbing problem with a toilet. Dad, ever the jack-of-all-trades, never called a serviceman. I tried my hand at fixing the problem but failed miserably. After Mom discovered that I had none of my father's how-to skills and would thus be of no help, she decided to do what he would have done, fix it herself. She tried to turn off the water at the wall, but succeeded only in bruising her arm and shoulder. I suggested she call a plumber. Though Dad had left her ample financial resources, she complained that plumbers cost too much. The next time I visited, her shoulder was well and the toilet fixed.

• two •

An Alabama Childhood

A moving van and a new school were symbols of my childhood. I attended twelve schools between the ages of six and fourteen. Our hegira began when we left northern Mississippi for Birmingham during the winter of 1941. But Birmingham was only a brief stop on the way to Sheffield. Although I have no memory of this event, Mother told me that I nearly frightened her to death as a toddler in the Tennessee River town when I disappeared one afternoon. With the river so close, she feared that I had wandered off and drowned. Actually, I had followed a man home who was returning with his cow from a summer's day grazing on the school lawn. When the neighbor had shut his cow safely in its stall, he returned me to my home, but not quickly enough to suit Mom, who was frantic.

My first memories resulted from our brief residence at Granddad Flynt's house on Buttermilk Road while Dad recovered from surgery. My kindly grandfather, who must have towered over me like a giant, would hold my hand while we walked to his strawberry patch to pick berries in April 1943. I loved them floating in fresh cream supplied by his brothers-in-law from their dairies. My grandmother introduced me both to the gourd dipper that they used to drink ice cold water from their well and to the mysteries of churning butter (it looked so simple when she did it and was so hard and endlessly monotonous when I tried).

When Dad returned to work, we moved into two rooms of a boarding house on Quintard Avenue in Anniston. The other residents were families of Fort

McClellan soldiers, and we shared a single bath in the hall. I was the only child among the families and received more attention than was good for me.

My favorite day of the week was when the garbage truck came. I would go through the garbage before the truck arrived, removing whatever seemed particularly interesting. One day when I retrieved a lipstick with enough contents remaining to smear both my face and clothes, I announced to Mother that I intended to be a garbage man when I grew up. For the next decade I seemed headed in that direction.

Our next house was a rental just north of Gadsden on a dirt road that ended at the Coosa River. There I first encountered Mom's heart problems. One warm day as she hung laundry on the line, she fainted, falling to the ground. I stood over her terrified, but after a few moments she regained consciousness and asked me to bring her water. It was no small accomplishment for a four-year-old, but I brought the water to her and splashed it on her face. Only afterward did it occur to her that the only place where I could have obtained water was from the toilet. She never forgave the owner of the house who saw her on the ground and did nothing because she believed Mom was drunk.

Our next move was to Red Oak, Georgia, near Atlanta, where I turned six. My October birthday would have prevented me from entering school in Alabama. But with a physician's certification of adequate maturity, a nearly six-year-old Georgia resident was allowed into school. Mother read to me constantly, and I was well-prepared academically though perhaps not emotionally. She enticed me into school with a flashy yellow rain slicker, and luckily the first day of school was rainy. I wanted to wear the raincoat more than I dreaded leaving Mom.

Midyear we moved back to Anniston, where I enrolled in Woodstock School. I spent most of my time there in trouble. When our teacher instructed us to bow our heads and close our eyes while saying the Lord's prayer, I decided to help the teacher monitor student compliance. My credibility with her went down when I reported a classmate for not closing his eyes.

Things went downhill from there. Our frequent moves and mother's overprotectiveness had made me insecure. One day when the teacher told me I must stay after school for talking too much, I waited until she formed our reading circle, then took the chair nearest the open door. As soon as she turned her back, I raced for the door and out of the building. Even at the age of seven, I knew my way to Aunt Ora's house near the school. She called Mom, who drove me back to school to take my punishment. That was the first of several school run-away incidents.

Toward the end of the term, Mom moved me to Tenth Street School, my

First-graders dream dreams, and I dreamed lots of them. At the time most of my dreams centered on no more moving vans or new schools. Courtesy Olan Mills Portrait Studio, Tuscaloosa, Alabama.

third school in first grade. I settled in there and felt right at home; when we moved to Goodwin Circle, I was able to begin second grade at the same place. It helped when Mrs. Downing, our boarding house landlady on Quintard, gave me a dog that summer. Buster was a mongrel mix of fox terrier and bulldog with an attitude. As my dad often remarked, "That dog would fight a circular saw!" We were inseparable, and he became my closest pal in a world where mobility made close friends a rarity.

I adjusted socially to second grade, and all went well until Dad, super salesman that he was, won a trip to Havana, Cuba, for Mom and him. They thought they could pay my way as well, but Swift and Company would not allow children on the voyage. As the departure date approached, Mom and I grew anxious. Dad insisted that he and Mom go, and she finally decided that I would be fine in Pinson with Mama Moore, Pop Fee, and my cousins.

As my parents left, I wept and begged them to stay. As soon as they were out of sight, I had a great time. Mama Moore let me wear my favorite clothes every day and did not insist I bathe. Pop Fee fed me candy and Cokes from his store and let me stand in a chair and work his cash register. Mama Moore also introduced me to her ritualistic way of wringing the necks of chickens. She marched out into the chicken yard, selected the victim, grabbed it by the neck, swung it around once, then snapped off its head on the second swing. What followed was a fascinating if macabre dance by a headless chicken, flopping across the chicken yard until it expired. My cousins Patsy and Arthur let me attend school with them. School, I discovered, was a lot more fun when I didn't have to complete homework or take tests.

Meanwhile, Mom was miserable. First came the seasickness on the boat from Miami to Havana. Then she worried whether I was all right. She spent most of the week making Dad miserable as well for separating us and bringing her to Cuba.

When I was nine we were back on the road again, selling our "dream house" on Goodwin Circle, where I had happily spent summers hunting balls on the golf course behind our house, building forts, riding my first bicycle, or engaged in harmless chinaberry fights and more dangerous BB gun battles with four neighboring boys.

Dad bought a duplex in Birmingham close to his sister Lillie Mae and her sons, George and Dale. George, later a brilliant electrical engineer and designer for National Cash Register Company, was older than me by many years, but Dale was only slightly older than I was. When I enrolled in fourth grade, Dale warned me of the coming apocalypse. I had drawn Miss Johnnie, the terror of Woodrow Wilson Elementary School. Whether she was really as mean as described or incoming students were merely the victims of urban legends, I do not know. I do know that her strict discipline and the fact that she had failed my cousin terrified me. So did mathematics, her favorite subject but already a source of bewilderment to me.

Perhaps I sought celestial protection from Miss Johnnie and mathematics at Hunter Street Baptist Church, where at age ten I was born again during an emotional revival. I don't remember thinking my sins were all that bad, but fear of Miss Johnnie far outweighed the prospects of hell. Just to provide double protection, I also joined the Cub Scouts. Our first television set also offered diversion from my fears.

Another move saved me from my fate. In January 1950 Dad was transferred to Atlanta where a fourth grade instructor, Mrs. Farmer, as kind as Miss Johnnie was formidable, became my favorite elementary teacher. This was my sixth school in four years. We bought a house in a new subdivision called Lakewood Heights and found a friendly Baptist church.

Less than a year later, we moved to Augusta, Georgia. Construction of the H-bomb plant in Aiken, South Carolina, across the Savannah River from Augusta, had created a heterogeneous population, bustling prosperity, and McCarthyite paranoia. I listened with rapt attention one day on a school bus while an obviously well-informed older student pointed out a house on our bus route where a "known Communist" lived.

Newcomers were nothing strange to Augusta. Indeed there may have been more of us than older residents. So we had no problem fitting in. I was selected for the fifth grade safety patrol, got my first job delivering the local newspaper, and began to notice that girls were different from boys.

Though I was not precocious in matters of sex, my mom probably slowed down my maturation by entering a conspiracy with one of her friends. The Swanns had a daughter named Brenda. She was cute, and under different circumstances I might have been smitten. But the conspiracy entered into by mother, without my knowledge or consent, designated me as Brenda Swann's partner in dancing class. Admiring girls secretly from afar was one thing. Exposing a twelve-year-old male to the scorn of his friends by making him a co-erced dancing partner to a girl was another matter entirely.

Remembering none of my promises to God during my conversion nor any ethical teaching since, I determined to sabotage mother's plans at the expense of poor Brenda. On the first night of dancing class, I pouted and purposely stepped on her feet at every opportunity. By the end of the evening, Brenda hated me and begged her mother to let her drop dancing lessons. When my wife implored me to take ballroom dancing lessons five decades later, I successfully used the trauma of that earlier misadventure to delay the inevitable for years. Finally worn down by a wife I loved who asked nearly nothing of me save to dance, I finally consented. I learned to love dancing in my senior years as much as she did.

My meanness to Brenda was not my only outrage. Never happy in school, a friend and I contrived schemes for an unscheduled holiday. In conception, the plan was brilliant. Unfortunately, our knowledge of chemistry and biology did not match our strategy. My idea was simple. Bring two candles, matches, and cake coloring from home. Melt the candle wax, spread it on the side of our faces, add cake coloring to a gash in the wax, pretend we had been injured in a fight, and ask the teachers to let us go home to be treated. Of course, I had reckoned without the fact that freshly melted wax applied to the skin burns, creates considerable pain, and results in a real emergency that gets you sent to the doctor. We won our freedom for a day, but the price wasn't worth it.

I also asserted my identity while conforming to my new peer group, where the boys were bleaching a bit of their hair white. Mom reacted negatively at first, but then became suddenly compliant. She agreed that I could bleach my hair if I would do it properly at her beauty shop. The idea of being seen by my friends in Mom's beauty shop was as repugnant as dancing class, so I abandoned the idea altogether, which may have been her intention all along.

After three house moves in Augusta, we returned to Lakewood Heights. Men from our former Baptist church surprised us the day our moving van arrived, waiting to help us move in. Such were the dimensions of religious community in the 1950s. We were soon back actively engaged in church; I returned to my old school; and in the summer I began a grass mowing business. Big for my age and not afraid of work, I earned good money mowing heavily fertilized lawns in the new subdivision. Only much later did I question the wisdom of mowing large, thick lawns with a push mower in the blazing Georgia sun for fifty cents a lawn.

Our next move came when Dad was selected to manage the Swift unit in Dothan. We rented a duplex, and I entered Young Junior High School. Always before, when moving back and forth, I had coasted when arriving in Alabama from Georgia schools, but had to work hard to catch up when moving to Georgia. Not this time. The little Wiregrass town of Dothan expected much from its students. Latin was offered beginning in ninth grade. Teachers were demanding and conducted no-nonsense classrooms. My teacher in 1954 wrote personal notes of encouragement, praising my efforts if not my accomplishments, ending one note: "The truest wisdom is a resolute determination." I suppose she had concluded that "resolute determination" was my only asset, and she was only partly correct even in that.

My school contained some remarkable people. William Joseph (Bill) Baxley would go on to law school, be elected attorney general of Alabama, prosecute the Ku Klux Klansmen who bombed the Sixteenth Street Baptist Church, and lose a race for governor that he should have won. I played baseball (though not very well) with Bill.

Another classmate, Travis Casey, would end my embryonic football career the following fall. I was a big kid at thirteen, weighing 175 pounds and standing more than six feet tall. I also thought I was tough. Casey—who was bigger,

Rev. Eddie Martin speaking to students at Dothan High School during his evangelistic tent revival in 1955. Despite my youth, I served as a counselor for teenager "enquirers." I am in the second row (*fourth from right*) next to my friend Bill Baxley, a future Alabama attorney general. Courtesy Southern Baptist Historical Archives.

taller, and tougher—played tackle opposite me in football tryouts for Dothan High. One week of practice was enough to disabuse me of any notion that I was tough and end my gridiron career. I was slow, soft, and averse to physical contact, not a good profile for a southern boy aspiring to play football. Travis went on to a scholarship playing for Bear Bryant at the University of Alabama. I went on to a job delivering the *Dothan Eagle*.

The flat terrain of the Wiregrass strengthened my argument that Dad should buy me a Cushman motor scooter despite Mom's protestations. The scooter sped me on my way through a transitory, working-class neighborhood. I discovered quickly that not everyone was like my rigorously ethical father. Customers moved away owing me for a month's papers or claimed they had paid when they had not. I learned hard lessons in a hurry. Collect every week in advance and keep careful records.

My hard work and reliability caught the attention of my bosses, including the circulation manager. One day he asked me if I would be interested in the job of route supervisor over all the paperboys. My duties would include delivering their routes when they were unable to do so, filling all the paper dispensers, and collecting money from the coin machines. For a boy of fourteen, the job involved lots of responsibility. I relished it despite onerous duties. (Why was it that newsboys tended to get sick or miss delivering papers to their customers mainly during rainstorms?) By the standards of the time, I also made good money.

Possibilities for spending the money beyond gas for my scooter were limited by my involvement in Calvary Baptist Church. When we first moved to Dothan, we had joined the prestigious First Baptist Church. But we soon moved our membership to less pretentious Calvary, a new mission of First Baptist. During a youth revival preached by Charles Worthy, a local "preacher-boy" from Dothan who was attending Howard College, I felt a powerful stirring of the spirit. I had long since forgotten my conversion, and the blur of intervening churches had left little impression. But the moment and my sense of purpose merged that night.

One of my Baptist heroes, Harry Emerson Fosdick, longtime pastor of Riverside Church in New York City, once wrote that in every person's life there are two beginnings: *When* we are born and the discovery of *why* we were born. That night at Calvary I became convinced that I had been born to preach. Worthy, who remained a lifelong friend and faithful advocate of social justice both as pastor in Washington, D.C., and as employee of Bread-for-the-World, returned to his ministerial studies at Howard College. Calvary's pastor, John Thomas (who later headed the Religion Department at the University of Mobile) proved a talented and patient mentor.

I spent much of my earnings traveling to Youth for Christ rallies throughout the Wiregrass, where I frequently preached. I witnessed to fellow newsboys, sometimes successfully, sometimes not. These were euphoric times of single-minded purpose. Latin could wait. God could not.

Actually, neglecting school was a familiar habit by now anyway. I was not a bad or hostile student, just an indifferent one. My elementary teachers had criticized me for talking too much in class and for lack of effort. One gave me a "poor" in history and reading, without high achievement in any subject. At Monte Sano Elementary School in Augusta, a seventh grade teacher wrote on my report card that Mom needed to ask me to explain a series of categories in which I needed improvement. The list included lack of respect for school regulations, refusal to follow directions, lack of attention, absence of self-control, and less serious lapses of dependability. I assured Mother that other than these offenses, I was doing fine. Luckily, Monte Sano had moved to the trendy grades of "superior," "satisfactory," "passing," and "unsatisfactory" in order to spare our fragile psyches. Out of forty-eight possible grades for the year, I had forty-six satisfactories and two superiors, in my favorite subjects, geography and history. Regrettably, this progressive grading had not yet taken hold at Fulton High School the following school year (1953–54) in Atlanta. A D in math and C in industrial arts neutralized As in English, social studies, and music. Although God replaced football as my chief diversion at Dothan High, I still managed no more than a B in English and science, balanced by an A in history and D in algebra. Dothan High was my eleventh school in nine years, and no evidence suggested a good outcome.

Family

During these years there were five constants in my life: moving; my dog, Buster; Dad; Mom; and my extended family of aunts, uncles, and cousins. Buster was my faithful companion from age six until he died the year I married and entered graduate school. I admired him for many reasons, chief among them the fact that he never realized how small and insignificant he was. With the size and digging proclivities of a fox terrier, he had the chest, legs, and ferocity of a bulldog. Like the Flynts, he would fight anything that strayed onto his turf or insulted his honor, including one huge boxer many times his size. I watched as Buster positioned himself between the big dog's stomach and front legs, biting its belly and throat, maneuvering left and right to stay beyond the boxer's teeth as it tried in vain to reach him, until the larger dog finally broke and ran.

He was less effective protecting me from Dad. My father did not whip me often, but every occasion was memorable. I am sure I deserved them all. I was spoiled, pampered, and selfish. But Dad used his belt in the white-hot fury of the moment. Off came the belt, he grabbed me by an arm, and I began a peculiar dance to keep my legs just beyond the belt's reach. I learned to lean into the strike; the further away I moved, the greater the force of the belt. Staying in close minimized Dad's striking power. Because the incidents were infrequent, Buster reacted as if my father were a mugger and I his victim. Tail stuck straight out, teeth bared and snarling, Buster lunged at Dad's vulnerable and heavily scarred legs. When he reached his target, Dad's fury quickly escalated. In time, Dad learned to aim the first blow at Buster, knowing a canine attack was inevitable. A couple of good blows and my protector tucked tail and ran, leaving me worse off than if he had not intervened in the first place. After the fact, Dad was remorseful because he had whipped me in anger. That played to my favor, and I used my tears for all they were worth. Mom sided with Dad before the whipping and with me afterward, which made his case even less tenable. In time, he simply gave up. In a thousand ways he demonstrated his love for me. The belt was just one of his ways.

I am holding Buster, my fierce fox terrier and faithful defender, at our home on Michael Lane in Anniston during the late 1950s. Behind me is a rock wall terrace that my father had me help build when I told him I had decided not to attend college. Pick and shovel work in the hard north Alabama clay during a scorching summer changed my mind, which was probably Dad's intent. Flynt family photo.

Mom was more of a problem. She seldom whipped me and never in anger. But her psychological warfare was more effective. She quite calmly made me go into the yard and cut a switch for her, warning that if my choice was of insufficient size, she would whip my bare legs longer and harder. The switching was never as bad as the selection, cutting, and anticipation. Nor was her remorse so great as Dad's.

Dad was seldom home long enough to play ball with me or take me fishing or hiking. He was a workaholic. I was not athletic anyway, nor an outdoors man, so it really didn't matter. Besides, I had Mom's full attention. There is a saying in the Talmud that God created mothers because he could not be everywhere. The saying never fit any woman better than Mae Ellis Flynt. Southern men love to write about their mothers. Usually they slobber right through the story until woman and mythology are indistinguishable. And it's a truism in Dixie that if you insult a man's mother, you had better be bigger, tougher, or faster than the family you insult because they will test your manhood. More than one man has died for such disrespect. I have read memoirs written by southern men who confessed to all manner of sins, but never one that admitted to being a "Mama's boy." I was one. The evidence is inescapable.

Though I have never been an intellectual pacifist nor felt compelled as a Christian realist to renounce all forms of violence and war as Jesus commanded, I was either born a genetic pacifist or became one under my mother's tutelage. Dad demanded that I fight the boys next door who pulled my hair. Instead I began wearing a cap with long ear flaps to protect my head. I attribute this practical pacifism to Mom's gentleness, her revulsion at cruelty, and her belief that family and personal pride began with self-restraint.

The first test of her influence occurred in Augusta when an older, tougher, streetwise boy tried to pick a fight with me while I delivered newspapers. He called my mother a name. I hated him for it, but I did what she had told me to do: I rode off on my bike as he shouted "Coward! Coward! Coward!" Had my father heard the conversation, he would have kicked my rear end or insisted that I kick the boy's rear end. How could my violence vindicate my mother's honor or his insult diminish her honor, I reasoned. Names shouted in anger changed nothing one way or the other.

Later my revulsion at hunting and the degrading aspects of high school football (one Dothan High football player delighted in throwing dirt in my eyes and spitting in my face when we took our three-point stance at practice) deepened my rejection of physical violence. By the time I turned fifteen, I had rejected three ideals of southern manhood: I would not kill animals; I would not fight other boys over family honor; I would not play football. Mother was pleased. Dad worried about me.

Mom was also ever present as my Cub Scout den mother, my preschool Sunday school teacher, my shopping companion, and my best friend. And our regular pilgrimages to Pinson provided my peer group. My cousins taught me many lessons, good and bad. And they were always fun to be with. When we arrived in Pinson, I became reacquainted with outdoor privies, Mama Moore's unique approach to beheading chickens, and my cousin's games. Nine cousins lived within a hundred yards of each other. A creek ran parallel to Sweeny Hollow Road across from the store and occasionally flooded during rainy season. At other times I could help my cousins set out minnow traps to catch bait that Pop Fee sold to fishermen.

A hundred yards south of the store on Center Point Road lived Jan, Joan, Leo, and Rex Hagood. A hundred yards to the east up Sweeny Hollow Road lived Patsy, Arthur, Jack, Donna Faye, and Paula Moore. As the eldest, Patsy, Arthur, Jan, and I declared ourselves to be the overlords and tried futilely to

In the absence of school chums, I bonded with my Pinson cousins, among them Patsy and Arthur Moore, who were visiting us in Gadsden. Flynt family photo.

rule our younger siblings and cousins. They resented our direction shrilly and demonstrably. Our parents generally sided with the younger ones, but since I seldom visited, at first Virginia Moore and Ina Hagood came down hard on Patsy, Arthur, and Jan, barely mentioning me. More often than not, I was ringleader of the mischief but usually escaped unscathed.

After a while, Virginia figured things out and included me in the group of miscreants. Ina soon caught on as well, though her special relationship with Mom moderated her discipline, and she continued to view me as essentially harmless and trustworthy.

There were moments of high drama, none more memorable than when Leo Hagood bought his children a Shetland pony that had a wild streak. When "Little Leo" mounted it, the pony began to gallop, heading directly for a tree, then dodging just before collision. It ran through the woods between the Moore and Hagood houses, then back again. Little Leo was terrified, but his father just shouted, "Stay with him, son, stay with him." The pony made four or five circuits of the trail, each punctuated by Leo's admonition, until Little Leo finally spotted a patch of grass and weeds and dove for safety.

Not all memories are so funny. At the top of the hill where Center Point highway dead-ended onto Highway 75 toward Oneonta, the Rock House honky-tonk proved an irresistible temptation to Curt, Leo, and Dad when they had had their fill of our antics. A few beers late at night turned into loud talk and more serious drinking, as well as growing anxiety for Mom, Ina, and Virginia. Fights were not uncommon at the Rock House, and men sometimes were knifed and shot there. When anxiety levels reached their zenith, the women piled us into a car and headed for the honky-tonk to retrieve our fathers. Knowing that the men would resent the embarrassing intrusion of their wives, the women dispatched Patsy as their emissary to persuade the men to come home.

My cousins and I bonded in childhood, separated in adolescence, and renewed our friendship in adulthood. They paid me the ultimate compliment by asking me to perform their marriage ceremonies. I also helped conduct Ina's funeral.

My Flynt cousins taught me lessons as well. Lynda Beason, Lillie Mae's third child after George and Dale, was born with Down syndrome. Lillie Mae rejected the conventional 1950s wisdom that such a child could not learn or successfully cope with other children. All who knew Lynda marveled at her happiness, friendliness, joy, and kindness. Was that the compensation for the dreadful syndrome? We who are "normal" struggle to maintain our wonder at life. She, among the afflicted, who lost her independence and autonomy, never wavered in the joy of interdependency and relationships. She exuded love and simplicity. And she never lost her innocence or understood how people could be cruel and unkind to one another. These were lessons Lynda and Lillie Mae taught me early in life that I did not learn from books or college courses.

If not idyllic, my childhood was always tolerable and mostly joyous. Because of the combination of constant moves and life as an only child living a substantial distance from my cousins, I grew up in a solitary world. Although counter to my extroverted personality (which was more like Dad's than Mom's) that was not altogether a bad thing. If you wanted friends (and I did), you couldn't sit alone at a table in the school lunchroom. I learned to barge right in to other people's lives. Sometimes the intrusion worked; other times it did not.

In later years, my two favorite presidents became Abraham Lincoln and Franklin Roosevelt. I considered Lincoln to be the man who saved the nation and abolished its most abhorrent institution. When the nation most needed him, poet James Russell Lowell wrote, "Out of the very earth, unancestried, unprivileged, unknown," he came among us, a man of integrity, moral authority, eloquence, and enormous strength of purpose. I liked Roosevelt because I envisioned him as being in so many ways like me. True, he was born into a rich, patrician, northern family. But he was also an only child. His overly protective mother spoiled him. His boyhood was ordered and harmonious. He was not athletic and did not fit in well at Groton or Harvard. He was neither popular nor an outstanding student. He spent more time with adults than children. In his solitude, he retreated inside himself, into hobbies such as stamp collecting. Living in a pastoral setting, he roamed the forests between his house and the Hudson River. At Harvard he preferred liberal arts classes, especially history.

Like Roosevelt, I roamed woods near our Anniston home, Buster by my side. Like him, I collected stamps. Like him, I was in the company of adults more than children. Like him, my mother and father doted on me.

I did, of course, grow up in a different generation, although my childhood was in many ways closer to his than to the baby boomers who followed me. My generation was secure in our social enclaves. Everyone—blacks, whites, men, women, children—knew their place. History meant the same thing to most southern whites: autonomy, democracy, capitalism, Protestantism, pride in family and regional identity, parochialism. Marrying "outside the faith" still meant a Baptist marrying a Methodist, and we were warned against it.

Before my parents bought a television, nights in the safe neighborhoods where we lived meant outdoor children's games, quiet reading, a favorite radio program, and an early bedtime. I especially enjoyed the eerie mystery program *The Shadow*. I also learned to love country and gospel music. I even got an autograph from Nashville Grand Ole Opry star Red Foley. Saturdays were consumed by the movies, a cowboy double feature along with news, cartoons, and previews, all for a dime.

Contraception had limited the size of families, and in time air-conditioning and television drove us inside our houses. Dinner trays in front of the television assured that we would not miss our favorite programs. Front porches ceased to have a function; individualism began to replace communitarianism; and soon we neither knew our neighbors nor cared to.

Things took over spaces once occupied by people. By 1951 nearly 90 percent of American families owned refrigerators and almost 75 percent had washing machines, telephones, vacuum cleaners, and gas or electric stoves. Americans owned 80 percent of the world's electrical contraptions and produced 40 percent of its electricity, 60 percent of its oil, and 66 percent of its steel. Of the 7.5 million new automobiles sold in America in 1954, 99.93 percent were made in America. Things we did not have to worry about because they had not yet been invented or they were new and impractical included interstate highways, fast foods, ballpoint pens, electric can openers, shopping malls, supermarkets, suburban sprawl, domestic air-conditioning, power steering, automatic transmissions, contact lenses, credit cards, garbage disposals, dishwashers, and major league baseball teams west of Saint Louis.

As greater affluence and urbanization reduced my family's dependence on the community and heightened our sense of self-sufficiency, we felt quite consciously middle class. Although I overheard Dad's stories often enough to know he had experienced hard times, I never thought of him as poor. He and Mom carefully shielded me from the harsh reality of their upbringing. Even with Dad's modest income, I felt no sense of deprivation. And if they seemed careful with every dime, that just seemed prudent and logical to me rather than the consequence of their economic insecurities.

I often shopped with mother. We had only one car, so where city buses were available (Birmingham and Atlanta), we rode them downtown to shop. Such trips usually involved a ritual visit to a dime store lunch counter for a grilled cheese sandwich and a milkshake. Department stores during the 1940s and early 1950s reflected a nation at war, with toy jeeps, planes, and child-size military uniforms (I had both army and navy). I also collected full-color photos of military planes provided by their manufacturers.

Vacations didn't last long but were keenly anticipated for months in advance. We usually stayed close to home, preferring Civilian Conservation Corps–built cabins at Cheaha State Park or the beaches of Panama City. Once we drove to Elkhart, Indiana, to visit the Rabideaus, our World War II friends from Mrs. Downing's boarding house. Our stop in Chicago made the trip my most exotic vacation. But my favorite was our summer trip to Washington, D.C., with stops along the way at each Virginia Civil War battlefield we passed.

I learned about the battlefields from a new source. The same year Dad bought a television, he purchased *Compton's Encyclopedia*. It was a tough decision financially, but he believed the set would help me in school. We had few books other than those volumes, and I buried myself in them. Though considered inferior to *Britannica, Compton's* was perfectly acceptable to a preteen boy. The introduction promised that the set would "inspire ambition, . . . stimulate imagination, . . . provide the inquiring mind with accurate information told in an interesting style." In time I would come to know the larger works of many of the encyclopedia's editors: historians William E. Dodd, John D. Hicks, Allan Nevins; historian/archaeologist James Breasted; poet/writers Stephen Vincent Benet and Carl Van Doren; folklorist Carl Carmer (whose *Stars Fell on Ala-*

bama was a classic that I would later introduce in a reprint edition). I raced through articles about World War II, the Civil War, airplanes, ships, navies, and all things military. My imaginary world was full of warriors.

Compton's accomplished its goal of inspiring my ambition and stimulating my imagination. Thanks to a mother who never threw away any of my projects and documented every major event in my life with photographs, I have samples from my first "book" written at age eleven in a "Yellow Label Syrup Jot It Down Book." My first chapter explored the U.S. Navy, fully illustrated with drawings of various kinds of ships. The second chapter explored the theory of flight (gravity, thrust, drag, and lift), complete with graphs and charts. I carefully outlined a third chapter on the history of flight but never finished it. Apparently I decided that *Compton's* and my own imagination made school redundant or irrelevant because I invested far more effort in my solitary learning than in school, at least until we moved to Anniston, where I began my sophomore year of high school.

Anniston was an unusual southern town. Dating only to Reconstruction, it was founded by two Yankees, Samuel Noble and Daniel Tyler, as a private, idealized, industrial, and conservative Christian community. They laid out a "model town" with a grid of streets, each allocated factories, businesses, schools, churches, and residences. It became one of the most successful southern industrial towns, briefly vying with Birmingham for dominance of the New South. The founders opened their private town to the public in 1883. Its cast-iron pipe shops, which made it the "sewer pipe capital of the world," thrived along with its textile mills. Conveniently located on the main Central of Georgia Railway line from Atlanta to Birmingham, the small city produced corporate lawyer John B. Knox, who served as president of the 1901 Alabama Constitutional Convention, and progressive banker Thomas Kilby, who was elected governor in 1918.

During World War I the U.S. Army established Camp McClellan just north of the city, and in 1929 the federal government gave it permanent status as Fort McClellan. In 1941 the Chrysler Corporation constructed Anniston Ordnance Depot west of town. By the time we moved there, Anniston was a bustling county seat of more than thirty thousand. Dad committed to staying put until I finished high school, then prolonged his residence until I was out of college. That allowed me finally to put down roots.

Two factors deflected my education in new directions, my recently discovered religious commitment and a remarkable Yankee teacher. Religion for me was more process than event. I compare my spirituality to the life cycle of a twin oak tree that grows next to my screened porch in Auburn. When my young family moved to Auburn in 1977, the tree had a small, rotting depression where the trunk divided. Water filled the depression when it rained, endangering the tree. I dug out the rot, filled the depression with a special compound to seal it, and the healthy twin oak now soars above my other trees. Watching that sapling as it slowly grew into a tall tree provided a wonderful analogy for my own spiritual pilgrimage.

Spirituality occasionally occurs as a great burst of insight, a sudden "aha" or "eureka" moment. Usually it is an imperceptible healing, maturing, growing, changing of direction. One day we are one person. A decade later we are a different person. And spirituality can die a day at a time just as it can grow the same way.

In the earliest manifestation of religious zeal, I was immature, self-righteous, and offensively judgmental. This constituted part of my spiritual "rot." As the modern Baptist theologian Fisher Humphreys has written, young Christians often test the sincerity and intensity of their faith by how loudly and militantly they proclaim it. In my teenage years, my zealous denunciation of dancing, consuming alcohol, and listening to rock-and-roll music must have made me a thoroughly objectionable Christian to many of my peers. Only slowly did I realize that the true test of discipleship was the integrity with which I lived my life, which was also the truest witness to my faith.

I was slow to learn another principle of Fisher's theology. There is a thin line between spiritual arrogance and paralyzing self-doubt and indecision. Only slowly did I learn to affirm both what I believed and that I could be wrong. For Protestants like me who trace our authority to careful and serious study of scripture and experiential engagement with Jesus, there is the added problem of our internal disagreement about the nature of divine revelation. With neither pope, bishop, nor churchly tradition to determine these issues for us, we inevitably differ about the meaning of both scripture and the kingdom of God. This revelation dawned slowly on me as well. Yet it did dawn, and I did change.

Not long after we moved back to Anniston when I was fourteen, I replaced *Compton's Encyclopedia* with the Carnegie Public Library. Though Mom had read to me as a child, and I had long consumed Civil War biographies for myself, I became a serious reader only after our move to Anniston. Carnegie Library was the perfect place for this second baptism of the spirit. The library was not only packed with wonderful books, but the nationally renowned H. Severn Regar ornithology collection stared down at me from the top of bookcases and out from glass cases, adding a touch of international exoticism to the experience of reading. The incredible lifelike expressions of the birds sometimes made it difficult for me to concentrate on the books.

Of course, I sought out giants of the Baptist persuasion such as John Bunyan's *Pilgrims Progress.* But I also wanted to know how my opponents thought. So I read British physicist/philosopher/atheist Bertrand Russell's essay "The Expanding Mental Universe" in an anthology titled *Adventures of the Mind.* The book included mind-expanding essays by Jacques Barzun, Paul Tillich, Robert Oppenheimer, Edith Hamilton, H. I. Hayakawa, Aldous Huxley, and the composer Aaron Copland, as well as by historians D. W. Brogan and Arthur M. Schlesinger Jr. Later I labored over Russell's *Why I Am Not a Christian.*

I borrowed what I found congruent, such as biological evolution, and rejected what I found objectionable. I learned that atheists can sound a lot like Southern Baptists in their arrogance, dogmatism, and patronization of those who disagree with them. More importantly, I learned the wisdom of an Albert Einstein observation about the universe even before I read the great physicist's quote myself: "There are only two ways to live your life. One is as though nothing is a miracle. The other is as though everything is a miracle." The physical universe described by physics, astronomy, biology, and geology was so miraculous that it overwhelmed me. But that was nothing compared to the expanding mental universe described by Einstein, Huxley, and Russell. Just to be alive and part of it shook me to my core.

Parker Memorial Baptist Church became part of my expanding mental universe. My parents let me select our church home, so excited were they by my budding spirituality. During a youth revival, I joined Parker Memorial. The Victorian church, with its liturgical and aesthetic richness, seemed an odd fit for us, but the mixture of people from many backgrounds suited us well. Among the prominent members were Charles Bell, the banker who had owned my grandfather's sharecrop farm, and Harry Ayers, whose father had been the first Southern Baptist medical missionary to China, where Harry had grown up. Ayers was an unorthodox Baptist who drank alcohol, owned the city's newspaper, taught the Baraca Sunday school class, and unfailingly endorsed Democrats for president, including John F. Kennedy in 1960. In a book about Alabama missionaries in China, I spent much space reconstructing Ayers's family history.

Our pastor, B. Locke Davis, was a Texan, a World War II chaplain in the Pacific, a history major from Baptist-affiliated Hardin-Simmons University,

Anniston's Parker Memorial Baptist Church in the 1940s. This church and its controversial pastors Charles R. Bell and B. Locke Davis were formative influences on my
theology and ethics. Courtesy Parker Memorial Baptist Church.

a voracious reader, open-minded, and ecumenical. He was entirely orthodox
in his opposition to local liquor sales and Roman Catholic presidential candidates, disagreeing with Ayers on both issues. A denominational statesman
who served a term as president of the Alabama Baptist State Convention,
he was only a mediocre preacher, though a careful Bible scholar and a well-
informed Baptist historian.

Further back in time the church's history was even more fascinating. At the
turn of the twentieth century, a series of pastors had implemented major elements of the social gospel, the idea that the kingdom of God was not some

event that would occur at the end of time but must be implemented by us now in acts of righteousness and justice.

Charles Bell's sons, Charlie and Tartt, grew up in the church with those same ideals. Charlie attended three Baptist schools—Howard College, Brown University, and Southern Seminary—before returning as pastor of Parker Memorial in the 1920s. He was a pacifist who talked with Mahatma Gandhi in India, introduced the confessional Oxford movement to the congregation (sins could be forgiven only when publicly acknowledged and confessed), invited black families to dine with him in the parsonage, established an interracial farm, and voted multiple times for socialist presidential candidate Norman Thomas. His brother, Tartt, was an even more radical pacifist who was imprisoned during World War II for his beliefs, became a Quaker, and worked most of his life for the Fellowship of Reconciliation.

On D-Day 1944, Charlie refused to allow an American flag next to his pulpit, contending that to introduce the flag into the church at a time of violence and death was tantamount to a Christian endorsement of war. Shortly thereafter, amid great controversy, he resigned to become pastor of an American Baptist church in Madison, Wisconsin.

Charlie's influence was still palpable when we joined Parker Memorial church eleven years later, and some of the congregational wounds remained unhealed. He returned once to preach while we were members (the sermon was brilliant and marvelously delivered), and I later authored essays about him, directed a thesis based on his life, and persuaded him to deposit his papers in the Samford University archives.

All these discoveries came later and connected me to a radical Baptist tradition that I knew nothing about as a teenager. I did know that Parker provided a warm, loving, nondogmatic, evangelical community. I loved singing in Griff Perry's youth choir. I finally had found a congenial, fervent, and intellectually stimulating circle of teenage friends, a nurturing pastor, and mature adult leadership. Summers were punctuated with youth retreats and weeklong trips to Ridgecrest Baptist Assembly in North Carolina. I was chosen pastor during youth week and spoke at both Baptist and interdenominational youth services. Mom and Dad loved the church as much as I did, and we soon became fully immersed in its life.

Anniston High School was not as exciting to me as Parker church but was satisfactory nonetheless. The school had no Latin courses, so my class schedule in the fall of 1955 had to be modified. In the way of casual academic advisers who perused my checkered academic past, they shuffled me off to a speech class, assuming, I suppose, that it would do me no harm and might even allow me to graduate.

That demonstrated how much they underestimated their new speech and theater teacher, Janet H. LeFevre. A Pennsylvania native and Cornell University graduate with clipped, precise diction, she came to Anniston with her army officer husband when he was transferred to Fort McClellan. She was a no-nonsense teacher who criticized what even my father agreed was my "mushy mouthed" southern accent that eliminated most consonants, especially "t" and "d" at the end of words.

At first thinking me fine material for drama (probably because I was determined to be a Baptist preacher), Janet drafted me for theater. My debut in a play titled *What's Wrong with the Girls?* required an on-stage kiss. I had never kissed a girl and was not about to begin on a stage in front of my Parker Memorial friends. LeFevre criticized my prudishness but finally omitted the kiss (the omission of which did not properly advance the story line of the play).

I was still not precocious in the mysteries of sex, having used my newfound faith to rationalize my inherent shyness around girls. My infrequent dates with Parker Memorial girls did not press me to misadventures in this regard. My first date at age sixteen using the family car brought no more instruction from my father than to remember that I was a Flynt. It would have been hard to forget that fact in Anniston amid so many relatives and family friends, where it seemed that everyone knew me or my family. Anonymity would not be a factor in my morality or lack thereof.

Dad had never chatted with me about sex, assigned me a time to be home from a date, or seemed to worry about my conduct. I gave him no reason to do so until my senior year in high school when I took a beautiful girl, the daughter of a divorced textile mill worker, to a football game. Dad grilled me carefully before and after the date. And her forwardness in sticking her cold hand into my overcoat pocket to hold hands seemed to have more to do with romance than the weather, so I listened carefully to his wisdom in my after-date-report. He stammered a lot, started over several times, and never really got to the point. But I understood the essence of his advice. Textile mill girls from divorced families might try to entrap me in some as yet undefined way, so I needed to be careful. We were both embarrassed, so we left it at that. In the decade that followed, few would have believed it possible that June Cleaver's world actually existed outside of television. I was proof it did.

Dad's concern for my welfare was obvious. And it was even more demonstrable the night I drove two teenage girls over "thrill hill" after a football game and church fellowship. Thrill hill was not what it sounds like. The steep hill had a sudden dip where your stomach seemed to come up into your throat if you drove at the appropriate speed. We had just completed the maneuver when I noticed a car behind me. The driver suddenly passed, then cut in front of me, blocking my car against the curb. He opened the door, came around in front of my headlights clad in an undershirt, pants, without shoes or socks, and holding a long knife. All three of us were terrified.

The man was furious. Someone driving a car similar to mine had stolen his hubcaps. He had driven around Anniston for hours looking for the car until he saw me. Insisting that I knew nothing about his hubcaps, I invited him to drive behind me to the police station where they could search my car. Somewhat mollified, he agreed. When the police search turned up no contraband, I drove the girls home, then returned to Michael Lane where we lived. It was after 1:00 a.m., the house was dark, and I assumed my parents were asleep. Wrong! They were in an absolute panic. I had never been so late without telling them, and they feared the worst. Dad demanded to know where I had been. When I mentioned the police station and the man with a knife, he flew into a rage. He demanded to know the man's name. I had no idea, so he called the police station. The dispatcher refused to tell him. Dad explained that he knew all the Anniston policemen and said one of them would supply the information if the dispatcher declined to do so. With the name in hand, Dad called the offender and threatened to shoot him if he ever bothered me again. Mother and I were terrified for days, knowing that he was fully capable of doing what he had threatened.

With my thespian career stunted by my timidity around girls, Janet LeFevre changed strategies. Having just launched a forensics program, she relegated me to stagehand duties in the theater and drafted me as a debater. I had found my niche. According to contemporary Gallup polls, Americans rated 1957 the happiest year ever recorded. That fall, I began my senior year of high school and had I been polled, I would have agreed.

Debate fit my proclivities for solitary reading and research, allowed me to excel in something other than athletics where I was so inept, appealed to my growing appreciation for the life of the mind, and harnessed my Baptist penchant for argument and my Flynt gift for gab. I won Civitan Club and *Birmingham News* regional oratorical contests. In the state newspaper finals, I finished second in a field of eighteen contestants. My debate partner (Donald Stewart, who later served as president of the student government association

at the University of Alabama and as U.S. senator from Alabama) and I finished second at the University of Alabama forensics tournament. I was ranked
among the top five debaters in the state, high enough to win college scholarships to the University of Alabama (at a time when its reputation in debate
vastly exceeded its woeful football team) and Birmingham-Southern College.

Dad lobbied strongly against the University of Alabama, which he denounced
as a country club school full of spoiled, rich, fraternity boys (his implication
being that they would never accept someone like me). The ready acceptance
shown to sharecroppers' sons like John Sparkman and Carl Elliott proved him
wrong, but I suppose his early participation in Future Farmers of America
youth programs at Auburn had sealed his loyalties in that regard. Birmingham-
Southern had the state's best academic reputation but as a Methodist school
seemed a strange staging ground for a Baptist ministerial career. So my pastor,
Locke Davis, wrote Harwell Goodwin Davis, the president of Howard College,
a Baptist school, asking him to match my other scholarships. Howard was a
poor school just moving to a new campus south of Birmingham, was about to
inaugurate a new president, and had only recently begun a forensics program.
Nonetheless, the school offered me a modest work scholarship in debate and
lots of encouragement. Tuition was only $150.00 a semester, half of which was
provided by a ministerial scholarship, so the school was affordable even for my
family's modest means. Dad thought well of the idea and agreed to help me as
much as he could.

Despite winning honor roll recognition virtually every semester in high
school, serving as president of both Anniston High and state chapters of the
National Honor Society, and achieving various oratorical and debate honors,
I was terrified at the prospect of college. Three years of striving could hardly
redress the problems created by nine years of inattention and academic dis-
ruption.

Even those three good years were flawed. Anniston High had some outstanding teachers: Janet LeFevre; history teacher Charles A. Nunn (who moon-
lighted as a professional wrestler, usually playing the villain, in order to earn
enough to continue teaching); W. H. (Billy) Bancroft (former Howard College
football and baseball star, premed student, and briefly my baseball coach until
he told me that I had no athletic talent, who proved that a high school coach
could also be a fine biology and geometry teacher); and Opal Lovett (my beloved English instructor who enthusiastically explained the beauty of English
literature and the intricacies of its construction).

Beyond that list, the quality of my instruction declined. Three Spanish teachers in two years left me thinking that Spanish and Latin shared one thing in common: they were equally incomprehensible. Math, as always, made Latin seem entirely logical by comparison. Other English and history teachers generally filled up time I would rather have spent reading or researching a debate topic. My standardized test scores, assuming I took any, must have reflected the vagaries of my childhood and my transitory education.

Since neither parent had attended college, they could offer no advice about how to prepare for the next stage of my life. Nor could my uncles, aunts, or cousins, none of whom had finished college by then. Pop Fee was our only college grad and he had earned his baccalaureate in 1924. Counselors in Alabama's underfunded public schools were as rare as Rhodes scholars. I remember none. My four favorite teachers offered advice and encouragement. I think Janet LeFevre was most realistic about my future. She told me that I could succeed in college but only with great effort.

I graduated from Anniston High School on Friday evening, May 30, 1958, and began the summer term at Howard College three days later. I explained to my parents that I needed the summer to research the national debate topic on the development of nuclear weapons. At a deeper level, the decision traced back to all my insecurities: fear of losing my parents, of sitting at lunch tables in a dozen schools by myself, of failure in the manly venture of athletics, that my academic deficiencies would finally catch up with me; my unease around girls; my fierce desire to excel at something despite my limited natural ability. At least, I reasoned, if I flunked out of college in the summer, I could enter the local Anniston labor market in September with my Anniston High classmates none the wiser. No one but my parents would have to know of my failure.

• three •

Discoveries and Awakenings

Howard College in 1958 was a lot like me. Everything was new and exciting, and it seemed a time of limitless possibilities. After more than a half century in East Lake (where my grandfather had been a student), with inadequate and rapidly declining facilities in a similarly challenged neighborhood, the college had just moved to a new campus in Homewood, an affluent suburb south of Birmingham. After nineteen years as president, Harwell G. Davis had retired. New president Leslie S. Wright and I both entered as "freshmen" that year, though he remained at the school a lot longer than I did.

Although the college was conservative and traditional in the way most southern denominational colleges were in the 1950s, it contained countervailing tendencies from its early days. One of America's one hundred oldest colleges, Howard had been established in 1841 in Perry County, deep in the Alabama Black Belt. Baptist leaders named the school in honor of English prison reformer and Baptist layman John Howard, who had expended his life and fortune trying to obtain justice for the poorest and most wretched Europeans. From the school's earliest days, one could find validation on campus for either the cultural captivity of Christianity to southern traditions or the liberation from culture by the radical teachings of Jesus.

The institution survived fires, the Civil War, financial depressions, bankruptcy, and the humiliation of a forced auction, before moving to the boom-town of Birmingham in 1887. After a brief interval of prosperity and growing academic experimentation—administrators, faculty, and students alike dab-bled in the new biblical liberalism spawned in Germany and the social gospel spreading across the urban Northeast and Midwest—the school settled back into its conservatism. The Great Depression again threatened Howard's sur-vival before Harwell Goodwin Davis (who, as the state's attorney general, had been a fervent prison reformer like the school's namesake) became president in 1939 and barely fended off financial wolves gathering at the school's gates. Ac-quisition of a V-12 Navy College Training Program during the Second World War, the GI Bill that followed, unwavering support by Alabama Baptists, and prodigious efforts on the school's behalf by Liberty National Insurance chief executive Frank Samford, had stabilized enrollment and finances by the time Wright took charge.

Although the student body was exclusively white, overwhelmingly Baptist, and mainly middle class, many of my classmates were first-generation college students. Not a few were from poor families who struggled to pay the nominal tuition. Scattered among us were pockets of Greek Orthodox and Catholic students from Birmingham's diverse ethnic communities, a handful of Jewish students, an agnostic or two, a Hungarian refugee who had driven an ambu-lance during the just-defeated national uprising against Soviet occupation, and Baptist missionary kids (MKs as they were known on campus), whose world perspective, language skills, and sensitivity to the problems of the global com-munity enriched education for all of us.

Football, though a long and revered tradition in earlier years, had fallen on hard times. A resurrection similar to the college's was under way, directed by new football coach Bobby Bowden. Many of us dutifully attended games and cheered the team, though none of us confused the school's purpose or identity with an oblong piece of pigskin.

When I moved into my nearly deserted dorm in late May 1958, I came in a state of near panic. But two summer terms instilled some confidence in me. My woeful background in Spanish allowed me into second year classes where I did not belong but made Bs anyway from two professors who had long since given up on language facility among their students and were marking time until re-tirement. Without athletic facilities on the new campus, the only physical edu-cation possible consisted of table tennis, the one sport in which I seemed com-petent. The course introduced me to the capricious professoriate. I defeated football players in the class tournament and on the final exam fully explained the rules of the game. The coach gave me a C anyway and them As. But I received higher grades than I deserved in Spanish, so I figured it evened out.

My two Western civilization courses were a delight. George Sarkiss, an Armenian refugee from Turkish genocide, had come with his family to America and earned his Ph.D. He did not teach Western civilization so much as his philosophy of history, punctuated by diatribes against the Ottoman Empire and Turkey. I still remember a quotation from Friedrich von Logau via Longfellow ("the mills of the gods grind slowly but exceedingly fine"), as well as Napoleon's axiom that "God fights on the side with the largest battalions." He was remembered by my wife as the teacher who threw her ungraded final exam into the wastebasket as she left the room, then arbitrarily assigned whatever grade he chose, but I was blessed to be an eager pupil of his offbeat wisdom and a class favorite who earned As.

Academically, that first summer was not memorable either for my performance or that of my instructors. Better times were ahead for me, and at least I spent considerable time reading and conducting research for the approaching debate season.

With my voracious appetite for learning, I naively concluded that if I truly applied myself I could pretty well master human knowledge in my three years of college, minus, of course, mathematics, physics, and chemistry, which were as incomprehensible to me as Sanskrit or Swahili. That first year I read Boris Pasternak's new novel *Doctor Zhivago* and became hooked on fiction. I also stumbled across the Classics Club, which published cheap editions of the great books of the Western intellectual tradition. I plunged into Marcus Aurelius's *Meditations* and became fascinated by Stoicism. Next came Homer's *Odyssey* and *Iliad*. Then the avalanche buried me until, feeling guilty that I could not read them all, I canceled my membership. Gradually, it occurred to me that the more learning I obtained, the more elusive my goal of mastering all learning became.

Religion: Academic and Personal

I was no less eager within the smaller intellectual realm within which I confined myself. Ministerial students were not required to major in religion. Indeed, history claimed as many of them as religion. I chose this direction, although I loved my Old and New Testament classes with yet another "freshman," W. T. Edwards, a newly arrived professor. Provocative, witty, and inclined to prick the pious, sanctimonious, and self-righteous, he also delighted in complicating simplistic theology. Despite a B in Old Testament, I stuck with Edwards, who became a lifelong friend and one of my most influential mentors.

Like everyone in the religion department, Edwards identified with the neo-orthodox theology that became so influential in the postwar years. Heavily influenced by brothers Richard and Reinhold Niebuhr and Paul Tillich, my professors blended biblical criticism (the application of archaeology, anthropology, history, linguistic analysis, and psychology, among other disciplines, to biblical study) with a strong sense of the limited scope of human inquiry. With their Baptist forebears and especially like emerging denominational superstar Billy Graham, they affirmed the sinful nature of human kind (which was easy to do following the Holocaust, World War II, atomic bomb attacks on Hiroshima and Nagasaki, the Cold War, and the prospect of nuclear annihilation), the urgency of repentance, and the necessity to be "born again." Though warmly evangelical and closely bound to the denominational life from which they came, they were overwhelmingly ecumenical.

Nor did they flinch when confronted by the wholly mysterious. In a philosophy of religion course my senior year with Mabry Lunceford, we tackled the problem of irreducible evil, the issue embedded in the anguished argument that Job (my favorite Old Testament character) had with God. It was no small issue for my generation. While we wrestled in class with the question of why good people suffer, die, are incinerated, nuked, napalmed, raped, and tortured, Archibald MacLeish explored the same issues on Broadway in America's greatest poetic drama, *J.B.* MacLeish put the argument on the tongue of his cynical character, Nickles:

I heard upon his dry dung heap
That man cry out who cannot sleep:
"If God is God He is not good;
If God is good He is not God;
Take the even, take the odd,
I would not sleep here if I could
Except for the little green leaves in the wood
And the wind on the water."

We read, debated, and philosophized about the problem of unjust suffering for a full semester. Only those who knew the answers before enrolling had solved the problem by the end of the course.

Beyond academic aspects of college, I treasured opportunities for service. My choice was a weekly trip to the boy's industrial school near the airport. Born in the progressive prison reform movement earlier in the century, the school was intended to separate youthful offenders from adult criminals. Some of the teenagers had already launched careers that would land them in adult prisons. They were in the school for rape, attempted murder, and armed robbery. Others were simply poor white boys who had become incorrigible, had been abandoned by their parents, or had no one to take responsibility for them.

My sheltered adolescence had not prepared me for these urchins, for their streetwise manipulation, lies, survival strategies, or their violence toward one another. Nevertheless, during my freshman year I bonded with one of them who had been abandoned by his parents.. He told me just before Christmas 1958 that he would not be at the school when I returned from break. Relatives were picking him up to come live with them. Afraid of older boys in the school, he was excited at the prospect of a new start in life. When I returned in January, he met me, deeply depressed and more cynical than before. I did not ask what had happened, but one of the staff told me that on the day appointed for his dismissal, no one came for him. That was my first encounter with Alabama's throwaway children. It would not be my last.

Many Sundays I availed myself of opportunities to preach in Howard's H-Day program. Part of the school's innovative extension effort, H-Day opened pulpits to aspiring ministerial students. Possessing as I did a strong democratic bias, I welcomed the opportunity to preach in churches of every kind. I preached to congregations of the well-educated and affluent in First Baptist churches; to poorly educated farmer Baptists in isolated rural congregations; to textile workers in mill village churches; to fundamentalist Baptists pastored by bivocational pastors who believed God had dictated every word in the Bible to scribes who wrote it down. I loved them all, although their racial comments over lunch sometimes raised serious questions about their willingness to allow the book they so treasured to liberate them from the culture they so revered.

By no means was I a full-blown convert to integration myself. But I was on my way to that promised land. I simply could not reconcile my reading of scripture with the racial norms of southern life. Bible stories such as the Good Samaritan must either be confined to irrelevance in ancient Israel or must address the enigma of race relations in modern America. It was not my parents, peers, school, or church that began to unshackle me from the chains of racism. It was the Bible. I was only a teenager in high school when the first tensions appeared between the teachings of Jesus and the teachings of John Patterson and George Wallace. Somebody was wrong. And it wasn't Jesus.

Race

My high school and undergraduate years (1954 to 1961) were seminal in the origins of the modern civil rights movement: the Brown Decision (1954); Montgomery Bus Boycott (1955–56); attempted integration of the University of Alabama (1957); the Freedom Rides (1961). These events provided the distant thunder that disturbed my ease in Zion.

In 1961 I penned my first letter to the editor. I wrote in response to a Tuscaloosa resident who congratulated "the good Christian men believing in our Anglo-Saxon heritage of freedom" who had mercilessly beaten freedom riders in a Birmingham bus station (with the connivance of city police). Where in scripture did the writer find justification for the attacks in Anniston, Birmingham, and Montgomery, I inquired. What biblical text conjured up an image of Jesus swinging a piece of lead pipe or kicking a human being writhing in pain? As for glorification of Christianity's Anglo-Saxon origins, I expressed surprise because I had always thought of Jesus as a Jew. Perhaps the writer had Jesus confused with Hitler and the Bible with *Mein Kampf.* As for threatening Alabama traditions, I ended my intemperate diatribe, best not to begin with "outside trouble makers" in 1961. Much earlier than that the Anglo-Saxon ancestors of the hoodlums at the bus station had pillaged land from the original Alabama inhabitants and destroyed Native American civilization. I acknowledged his right to protest integration or even defend mob violence, but I thought it best to leave Jesus out of it. The mean-spirited incivility of my letter, which I now regret, was constructed in equal parts of Flynt temper, my sense of moral outrage at unfair treatment of powerless people, and my meandering journey from racial captive to my culture to something quite different that would come to define my life. I took some consolation in the discovery that many other southern Christians were traveling this path alongside me. Their courage became my inspiration.

Across town at Birmingham-Southern College, a friend who was president of the student government association (SGA) boldly challenged segregation and was backed by his college president, leading many donors to withhold financial support from the fine Methodist school. An Alabama minister without a pulpit (meaning that he could exercise the gift of prophecy, which is always

easier when a preacher has neither ministerial job nor family) worked unsuc-
cessfully for racial reconciliation:

> What can a southern man who loves his region and his church, his segregationist
> congregation and his antisegregation convictions do here today and still not be
> cut down by the powers-that-be? We've seen the teachers and preachers speak—
> and leave. We've seen the college trustees and church boards build the campuses
> and get rid of the faculty, build the churches and get rid of the ministers. When a
> group of civic leaders came to me and pleaded with me not to hold an interracial
> group meeting in one of the city buildings, I was so heartsick I could only say,
> "Gentlemen of good will and bad conscience, I abdicate."

On the Howard campus, most faculty and students I knew, if not unanimous in their rejection of racism, were close to it. MKs were appalled at the
message sent round the world by the South's discrimination. Students from the
fringes of the South—Virginia, North Carolina, Texas, and Kentucky—where
desegregation was already under way, dissected the contradictions inherent
in a racially segregated Christian college. Even segregationists deplored white
violence. I shared their sense of dismay. My notes from a course in persuasive
speaking, which I took during the last semester of my senior year, are filled
with my musings about the contradictions between religion and racism.

Christian Higher Education

Already these issues were defining for me the essential purpose of Christian
higher education. Baptist theologian Fisher Humphries has explored four possibilities. Was the purpose to brainwash students, whether from the ideological
right or left? Was it to indoctrinate them by claiming that all truth resided in
the professor and his ideology, that any other claims to truth were wrong and
should not be discussed except for purposes of refutation? Was it for exploration, transmitting and affirming traditions, while urging students to think
for themselves and finally to embrace whatever their minds and consciences
told them was true? Or was it intellectual relativism, where no value or tradition is affirmed and students are urged to adopt whatever ideas appealed to
them? Most of my professors fell into the pedagogy of exploration category:
they transmitted and affirmed their own traditions and values while leaving
the final resolution to the student.

For many of my classmates, this exploration began their journey out of the

South, the church, and their inherited culture. For me, it was the beginning of a lifelong struggle to keep the faith, to reconcile as much as I could of my traditions with an emerging consciousness about the injustice embedded in American society.

The college's faculty, many state Baptist leaders, as well as my pastor and the staff at Parker Memorial, never wavered in their support of me wherever my journey led. In the spring of 1961, I served the church again as Youth Week pastor. I continued to preach H-Day sermons, though with a growing sense of uneasiness. I faithfully attended Dawson Memorial Baptist Church, my adopted college congregation, speaking to Sunday school classes when invited. And when my home church asked me to serve on staff as full-time youth minister during the summer of 1961, I quickly accepted and was ordained to the ministry by the people who knew me best and loved me most. Mine was, I believe, a generation that struggled hard to reconcile our traditions and flawed institutions with a new vision of the future.

Academics

Meanwhile my academic banquet continued uninterrupted. Professors in English, history, biology, religion, and speech were uniformly inspiring. The best of them—David Vess, William P. Dale, and Hugh Bailey in history; W. T. Edwards and Mabry Lunceford in religion; Sam Mitchell in English; G. Allan Yeomans in speech—were superb and shaped my life. Vess was a Harvard-trained historian of Europe; Bailey a prolific scholar of southern history and a Guggenheim Fellow; Dale a Duke-trained Latin Americanist; Edwards and Lunceford, warm-hearted, critical thinkers who forced me to confront hard religious issues; Mitchell a witty teacher and rigorous critic of my writing; Yeomans my closest faculty friend.

Every one of them stretched me until I feared I would snap. They made me write, write, write, then write some more. In all, there were fifteen major research papers, which they meticulously critiqued despite teaching loads of five courses per semester. I considered the writing requirements typical until I went to graduate school and discovered that some of my classmates from prestigious universities had written no research papers at all.

Though not highly refined, at least my topics were ambitious. For freshman English, I surveyed the influence of the Civil War on American fiction. In speech and drama classes, I compared Aristotle's theory of criticism with the work of seven New York City drama critics, wrote a rhetorical analysis of

Franklin Roosevelt's fireside chats, and discussed General Douglas MacArthur's use of logic in his 1959 address to Congress. In East Asian history, I explored the origins of Japanese militarism. The demands made on me undoubtedly would have been greater at an Ivy League school. Certainly the academic credentials of my professors would have been more impressive. But I have learned over four decades of teaching that ordinary colleges accomplish amazing feats with students willing to work hard for professors who care deeply about them.

Debate

My single most transformative undergraduate experience was extracurricular but not athletic. All those aspirations in sports, which had left my competitiveness unfulfilled but my course deflected, now converged on intercollegiate debate. Like any team sport, debate is a corporate enterprise. Coaches matter, as do colleagues. As part of a relatively new forensics program begun by Allan Yeomans in 1952, I was fortunate in both.

Yeomans was the most influential of my professors, undergraduate or graduate. Like Sarkiss, he did not teach his subject so much as he taught himself. At first the principal joy of tournament life consisted of victories and trophies. Before long, I most looked forward to the long rides to tournaments when we could talk about life.

A midwesterner by birth, orphaned early and educated at Methodist-affiliated DePauw University, Al had served in the U.S. Army Air Force during the Second World War. As a company adjutant for a heavy bomber squadron, he had watched his mates take off from North Africa on a 1,500-mile flight across the Mediterranean and the German-occupied Balkans, to the Third Reich's oil refineries in Ploesti, Rumania. Of the 1,733 men who flew that 1943 mission, 446 were killed, and only 33 of the original 178 planes returned fit to fly again. As Al described waiting in North Africa for his friends to return and seeing so few land, his eyes became misty, his voice went quiet, and silence settled over the car. Al taught me about the war as Mom and Dad had taught me about the Depression.

Al and his wife, Jo, sometimes invited us to their home for meals, but it was his letters that meant most to me. He taught me the power of thoughtful, carefully constructed correspondence to communicate what is most elemental in human relationships. Oral conversation is spontaneous, unplanned, and sometimes scintillating, but other times it is vacuous; almost always it is short-lived or one-sided. Even debate flirted with sophism, a mere contest to see who wins. But a carefully constructed letter enters both consciousness and history. Speakers can deny their words; writers have no such luxury.

Writing to the debate team in March 1959 following a memorable debate season, Al ruminated not about the national debate question but "what should be Christian education's candid commitment to truth?" Christians surrendered a certain freedom of conduct, he argued, but not their freedom of inquiry, reason, investigation, or critical judgment. Christian churches and schools could preserve their integrity and identity only if they produced students committed to excellence and free inquiry. Deeming us such a cadre of people, he ended his letter with a revolutionary challenge in the context of Alabama public life in 1959: "Christianity is not worth the breath it takes to say the creed unless it can produce individuals who have found in concrete living a new community commitment in every dimension. A rabid sectarian, a racialist, a sectionalist, a nationalist shows by his fruits that his heart is full of something that is not Christianity." That paragraph resonated through the decades that followed.

Near the end of my debate career, in January 1961, Al wrote how much he valued the hours of preparation required by debate, how he cherished our conversations on tournament trips and the conduct of Howard debaters. Not a word about our victories; only pride in our values and ethics. That was so like him. Congratulatory letters piled up from President Wright and other college officials. But they were pro forma and perfunctory good wishes rooted in valuable publicity for the college because of debates won against schools more highly touted than ours. They massaged my ego without expanding my conscience. Al's letters touched me profoundly.

The twenty or so debaters on our team furnished many of my closest college friends: Max Gartman, Paul Barefield, Don Ragsdale, Harold Holder, Nelda Chadwick, Jack Haley, George Bryant, Richard Wise. I am still in touch with some of them. Days and weeks conducting research, practicing debates, taking courses, traveling to tournaments, as well as the electrifying energy of competitive argument against some of the finest debaters in the English-speaking world, drew us together within Yeomans's magical web.

Debate also expanded my mental universe. The national topics—control of nuclear weapons; provision of compulsory, universal, national health insurance; giving Congress power to reverse decisions of the Supreme Court—demanded that we explore both affirmative and negative sides of three of the most important public policy issues of our times. Through debate, I learned again the wisdom of one of my father's aphorisms: "No dime is so thin it doesn't have two sides."

From the day the topic was announced, I disappeared into the bowels of the Harwell Davis Library, which contained government documents. My closest companions became government reports and publications on all sides of the issue. I learned both the strengths and weaknesses of newspapers such as the *New York Times* and *Christian Science Monitor,* and magazines such as *Nation, Time,* and *Newsweek,* all of which became routine reading.

I worked hard, and I learned a valuable life lesson. Although work is not always rewarded as it should be, more often than not it is rewarded. One of our first tournaments was at Louisiana State University where I won Superior Debater. Shortly thereafter, we won the tenth annual Florida State University Invitational against a field of twenty-three teams, beating opponents from Tulane, FSU, LSU, and Georgia Tech, among others. My second year we swept the Dixie Tournament; I won Superior Debater at FSU and Men's Oratory at a Wake Forest University tournament.

My senior season was the highlight of my debating career. I won Extempore Speaking at the Carolina Forensics Tournament. Our team won the sweepstakes at the Dixie Tournament and the FSU Invitational, where I also won first in Oratory and Impromptu Speaking.

Don Ragsdale and I debated a visiting team from Cambridge University, renowned for its debating traditions, on campus in front of a packed auditorium. The topic, "That the American high school is the grave of American Greatness," first introduced me to the nation's education crisis. Don and I stood in defense of the American high school as a democratic bastion of open access and equal opportunity. Our opponents—Julian Grenfell and Roger Warren Evans—were an impressive argument for the position they proposed. Grenfell descended from Lord Deborough, whose son and Julian's namesake was a famous British poet and First World War hero killed in the 1915 Ypres campaign. Julian was a law graduate of Eton and King's College, Cambridge University, who had served as president of the Cambridge Union, a member of the University Conservative Association, a polo player, and an officer in the King's Royal Rifle Corps in the Middle East. He planned a career in journalism and politics. Evans, who took a first in history from Trinity College, Cambridge, served as secretary of the Cambridge Union, editor of the university opinion magazine, president of the Sociological Society; was in the Royal Navy; and was an accomplished actor, guitarist, singer, and Rugby player. He later finished an advanced degree at the London School of Economics, led the Welsh Social-ists, served as an undersecretary in a Labour government, practiced law, and headed a real estate firm. Greenfell and Evans beat us like a drum. After having won forty-six victories in sixty-five debates, we received a British-administered dose of humble pie. After it ended, my mother assured us we had won. But my high school debate coach, Janet LeFevre, who had driven over from Anniston for the big event, would have none of this home-cooking. Ever my candid critic, she said, "You were beaten and beaten badly." The audience vote confirmed her judgment.

Years of researching and discussing public policy and social justice left their impression on me. So did head-to-head contests with some of the smartest people I ever met. Slowly debate pushed me deeper into politics.

Politics

Not that I first thought about political partisanship or ideology at Howard. That had begun in high school. As I slowly changed my mind about race, I also drifted toward Republicanism. Lots of issues were involved in the evolution. Alabama's Democratic Party in the 1950s still entered election cycles under the logo "White Supremacy for the Right." Furthermore, voters' slavish devotion to the Democratic Party marginalized Alabama in national politics. Democrats took the state for granted, Republicans conceded it, and we never saw a serious presidential candidate of either party. Also, my years of emersion in Confederate genealogy and Civil War history prepared me well for a states' rights approach to national politics, at least one purged of racism. My ideas about individualism, personal accountability, internationalism, and fiscal restraint conditioned me to depart from my family's fidelity to the Democratic Party. Until John Kennedy stood up to Castro and Khrushchev during the Cuban missile crisis, I also considered Democrats vacillating and weak in their anti-Communism and defense policy. Perhaps Kennedy's Catholicism was an issue as well. These were years when southerners wrestled with race and religion in new ways, and I was no exception.

As a twenty-year-old too young to vote in 1960, I was furious with my disfranchisement and became an ardent advocate of allowing eighteen-year-olds to vote. Meanwhile, I found other ways to have my say. I had discovered the power of the pen and began to use it regularly in letters to the editor. I wrote on behalf of prohibition, racial justice, and Republicanism. Arguing that true Jeffersonian democracy—devolving authority to the states, frugal government, fiscal restraint, individualism, and internationalism—favored modern

Republican principles over Democratic alternatives, I endorsed the ticket of Richard Nixon and Henry Cabot Lodge. The newspaper publisher and my fellow church member Harry Ayers was one of the few Alabama journalists to endorse Kennedy and had some fun at my expense. He titled my overly long letter, which to his credit he published in full, "Mr. Flynt's Manifesto."

Though I did not convince Mr. Ayers, I did convince my father to cast his first ballot for a Republican presidential candidate. After the Watergate scandals and Nixon's resignation, he never let me forget that I was the one who had persuaded him to vote for the disgraced president. Henceforth, whenever I offered election advice, he would remind me of my flawed reasoning in 1960 and only half jokingly dismiss me as an untrustworthy political pundit.

I also wrote a series of three essays on "politics, 1960 style" for the Howard College *Crimson*. And I agreed to serve as Alabama coordinator for College Youth for Nixon-Lodge, earning a chance to meet the presidential candidate at a giant parade/rally in Atlanta. A Republican publication circulated on campuses contained my endorsement along with ten others from across the United States, including the president of the student government association at the University of California, Berkeley (how quickly that campus would change during the following decade). Other student leaders from Notre Dame, Harvard, Smith College, UCLA, and elsewhere added their endorsements. Targeting students obviously did some good, at least on the Howard campus, where Nixon won a straw poll over Kennedy by a margin of four to one.

Politics had become a strong interest of mine if not an obsession. In the spring of 1960, I decided to run for president of Howard's SGA. With strong ties to ministerial students and independents and with a high profile in both debate and academic honoraries, I believed I stood a good chance of winning. But my opponent in the run-up to election day was a popular student and a member of Sigma Nu fraternity who was strongly backed by Greek social organizations.

Although Howard's Greek system never influenced campus politics as it did at the University of Alabama, it was increasingly formidable as the student population began to reflect postwar middle-class prosperity. I had not joined a fraternity for two reasons: I couldn't afford it, and I harbored deep-seated reservations about any sort of exclusion based on economic status, physical appearance, race, or any other social construction of the 1950s. Although the exclusions at Howard were minimal compared to the Greek system nationally, I still preferred independent status. I might well have lost the election because of that had my opponent not withdrawn just before students voted.

My election and subsequent visibility in the Students for Nixon national organization misled many of my friends, who believed I was headed for a career in politics. One of them even predicted in the *Crimson* (humorously, I think) that I would be elected the next governor of Alabama. Had I believed such a miracle possible, I might have run. The year after I graduated, Alabama voters elected George Wallace to the first of his four terms as governor.

During my year as SGA president, I did my best to represent student interests. It was reflective of the times and generation that students' major complaint was the quality of food in the cafeteria. So persistent were complaints that I asked President Wright to meet with students. He reluctantly agreed. Knowing that he would argue that though the food was not home cooking, it was nutritious and adequate, students urged me to take a tray of food to the meeting to demonstrate how bad it was. The spareribs that evening consisted mostly of globs of fat swimming in pools of grease and seemed a perfect exhibit. So, off I marched, tray in hand, followed by my faithful legion, who could hardly believe that I actually would do such a thing. We filled the new chapel, and when President Wright began his familiar defense of the food, I picked up my tray from the seat beside me and offered him a tasty morsel from our supper as rebuttal to his argument. He was not amused and declined my invitation. The incident, greatly embellished, became a part of campus folklore for decades. I had demanded the president eat the food. I had thrown it at him. I had denounced him before my student cohort. None of this was true. I was respectful. I did not press him when he declined to eat. I wrote him thanks for meeting with us. For his part, he was later good-humored, thanked me for arranging the meeting, and praised my leadership of SGA.

Transitions

As graduation approached, I entered the panic mode typical of college seniors. Where to go? What to do? Blessed with a booming national economy and a plethora of opportunities, I was uncertain which path to take. All the old insecurities resurfaced. True, I had excelled at a little Baptist college that no one outside Alabama and the denomination had ever heard of. But how well was I prepared for a more competitive world? Graduate school seemed an obvious alternative to seminary until the racial climate changed. But which should I attend? And in what area of history should I specialize?

William Pratt Dale, dean of men, directed academic scholarship programs at Howard, and he called my attention to Woodrow Wilson and Danforth

Foundation programs for graduate study. Because of the unfolding crisis with Cuba and the strategic importance of Latin America, he urged me to consider that field. I had enjoyed his courses in Latin American history, had at least a modicum of Spanish, and the field fit my growing interest in public policy studies. He advised me to apply to his alma mater, Duke, as well as to Latin American programs at Vanderbilt and Alabama. Hugh Bailey, whose courses in U.S. and southern history had enthralled me, urged me to apply at Florida State whose department head was a well-published historian of antebellum Alabama. David Vess, the Europeanist on our faculty, knew that I was not interested in his specialty for graduate study, but he gave me a copy of C. Vann Woodward's newly published book *The Burden of Southern History* as a graduation gift. David also gave me good advice: you are about to begin a multiple-year humility lesson to teach you how much there is to learn and how little you know. His advice served me well.

I followed Bailey's suggestion to apply at FSU, filled out applications for the Woodrow Wilson and Danforth Foundations focusing on Latin America, and waited anxiously. Danforth Foundation invited me for an interview in Atlanta, which proved to be a troubling experience that sent me reeling. I felt uncomfortable from the beginning of the session, which started with a totally unexpected question: "Suppose you knew you had only twenty-four hours to live. Tell us how you would spend the day." All those years preparing for extemporaneous speaking had not prepared me for this struggle with my deepest identity. I offered a feeble response, including books I would read, music I would listen to, and people I would call. The next question was equally confounding: "If these books, this music, these people are so important to you, why haven't you done these things before you came to the end of your life?" As an exercise in value clarification, the interview was effective. As an attempt to win a coveted fellowship, I walked away knowing that I would not become a Danforth Fellow. I also knew I had lots to learn about myself.

The more conventional Woodrow Wilson interview went well. In March I received word that I had received the prestigious scholarship for study at any graduate school in the United States that admitted me. That would have resolved my dilemma except for my indecision about what field and what university I preferred.

Other complications arose. Thanks to Alabama congressmen Lister Hill and Carl Elliott, Congress had passed the National Defense Education Act (NDEA) in 1958, funding a massive program to upgrade higher education. A reaction to perceived Soviet technological superiority after the launch of Sputnik, NDEA was designed to attract the brightest college students into graduate school in order to provide faculty for baby boomers about to flood colleges. Unlike Woodrow Wilson and Danforth fellowships that, though renewable, guaranteed only the first year of graduate study, NDEA grants provided three years of funding for a student and dependents, prohibited other employment as a graduate assistant, and focused on speeding up the graduate education process. (When I entered graduate school, the average age at which Ph.D.s in history were completed was thirty-four.) Within a matter of weeks, both Alabama and Vanderbilt offered me an NDEA in Latin American history, Tulane granted a wonderful scholarship as well, and Duke admitted me as a Woodrow Wilson Fellow. With head already swirling, I opened a letter from FSU awarding me an NDEA in southern history.

Probably it was reading Woodward's book that tipped the scales in favor of FSU. His essays about the South, so gracefully written and theologically grounded in a sense of tragedy and hope, hooked me for a lifetime. Latin American studies appealed to my head, but the southern United States had taken hold of my heart.

More investigation of FSU revealed a sterling young faculty of southern specialists. Besides, familiarity with the school gave me confidence in my ability to compete there. And perhaps my own ambivalence about my ability to succeed at Duke, Vanderbilt, or Tulane, much less at Ivy League schools to which I did not even apply, entered into my decision as well. It was true that no one knew of FSU's doctoral program. But I could help change that.

I graduated college on May 29, 1961, and was sent off to a new life with prophetic words ringing in my ears. Our graduation speaker, Rufus C. Harris, longtime president of Mercer University, warned that graduates would confront not only bitter local race relations but also terror and disorder. We must uphold spiritual values, keep public schools open, and make sure that all students had opportunities. We must at all cost avoid mob rule.

In the near term, however, I had a wedding on my mind. I met Dorothy Smith ('Dartie" to her friends because of her rapid movements as a fencer and walker) my freshman year in college. She worked in the largely deserted government documents division in the library basement. Though I knew she was beautiful, she was mainly of value at the time as the human conveyor who retrieved heavy tomes and statistical data for me. She was a speech-drama/English major, so we had classes together where I also noticed her. But not until late in my second year at Howard (her senior year) did a mutual friend confront me as I paid tuition and inquire why I didn't ask Dartie for a date. I couldn't think of any reason why not, so I did. That is how it all began.

I had largely avoided dating my freshmen year because I didn't have time or money. Although there was no truth to rumors begun by one of my fellow debaters that I wrote time for bathroom breaks in my schedule book, I did carefully organize each day. In another life I would have made a great time-management/efficiency expert. At least until that first date with Dartie.

Before I met her, I also had a love affair with basketball. I played on the ministerial association intramural team until a bad ankle sprain ended yet another athletic effort. So it was entirely logical that our first date was to a basketball game. After we left the coliseum headed for a restaurant, my lack of dating experience nearly proved lethal. Though an experienced debater, I could think of nothing to say. The silence seemed to last for hours. I had just been elected SGA president, so finally in desperation I blurted out the most inane, egotistical sentence of my life: "How does it feel to have a date with the SGA president?" After a long embarrassed pause, Dartie (whose background included a more robust social calendar than mine, especially involving SGA presidents) blurted in response: "Haven't you heard? I specialize in dating SGA presidents." For the first of many times, she had the last word. The conversation again lapsed into silence as we both pondered our words, convinced there would be no second chance. Of course, there were other dates, and by the time she graduated, we were deeply in love.

She had applied for a summer mission program in California and was soon on the train traveling west. After returning in August, she had a job teaching English in Gadsden, so our courtship continued long distance through my senior year. We sometimes spoke together at Baptist youth meetings while I served as youth director at my home church. We married on August 20, 1961, moved into a secondhand mobile home at University Trailer Park in Tallahassee, and I began graduate school.

Church Life and Race in Tallahassee

Shortly after arriving in Florida's capital, we found a church in which we grew and thrived. Throughout our lives, churches were our chief entry point into communities. They provided our closest circle of friends, our greatest inspiration, and our most reliable source of comfort. Tallahassee First Baptist was no exception. Our Sunday school teacher was a geologist who had earned a global

As we left Parker Memorial Baptist Church in Anniston on August 20, 1961, Dartie and I began three new lives together. I left my ministerial duties as summer youth director at the church for a new career as graduate student. She left her teaching job for the uncertainty of helping me complete my Ph.D. And we began married life together. It was my happiest day ever. Courtesy of Benny Benefield, Benny's Hollywood Studio Photography, Gadsden, Alabama.

reputation for his studies of beach erosion. He moved easily beyond the silly science-faith conflicts troubling our times, which had ended for us in under-graduate school anyway. Howard faculty overwhelmingly had been theistic evolutionists (God created the natural order, then allowed scientific processes to function).

C. A. Roberts—a young preacher from Oklahoma who spoke prophetically about race and was a rising star in the Southern Baptist Convention—became our pastor to the consternation of many racial conservatives in the community. Many of our members were powerful state and local officials who led Florida's resistance to integration, and they did not appreciate prophetic voices in their pulpit.

One Sunday morning in 1963, Rufus Harris's prediction that we would confront bitter race relations was fulfilled outside First Baptist. A group of black students from Florida A&M University walked up the steps leading into our sanctuary as we were coming down. As they reached the entrance, a "greeter" told them they were not welcome. We were stunned by the hatred in his voice. As the young men turned to leave, I told them I was sorry for what had been said, that the man had not expressed my views nor those of my church friends. The greeter overheard my comments and told Dartie and me that if we felt that way we should go with them to "the nigger church." My Flynt temper spun quickly out of control, and I told him that I would more likely encounter Christ there than in his church. He challenged me to meet him there the next morning where we could settle this man to man. I heard Mother's words as he spoke: "You never defend honor by engaging in violence." So I walked away. Away from him. And, ultimately, away from First Baptist Church.

Weeks later at Wednesday night prayer meeting we voted whether or not to admit African Americans to the church. In what must have been the best attended business meeting in the church's history, members (and probably more than a few nonmembers) voted, according to my memory, 340 to 327 against integrating First Baptist.

It is amazing how we empower people and institutions we love the most to hurt us the worst. After the vote, we wept and left. We have never been back. That evening ended our innocence about the church, which had always been so generous, kind, and loving to us. Not until later, when I read Richard Niebuhr's book *Christ and Culture,* did I fully understand how difficult it is to pry the teachings of Christ from the tentacles of culture. For our remaining year in Tallahassee, we attended a Lutheran church, more comfortable with its racial openness than with its regional differentness.

The racial conflict at First Baptist also branded me locally in a strange new way. Having defined my political identity in Alabama as conservative and Republican, I sat in disbelief one day as my conservative friend Chuck Dunn (who would later become special assistant to the Republican governor of Washington and then to the Republican minority whip in the U.S. House of Representatives) related a conversation he had overheard in his barbershop after the incident at First Baptist. One barber described in absolute seriousness the activities of a Communist graduate student in history who had been trained in Cuba, smuggled into the United States, and embedded in FSU and First Baptist Church in order to foster racial turmoil. Knowing my devotion to both Christianity and Republicanism, Dunn chuckled his way out of the shop and hurried to relate the story to me. I was dumbfounded. I should not have been. After all, these were the years the cuckoo claimed.

FSU

Having severed ties to our church, we forged closer ones at the university. Our circle of friends included Baptists, Catholics, agnostics, members of the Church of Christ, Democrats, Republicans, conservatives, liberals, and even one socialist. The Molays, a black couple from Florida A&M, visited us at the trailer park. Carlton Molay directed theater programs, and his wife, from southern California, had never eaten homemade ice cream, which we introduced to her.

Debates on campus grew fierce, especially as the Vietnam war escalated and civil rights demonstrations increased. One of our friends from church and graduate school left FSU for the jungles of Southeast Asia. My Ph.D. years (1961–65) were incredibly heady ones both intellectually and politically. Not long after arriving on campus, the Liberal Forum began picketing the Mecca Restaurant, the history department's favorite eatery across from the main entrance to campus. The Mecca certainly belied its name for FSU's small contingent of black students, whom it refused to serve. I honored the picket line and ate elsewhere.

Meanwhile, the racial situation in Alabama worsened. Wallace's stand in the schoolhouse door at the University of Alabama, the 1963 demonstrations in Birmingham, KKK bombings of churches and synagogues, the murder of four young girls at Sixteenth Street Baptist Church, violent suppression of marchers on the Edmund Pettus Bridge in Selma, the Selma to Montgomery march, and passage of the Voting Rights Act in August 1965 punctuated my graduate studies. I well remember returning home from church the day of the Sixteenth Street bombing, hearing the news, weeping (we wept often for Alabama then and later), and telling Dartie that, though I did not know where we would go after graduate school, I would never return to Alabama.

My politics began to change as well. As late as August 1962 I wrote one of my letters to the *Anniston Star* responding to a Harry Ayers editorial that blamed the GOP for political scandals and the South's poverty. For every Republican "robber baron" who looted the South, I wrote, there had been a Democratic

Boss Tweed who plundered the public treasury. The South's poverty owed
more to its Democratic planters than to its Reconstruction Republicans.

But the increasing identification of southern segregationists with the GOP
made me nervous. When Barry Goldwater was nominated for president in
1964 on a platform of states' rights that appealed strongly to Deep South segregationists, I helped organize a "Republicans for LBJ" club and canvassed
neighborhoods for Lyndon Johnson. His victory in Florida (the first Democratic presidential win in that state since 1948) helped accelerate my political
ideology in a new direction.

In previous years, there had been little discernible difference in attitudes
toward race between the two parties. In fact, the Democratic Party had not
even allowed black delegates to attend its national convention until well into
the century and even then had separated them from whites with chicken wire.
The party of Lincoln had been more inclusive and welcoming and had received most of the black vote until the 1930s. But white backlash against the
civil rights movement drove many segregationists out of the Democratic Party
during the 1960s and 1970s, first to George Wallace's Independent Party, then
into the GOP once it honed its "southern strategy." Meanwhile I was headed
in the opposite direction.

As at Howard College, I thrived in graduate school. Historians Weymouth
Jordan, William Hair, James Jones, Maurice Vance, and my major professor,
William W. Rogers (a native of Butler county, Alabama, and a graduate of Auburn and the University of North Carolina) were as fine a group of teachers as
I have encountered anywhere. They were a wonderful mixture of mature senior scholars and liberal young ones bursting with energy. And the times were
electrifying. History faculty and graduate students argued about everything.
Conservative grad students (and there were many despite popular myths about
graduate schools as liberal indoctrination centers) took exception to the opinions of liberal students and faculty. As usual, I was somewhere midway between the ideological ends of these debates.

I relished my study outside history as well. I took courses on Southeast
Asian politics with a well-published scholar and former State Department official who had been posted to Indonesia during the Eisenhower administration. In my minor field, rhetoric and persuasion, I studied under two of the
best minds in the country, Greg Phifer and Wayne Minnick.

Dartie served as a substitute teacher during our first year in Tallahassee,
then taught full time our second and third years. Freed of financial pressures
and the need to teach or assist, I devoted every waking moment to research,

reading, and studying for language exams. I also wrote articles for submission to professional journals. To my surprise, all of my submissions were accepted, leading to articles published in the *Florida Historical Quarterly, Civil War History,* and two in the *Southern Speech Journal.*

With my coursework finished and doctoral exams completed in a little more than two years, I applied for a Woodrow Wilson Dissertation Fellowship to spend a year finishing research and writing my dissertation on U.S. senator Duncan U. Fletcher, a major figure in American politics between 1912 and his death in 1936.

Once again providence smiled on us. The Wilson grant allowed Dartie to quit teaching and join me as a research assistant on a long journey through East Coast archives: Duke, the University of North Carolina, the University of Virginia, the Library of Congress, the National Archives, and the Franklin D. Roosevelt Presidential Library at Hyde Park, New York. With our little Volkswagen loaded down with notes, we returned to Tallahassee in September 1964, where I gestated a dissertation and Dartie a baby. They were born about the same time, my work in the spring, her baby in August.

With new life to support and anxious to find a teaching job, I began submitting my résumé. The market was robust, and I soon had numerous prospects. FSU tendered a one-year appointment. Kentucky Southern College offered me a job at the exciting new college in Louisville. My alma mater wrote as well, offering me an opportunity to return to a place that I was not sure I wanted to be. But the possibilities for change in Alabama excited me, as did the prospect of being close to our parents. I had read Harper Lee's Pulitzer Prize–winning novel, *To Kill a Mockingbird,* and concluded that if Monroe County, Alabama, could produce a novelist as gifted and tolerant as she, there must be hope for the future.

George V. Irons, head of Howard's history department, sweetened the salary with a postdoctoral proposal. With the growing U.S. involvement in Southeast Asia, the Ford Foundation was funding a number of summer institutes in Asian studies designed to provide faculty for small colleges unable to hire a specialist. The institutes were interdisciplinary crash courses in history, politics, religion, and literature, taught by some of the nation's foremost Asianists. If I agreed to return to teach Asian and southern U.S. history, Howard would nominate me for the institute scheduled for FSU during the summer of 1965.

I signed the fateful contract and settled into yet another life-changing intellectual experience. Led by Albert Craig and Edwin Reischauer of Harvard; Charles Hucker of the University of Michigan; Minoru Shinoda of the University of Hawaii; and Edmund Clubb, former U.S. consul general in Beijing and professor at Columbia University, the three-month seminar immersed me in modern East Asian history. The Ford Foundation presented us a library of basic books about the region. I took from the postdoctoral experience a fascination with Asia that later carried me there many times, including a semester's residence in Hong Kong and a lecture tour of India. I taught Asian history at both Samford and Auburn, coauthored a book about Alabama missionaries in China, and read Asian history, religion, and literature all my life.

My intense postdoctorate was at an end and our son David was born (characteristically of him) exactly when he was due on August 1, 1965. The first two weeks of life he slept in the open drawer of a dresser, our only available space in the suddenly shrunken trailer. Then we sold our mobile home, loaded David into an unair-conditioned Buick with terminal transmission problems, and prayed that we made it through the heat (both physical and metaphorical) to our new life in Birmingham.

• four •

Going Home

Life might have been lots easier teaching somewhere other than Samford University. The school was crippled by money problems, wretched salaries, and horrendous teaching loads. During my first year of full-time teaching, our family income dropped below my last year of graduate school. The standard teaching load during most of my years on the faculty was five courses per semester, plus a January term offering and two summer classes for a total of thirteen a year. Typically, I taught eight or nine separate preparations.

As baby boomers swamped the campus, classes reached unmanageable size. My first semester (fall 1965) the five courses I taught enrolled nearly two hundred students. Conditions worsened in the late 1960s. During the summer of 1969 I taught sixty-seven students in New South. Modern East Asia regularly enrolled between thirty-five and forty, and my spring 1969 American Intellectual History class numbered sixty-six. By the 1970s, I was teaching small honors classes, graduate seminars, and smaller advanced classes. But I gave essay exams and assigned research papers in all junior-senior level courses, so the burden slackened only slightly. As a consequence, I barely saw my wife and new son, Sean, born in 1969.

My teaching load was not unusual for new professors at small liberal arts colleges during the 1960s. But I tried to do too much and worked the students hard. I was a strict grader (14 percent of my freshmen earned As, 10 percent failed, and 23 percent made Ds) and even tougher evaluating research papers.

My night class that first year was traumatic for a different reason. At the first session, older students who mostly worked full time during the day continued to chat long after I was ready to begin. Suddenly I realized that they thought I was a fellow student rather than the professor. I was twenty-four but looked much younger. As I began to lecture, they stared in disbelief, then smiled at the incongruity of mature people like themselves busily taking notes from someone half their age. I was closer in age to my freshmen than to them and I more easily identified with the eighteen-year-olds.

After several years of this problem, I grew a mustache in order to look older. Dad was not pleased, believing this was the first step on the road to hippiedom. I reminded him that his father once sported a handsome mustache and the argument subsided.

Despite all these problems, I was euphoric. Every day I hurried off to school filled with high purpose. Ever the idealist, I was convinced that in one generation teachers could melt thousand-year glaciers of selfish and fearful tradition, destroy racism and sexism, unleash the ethical power of the Sermon on the Mount, and change the world.

Believing with the Roman philosopher Cicero that "the man who does not know what happened before he was born has the mind of a child," I arrogantly concluded that history trumped all other disciplines. In time, I became more measured and skeptical about the lessons of history and the prospects for change. The contexts in which events occur are never the same, so whatever lessons we learn from the past are imperfect. The historian Julian Barnes came closer to the truth when he wrote: "Does history repeat itself, the first time as tragedy, the second time as farce? No, that's too grand, too considered a process. History just burps, and we taste again that raw onion sandwich it swallowed centuries ago." The art historian Simon Schama of Columbia University phrased the argument more elegantly: "Historians are left forever chasing shadows, painfully aware of their inability ever to reconstruct a dead world in its completeness however thorough or revealing their documentation. We are doomed to be forever hailing someone who has just gone around the corner and out of earshot." The novelist Victor Hugo captured the pathos of historical lessons left unlearned: "For over six thousand years, war has been the pleasure of the quarreling powers. One would think that God wastes his time making for man the stars and the flowers."

I suppose it was inevitable that Hugo's words should shape my philosophy of history, because his conclusion is rooted in the experiences of the ancient Hebrews and the teachings of Jesus. Humankind really is selfish, narcissistic, and sinful (an old-fashioned word I prefer to "mistake," which implies no malice of forethought). Seeking one's own advantage, protecting one's own national interests, pervasive materialism, hubris, blind ambition, lack of public engagement, reluctance to sacrifice for the common good—all of these sicken civilizations and play roles in their demise.

One of my favorite lectures dealt with Socrates's heresy trial. He was accused of subverting his pupil's loyalty to the Greek city-state of Athens by his philosophic questioning of their priorities. One of his students thought he testified in defense of his teacher, when in fact the student may have sealed Socrates's doom: "He taught me that I ought not live as I do, neglecting the wants of my own soul and busying myself with the affairs of Athens." During escalating campus debates about the justice of America's war in Southeast Asia, I knew this discussion had historical relevance quite beyond events three thousand years ago. Students who were facing the draft and the jungles of Vietnam never doubted that ancient Greeks could speak to their existential situations.

Given my family responsibilities, I should have been content with teaching classes, grading exams, marking research papers, and going home. I could not be content with that, probably because I remembered the way Al Yeomans had imprinted my life outside the classroom. So I became sponsor of the Young Democrats, organized a tutoring program at all-black Rosedale High School in Homewood, and agreed to serve as Woodrow Wilson Fellowship adviser. Dartie and I invited history majors who were contemplating graduate work to our home, where she cooked for them despite her obligations to two young sons. We talked far into the night about all manner of things, much as Al and I had once done.

My Samford Family

Given the temper of the times, it was inevitable I suppose that many of my student involvements were controversial. Some of my finest history majors participated in the Rosedale tutoring program. The literary club we began became not only the gathering place for alienated and liberal students, but one of the most intellectually stimulating parts of my life. We read a book, typically from the panoply of new and controversial publications pouring off presses during those years: John D. T. Robinson's *Honest to God;* Dietrich Bonhoeffer's *Letters and Papers from Prison;* Jean Paul Sartre's *Of Human Freedom;* Albert Camus's

The Fall. One of us led the discussion to the degree that the ensuing verbal free-for-all permitted. As was common across America, college students showed little deference to their elders, and I was barely even an "elder."

Sometimes we brought speakers to campus who did not reflect a Baptist perspective. None was more memorable than radical poet John Beecher. Though born in Birmingham, the son of a U.S. Steel official, John had drifted sharply left during the 1930s and 1940s. Considered by many to be a Communist, he certainly was radical on race, which was all that was necessary in those years to brand him as a subversive. We invited John to speak, and President Wright literally and figuratively saw red. At first he tried to withdraw the invitation. When students refused, he permitted the reading but saturated campus with Homewood and university police. Naturally this commotion and free publicity turned our normal audience of twenty to thirty students and faculty into a standing-room-only auditorium filled with hundreds. Beecher, who was a pariah in his hometown, was shocked by the size of the crowd gathered to hear his poetry as well as by the burst of applause that greeted him (which had more to do with southern hospitality and opposition to Wright's attempt to prevent him from speaking than agreement with his poetic sentiments). The contentious poet considered the evening one of his most satisfying, never fully realizing the unique set of circumstances that accounted for it.

Other of our contrarians were homegrown. Randall Williams, though not a history major, took several courses with me. He was a bright student from a poor family who was blessed with a scholarship established by a wealthy donor for young people from the red clay hills of Chambers County. Indoctrinated with the teachings of Jesus by his church and with the ethics of journalism by Richmond Brown, head of Samford's Journalism Department, Randall took his responsibilities as *Crimson* editor seriously. The quality of the paper, which had always been high, improved even more under his relentless editorship. I expected a campus eruption over race, Vietnam, sex, drinking, or some similarly contentious subject. Instead, what precipitated the 1973 crisis was an article about Samford clearing land in a Homewood floodplain, a policy strongly opposed by environmentalists and local residents. Randall and fellow journalism student Bill Steverson couched their editorial in a clever triplet: "First they cut down all the trees. Then they channelize the creek. Then they name it Brookwood Mall." The students, backed by Richmond Brown, resigned rather than comply with administrative censorship. Randall began an alternative newspaper, *Another Voice.* By contemporary campus newspaper standards, the paper was wonderfully written and impeccably responsible: no obscenity, Communism, socialism, or advocacy of free sex, drugs, or abortion. It provided the campus exactly what it promised on its masthead, "another voice" from the university line. It received no financial backing, though it was subscribed to and widely read by students and faculty. At first Wright merely refused to allow distribution of the paper on campus. In time, he turned vindictive, canceling Randall's scholarship and forcing him out of school.

Unwilling to yield, Randall began the *Paperman* in August 1973 as an alternative weekly directed toward the twenty-five thousand college students living in the Birmingham area. Like many worthy projects spawned by the age of Aquarius, this one failed financially despite a superb staff. The *Crimson/Another Voice* episode inflicted lots of pain but never dissuaded Randall from a lifetime of courageous battles over freedom of speech and social justice. He later combined intellectual freedom with a viable career, launching New South Books, a commercial publishing company in Montgomery.

Many of my Samford students wound up like Randall, casualties of one kind or another. Some left the church altogether. Others remained within the fold of traditional religion, but with the walls greatly expanded. They shared their stories of theological liberation with me over a lifetime. If I played a small role in any of their lives, I'll gladly take credit. They were an amazing generation of students, the best and most intellectually curious I would teach. Perhaps it would have been the same had I been on the faculty at Auburn or any other university between 1965 and 1977. It may have been more the times than the place.

Each story differed from the others, but their collective experience was impressive. Carolyn Johnston won Woodrow Wilson and Danforth fellowships, took her Ph.D. at the University of California, Berkeley, became Elie Wiesel Professor of Humane Letters at Eckerd College, and authored a shelf of fine books about socialism, gender, race, and ethnicity. Jim Huskey took his Ph.D. at the University of North Carolina at Chapel Hill and became an Asian specialist in the State Department, was on Tiananmen Square in Beijing the night the Chinese army massacred students there, as well as in the U.S. embassy in Nairobi, Kenya, when terrorists bombed it. Kerry Buckley, Eddie Akin, George Sims, and others took Ph.D.s at some of America's finest universities, the kind to which I was too timid to apply for admission. Andy Collins became one of the nation's most frequently cited child psychologists at the University of Minnesota. David Chestnut turned down a National Medical School Scholarship at Harvard in order to attend UAB medical school because he wanted hands-on relationships with ordinary people like the ones in his hometown of

Selma, rather than conducting biomedical research. Philip Wise studied at Oxford University and became a prominent moderate Baptist leader and pastor, Cynthia (his wife) a college history teacher. George Sims wrote a fine biography of Alabama governor James E. Folsom and served as a university administrator. His wife, Ellen, became a Baptist minister. All of them and many others radiated a sense of decency and justice that I believed then and now should be at the heart of Christian higher education.

Although I developed closer relations with some students than others, I counted my Samford student friends in the hundreds. Over the decades we conducted extensive correspondence that filled file drawers, a far more extensive record from those twelve years at Samford than from my twenty-eight years at Auburn. That, I suspect, resulted more from differences in schools than in students. Samford afforded me relationships with undergraduate students, even freshmen, that was matched at Auburn only by my doctoral students. This correspondence owed much to those influential letters Al Yeomans had sent me. Having experienced the transforming power of a thoughtful letter, I strove for similar effect.

In response to one student who aspired to teach, I wrote in December 1970 that a teacher should obtain a thorough knowledge of the subject and dedicate his life to communicating it well. "We come from the past," I wrote, "and in many ways are creatures of it, captured by its traditions and its ways of thinking. . . . I love history, and I want everyone to enjoy it as much as I do."

A former student who had become a social worker began a correspondence in July 1968 about her frustrations working in a poor-white hill county in northeastern Alabama: "I know you must feel the constant frustration too of running into so much opposition (I like to call it ignorance!) to any sort of change. I don't think we have any friends left in our hometown . . . , but I am convinced that my fulfillment or success can only come through helping less fortunate people." They invited black friends for dinner, her husband had just been drafted into the army, and she was leaving the South for Washington, D.C. Experiencing the double isolation of her liberal views on race and gender, she concluded her letter: "In some ways it is so frustrating being a girl because the prescribed role of a wife is so dull—at least for me. I didn't go to school to learn to cook and clean house, so I don't!" The revolutions under way at Samford in the 1960s and 1970s might have been quieter and less confrontational than elsewhere, but they were no less life changing.

Students reciprocated my affection. Several times they chose me friendliest professor, and I shared with my friend W. T. Edwards the John H. Buchanan

Despite tumultuous conflict that swirled around racial policies at Samford University during the 1960s, I experienced many wonderful times, most involving my students. In a 1968 student poll, my good friend and former religion professor W. T. Edwards and I were winners of the John H. Buchanan Award for excellence in classroom teaching. President Leslie Wright (*presenting plaque to Edwards*) was generous in his praise. Courtesy Samford University.

Award for Excellence in Teaching. My student evaluations were consistently good, my department head's annual evaluations flattering, and I was quickly tenured.

Academic Bureaucracy

President Wright particularly appreciated my work as Woodrow Wilson adviser. If students were going to become competitive for these prestigious grants, I had to identify them early. My work paid dividends when, during the three years between 1969 and 1972, Samford tied Auburn for the most fellowships awarded in Alabama. The president, who was obsessed with his belief that Birmingham-Southern received more favorable media attention than we did, reveled in the fact that we produced more fellows during those years than our crosstown rival.

Besides advising, I was also buried in university committees. Because many students disliked compulsory chapel, I was appointed to a committee with student leaders to craft a new chapel policy. (At the time it consisted of a steady diet of Alabama Baptist ministers—some fine, others dreadful.) Defining the chapel experience more broadly, we lobbied successfully for a wider range of speakers, subjects, and student options. Our list of proposed speakers included theologian Harvey Cox, conservative columnist William Buckley, media theorist Marshall McLuhan, Baptist congressman Brooks Hays, governors LeRoy Collins and Albert Brewer, and Johnson administration cabinet member Bill Moyers. Most on our list proved too expensive and our topics (Christianity's relationship to world poverty, overcoming racial barriers, helping the educationally disadvantaged, the war in Vietnam, black power, America's urban crisis) too controversial. But chapel did become a more challenging intellectual experience. My service on a long list of other committees, added to my work as faculty sponsor to the Young Democrats and the Rosedale tutoring program, kept me in a flurry of activity.

Were all that not enough, I regularly taught courses on China and Japan for the Samford after Sundown adult learning program, partly because we needed the extra money and partly because I enjoyed outreach programs designed for nontraditional students. Typically filled with retirees, divorcees, well-educated women whose children had entered school, or Birmingham residents merely interested in the subjects, these constituted some of my most thoughtful students. They brought to the classes rich life experiences, a variety of backgrounds and interests, and lots of maturity. I usually learned as much from them as I taught.

Once the university adopted a modified calendar that included an intensive three-week January term, I taught interdisciplinary or experimental classes such as America in the 1920s, The Developing World, and The Application of Christianity to Contemporary Social Problems. I taught in the honors program and began directing graduate students in the department's new master's program. Three of my colleagues and I also taught weekend seminars on Alabama folk culture for schoolteachers.

Outreach

Off campus, I spoke constantly to literary and civic clubs. The Highland Book Club, Birmingham's second oldest women's study club, became my favorite. It had enrolled many of the city's progressive women, including a number who had led movements to abolish child labor, reform prisons, and enfranchise women. Although some liberal colleagues believed that the club corrupted me by too close association with ritzy Mountain Brook matrons, I never felt that way. I found as many bigots in blue collar and black audiences as in Mountain Brook, and not a few wonderfully tolerant people in the affluent over-the-mountain suburb.

My most perplexing speech during those years was at Temple Emanu-El, the city's Reform synagogue. Rabbi Milton Grafman invited me to speak on Vietnam for the 1969 Men's Club and Sisterhood joint meeting. After initially supporting Lyndon Johnson's Southeast Asia policy, I had abandoned him following the Ohio National Guard's attack on students at Kent State University. My Jewish friends apparently mistook my Baptist roots and Samford faculty status for support of the war. I mistook their Judaism and historic liberalism for opposition to the war. We were both wrong. Having always prided myself on my ability to analyze an audience, I went badly astray this time. The evening turned into an uncomfortable confrontation for all of us.

Others reacted better to me. Duard LeGrand, highly respected editor of the *Birmingham Post-Herald,* the more progressive of the city's papers, and chairman of the State Committee for the Humanities, recommended me as one of one hundred "opinion leaders" for a nine-state conference on "people of the South" in Nashville. A stellar group of speakers offered a robust agenda for change that helped move me farther along the path toward political advocacy.

My wife and I were also selected as Danforth Associates, a program designed to promote moral and ethical values, humane relationships, and civility on college campuses, all much needed in the volatile 1960s and 1970s. The program brought us in touch with compatible faculty nationwide but especially from within Birmingham's academic community. I proposed the creation of a citywide dialogue, consisting of monthly seminars rotating between our campuses and hosted by one of the nine Danforth couples. I received a grant from the foundation, and we began our sessions. Among our speakers were David Vann, advocate of countywide consolidation and a future Birmingham mayor; the city's police chief; the superintendent of county schools; civil rights leader and future federal judge U. W. Clemon; a session at Miles College with writer William Bradford Huie on the death penalty; and respected social worker Betty Bok, who spoke about the city's poverty.

Although our circle of friends was expanding from campus to city and region, our closest and most meaningful relationships remained Samford colleagues. Within the department, George Irons, Hugh Bailey, Lee Allen, David

Vess, Marlene Rikard, James (Jim) and Linda Faye Brown, David and Judy Gillespie, and Leah Atkins became fast friends. Jim, one of the brightest and best teachers I encountered in my career, also enriched my life by teaching me how to fish Alabama's bountiful creeks and rivers.

Outside the department, our closest friends were theater director Harold Hunt and his wife, Barbara, and chemist Jerry Barrett and wife, Lynn. My wife's love of theater made us faithful patrons of Samford's drama program and later the Alabama Shakespeare Festival in Anniston and Montgomery. The Barrett children made wonderful traveling companions for our sons on monthlong camping trips each summer. Mathematician Ruric Wheeler, Jerry, Harold, and I also took out our frustrations two or three days a week playing handball at lunchtime.

Beyond these, my professors and colleagues from undergraduate school (Sam Mitchell, Al Yeomans, W. T. Edwards, and Max Gartman—then back on the faculty as a professor of French) became close friends. Younger professors demonstrated one of the best features of a liberal arts college, the ease with which faculty move beyond their disciplines to engage colleagues and issues different from their own. One in both genteel poverty and complaint, we spent much time together.

Writing

Weymouth Jordan, department head at FSU and initially my major professor, sent congratulations when I received the job at Samford. He included two pieces of advice: write on average one article a year and at least one book every decade. Avoid administration: "Be careful, for the powers that be will draw you into administration. Someone has to do that type of work around a campus, but I hope that it will not happen to you."

As I gained confidence in my teaching and taught less, I did as he suggested regarding writing. I have always believed that scholarship operates like a virus. Once you are infected, it takes over all aspects of your life. I never believed that research, writing, and teaching were mutually exclusive or that one should be rewarded and the others ignored. Teaching, research, and writing are alternative aspects of a process of transmitting knowledge from one generation to another, and each enriches the other. But something has always compelled me to get inside archives for long, solitary hours of research, followed by laborious months of organization, analysis, and meticulous composition. I began in graduate school and never stopped. It proved to be the hardest work I ever did.

Several themes captured my attention. Some remained for a lifetime. Others slipped by the wayside as competing interests crowded them out. I had begun to write labor history while in graduate school and became more interested in the subject after moving to Birmingham. The city contained the highest percentage of union workers of any southern metropolis. I and a group of like-minded professors organized the Association of Southern Labor Historians (ASLH). They elected me secretary-treasurer, and for a decade I edited and distributed a newsletter and helped organize sessions on labor history at the Southern Historical Association. The ASLH combined historians, economists, and labor leaders. Colleagues from FSU such as W. I. Hair and George Green formed the core of the group, to which we added James A. Hodges, Durward Long, Jim Green, and other prominent labor historians. Labor leaders included Barney Weeks (president of the Alabama Labor Council, AFL-CIO), Claude C. Ramsey (president of Mississippi AFL-CIO), and H. L. Mitchell (cofounder of the Southern Tenant Farmers Union). The economist Ray Marshall, later President Jimmy Carter's secretary of labor, added his considerable knowledge to our group.

The cross-fertilization of so many different backgrounds and viewpoints inspired many lectures, conferences, and publications, including my article on Florida labor and socialism published in *Labor History* (1968). I also keynoted a session on labor history at an NDEA institute, the Advanced Study of History, at the University of Mississippi in 1966. Labor activists who had actually participated in the events that historians described spoke at our conferences, making the sessions unique in the profession.

Although in time other interests diverted my attention from labor history, I never retreated from telling America's story from my mother's and father's perspectives, from the bottom up. Before the 1960s, American history concentrated on winning politicians, dominant religious denominations, CEOs of major corporations, middle and upper classes, and white men. Women, African Americans, other ethnic minorities, fringe political movements, poor whites, laborers, Pentecostal and holiness sects, and other marginal groups seldom made an appearance. My generation of historians may have overcompensated in our attempts to provide a fuller, more complete account of America, but if so, future generations could balance our mistake. Our collective legacy to the profession was shining a spotlight into the crevices of American history where few had looked before.

My interest in religious history also began at Samford. Ever since historians Charles and Mary Beard had inserted economics and class interests at the heart of the nation's story early in the twentieth century, religion had slipped to the edges. An increasingly secular professoriate, especially after the 1950s, considered religion and its excesses to be a central part of America's problem, not one of its assets. Whether in satirical descriptions of the 1925 Scopes trial in Dayton, Tennessee, overemphasis on evangelical emotional excesses and anti-intellectualism, or discussion of the persistent racism and sexism of American churches, scholars either marginalized or criticized the role of religion in American life.

I could not deny many of their indictments, but I believed the narrative was one-sided and incomplete. Evangelicals had led the abolitionist movement. They had established many of America's finest colleges. They had lobbied for separation of church and state, fearful that any state-supported church would trample freedom of conscience. Many of the labor unionists I studied were informed more by biblical visions of justice than by Marxist conceptions of class struggle. And the modern American civil rights movement was born in the theologically fundamentalist black church, not in New York salons or left-leaning academic communities.

So, when the *Birmingham News* invited me to write a special July 4, 1973, feature on "religion and the revolution," I gladly accepted. Religion pervaded early American history, I wrote, and was a partial cause and justification for armed rebellion. But the Revolution also occurred at a time of the lowest church membership in American history, serious religious differences among the founding fathers, and strong impetus for disestablishing state-sponsored churches that reigned supreme in nearly all the colonies. The greatest legacy of the Revolution, save for America's actual political independence, was separation of church and state, to which religious dissenters such as Jews, Baptists, Quakers, Deists, and others made major contributions.

As for widespread historical assumptions that the southern church was essentially racist, fundamentalist, and conservative, I waged a career-long assault on three fronts. One was to educate my fellow historians that at least between 1890 and 1945 there was another tradition, a strong social gospel impulse based on biblical principles of justice toward all people, especially the poor. Beginning with my first article in the *Journal of Southern History* ("Dissent in Zion: Alabama Baptists and Social Issues, 1900–1914," November 1969), I staked out ground that would result in dozens of published articles and book chapters about Baptist, Methodist, and Presbyterian advocates of social Christianity and progressive politics. Over the years, other historians joined the chorus. I also began research that turned into a thirty-year project on Alabama Baptists, which would balance negative and positive views of this most stereotyped of denominations. Finally, I reminded my colleagues that the southern church included African American congregations that confounded many of their assumptions.

Like my lectures to Baptist groups and colleges around the South, my intent was partly to educate fellow Baptists to their own misunderstood and complex heritage. I was determined to rescue the Baptist social justice tradition not only from academic neglect but also from denominational amnesia.

To do that, I had to move beyond traditional academic publishing venues to other forums. For instance, I won the 1973 Alabama Baptist Sesquicentennial essay contest with an article about Alabama Baptist opposition to child labor, which was published in the *Alabama Baptist,* a weekly newspaper that entered the homes of tens of thousands of church members. In later years, I chaired the Southern Baptist Historical Commission, wrote frequently for its journal, spoke at annual meetings of the Baptist History and Heritage Society, served three years as coordinator of a Baptist history symposium for church historians teaching at Baptist colleges, delivered lectures on Baptist history at Mississippi College, as well as Carson-Newman, Judson, and Wayland colleges; at Baylor, Ouachita, and Palm Beach Atlantic universities; and at the Alabama and Virginia state Baptist historical societies. In time, I broadened my interests to include Methodists and Presbyterians, speaking at their churches, historical societies, and colleges, as well as writing for their journals.

Although this was not considered scholarly activity by many of my colleagues, it fit a central career pattern for me, taking history off campus to educated, ordinary people who wanted to understand events that too often are obfuscated by professional historians. This became as important to me as my call to preach, and perhaps in a way represented an extension of that original vision.

The final theme of those early years of scholarship explored an entirely different aspect of history, though in later years I would merge it with my interest in southern religion. Unlike religious history or history from the bottom up, biography had long been at the center of historical inquiry. Explaining the lives of important men and (infrequently) women, had located history within familiar and common human terrain. Biography had a history of twenty-five centuries, though the art had no name until the seventeenth century. By the nineteenth century, biography served the purpose of Victorian elegiac, glorifying the heroic qualities of men (and a few women). More recently it had become the medium for exploring the subterranean recesses of human personality, often appropriating half-understood Freudian assumptions.

Biographers are in some ways like portrait painters. Their scope can vary from a pencil sketch to a Rubenesque canvas, from light brush strokes to complex layers and multiple shades of light. They reduce the incomprehensible complexity of human experience to a single object, connecting one intrinsically interesting human being (the painter/writer) to another (the subject/reader).

I consider biography to be one of the highest forms of storytelling. Rather than merely explaining what happened to transform an ordinary person into an extraordinary life, biographies explain how and why events occurred as they did. Biographers also have double vision. They view the world through the lens of another person in order to understand why that person acted as he did. They view the world independently so they can determine what alternative ways of understanding, seeing, and perceiving reality existed for their subject.

Biographers must respect the sequence of life. They cannot rearrange events to make the story more dramatic. Life contains passages, phases of maturation, and change. Authors cannot make a person know more at one stage of life than it was possible to comprehend (judging people who lived long ago by our own moral standards or enlightenment, for instance).

Biographers are both diggers and dreamers. They gather as many facts as they can unearth. Then they transcend facts for the purpose of analysis and interpretation. Digging puts a person on the page. Dreaming lifts the person off the page and into another realm.

The chief danger of biography is that the author becomes an apologist for his subject. The biographer stands in the subject's shadow for so long that the shadow will not go away. The writer begins to rationalize the foibles of the subject, explains away inconsistencies, even falls in love with the object of the story.

I had apprenticed for the craft of biography while in graduate seminars, where I wrote biographical essays on Samuel E. Morison, Tyler Dennett, Francis Parkman, and Theodore Roosevelt, four American historians who participated in the events they described. They crafted history by living it, engaged fully in the issues of their times, and mobilized prose narrative on behalf of a conversation with literate, nonprofessional audiences. All these patterns influenced my own career.

I first applied the biographer's craft to two Florida politicians, influential U.S. senator Duncan U. Fletcher and demagogic governor Sidney J. Catts. Much later I returned to this genre with a more ambitious project in mind. Jerry Berkley, a colleague at Auburn University Montgomery (AUM) specializing in Chinese history, asked me to coauthor a book about Alabama missionaries (Baptist, Methodist, and Presbyterian) who served in China between 1850 and 1950. Collective biography posed unique problems. How to combine many lives into common themes? How to merge forty-seven missionary stories while maintaining individual distinctions?

Although I wrote the first draft of the book in Auburn, I revised it during three months as research scholar at Hong Kong Baptist University, where long-time Samford friend Jerry Barrett then served as provost. We lived in a high-rise in the New Territories surrounded by Chinese neighbors. We shopped in Chinese stores, ate Chinese food, traveled on Chinese public transportation, and submerged ourselves in Chinese culture. I learned much about the initial missionary experience from being a white man from Alabama living in a society where I did not speak the language or entirely understand the culture. Since that was the initial missionary experience about which I wrote, Hong Kong seemed a perfect setting for my revisions. Like the four historians I wrote about in graduate school, I was learning history by living it.

Politics

During these years I not only wrote politics, I also lived it. As sponsor of Samford's Young Democrats, I came to know many Alabama political leaders. In 1971 I wrote state legislators, urging them to support stronger environmental legislation. Chriss Doss—my representative in the house, later an excellent county commissioner, Samford colleague, and fellow church member—introduced such a bill. I also supported One Great City legislation introduced in 1971 to consolidate separate Jefferson county political jurisdictions into a single metro government.

Nevertheless, my reservations about Democratic corruption and incompetence remained. Although I backed Democrats John Sparkman and Lister Hill in U.S. Senate races, I supported progressive Republican congressman John Buchanan for the sixth district congressional seat. I was nonpartisan in gubernatorial elections, the constant being my opposition to George Wallace, for whom I can proudly say I never voted. In 1970 I supported Albert Brewer in the Democratic primary, then voted for John Cashin, an African American dentist from Huntsville who established the National Democratic Party of Alabama in order to oppose Wallace in the general election. When Wallace or his wife, Lurleen, ran multiple times for governor, I cast protest votes for Prohibition, Socialist, and Republican candidates against them.

In presidential contests, I voted Democratic, supporting Hubert Humphrey in 1968, reluctantly voting for George McGovern in 1972, and enthusiastically voting for virtual next-door neighbor and fellow Baptist Jimmy Carter in 1976. For Carter, I worked the phones at Democratic headquarters with African Americans, college students, and United Mine Workers to turn out the vote that helped a Democratic presidential candidate win Alabama for the last time in more than thirty years.

During these years, I began to understand two pieces of political wisdom. British prime minister Benjamin Disraeli once said that "a successful politician must understand his times and himself." Perhaps in the United Kingdom. But in America, and especially in Alabama, I was appalled at the number of successful politicians who understood neither. That does not speak well for our electorate. The British novelist Jane Austen spoke more personally to me: "Where so many hours have been spent in convincing myself that I am right, is there not some reason to fear I may be wrong." My youthful exuberance for Richard Nixon in 1960 provided an object lesson in Austen's wisdom. Since 1960 I have often regretted my political decisions and would have voted to remove many politicians I helped elect were recall an option under the Alabama Constitution. Having to live with my past political mistakes, I am not inclined to argue with people about how they vote or urge my own preferences too strongly.

Family

The tsunami of teaching, research, speaking, and endless activity overwhelmed me, even with my schedule book accounting for every minute. I found safe haven and sanity within my family and church.

Just as the music, fashion, religion, and reading preferences of Depression-era children seemed quaint to generations that followed, so did our family structure. My generation's divorce rates were low, though our index of marital happiness probably was not much different from other generations. My generation rushed from big cities into suburbs without asking important questions either about the cities it was leaving or the suburbs it was constructing.

Our home on Queensview Road atop Shades Mountain in unincorporated Jefferson county was made possible by a kindly registrar at Samford who was leaving with his nurse-wife for missionary service in Africa. They wanted us to have the house and priced it within our reach, yet another kindness attached to the religious community to which we belonged. Our neighbors, especially Walter and Dot Johnson, were salt-of-the-earth, God-fearing, churchgoing, friendly people willing to fix our furnace or provide role models for our children. The street teemed with kids about the ages of David and Sean. Shades Mountain Elementary school, several blocks away at the foot of the mountain, was within easy walking distance.

Dartie's decision to become a stay-at-home mom compensated for my practice of being a mostly absent dad. If the cultural preferences of two adults born in 1938 and 1940 seemed antiquated to baby boomers, our gender roles must have seemed even more old-fashioned. We were stranded between two societal patterns. We had the birth control pill but were already content within a strong marriage. We had books on child-rearing by Dr. Spock but were products of spanking and believed it had done us no harm. Women in our generation still defined their identity largely by their husbands and children, not by their careers. They exercised influence indirectly through families, churches, and communities. Most were celibate until marriage and monogamous afterward. Men should follow the same rules, but (wink, wink!) we knew they would sow wild oats. High school girls who became pregnant—but not the boys—had to drop out of school.

Within five years after arriving at Samford, I discovered from my students that many of the rules my generation lived by or at least claimed to live by had changed dramatically. Affluent coeds traveled to Europe for abortions. Less affluent ones, sometimes pregnant but in stable relationships, blackballed allegedly promiscuous coeds from campus academic honoraries. One of our handsome young married male professors allegedly "hooked up" with some of his students. Feminism was on the march, bras were out, careers were in, marriage was postponed or irrelevant, and traditional rules seemed to be hypocritical. To steer our own independent lives through so many shoals made for perilous journeys.

Dartie piloted her life brilliantly. Her choice to remain home with our sons did not result from failure in her career. She had been a successful teacher both in Gadsden and Tallahassee. She was ninety-two pounds of dynamite, as a group of failing football players enrolled in her English class at all-white Emma Sansom High School had discovered. When two of them began a fistfight in class one day in 1961, she first tried to separate them, only to be swatted aside by one of the giants. When she recovered, she gathered students cowering on the edges of the fight and escorted them out of the room, shutting the door

I am with my sons David (age five) and Sean (one) in front of Beeson Hall on the Samford campus, where the history department classrooms and offices were located. I was twenty-nine when this picture was taken. Flynt family photo.

behind her. They stood in the hall until the fracas ended. Then she returned to the room, took the two bloodied and considerably weakened boys by the arms and marched them to the principal's office for punishment.

Punishment was neither swift nor certain in her school. One incorrigible student disrupted class so often that Dartie finally took him to the principal for discipline only to have him return minutes later with a note readmitting him to class. Furious, she marched to the principal's office and announced that it would take her five minutes to gather her purse, keys, red pens, lesson plans, and notebooks and leave. Thereafter, the student sat in a desk by himself in the hall where he could hear her lessons but not disrupt the class.

The following year in Tallahassee she obtained a teaching job by substitute-teaching in a large university town where prospective teachers often waited years for full-time jobs. The chief challenge for substitutes was discipline. Students tested them to see how much they could get away with. In Dartie's case the answer was, "nothing." She had already taken her Ph.D. practicum in discipline at Emma Sansom. She obtained an offer of full-time work after substituting for a retired military officer who had lost control of the class so completely that students threw chalk and erasers at him.

When students wanted to learn, they found her a supportive mentor. When they didn't, they found her a formidable adversary. Her favorite class consisted of a group of eighth graders. Every boy had failed English at least once, and the only girl who enrolled quickly transferred. The boys were all from working-class families with weak support systems. But they were also streetwise, competitive, and resourceful. They repaired cars, built things, worked odd jobs, and were fiercely proud. Rather than belabor grammatical constructions, Dartie introduced them to debate. Selecting topics that would interest them, she divided the boys into teams and sent them to the library to conduct research. Within weeks they had become immersed in their subjects, secretively conspiring with their partner, covering their books, magazines, and notes when an opposing debater came near, and furiously arguing their points before classmates. Their grades improved, discipline ceased to be a problem, parents beamed with pride, and Dartie spent her most satisfying year of teaching.

So her retirement from teaching was by choice, not the result of revulsion or failure. She was increasingly attracted to a variety of feminism not always popular in the mainstream women's movement. Feminism for her meant the right of a woman to choose for herself. If other women chose abortion, that was their right but not her choice. If other women chose career over having children, she did not criticize them, though she preferred to be home with the boys. As a tomboy, tinkerer, fixer-upper, as a strong-minded, intelligent, self-contained, stoical woman who grew up with two brothers in a neighborhood of boys, she explained that she was not even aware she was a girl until age twelve. She fell out of trees and beat up a much larger girl in elementary school for picking on her best friend. Sent to the principal's office after the fight where she was asked why she hit the larger girl, Dartie sputtered that she was furious at the girl for picking on her friend. The astonished principal informed her that she was much smaller than the girl she was defending.

Quiet, private, and introspective, Dartie was my opposite. House-bound, a wonderful cook, a true soul mate, she also opened our home to friends, students, and colleagues. Intellectually curious, she read more widely than I and enrolled in biblical archaeology and art courses.

In a classic role reversal, Dartie relished all things mechanical, which I despised. Dad had been much too impatient to teach me anything, so I had no confidence in my domestic skills. She, on the other hand, would not buy an appliance unless it had external screws and could be disassembled for repair. Once when our gas furnace malfunctioned during a cold winter, she asked our neighbor, Walter Johnson, to look at it. He told her we needed a new motor. I told Dartie to call a repairman. With no financial resources, and having grown up in a frugal Baptist minister's family, she ignored me. When I returned from school that night, she had taken the motor out of the housing, located a store downtown that sold them, and sent me on my way to buy a new one, which she installed. My pride bruised, I was furious, but in time I came to treasure her skills and defer to her mechanical judgment.

She was also a master at stretching our tiny budget. When I came home from the barber in 1965 with my hair butchered, she inspected his work and vowed that she could do better than that. She went to the store, purchased a hair clipping set, and demonstrated her point with humor. Before I was filmed for a television documentary, she cut and sprayed my hair so thoroughly that she concluded, "That's sprayed so well that if the wind blows your head off onto the street, people will say, 'but doesn't his hair look good'!" She also cut our sons' hair until they went off to college, saving us thousands of dollars in the process. A wonderful seamstress, she made most of her clothes and many of ours. She purchased the rest of her elegant wardrobe in thrift shops, assisted by her tiny size, which assured a steady supply of fine dresses and suits too small for most shoppers. When driving our 1961 Volkswagen Beetle, she entertained the boys by cutting off the engine and coasting down hills. They thought it a fine game. She knew it to be a way of making ends meet until the end of a month.

Dartie was never more queen of her realm than when organizing our annual camping trips. In 1971 we bought a two-year-old Volkswagen camper and, from that time until we left Samford, traveled across the Eastern Seaboard with the Barretts or Dartie's brother Everett and his family. Our boys bonded with their four Smith cousins as well as with the Barrett children. On those monthlong excursions, I really did decompress, directing all my time and attention toward Dartie and the boys. Trips ranging from Appalachia (we particularly loved western Virginia) all the way up the East Coast as far as Canada's Maritime provinces and west to Arkansas and Texas required Dartie to master both the technology of the camp stove and a pared-down cuisine palatable enough for two growing boys and within our limited budget. She became an imaginative camp cook who would have done justice to a nineteenth-century wagon train or cattle drive.

At a more profound level of companionship, Dartie and her family expanded my mind, soul, and experience. Her family lived in the same Appalachian foothills as mine, though they came from Clay and Coosa counties, a bit farther south than Calhoun. Her desperately poor father had moved into Sylacauga when he felt called to preach because the remote mountain where they lived had no high school. He worked a year at Mignon Mill in order to earn enough money to attend a year of high school. By alternating three years of high school around three years in the mill, he was able to graduate, then work his way through Howard College. At Southwestern Baptist Seminary during the Depression, he worked multiple jobs to sustain his family, pastored, and suffered a nervous breakdown. Dartie's resourceful but quiet mother held the family together while he recovered.

Her maternal grandparents, Mr. and Mrs. L. A. House, also lived in Sylacauga, where he worked at a coffin factory and she in the mill. Mrs. House became the subject of one of my first oral histories and furnished many of the insights for my sixth book, *Poor but Proud*. She had a folksy way about her that could charm birds down from the trees. We visited Mrs. House when she was ninety-four years old and in poor health. She didn't have her false teeth in place, had on no makeup, and wore a faded dress. Worn out by a lifetime as a spinner in the mills, three times a widow who had also outlived four of her five children, she told me in exasperation: "I can't hear, I can't see, and I don't even chew. It's so bad when you lose all your qualities." But she added, "Mr. House [her long-deceased husband] comes to visit me often nowadays. Sometimes he stays all day."

While we lived in Birmingham, Otis Brooks, our pastor at Vestavia Hills Baptist Church, asked Dartie to help him with an article he was writing on the theme "don't make your children hate the church." He asked her for insights from a "preacher's kid" (PK) perspective. Professional church staff, she responded, needed to remember that their children did not volunteer for full-time Christian service. When vacations had to be rescheduled or even abandoned because a church member died, parents needed to explain to children why they couldn't go on the trip and apologize. Parents needed to take children's plans into consideration before they scheduled church commitments beyond regular duties. They should spend quality time with their children. Sometimes PKs preferred to stay home rather than attend church. On special occasions, parents should permit them to do so. Although parents might need to avoid close friendships with church members lest they appear to show favoritism, that should not be a requirement for children. And parents needed to confront the likelihood that teenage PKs at some point would rebel by pulling away from the church and religion for a while. I thought her advice the wisest I had read about the relationship of ministers to their offspring.

Dartie also shrewdly analyzed our family. When I overreacted to David's long hair, she reminded me how fine our sons were and admonished me to ignore the little stuff that didn't matter. One Christmas she gave me a copy of psychologist Wayne Oates book *Confessions of a Workaholic*. I recognized myself on every page. So did she. I tried to change but was not very successful. Pablo Picasso spoke the truth when he said, "It is the work in life that is the ultimate seduction." Like drugs or alcohol, I allowed the work I loved to consume my life. Luckily, Dartie and our sons understood what had happened to me and avoided the trap. Dartie was quite content, like Annie Flynt before her, to place home maintenance farther down her list of priorities, preferring to enjoy her sons, to dig wildflowers for her garden, or just sit in the library sipping coffee and watching birds at our feeders. When I did that, I was filled with guilt at neglecting unfinished business.

In 1988, when Sean was a student at Samford's London Study Center, we flew to England to spend our holidays with him. On an unusually balmy, sun-drenched day, we strolled through Saint James's Park. I was exhausted from reading doctoral dissertations, finishing one book, writing a second, and researching a third, all with tight deadlines, not to mention a heavy load of lectures and speeches around the country. Meanwhile, Sean demonstrated how birds would land on our hands, arms, and shoulders to eat seed. I began to relax, surrendering to the easy seduction of a glorious day in London. After minutes of joyful hedonism, I announced: "I have the title for my memoir: 'Feeding the Birds in Saint James's Park: The Confessions of a Former Workaholic.'" Without hesitation, Sean replied sardonically, "I didn't know you wrote fiction."

Despite his good-natured skepticism, I was learning an important lesson. In order to survive, I had to follow orgies of work with times of self-indulgence. Our long camping trips were my first clue how this could be done. Find a pastime (camping, backpacking, fishing) that required undivided attention.

At Vestavia Hills Baptist Church, I volunteered to sponsor a group of boys called Royal Ambassadors (RA), who studied missions and the Bible while engaging in a rigorous regimen of crafts and backpacking. On Wednesday nights we did the church stuff. Five or six weekends a year, we disappeared into the forests, creeks, and rivers to live as simply as we could, fashioning tents from pieces of polyethylene and rope, cooking, hiking, rappelling, swimming, fishing, and learning about nature. The biologist Tom Denton and historian/folklorist Jim Brown, fellow Samford faculty and church members, supplied the expertise. Our sons were members of the group, and we all bonded in special ways as we explored Alabama's magnificent diversity and physical beauty. I became a devoted environmentalist, not from reading books or attending lectures about nature, but from encountering it firsthand. I would lead wilderness RA groups until Sean departed for college. After twenty years of backpacking and camping, however, my idea of roughing-it became the nearest Marriott.

Our international adventures began in 1971. With six-year-old and two-year-old sons at home, Dartie was frazzled. I was exhausted from six years of nonstop teaching and work on my recently published first book. Mother and Dad were energetic grandparents in their early fifties who volunteered to keep the boys, a gift that exceeded all their generous financial support. So we bought discount airline tickets with the Huntsville German Club for a brief trip to Europe.

During March 1971, before our departure, we took the boys to Birmingham's International Festival of Arts, which that year featured Spain. Tired from a half day of walking, talking, and sampling Spanish food, crafts, and culture, we were on our way out when David spied a booth where people were registering for a free trip to Spain. Sean was fretting, so I ignored David's plea that we register. He was persistent, so more to pacify him than to win a trip, I filled out a form and dropped it into the box.

Several weeks later on April Fool's Day, I received a call at the office. The caller informed me that I had won two plane tickets to Spain on Iberia Airlines. Of course I had, I replied tersely, hanging up the phone. Made wise by years of students' April Fool tricks, I was not about to be fooled again. Some time later, the frustrated man called again and began the conversation: "Please don't hang up. Did you attend the International Fair?" Yes, I replied. "Did you register for a free trip to Spain?" Yes, I confirmed. "I called you earlier to tell you that you had won the trip. You hung up on me. I phoned your wife at home to tell her, and she hung up. I am a Birmingham lawyer and fair volunteer and you *did* win the tickets." We canceled our flight with the German Club, used the refund to buy Eurail passes, and spent four glorious weeks in Europe, followed by two miserable ones pining for our sons.

After we returned, David did not assuage our guilt (he had marked off each day on the calendar that my mother bought him and eagerly listened as she read our daily letters). Later we overhead a friend ask him if he had gone with us to Europe. "No," he replied, "but I've been to Alabama Mills store" (a landmark Birmingham establishment where Dartie bought cloth and sewing supplies while David and Sean played beneath tables of fabric).

That summer Mother and Dad bonded with the boys in special ways. Her indulgent presence reassured them. Sean was malleable and easily entertained. David's personality drifted more into the Flynt orbit. Watching David and Dad together, Dartie observed during a stressful vacation when David was three, was like watching two three-year-olds interact.

We promised the boys we would take them to Europe next time we went. In 1977, we kept our word. I bought a new VW camper to be delivered in Luxembourg. We picked it up in June, then spent six weeks camping across Europe, ending up in England, where we shipped the vehicle home.

After our move to Auburn, we took the boys on overseas trips almost every year, funded by book royalties and honoraria from lectures, which we set aside solely for travel. We stayed sometimes with Dartie's younger brother, Charles, his wife, Sandy, and their three children. Tiring of Baptist theological battles, he opted to pastor churches in Pozzuoli, Italy; Stavanger, Norway; and Dubai. In addition to Italy, we took the boys by ferry to Athens, Greece, to every western and central European country, to Britain and Ireland, and in 1982 to Hong Kong and the People's Republic of China. David just missed celebrating his seventeenth birthday on the Great Wall of China. The boys did not live a life deprived of adventure. Though they learned much from teachers in Auburn's excellent schools, they probably learned as much from our travels.

Lest all this seem a romanticized rationalization of a perfect marriage, the story is not quite so simple. Years later Dartie described to me what she called "housewife's fatigue" brought on by her endless chores and child-rearing duties and my nearly complete submersion in my career. I often arrived home after she and the children had finished dinner then plunged into grading as soon as I wolfed down some food. She began to live as a single mother in a married household. More than once she confided to me in saner, less stressful years that she had considered taking the keys to the Volkswagen, driving off to some uncertain destination, and letting me raise the children and tend the house. I had not a clue she once harbored such thoughts, which is a clinching argument of how I sometimes failed as a spouse.

Church

Beyond family, the other pole of my nonwork existence was Vestavia Hills Baptist Church. The church was as unusual as the building in which it met, a poor twentieth-century replica of the Roman temple of the vestal virgins. The Birmingham mayor who built it as a home reputedly made it a center of bacchanalian depravity unworthy of its Roman origins. The building dominated the crest of Shades Mountain, facing down toward Samford's campus in Shades Valley. The church was barely a decade old when we joined, attracted by our friend Max Gartman, who directed music, and a minister as unusual as the building in which he preached. John Wiley was a no-nonsense former marine, a man's man if there ever was one. At the same time, he was one of the first professionally trained pastoral counselors in the Deep South, with a degree in the subject from Boston University. He attracted a diverse congregation of mainly affluent, well-educated, independent-minded members.

That he danced to a different theological and cultural tune became clear in his crisp, thoughtful sermons as well as in his reaction to me. Not long after we joined the church, he took me aside to relate a telephone conversation he had had when the church requested confirmation of my membership at Tallahassee First Baptist. Someone from that church had contacted John to tell him that I was a Communist trained in Cuba and smuggled into America to agitate for civil rights. We both laughed. Not until years later did I discover that this mythology of Cuban origins had been a central tenet of the far-right anti-integration movement.

For years, I taught a college Sunday school class consisting of forty or fifty Samford students. I also served as RA leader, deacon, and director of Training Union (a Sunday evening program devoted to the study of Baptist missions, doctrine, and history). My Training Union series included studies of religion in China, women's roles in the church, and the intersection of faith and psychology, among others.

When John Wiley retired, I was elected to the pulpit committee to identify his replacement. Our choice was one of the great Christians of my acquaintance. Otis Brooks had been a student at Emory University in 1943 when he was drafted and assigned to the Seventh Army as a medic. This placed him at the Battle of the Bulge, where the endless line of mangled bodies and corpses profoundly affected him. Following the war, he became a chaplain's assistant and was recommended for study at the University of Glasgow, where one of the leading Bible scholars of the century, William Barclay, taught. Upon his return from Europe, Otis finished his studies at Emory and Southern Baptist Seminary in Louisville.

Otis was a gentle man of uncommon moral courage. He was spiritually mature, theologically insightful, and prophetic in his application of the gospel to society. He successfully led a diverse congregation of differing political ideologies and theological positions. He was empathetic and a wonderful preacher who avoided clichés. I remember to this day lines from sermons he preached. In October 1969, while preaching about economic and racial justice for the poor, he exclaimed: "Tell me what you know about the suffering all around you, and I will tell you how much you love mankind." During a sometimes rancorous debate about women's roles in our church, Otis spoke both prophetically and—for the only time I witnessed—in anger. In a sanctuary that grew so quiet you could hear a pin drop, he thundered: "I will not spend my ministry painting rouge on a corpse! Let me say that again." Then in measured, dramatic cadence he repeated: "I-will-not-spend-my-ministry-painting-rouge-on-a-corpse!"

Otis metaphorically opened the windows of our church on both the sanitized, affluent suburb of Vestavia Hills and on the larger, wounded world of Birmingham. Despite our small size, the church furnished Vestavia Hills two mayors and many financial and civic leaders. But when we joined the church, not a single African American lived in Vestavia so far as I know.

Early in the 1970s, one of my Nigerian students asked if he could ride with me to church. We had never voted on the issue, so I told him I would pick him up. On the assigned day, I couldn't go, so I asked a surgeon friend in the church if he would pick up Benjamin Idiong. The reaction was incendiary and my poor friend caught the flack. After much debate, deacons voted for an open-door policy despite a residue of unhappiness, and Benjamin, resplendent in his tribal robes, became our first black member. That was the last debate about race in the congregation's history so far as I know, and in time the church took justifiable pride in being one of Birmingham's first white churches to accept black members.

Paradoxically, we experienced more strife over the issue of women deacons. At a March business meeting in 1976, after leading a Training Union series on the subject, I proposed a change in church bylaws to allow women to serve as deacons. Our practice was so contradictory as to be ludicrous. Our church treasurer, who supervised the church's finances, was a female Ph.D. in accounting at UAB. But under our policies, her gender disqualified her from serving as deacon. Once again, the church's essential sense of decency and fairness prevailed. Meanwhile, Otis had begun a dialogue group with Saint Peter's Catholic Church. Our congregation met with them, and they and their priest participated in our services.

Slowly and painfully our church was moving away from being in lockstep with its culture to being consciously in tension with it. That I played a part in this transformation is a source of considerable satisfaction to me, though the journey was not without pain and misunderstanding. Our membership lost some who could not abide the changes and attracted others committed to the effort. During the pilgrimage, I often thought of the prayer that the Great Awakening revivalist George Whitfield recorded in his diary before the American Revolution: "When Thou seest me in danger of nestling down, O Lord, in pity, in tender pity, place Thou a thorn in my nest to prevent me from it." God seemed to have a fine supply of thorns for Otis and me.

On the fifteenth anniversary of our founding, the congregation dedicated a new sanctuary. I briefly summarized the history of the infant church. Then we engaged in a prayer-litany that spoke movingly of the church we were becoming:

> Let this be the church of the free, whose daring has called them upon religious pilgrimage. Let this be the church for those who are confused and baffled, that they may find light for their darkness. Let this be the church for those who are sick in mind and body, that they may find healing for their illnesses. Let this be the church for those that are stabbed by the guilt of sin, that they may find forgiveness in the God of a crucified Christ. Let this be the church of the family, that the home may be strong and secure. Let this be the church of the young, that the future may be a meaningful adventure. Let this be the church of parents, that they may be a source of joy to their children. Let this be the place of singing, where the real faith we hold to becomes a song in our hearts. Let this be the place of prayer, where the lonely may come and not leave alone. Let this be the church where all men know their oneness in Christ and are no longer divided in their ways.

Some of the words may have been circumscribed by gender, but the aspiration was inclusive and expansive.

The journey toward that good day reached its climax at the New Baptist Covenant which met in Birmingham in January 2009. A coalition of black and white Baptists packed Sixteenth Street Baptist Church twelve hundred strong to attend seminars on poverty and justice (one of which I led) and to hear former president Jimmy Carter and Marion Wright Edelman (a black Baptist and founder of the Children's Defense Fund) speak. The meeting was coordinated by Sixteenth Street Baptist Church, where four girls were murdered in September 1963, and by Vestavia Hills Baptist Church.

Race

Down the mountain from the church, campus attitudes about race changed just as slowly amid even greater stress. It was a good thing I had my church, students, and faculty friends because all was not well with Samford's leadership. Of course, Dartie and I were under no illusions about the pace of change when we returned to Alabama. We had been disabused by a visit to the Alabama State Archives in Montgomery during the fall of 1964. While I read manuscripts on the second floor, Dartie checked books for me in the reading room. Suddenly she appeared at my desk, red-faced with rage. She announced that we had to leave; we had been kicked out of the State Archives. She told me that she had selected some books and sat down at a nearly empty table, when a staff person motioned for her to come inside her office. Greatly agitated, the woman warned Dartie if she did not move to another table, she would call police and have her arrested. Dartie asked what she had done wrong. The woman chided her not to pretend she was unaware of what she had done. Only then did Dartie observe that the only other person sitting at the long reading table was African American. Before we left, I went into the librarian's office for an impolite chat. I was a resident of Alabama, I informed her, whose taxes helped fund the archives and pay her salary. Therefore, I would sit wherever I pleased when using the building. She was not impressed by a lowly graduate student probably the age of her grandchildren and reaffirmed her intention to call the police. We stormed out of the archives to the woman's obvious relief. From that time forward, I knew that Dr. King's vision of the beloved community had not yet taken root in Montgomery. I soon discovered that it had not arrived at Samford either.

We have the capacity in memory to reinvent ourselves, to cast our motives in the most favorable light. So I tell myself that reading the Bible as a teenager constituted the pivotal moment in my changing racial consciousness, between the inherited traditions of my childhood and the acquired wisdom of my adult years. But the debater within me who challenges all assumptions about motives and the historian within me who scrutinizes all points of origin force me to consider other possibilities.

I read scripture about biblical justice between ages fourteen and seventeen. I attended a Baptist university where the topic was present if not pervasive between ages seventeen and twenty. I also came of age during a critical period of American history, when the courageous actions of African Americans every day challenged my beliefs about states' rights and the efficacy of gradualism. My habit of watching network news every night, as well as reading newspapers and news magazines, placed local events in national and even global perspective. As I came to know black families like the Molays at Florida A&M or talked with black students on the steps of our church in Tallahassee, I began to see life from different racial perspectives. So, in the final analysis, it was not merely scripture, godly instructors, enlightened friends, or Christian ethics that changed my thinking. It was all those played out in the context of a social revolution. Had I been a southern white teenager reading scripture between 1900 and 1906, or 1920 and 1926, or 1940 and 1946, I might have felt differently. For certain, I had changed my mind about race between 1954 and 1961. I had changed even more between 1961 and 1965. Now I was about to enter postdoctoral studies in race relations.

Birmingham could not have been a better laboratory for my quest. Pummeled by the international press, chastened by murders, bombings, and terrorist violence, "brought low" (in the memorable words of evangelicalism) by its collective sins of hatred and silence, the community was ready for conversion. Two novelists have captured the city's mood in 1965. Vicki Covington wrote in *The Last Hotel for Women* about the racial violence of the 1960s. Her narrator speaks of Gracie, a thirteen-year-old white girl keeping track of events for school reports: "Birmingham *is* a current event. Living in this city is beginning to make Gracie feel like she needs a bath." Novelist Sam Hodges (*B-Four*) has a cynical reporter for the *Birmingham Dispatch* suggest that the city's promotional campaign to change its wretched image should be: "Birmingham: Better Than Tulsa."

As we moved to town, we entered a world torn between two resolute forces, one determined even at the cost of life to change Birmingham, the other willing to risk wealth and power to preserve it. My vantage point for this contest became the Samford campus and the surrounding community of Homewood.

One of my students, David Graves, had entered college as a freshman just after I graduated, and we overlapped one year after I returned. He had grown up in Louisville, Kentucky, and attended Crescent Hill Baptist Church, a congregation favored by Southern Baptist Seminary faculty and pastored by a prophetic preacher, John Claypool (who would later become an Episcopal priest at Saint Luke's Church in Mountain Brook, only a few miles from the Samford campus).

As a border-state Baptist with a keen sense of moral righteousness, David became Howard's go-to person on race during the city's 1963 racial agony. He was present at Kelly Ingram Park the day of the fire hoses and police dogs. In March he visited Dean Dale to discuss ways Howard students could help desegregate the college. Dale warned that he would probably be expelled if he tried. Because President Wright had also grown up in Louisville where his father was a pastor, had played basketball at the University of Louisville, gone to law school there, and then earned his doctorate at the University of Kentucky, David decided to take his plan directly to the president.

Wright was surprisingly accommodating, admitting that the college should assume leadership in solving racial divisions. But that was not realistic amid such bitter resistance. If the school tried to do so, its funding would likely dry up and it would have no influence at all. "In other words," David wrote a friend summarizing the conversation, "the spiritual realm cannot be separated from the financial."

David would not relent despite this dawning consciousness about how religion worked, and the next day he talked with Wright again, suggesting that recruiting even one Negro student would "get people used to that race." Since the trustees had established no policy on integration at the time, Wright "was in favor of the idea."

The president's tacit approval set David to work on how to implement his plan. He called President Lucius Pitts at all-black Miles College and arranged a meeting. David and his roommate visited Miles to talk with students. He also talked with his religion professors at Howard. They applauded the idea but hesitated to accompany him for fear of retaliation. They advised David to talk with Gilbert Guffin, dean of religion, who warned him to be "very cautious." If he visited Miles, he must do so as an individual, not as a representative of the college. Yet Guffin was also encouraging, telling David that eleven years earlier Howard had conducted a Negro extension division (in fact, Dartie's father had taught in Courtland, Alabama, each Thursday night for the program while he pastored Sheffield's First Baptist Church). After the 1954 Brown decision, Howard had terminated the program. Guffin told David that he was eager to "rebuild these broken lines of communication without publicity."

David's visit to Miles went well. He found that Birmingham-Southern students already participated in a discussion group, which he and other Howard students joined. He also conspired to sneak a black friend from Miles into the Birmingham Symphony's Summer Pop Music concerts held on Samford's campus.

Wright had told David the truth about the peril that integration posed to the college both from white Alabama Baptists and college trustees. Leon Macon, editor of the *Alabama Baptist,* opposed integration because he believed it would create a "mongrel race," "the half-breed children of an integrated marriage." A letter published in the paper congratulated Alabama Baptists for supporting segregation and preserving "the true teaching of the Bible and the 'pure . . . blood of the white race.'" A letter to Wright warned that integration corrupted "the white youth of the south."

Dean of Women Margaret Sizemore and other conservative administrators made the school a regular stopover for visiting right-wing luminaries. The campus chapter of Young Americans for Freedom invited South Carolina senator Strom Thurmond, who tied integration to Communism and mocked the idea of equality (students did not then know of his own contributions to integration—interracial sex and a mixed-race daughter). The right-wing Freedom Foundation regularly granted the school awards for its emphasis on Americanism, which became a source of pride among college administrators, trustees, and conservative Birmingham whites. Many students eagerly listened to speakers such as Thurmond and supported the administration's determination to preserve segregation.

Trustees took a keen interest in these issues. Insurance executive Frank Samford had played the major role in selecting Harwell Davis and Wright as presidents. He was also the school's largest financial contributor and booster. Indeed, it would be his influence in connecting the college with the Beeson family of Liberty National executives, who, over the next half century, would transform it from a provincial college to a nationally respected doctoral university. Recognizing its debt to him, and unable to call itself Howard University because there already was one, which ironically was predominantly African American, the school changed its name to Samford University in 1966 after acquiring Cumberland Law School.

Whatever other legacy Samford bequeathed the school, he was determined to perpetuate the racial views of his Black Belt ancestors. He made clear that he did not want blacks present at the 1964 dedication of the law school. When he discovered that students had begun tutorial programs in various black schools, he called Arthur Walker, vice president for student affairs, demanding an explanation and instructing him to contact the board chairman before initiating future biracial programs.

I suppose I was responsible for poor Arthur's troubles with Mr. Samford. I had suggested to the Young Democrats, the Baptist Student Union, and the Student National Education Association that they cosponsor the tutoring program at Rosedale High School, Homewood's ghetto-bound secondary school several miles north of campus. The wretchedly funded institution had no science laboratory or advanced math courses. Bright students simply languished. Dozens of my most idealistic Samford students, MKs, and future missionaries responded. Every Wednesday afternoon we trekked across Homewood to tutor all levels of students, from those who could not read to college-bound teenagers without adequate preparation, for two hours. It was there that I tutored Elizabeth Sloan, a bright, articulate, teenaged steelworker's daughter with dreams of greatness. From this small beginning, with the help of education faculty from Samford and UAB, the tutoring program expanded to Ensley, Wenonah, and elsewhere. In my student orientation to the program, I discussed economic development, health, politics, religion, and race. I forced white students to consider how they felt about a black roommate, racial stereotypes, and interracial friendships.

It was this tutoring program that brought me into direct contact with my first black Birmingham friends, teachers at Wenonah High School. They asked if I would write letters on their behalf to Jefferson County's superintendent of education. Given their extra effort to help disadvantaged students after school, I was delighted to praise their dedication.

Wenonah, which had once been a thriving iron ore mining camp, also demonstrated how long and hard these kids' journey toward equality would be. One day I planned a special project for accelerated students, a slide show about European sites they had read and heard about in my tutorials. But I used an entirely inappropriate introduction to the session. If you had all the money you needed to go anywhere in the world, I asked them, where would you go? I had organized my slide trays by country to expedite the presentation. If a student answered "England," I would insert the tray in my projector and show them what England was like. Same for Spain, France, Germany, Austria, and Italy. Obviously, I did not understand the limitations imposed on their dreams. The farthest any of them could imagine traveling to was Tuscaloosa, and I had brought no slides of "T-Town."

During these same years, the Young Democrats sponsored a voter registration drive in Homewood's black neighborhoods. We knocked on doors and transported blacks to register. When we returned to the neighborhoods in 1968 for the elections, we transported some of those newly registered voters to the polls. One of my most vivid memories involved a sullen, older white voting supervisor who refused to allow me into a voting booth to assist an illiterate, nearly ninety-year-old black woman. I patiently explained that if Alabama had given her a chance at a decent education, she wouldn't need my help. That argument fell on deaf ears, partly because the registrar had been complicit in the woman's illiteracy. Instead she threatened to call Homewood police.

Since I had failed with the firm, professional approach, I switched strategies. Was she aware of the Voting Rights Act of 1965? Well, then, she must know that the act provided for just this circumstance. She could call the Homewood police if she wished while I called federal voting observers who had poured into Alabama for the election. Then she, they, and the police could chat about requirements of the Voting Rights Act. The supervisor relented, though with hostility that could have slain me with expression alone.

Although Samford trustees tried to shift blame for continuing segregation to the Alabama Baptist State Convention, internal university documents do not support their claim. My future pastor at Auburn First Baptist Church, John Jeffers (who would soon launch an integrated child development center in his church), chaired the convention's Christian Life and Public Affairs Commission in 1965. The state convention assigned John's group responsibility for determining whether or not its institutions should comply with the Civil Rights Act of 1964. Although sentiment in the convention seemed to oppose compliance, the commission realized that this would create hardships for Baptist schools and hospitals and promised to do "whatever we could to help our constituency adjust" to integration if the trustees deemed it wise.

The trustees did not deem it wise. As a consequence, neither did Wright. Leon Macon complicated John's attempt at accommodation by editorializing in the *Alabama Baptist* that "it would be a tragedy if our colleges bowed down to the federal government and in any way signed agreements by which they could lose their freedom of action." Buoyed by Macon's resistance, Mr. Samford hunkered down for battle.

The same month as Macon's editorial, Wright secretly convened an advisory group on integration and compliance. Participants included corporate CEOs R. J. (Dick) Stockham of Stockham Valves and Fittings; Allen Rushton of Birmingham Ice and Cold Storage; W. R. Bond of Woodward Iron; John Hand of First National Bank; Earl Mallick of U.S. Steel, Fairfield-Ensley; and

C. P. Rather of Southern Natural Gas. Mr. Samford played a role in the meeting, suggesting and inviting participants, but did not attend. Other trustees were informed of the meeting as well. Fragmentary notes scribbled during the meeting were cryptic but revealing: "breakdown of historic constitutional relationships"; "states' rights"; "extension of Federal control over every area of life ('creeping socialism')"; "control over all levels of education."

Advised by so many conservative businessmen to resist integration, Wright complied. Speaking in February 1967 to the Childersburg Chamber of Commerce, he accused the Supreme Court of political and sociologically motivated "judicial activism" and called for a return to the original intent of the founding fathers. He also attacked President Johnson's war on poverty.

With the Baptist convention's lateral of the issue to the board of trustees, that body was forced to resolve integration. The rapid expansion of federal funding during the 1960s involved not only student loans, but science equipment, buildings, and other educational facilities as well. To receive these funds, the university had to sign a nondiscrimination compliance agreement. Wright rejected such action, echoing Leon Macon: taking federal money inevitably led to federal control.

By 1967 this position had become the university's Achilles' heel and potential doom. Samford was among fewer than 5 percent of all accredited colleges to reject federal funds. Creation of the University of Alabama in Birmingham and three state junior colleges in the city threatened the school's enrollment. Finances were precarious. Nine-month salaries my first year (1965–66) for full-time professors averaged 25 percent below the national average. After a successful National Science Foundation summer teacher institute (which included five blacks) pumped money into the university, a trustee's wife called the director, demanding to know why blacks were on campus. As a result, a follow-up institute was canceled.

More critical than the canceled institute was accreditation of Cumberland Law School. Both the American Bar Association (ABA) and the Association of American Law Schools (AALS) required desegregation as a condition of accreditation. Wright took the issue to the trustees in January 1967, warning that ABA and AALS censure "would be disastrous" for Cumberland. Rumors that the University of Alabama might move its law school to Birmingham added urgency to the warning. Furthermore, Audrey Lattimore Gaston, daughter-in-law of reputedly the wealthiest black resident of Alabama and a Republican, became the first academically qualified black to apply. Several south Alabama trustees supported her admission, saying that they had been praying about the matter and believed it was time to act. Denominational representatives on the board, including state convention president Dotson Nelson agreed. Former president Harwell Davis also endorsed integration.

Following trustee approval of Gaston's admission, Wright wrote law school dean Arthur Weeks that her admission was "for this time and this time only." He planned to "sit on" any future applications by blacks sent to him. Weeks subverted the president's strategy by sending a file on the next qualified black applicant together with a cover letter telling Wright that he would accept the applicant unless the president specifically sent a rejection letter. Wright was furious with Weeks but relented.

Meanwhile, pressure built from another direction. At a 1968 faculty meeting, my friend Max Gartman proposed a faculty poll about integration. I spoke in favor of the resolution, arguing that we should also send results to the board of trustees. Debate turned hot after that, with most opposition coming from faculty in the professional schools. A business professor was aghast that the faculty would meddle in trustee affairs. A pharmacy professor argued that as a private school, Samford could admit whomever it pleased. As a top-down institution where trustees ruled and the rest of us were expected to do what we were told, faculty were under no illusions about our power to change university policy. Shared governance was no more than a glimmer in our eyes.

Dean of Religion Gilbert Guffin listened to our debate and responded in his own way. He had been timid in his reaction to David Graves but demonstrated considerable courage over NDEA compliance. Sweeping aside cobweb rhetoric about states' rights, he wrote President Wright that the real issue was segregation, which the tide of world opinion and even Southern Baptist thinking (except in the Deep South) had turned against. Segregation was "contrary to Christian teaching, even as we now see slavery was objectionable": "If the issue before us were only a social or political one, as some of our friends insist it is, the stakes would not be as high. But despite its other overtones, it seems inescapably at its depths a moral issue; and it is exceedingly important that an institution like Howard finally come down not on the pragmatic but on the right side of a moral question." Though he did not plan on mounting a crusade, he nonetheless knew that many students and faculty agreed with him. Given the fact that Frank Samford chaired the board and his pastor at Southside Baptist Church (where Samford was a deacon) served as vice chairman, the center of power was quite beyond our reach. Samford presided at all trustee meetings, appointed all committees, decided all questions of order, and rejected integration. He blamed the school's worsening financial problems not on his own intransigence against taking federal funds, but upon national foundations that refused to fund segregated colleges. "I believe," he wrote a Baptist minister friend, "that by adhering to our principles of having a college for white young men and women we will attract support we have not previously enjoyed." Though he conceded that the school might someday have to admit blacks to its undergraduate college, "I know that as long as I am connected with it, I will oppose it." He was as good as his word. But over his bitter objection, the university named in his honor signed a compliance agreement on August 14, 1968, accepting both black students and federal funds.

Wright decided to launch integration of the undergraduate school by recruiting black basketball players. Mr. Samford opposed the action, was voted down, and despite the humiliation, remained as board chairman for five more years. The first year of integration was worth $750,000 in federal funds. Enrollment began to increase, surging to thirty-eight hundred my last year in 1977.

The transition for whites was not easy, but it was far more traumatic for Elizabeth Sloan, who became the first black female to live on campus. When she moved into her dorm, she was taken to a large room with double beds but no roommate. Like so many civil rights pioneers, she forged her victory for human rights with few allies. But resistance was largely generational. When black students finally were assigned rooms with whites, more parents than students objected. Yet the yearbook did not contain Elizabeth's photograph, and in 1975 one fraternity insensitively raised money for summer missions by sponsoring a "slave day."

One day Frank Samford visited Wright's office and asked to see the new gymnasium and the suddenly competitive basketball team at practice. Moments later head coach Van Washer received an urgent phone call from the president's office directing him to get our first black players out of the gym. Coach Washer gave them money, with instructions to go to McDonald's and buy something to eat. They never did understand why the coach interrupted a scrimmage to give them a snack break.

Despite Elizabeth Sloan's restraint, elegance, and high grades in speech (her major) and history, the experience left scars. But many students and faculty befriended her. In 1971 student members elected her president of the Young Democrats. I introduced her to Sidney (Sid) Burgess, a former Samford student working in her chosen field, and he helped her land a job at television station WBRC. That launched a career that carried her to Huntsville, where she eventually became director of educational television at Alabama A&M University.

Samford also dragged its feet on affirmative action. Individual deans integrated their schools with various degrees of resistance and enthusiasm. Ruric Wheeler, a nationally respected mathematician and vice president for academic affairs, urged Wright to implement good-faith efforts to recruit black students and faculty, attended national conferences on the subject, and reminded other administrators that at the end of the 1970s, only 1 percent of Samford's students were African American. He drafted a model affirmative action statement and released additional funds to hire two outstanding black faculty in law and nursing.

Every forward step had to overcome barriers. After years of grousing about segregated Christmas parties for "the Samford family" (administrators, faculty, and staff), Max Gartmen and I, along with like-minded faculty, decided to boycott the December 1970 event. On December 17, I wrote Wright that Dartie and I would not attend until blacks were allowed to participate. I congratulated him on his recent stand for desegregation with the trustees. But I could no longer "in good conscience attend when I know the same black people we asked for money at a mixed banquet some months ago are now confined to secondary place. This, of course, is my own private issue, but I have always thought it cowardly to . . . criticize behind someone's back. I appreciate the constant dilemma you are in on this matter with pressure from both sides; I have no simple answers, but I do feel duty-bound not to attend for this reason." The following year, blacks and whites met together in a joyous Christmas celebration. I sent Wright another letter, expressing my gratitude and congratulations for his decision.

My mercurial relationship with the president soon plunged again, this time over establishment of a campus chapter of the American Association of University Professors (AAUP). Ten faculty who were already individual members of AAUP decided in 1974 to establish a chapter because faculty were not consulted in decisions such as integration or accepting federal funds. I sent out invitations, which generated a strong faculty response and an administrative firestorm.

Ruric Wheeler came to our meeting because, he said, faculty were going to be hurt. Trustees considered AAUP to be a labor union and would never approve. Enjoy your individual membership, he urged, but "keep away from anything that would hurt your career if you plan to stay at Samford."

I interpreted the remarks as a threat, as did nearly everyone else. Among twenty or so faculty who initially agreed to join the chapter, a few called to remove their names. I found it ironic that no one from religion caved in, whereas almost all the law faculty withdrew. I knew Ruric thought he was protecting us. But what is left to protect, I wondered, when time after time principle surrenders to expediency.

Despite his warning, we established our chapter on February 6, 1975, with chemist Ben Chastain as president, me as secretary, and a total of seventeen members. They were among the bravest faculty I ever knew, and the memory of their courage would later sustain me during similar times at Auburn.

One of my favorite novelists, Olive Ann Burns, has her character Rucker Blakeslee explain to his perplexed grandson, Will Tweedy, why he ignored community sentiment by marrying a much younger woman not long after his wife died. "Living is like pouring water out of a tumbler into a dang Coca-Cola bottle. If you are scared you can't do it." My band of brothers and sisters, who poured water with a steady hand and not a drop spilled, deserve names: from religion, W. T. Edwards and Karen Joines; Cumberland Law School, Ken Manning; foreign languages, Max Gartman; music, Harry E. (Ted) Tibbs; business, Fred Hendon; English, Nancy Witt; pharmacy, Stan Susina; biology, Mike Howell, Tom Denton, and Robert Stiles; chemistry, Jerry Barrett and Ben Chastain; history, James S. Brown, David Gillespie, and Leah Atkins. As it turned out, we were not fired; we were just ignored.

Perhaps this conflict was my bridge-too-far. After twelve years, two published books and another under contract, dozens of publications, hundreds of speeches, numerous teaching awards, and service on many committees, I had become a dangerous pariah in the view of some administrators. I suffered this vituperation for a salary of $17,000 a year, too little even to send my sons to college, assuming they decided on a university other than Samford. For my family's sake as well as my own, I began to cast about for another job. Over the years, I had received numerous offers that I had declined: at Judson College, Kentucky Southern, the University of Texas at Arlington, and the University of Florida. Now I went on the offensive, applying at many universities, including for headship of the history department at Auburn University. The speed with which that search proceeded was as impressive as its professionalism. I was pleased with the committee, the faculty, the administrators I met, as well as the impressive traditions of the department. Emotion tied me to Samford but by 1977 nothing much else did. Dartie was patient. Dad was impatient. I dithered, remembering what Weymouth Jordan had warned about administration. Finally I took the issue to Ruric. I could not remain as poor as I was. On the other hand, I loved my students and hated to leave. Could he help at all?

He promised to talk with Wright, though he warned me that I already was the second highest paid member of the faculty. When we met again, he wished me good luck in my new job.

Like a newborn bird, I needed to be tossed out of the nest. Ruric and Wright did the tossing. The experience, like most kinds of freedom following long bondage, was both traumatic and liberating. When bad times later engulfed me at Auburn, I never second-guessed myself about whether I had made the correct decision. And in a sense that only religious people would understand, I saw the movement of God in all this. My dad saw the 35 percent salary increase and wondered why it had taken me so long to perceive the hand of God in so obvious a sign.

Wright made my exit easier by telling denominational leaders that I left for more money because the school was so poorly funded. Worse than that was his speech to the state Beta Club, in which he told students: "Make the bold choice: Follow the path of the unsafe independent thinker, expose your ideas to the dangers of controversy, speak your mind, and fear less the label of 'crackpot' than the stigma of conformity." I copied that newspaper report to remind myself of what his administration had not encouraged, rewarded, or, in the end, even permitted. As president he did many good things, even a few courageous ones. He was certainly constrained by Mr. Samford and other trustees. But within five years, seven of the seventeen members of our AAUP chapter had left. To their credit, those who remained persevered with dignity, taught brilliantly, and served their students faithfully.

As I packed to move, I set aside time to answer numerous letters of regret (from Samford alumni and students) and congratulations (from colleagues inside and outside Samford). Through the decades, letters from those wonderful students continued to arrive, to be carefully read and promptly answered.

In time my wounds healed as I transferred my energy and passion to Auburn. I tried to think positively, give everyone their due at Samford, and remember that they were caught in the jaws of history as tightly as I was. As new administrations came and went, I tried to help the school in whatever ways I could. My son Sean attended the university happily, had some of those AAUP members as his favorite teachers, received a fine education, and later worked in Samford's Office of Communication. Both my sons married brilliant alumnae, one of whom returned to Samford as a classics professor.

The rapprochement was two-way. I was selected Alumnus of the Year, awarded a doctor of humane letters degree, and appointed to the board of overseers. I

By the 1990s our sons had married wonderful sisters, Shannon and Kelly Rogers, from Morris, Alabama. Both were Samford graduates with advanced degrees from the University of Alabama, University of Missouri, and Wake Forest University. They have enriched our lives (with the help of three grandchildren). *Standing:* David, Kelly, my mom; *seated:* Sean, Shannon, Dartie. Flynt family photo.

relished the changes wrought by Tom Corts, who created the Public Affairs Research Council of Alabama, supported the Alabama Poverty Project, launched Citizens for Constitutional Reform, and promoted international education.

Andrew Westmoreland continued Tom's opening to the world. When I mentioned to him the grievous injustice done to *Crimson* editor Randall Williams, he arranged to restore Randall's long-canceled scholarship. In 2010, Randall returned to campus to complete his senior year and graduated nearly four decades after launching *Another Voice*. For the time being, I sorrowfully moved on to a new life.

• five •

Sweet Auburn, Stormiest Village of the Plain

For reasons that will become obvious, beginning a description of my twenty-eight-year career at Auburn with a modified line from Oliver Goldsmith's poem "The Deserted Village" is ironic. Auburn could morph quickly from the loveliest to the most grotesque village. If some Auburn University alumni and boosters had their way, poetry such as Goldsmith's would be banned from campus along with philosophy, religion, history, sociology, music, drama, art, or anything else that smacks of liberal arts.

That said, another part of the celebrated Auburn family loved the poem as expressing their conception of the small village, the large university, and the Auburn mystique. Their vision of Auburn was as Eden's garden, desecrated, threatened, betrayed, violated, but always worth saving. That part of the Auburn family made my life a joy. University families, like human families, come as a whole piece, not in fragments. Take it or leave it. And there was much to be said in favor of the family that bled orange and blue.

Each year in my first World Civilization lecture, I would pass out a section of Goldsmith's poem, then lead a discussion of its historical context and meaning. Like all poetry, "The Deserted Village" can be understood in different ways. The immediate context describes the way the enclosure movement and industrialization swept away a bucolic village practicing subsistence agriculture in the eighteenth century. Metaphorically speaking, the poem describes what can happen to any idyllic community when crass, cynical people distort its origins and substitute material values for spiritual and communal ones.

From my father, I had learned about mythic, idyllic villages (Shady Glen and Auburn), beloved by all and uniting all in common purpose. To some degree, that is the way I found Auburn when we arrived in August 1977. Storms gathered quickly after we arrived.

Administration

In one of my interviews with Academic Vice President Taylor Littleton, I received my marching orders as department head. The history department had a new Ph.D. program (my friend and Samford colleague Leah Rawls Atkins had received the first doctorate in 1974), but Taylor did not deem it a productive scholarly department. Staffed by bright faculty who were well respected within both university and community, they had nonetheless produced little significant scholarship and were not well known within the profession. Most of the faculty held Ph.D.s from southern schools (four from the University of Alabama, two from Vanderbilt, and two from FSU). I should use merit pay as a carrot and retirement as a stick to motivate them. I would have to make some tough decisions. As I stood to leave, Taylor added that no administrator came to Auburn with tenure. In fact, only one second-year colleague and I were non-tenured, and most of the nonproducers were full professors. My predecessor as department head, Malcolm McMillan, confirmed Taylor's assessment.

This had not always been so. George Petrie—native of Montgomery, son of a Civil War chaplain and distinguished Presbyterian minister—had attended the University of Virginia, majoring in Latin and modern languages. He arrived in Auburn as a professor of modern languages and history in 1887. His thirty-seven recitations a week in four languages plus history (he had not taken a single history course at Virginia) left him reeling. He departed two years later to complete his Ph.D. at Johns Hopkins University in Baltimore. At Johns Hopkins, history replaced languages as his primary interest. Hopkins professor Herbert Baxter Adams had just introduced "scientific history," the systematic study of original documents discussed in a seminar format with the professor leading and all entering into the conversation. Before Baltimore, Petrie considered history to consist of nothing more than memorizing facts and dates. Under Adams's tutelage, history became "human life writ large: I felt like a boy in a storeroom full of preserves and jellies."

Petrie not only discovered scientific history in Baltimore, he also encountered "scientific football." Though he had been nurtured in the Lost Cause mentality of southern Reconstruction, his time in Maryland convinced him that New South advocates such as Atlanta's Henry Grady were correct. The South must move away from agriculture, ruralism, and provincialism on the way to modernity. To Petrie, scientific football offered southern men a chance to assert their masculinity and the South's physical supremacy short of actually taking up arms. It brought southern society in tune with northern innovation.

Petrie returned to the village of 1,500 citizens and 360 students in the fall of 1891 determined to install both a new kind of history and a new type of sport. He established a rigorous history curriculum, began one of the South's first graduate programs, placed his best M.A. students (Walter L. Fleming, Watson Davis, Frank L. Owsley, A. B. Moore, Herman Clarence Nixon) in the nation's finest doctoral programs (mainly at Columbia, Harvard, and the University of Chicago), and established his department as one of the university's finest. He also retained his love for the beauty and mental discipline of Latin.

Petrie's study of classics had instilled in him the Greek ideal of a strong mind in a strong body. No sooner had he returned to Auburn in 1891 than he began assembling a football team, which practiced on the lawn behind Samford Hall. Anchored by professors of electrical engineering and history/ modern languages, students eagerly filled in the roster. Having observed only a single game in Baltimore, Petrie was no expert coach. Quality instruction would have to wait on an experienced northern coach. But Petrie did his best. In February 1892 he and a Johns Hopkins friend then teaching at the University of Georgia organized the first major college football game in the Deep South. Having established football at Auburn, he turned the team over to a properly trained coach and redirected his efforts to organizing the school's first sports field day, building the first tennis courts, gymnasium, and bicycle paths.

Petrie led the department he founded for more than five decades and served as graduate dean, finally retiring in 1942 at age seventy-six. When one of his former students, the historian A. B. Moore, wrote that "men make institutions" and asserted that Petrie was responsible for Auburn's "best traditions," the aging icon responded with what became known as "the Auburn creed." It remains the most revered statement of the Auburn family, with its commitment to education, hard work, honesty, truthfulness, a sound mind in a sound body, obedience to law, love of country, and "clean sports."

When I became history department head in 1977, I was only the fourth since Petrie began the department nearly a century earlier. I was the first to have no Auburn connection. And I had no intention of continuing previous records of administrative longevity.

The faculty was comfortably embedded in a conventional academic lifestyle. At any given time, four or five professors and at least that many graduate students held forth in the coffee room on the seventh floor of Haley Center. Many of the faculty were Second World War veterans who had finished Ph.D.s on the GI Bill. Not a few of them told Depression stories about their experiences in the early 1930s. They were overwhelmingly Democratic, southern (the department had hired its first midwesterner, Robert R. Rea, in 1950), and liberal. Only recently had the department hired its second full-fledged Republican, medievalist Joe Kicklighter (some faculty kidded the good-natured new Emory Ph.D. that it seemed entirely appropriate that our new Republican specialized in the Middle Ages).

Like the graduate students, I found myself seduced by the coffee club. These professors were some of the state's brightest people and best storytellers. Some (notably Joe Harrison, Robert R. Rea, and Bill Maehl) were brilliant. Joe possessed total recall, lectured without notes, and seemingly never forgot a date, statistic, or story. No one at Auburn matched him as a raconteur. Bob Rea—distant, acerbic, sometimes terrifying to graduate students—was a fine writer and a generous man. Bill Maehl, our German historian, looked and acted the part of a Prussian field officer.

Loosely speaking, the department contained two factions, one erudite and somewhat elitist, the other populistic. They sniped endlessly at each other, frequently brought their grievances to my office, expecting me to side with them. My mandate from Taylor required a simpler division of the department into productive and nonproductive.

Fortunately, some of the scholarly nonproducers were excellent teachers. And some of the marginal teachers were among the best scholars. So everyone filled a niche. My job was to inspire and encourage them to remedy their deficiencies in published research. My age complicated this mission. I was thirty-six and the third youngest person in a department of twenty-one. I had no administrative experience. Furthermore, there was the problem of being Baptist and coming to Auburn from a denominational college. Finally, I neither drank nor particularly enjoyed cocktail parties, the social occasion of choice in the university community. One second-tier administrator asked my wife which of the punch bowls at our annual Christmas party contained alcohol. Learning that neither did, he expressed dismay and some agitation. Gradually our invitations to parties dwindled, and we were spared the multihour ordeal of fac-

Wickham Henkels, my skillful, artistic, and enormously astute administrative assistant for decades, drew a troll with appropriate advice on the front cover of my schedule book during my frenzy of speeches and meetings in 1992. Courtesy of Wickham Henkels.

ulty packed like sardines into tiny spaces, each shouting louder than others to be heard, no substantive conversation possible above the din, which continued long into the night beneath a fog of tobacco smoke.

With my social options limited, I had to find a creative way to become a successful administrator. I had an additional liability. I didn't like to tell people no. (One faculty member chided, "If you were female, you would be pregnant all the time because you can't tell anyone no.") My beloved administrative assistant Wickham Henkels covered my schedule book with a picture of a scowling troll and a huge NO!

One of my books on spirituality supplied good advice. Praise and promote the careers of all people around you. If they succeed, the entire unit prospers. In that event, there would always be enough credit for everyone. Luckily, I genuinely liked and respected nearly everyone in the department. I also had excellent coordinators in Bob Rea, who supervised the graduate program, and Joe Kicklighter and Allen Cronenberg, who advised freshmen and undergraduate majors.

Problems abounded, among them declining numbers of history majors and inadequate equipment. For twenty-one faculty members we had only six telephones, three secretaries, and nearly thirty graduate teaching assistants (GTAs). We had no computers. Salaries trailed most other departments in the university. In an attempt to marry me to the department's malcontents, one of my incendiary professors assured me that I was the lowest-paid department head. Of course, coming from Samford I was familiar with such conditions. Pharmacy and law profs are always going to make higher salaries than historians so just get over it, I told my needling colleague; besides, how would you like to teach pharmacology or torts the rest of your life? In addition, our GTA stipends were not competitive; we had too few of them for our classes; our maps were ancient even when intended to depict ancient places and hopelessly inaccurate about rapidly changing Africa; and our budget for equipment, supplies, and travel amounted to barely $20,000 annually.

I systematically began to address each problem. Improving our woeful resources proved the easiest task. I told my kindly and supportive dean, Edward (Ed) Hobbs, that I could hardly encourage publication without supplements for travel and faculty opportunities to present the result of their research at scholarly meetings. I created a departmental newsletter designed to connect us with alumni, who began to contribute to the department. George L. "Buck" Bradberry, a former assistant football coach and head of the alumni office, generously funded the newsletter for many years. I created student awards named in honor of beloved history faculty. I wrote a recruitment booklet explaining career options other than teaching to prospective history majors. Because much of our enrollment decline had occurred in the 1960s when political science became a separate department and an administrative home for prelaw students, I invited Cumberland School of Law's admission officer (who was a former Howard College debater, debate coach, and friend) to meet with history prelaw students.

I used merit pay to reward productive faculty. If it worked everywhere else, it might create incentives for improvement in public education as well. To the consternation of colleagues who rationalized that everyone made an equal contribution to the department, I rewarded faculty who authored books, taught well (as judged by student evaluations and alumni feedback), or engaged in innovative outreach. I also sponsored an author's reception each spring that drew families, friends, and top Auburn administrators to celebrate the department's scholarly accomplishments. Because the department had no money for entertainment, Dartie arranged her wildflowers and my roses into amazing bursts of color, baked cakes and cookies for days, made cheese straws and assembled heaping trays of fruit. We had four graduation parties a year (Auburn slavishly maintained the quarter system long after I arrived) for history majors and their families, also hosted by Dartie, where faculty socialized with their students. Few events did more to build support among alumni, who relished the opportunity to introduce siblings and parents to their favorite professors.

I also brought the director of the University of Alabama Press to campus each year to conduct seminars on book publishing. David Mathews, then Alabama's president, had asked me to serve on a committee to rethink whether or not the school should continue to have a press. With that decision resolved, he appointed me to the search committee to select a new director. Then he asked me to serve as the first non-UA representative on the press advisory board that made final decisions about whether or not to publish manuscripts. Over the following quarter century, I served longer than any other faculty member. As I came to understand the arcane, complex world of what is called "refereed publishing" (in which academic experts read a manuscript that they either approve, reject, or mark for revisions), I was able to share these insights with our graduate students and younger faculty. Many of them later published books with the press. In fact, during my last years in administration, the history faculty typically authored five or six books a year, and the press director's recruitment visits expanded to many other units of the university. The authors' receptions became a social highlight of the department and a central reason for its increased visibility. The graduate school even pirated my idea to honor all university authors.

I also persuaded the faculty to adopt what was, for us at least, ambitious tenure and promotion guidelines. Tenure within the first seven years of service generally required authorship of a book. Promotion to full professor required publication of at least two books or significant articles in national journals and anthologies. That full professors who had authored no books would vote for such procedures indicates their growing recognition of the fact that some of our new Ph.D.s published more than the professors who directed their dissertations. Although I realized how bright and well-read our faculty was, that compounded the failure of such well-informed people to subject themselves to the rigorous intellectual discipline and excruciatingly hard work necessary to produce a peer-reviewed book.

I tried to minimize the rift between teachers and scholars by insisting that both were equally important. Great teachers became better when they, metaphorically at least, walk straight out of an archives filled with new ideas, anecdotes, and insights and into a classroom. I knew from my own experience that such moments were not only the ones that lit my fire but also the ones that energized students. Students cared less about what their texts and other historians thought than what the teacher in front of them had learned from primary sources. Petrie had known that in 1891. Slowly we recaptured his vision. I was exceedingly proud of them for the effort.

Of course not all responded. One of my favorite colleagues simply would not write. I even offered to mail her revised doctoral dissertation to a press, but she refused. Other faculty regarded her highly; she had an Ivy League degree from arguably the best university in America; and she was one of our best teachers. But she was not tenured because I would not recommend her. Another of my favorite professors chose retirement when I explained to him that he would have to decide between using his considerable teaching skills in more classes, retaining his current class load by publishing, or retiring.

On the other hand, one of my proudest moments was the promotion of our medievalist (for whom publication opportunities were limited) to full professor based on some publications and a broad alumni consensus that he was the finest teacher at Auburn. When some of our most productive scholars raised questions about his promotion, I reminded them of the faculty commitment both to teaching and publishing. If he could not be promoted to full professor based on teaching excellence, who could? Ultimately the faculty chose a middle road with teaching at its core. We became one of the few doctoral departments nationwide to expect even holders of named chairs and Distinguished University Professorships to teach freshmen. While I was head, I voluntarily taught freshmen. Later I taught one of the two-hundred-student World Civilization sections that I despised (it was impossible to know all the students or assign writing projects) as a symbol of solidarity with those who taught them every semester. When given a choice of courses to teach my last semester at Auburn, I asked for two freshman honors classes, returning symbolically at least to my beginnings forty years earlier. Once again the department followed paths blazed by George Petrie: thirty-five years after coming to Auburn, he had still voluntarily taught freshman classes.

Preserving the course prerogatives of the old guard also helped my faculty relations. Several younger faculty urged me to usurp the graduate seminar in New South, which at the time was taught by an unpublished senior professor. This I flatly refused to do. I liked and respected him. I believed his dissertation, if properly revised, was publishable. Furthermore, I knew that the seminar was the initial exposure graduate students had to professors, and if I took over his class, I would also be taking incoming doctoral students, for whom I had inadequate time anyway. My confidence in him was rewarded by a fine book and a wonderful friendship.

I was able to resolve most of these problems over time by encouragement, retirement, and recruitment. By the 1980s the GI Bill faculty nationwide were approaching retirement, undergraduate enrollments had stabilized, and history graduate schools were pouring out talented Ph.D.s. We replaced retiring senior faculty with excellent younger ones. I also lobbied the administration successfully for additional funds to reduce class size (we sometimes taught fifteen sections of two hundred or more students, some taught by senior GTAs).

As we debated the disposition of these new faculty positions, I focused on the innovative History of Technology program through which David Lewis already provided Auburn an international reputation. This specialty seemed a natural in a land grant university with large enrollment in engineering and the hard sciences. Expansion of the program especially shored up our relationship with engineering because professors in these disciplines spoke a similar technical language. New professors steadily expanded the department's reputation, its doctoral fields, and its connections to other colleges within the university. Although the department never succumbed to my endless agitation to hire an agricultural historian, I was proud of them for at least departing from their traditional definition of what constitutes history to a more inclusive technological definition.

The department also became increasingly diverse. We had only one African American faculty member when I arrived but soon added others (though it was hard to retain them in so rural and white a setting as Auburn). When I came, we had no tenured females and had employed only one tenure-track woman in the department's history. We tripled the number of female faculty by the time of my resignation as head in 1985.

By ethnicity, doctoral degree, region, nationality, and field, we were more diverse than at any time in the department's history. But I was soon to learn that what we considered progress, external critics regarded as dangerous deviation from tradition. And within the department, pluralism became a source of division, sometimes infused with political correctness.

Critics from beyond the department made their appearance in 1980. Internal disputes became part of an ongoing dialogue in which I was increasingly part of the departmental backbenchers. The flash point came after my retirement as head. During one of our reaccreditation self-studies, the department adopted new guidelines. I agreed with most of them: the centrality of teaching to the department's mission; expectation that all faculty would teach freshmen classes. But unnecessarily prolonged discussion, complete with dollops of self-flagellation that reminded me of a Chinese self-criticism session during the Cultural Revolution, struck me as hypocritical and rooted in the fashionable academic political correctness of the times. We must recruit more blacks, women, Hispanics, and other marginalized groups. This sentiment of special entitlement for certain people tended to divide the department along generational lines. What about special set-asides for sons and daughters of poor whites, I inquired? Shouldn't we actively recruit retired military, conservatives, Republicans of any sex, color, or background, Pentecostals and other evangelicals, or homeschoolers, none of whom had any presence whatsoever in the department, save for our one lonely Republican? If we were serious about pluralism, wouldn't hiring initiatives in these underrepresented areas require highest priority, since we already had at least token representation of the other groups? Some of my older, liberal colleagues—knowing my record on tax, education, constitutional reform, poverty, and race—seemed mystified by my questions. Some new faculty were aghast, even horrified by such retro opinions. A few older colleagues sat silently amused.

More troubling was an incident involving a well-qualified southern-born job candidate teaching in a northwestern state. After the candidate revealed casually over lunch that he homeschooled his children, one of my graduate students overheard one faculty member vow to another: "I'll be damned if I'll vote to hire a candidate who homeschools his children."

Other areas of tension developed after I left the headship. As head, I practiced shared governance (using faculty committees, faculty meetings when we had business to conduct, open debate, and majority vote). But I was ambivalent when we voted to transition to a chairmanship system limited to two three-year terms, with faculty meetings several times a month, endless committee meetings, and a significant narrowing of merit pay. A majority of faculty voted to tenure faculty who did not meet our guidelines, promoted several faculty to full professor without a second book, and relied less on student evaluations and more on peer review, in which faculty evaluated each other and never seemed to identify anyone who wasn't a wonderful teacher.

It had taken me three years to learn how administrative systems operated at Auburn, and I felt my maximum efficiency occurred in years four through eight. That was more time than any chair served who followed me. They were all fine people and devoted to their work, but I thought they would have been more effective with longer terms. Of course, no system is better than the people it places in leadership, and the department was fortunate in those who agreed to serve. Being a department head or chair may be the hardest job in a university because the person is neither fish (faculty) nor fowl (administration).

I had many chances at higher administration at Auburn. But by then I knew too much about Auburn's administrative dysfunction to be interested. At Auburn, ambitious administrators were like moths irresistibly attracted to fire, only to be consumed by the flames, either ethically or professionally.

The Dysfunctional Auburn Family

All university presidents function within both historical patterns and contemporary systems of governance. Some presidents were better suited to some systems than others. So to understand why Auburn had seven presidents during my twenty-eight years on the faculty—an average term of four years (in 1986, the average tenure of a U.S. college president was 6.3 years, and in 2006 it was 8.5 years), meaning that the average undergraduate spent more time on campus than the average president—requires understanding the Auburn family, Auburn traditions, and Auburn's system of governance.

Southern families are strange configurations of the best and worst in the culture. Nearly every family has one or two members it would prefer not to claim. Often fiercely loyal to each other when confronted with external threats, members can turn on each other like starving jackals when they get in a spat. Being part of a loving, loyal, proud southern family does not preclude the prospect of bloody violence. Families can be functional sometimes, dysfunctional at other times, or even both at the same time. I had the misfortune to be present when the Auburn family was unusually dysfunctional.

I found the existence of the legendary Auburn family to be largely true. That family contained some of the best people I knew. That held true for trustees, administrators, faculty, students, and alumni. Other members of the family were mean as snakes.

Historically, Auburn was divided along sharp fault lines. The school's early history as a Methodist liberal arts college revolved around theology, classics, languages, mathematics, and sciences. Its later manifestation as land grant college grafted on to this earlier tradition a practical education, especially in engineering and agriculture. In theory, these interests can and do coexist in universities across America. But no other state relies so heavily as Alabama on volatile sales and income taxes to fund education. Other states rely on more stable and predictable property taxes. As a result, five or six times every half century, Alabama faces state-mandated proration of education budgets. When that happens, the battle for funding intensifies between K–12 and the universities, between professional schools and liberal arts, between universities and teaching colleges, and between Auburn and the University of Alabama.

The state's political culture doesn't help matters any. Auburn is a Deep South state university that relies heavily on underfunded public high schools to fill its classrooms. Many of these students are as poorly prepared for college as I was. Like me, many of them outperform expectations. But the faculty does not wrestle with hordes of National Merit Finalists. Such students generally travel out of state to elite northeastern or midwestern universities. Political pressure on Auburn has never been to make it elite but to keep it populist and affordable. Some trustees—notably R. C. (Red) Bamberg, Henry Stegall, and Senator Lowell Barron—made that goal the prevailing mantra.

Even if brilliant students had flocked to Auburn, the university was chronically underfunded compared to the University of Alabama, not to mention other regional state universities. Whether judged by faculty salaries, academic scholarships, equipment, endowment, or facilities, Auburn trailed its peers. Visionary trustee or administrative leadership can compensate for such inadequacies. That was seldom the case at Auburn for a variety of reasons, chief among them the highly politicized board of trustees.

Auburn had some fine trustees during my tenure—notably insurance executive Frank Samford Jr., attorneys Bob Harris, John Denson, and Morris Savage, congressman Bill Nichols, and publisher Emory Cunningham. We did not always agree, but I never doubted they had only one agenda—Auburn's best interests. Over the same time period, Auburn also had what I deemed to be wretched trustees, whose agenda was narrowly self-serving.

What united most trustees was participation in a pay-for-play system deeply rooted in Alabama's past and raised to a high art by George Wallace. During his four terms as governor (plus part of his wife's term), a 10 percent tithe of state contracts paid off the top to his brother Gerald became the entrance fee for doing business with the state. Aspiring trustees, whether good or bad, first must contribute to a winning governor's campaign. That allowed them to play. If they judged incorrectly in the governor's race, they could always come to the winner hat-in-hand to help pay off "campaign debts." Good trustees held their noses and wrote checks. Bad ones relished the sport. A few trustees refused to play the game and somehow managed to serve a term or two anyway. Governors feigned innocence when caught, which was rare because of the use of political action committee transfers that allowed them to hide such transactions. Unfortunately, corruption was so rampant in the state that control of a trustee board seemed inconsequential in the larger scheme of things.

This politicization was by no means unique to Auburn. I chronicled trustee conflicts at eight different Alabama colleges during my Auburn years. University administrations, sometimes potentially quite good, often failed because of bullying by intrusive trustees or politicians or because of timid responses from intimidated presidents.

Two personal case studies demonstrate the pattern. While I was department head, an associate dean solicited a campaign contribution for Governor Wallace, explaining that this was simply a prudent way to make sure the college remained in the governor's good graces. Never, ever, in a thousand years would I give the governor even the time of day, I replied, ending the conversation. On another occasion during a faculty search, the same administrator called to explain that a candidate who was completing a Ph.D. at Tulane was applying, and he was the son of a powerful legislator. The caller did not ask for favored treatment but thought I needed to know the circumstances. I explained that I would ignore this information because if my faculty learned about the call, it would so prejudice the search committee against the candidate that he would not receive fair consideration. I was never so glad as at that moment that I had changed the hiring procedure from arbitrary decisions by the department head to a faculty-directed search committee. In fairness to the intrusive associate dean, I never felt pressured to respond or experienced any retaliation.

In addition to state political patterns, Auburn traditions complicated decision-making. The first president of the new land grant university, I. T. Tichenor, straddled three academic cultures. As a former Confederate chaplain and sharpshooter, he satisfied Auburn desires for a true southern man. As a Baptist minister educated in the classics, he connected the school to its religious roots. As a self-educated mining engineer, entrepreneur, and New South promoter, he valued practical education. Furthermore, no sooner had he arrived than he became engaged in a fight with the University of Alabama. That institution's president disparaged the academic preparation of Auburn students. Tichenor responded by labeling UA an elitist school whose classical curriculum was ill-suited to "republican institutions," which required the services of practically educated scientists and engineers. By the early twentieth century, Alabama Polytechnic Institute (Auburn's official name then) was chronically underfunded and not highly regarded.

Subsequent presidents came from one academic tribe or the other, and clashes steadily escalated. Presidents from classics-oriented schools—Vanderbilt, Virginia, Wake Forest, Columbia—tugged the school in one direction. Presidents from land grant universities such as LSU pulled the opposite way. Finally, in the 1980s, Auburn resolved the tension by hiring only its own graduates. (After Harry Philpott, five of the next seven presidents and interim presidents graduated from Auburn, and a sixth was an administrator there at the time of his selection.)

By the 1930s tensions had reached such a state that trustees chose a three-man administrative committee to administer the college. Luther Duncan, head of the agricultural extension program, who was deeply enmeshed in Democratic politics, replaced the troika. He promptly clashed with the faculty over academic freedom and arbitrary faculty dismissal.

Ralph Draughon, whose tenure as president covered the years 1948 to 1965, was chosen from the history faculty to replace Duncan. Draughon tried to straddle the divide as Tichenor had, but by then the fissures were too deep. He ordered the director of agricultural extension to stay out of state politics after Auburn extension agents backed a gubernatorial candidate opposed to James (Big Jim) Folsom, so infuriating the new governor that he tried to pack the trustees with his own supporters. In 1957 trustees met in executive session, excluded President Draughon, and fired a new teacher who had written a letter to the *Plainsman* referring to racial segregation as "morally repugnant." A petition signed by seventy-six faculty (including many historians) protested the firing, causing the American Association of University Professors (AAUP) to censure the school. During the next five decades, the AAUP and NCAA vied with each other to see which could censure Auburn most frequently.

President Harry Philpott and I began our tenures in Alabama higher education at Auburn and Samford, respectively, on the same day, September 1, 1965. We both arrived from Florida where he had been vice president at the University of Florida. We were both Baptists (and members of the same church after 1977), and we were both ordained ministers. Frank P. Samford, then an Auburn as well as Samford trustee and chairman of the search committee, was largely responsible for the selection of Philpott as president.

Erudite, witty, and personable, Philpott was a popular president. His Ph.D. in religion from Yale and his career as a religion professor endeared him especially to arts and sciences faculty. Agricultural faculty and football enthusiasts thought him insufficiently attentive to their interests. He also resisted efforts by prominent Montgomery business and political leaders to establish a satellite campus in the capital and later refused an offer from Governor Wallace to establish a medical school. Given impending civil rights suits against the state's white colleges, he did not relish establishing an Auburn campus in a city that already contained a historically black university. Under pressure from powerful trustees who threatened that if he dallied longer, UA would open a campus in the capital, he finally relented. Some influential Montgomery leaders never believed he sufficiently supported AUM and sought a successor more attuned to their interests.

Another contentious Auburn tradition involved Petrie's godchild, scientific football. Almost from the inception of the sport, moralists condemned its excesses. Auburn president William Leroy Broun at first endorsed Petrie's innovation but developed reservations as players lost interest in academics. As a sport with few rules, excesses were common. One stout Irish immigrant newly arrived in America played football for Auburn without bothering to enroll in class. Football also replaced debate societies as the most popular extracurricular activity on campus.

Even one of Petrie's students, Leroy S. Boyd, class of 1892, condemned football in an article written early in the new century. Football players, Boyd charged, "utterly disregard all college discipline and are absolutely under the domination of an imported professional trainer, who in most cases . . . is a man of loose morals, and very often a deep-eyed scoundrel as well." No wonder, he concluded, that religious activities at Auburn had declined since the introduction of football.

President Charles C. Thach (1902–20) expressed similar concerns about football, as did his successor, Spright Dowell. Dowell was a graduate of two highly regarded institutions, Wake Forest and Columbia, a former state superintendent of education, and a prominent Baptist layman. His sense of propriety and fairness got him into trouble when he ran off the school's Southern Conference–winning coach, expelled a star quarterback for drunkenness, presided over a steadily worsening football program, and incited revolt among football-crazed boosters, led by Birmingham's antiunion coal mine owners Charles and Henry DeBardeleben. Despite energetic support from the state's religious leaders and Dowell's own heroic defense, the boosters lifted the president's scalp. His firing indicated which Alabama religion, Christianity or football, wielded the greatest power on the plains.

Dowell left Auburn to become a popular and successful president at Mercer University. One Mercer trustee listened to a flattering recommendation of Dowell by the search committee then inquired why, if he was such a great man, he was leaving Auburn. A physician on the committee answered with a parable: "Years ago there lived on the Western Plains a tall, strong, fearless cowhand known as 'Big Foot Bill.' During the terrible Grasshopper Scourge, they found his dead body on the plains covered with millions of grasshoppers. When they dug his body out, they found that just before his death he had taken from his pocket a stub pencil and a scrap of paper on which he had written, 'I do not mind dying in open battle with brave men, but I hate like hell to be kicked to death by grasshoppers.' Gentlemen, that is the reason why Spright Dowell is willing to leave Auburn." I shared that story with several former Auburn presidents. They smiled and nodded knowingly.

Auburn football reached its zenith under two coaches, Ralph "Shug" Jordan during the 1950s and Pat Dye during the 1980s. Both tenures ended tragically for them and for Auburn.

Jordan, my sports hero growing up, coached the team to its first national championship in 1957, a victory marred by two events. The NCAA penalized the team for recruiting violations. That same year both mechanical and electrical engineering departments lost accreditation because of underfunding, inadequate equipment, and miserable facilities.

In 1971 Jordan, near the end of his career, asked Philpott to appoint him athletic director as well as head coach, dual positions already held by his rival Paul "Bear" Bryant. Philpott refused, offering either title but not both. Jordan, according to one trustee, "never got over" the snub. Embittered at Philpott, he welcomed appointment to the trustees following his retirement. On the board, he chided fellow trustees for being a "rubber stamp" for Philpott's decisions. Alumni increasingly blamed the university's lack of football success against its cross-state rival not on inferior coaching or players, but on insufficient support from Philpott, whom they accused of spending too much money on women's athletics and minor sports. One letter complained that "an intellectual, non-competitive and non-violent person" could not "truly comprehend . . . the world of competitive athletics." Other letters to trustees insisted the head coach needed "unfettered authority," instructing the university president and trustees to stay "out of the football program" (no matter that lack of administrative oversight was one reason Auburn stayed in trouble with the NCAA).

Jordan's determination to get even with Philpott found an ally in Fob James, one of the coach's football stars who was elected governor in 1978. So the first crisis in my Auburn years involved a former coach and one of his players bent on revenge.

Governor James added other indictments to the charge of snubbing his old coach, accusing Philpott of requesting too much money for Auburn and poorly managing what he received. Although Philpott always denied that he was fired, one trustee alleged that James asked for his resignation. Other sources claim that trustee Morris Savage met with Philpott and told him the governor wanted him to resign. At any rate, Philpott, no doubt weary of such pettiness, called it quits. The ensuing presidential search must rank as one of the most bizarre in the history of Alabama higher education. Given the high standard the state set for sham presidential searches, that required some doing.

Trustee Bob Harris, a Decatur attorney, agreed to chair the search committee provided James would pledge to permit a legitimate national search and not meddle politically. The governor agreed. He kept neither promise.

According to Harris's narrative of events, James from the outset backed his highway director, Auburn engineering professor Rex Rainer, for president, with a subsidiary agenda of firing Herb White, director of university relations, and a variety of other Philpott administrators. Four other potential presidential candidates emerged, led by Steven Sample, vice president of the University of Nebraska. Sample by all accounts was a renaissance man, an engineer who also played percussion in the Nebraska Symphony Orchestra and was a splendid administrator. From the outset, Sample won support from a majority of trustees, with the others divided between Rainer and James Martin, an Auburn graduate who was then chancellor at the University of Arkansas. Unable to mobilize a majority for Rainer, the governor refused to hold meetings and dispatched his county political coordinators and business friends to lobby trustees. One allegedly dangled a junior college presidency before the friend of a trustee and promised other rewards to wavering board members.

James initially dismissed Hanly Funderburk, who served as chancellor of the AUM campus, as a lightweight. After Funderburk's interview with the board, the governor told Harris: "Shit! Can you believe that we have someone like that working for Auburn University." He ridiculed Sample as well, asking Jordan at one meeting, "We don't need a flute player as president of Auburn, do we, coach?" Jordan chortled, "No, Governor, we sure don't." Hoping to embarrass Sample into withdrawing, he refused to send the state plane to pick up the Samples, leaving them stranded in the Atlanta airport. Frank Samford Jr., Morris Savage, Superintendent of Education Wayne Teague, Bill Nichols, and Harris angrily held firm for Sample. As the governor grew ever more furious at recalcitrant pro-Sample trustees, however, he began to stress Funderburk's Alabama roots and finally brokered a deal to install Funderburk as president with Rainer as executive vice president. James pressured trustee Charles Smith to switch from Sample to Funderburk.

Harris threatened to resign as chair of the search committee and reveal everything that had occurred but was dissuaded from doing so by his allies. On April 7, after Sample withdrew, trustees elected Funderburk by a 10-1 vote. Harris stood alone in opposition. He also circulated a document apologizing to the Auburn family that his assurance of a search free of provincialism and politics had not been honored.

As Harris confirmed, this "national search," like so many after it, actually stretched all the way from the Tennessee River to the Gulf of Mexico, from the Tombigbee to the Chattahoochee. Anyone outside these boundaries had better have at least one Auburn degree.

Sample went on to a seventeen-year presidency of the University of Southern California (USC). While he was president, USC football teams won multiple national football championships (though not without scandal), the endowment quadrupled to $4 billion, and he renovated the campus. USC soared to twenty-sixth place on the *U.S. News & World Report* rankings of American universities, and received thirteen applications for every spot in its freshman class. Any one of those accomplishments at Auburn would have exceeded his competitors.

Funderburk moved on to a more problematical fate.

Under the best of circumstances, the flawed search would have been a huge barrier for him to overcome. While financial problems and prorated budgets during the 1978–83 national financial meltdown were difficult, Funderburk's poor communication skills, bean-counter mentality, and isolated administrative style complicated his problems. Early on, Funderburk summoned all Auburn administrators to a meeting where he read them selected passages from a basic management text. He surrounded himself with AUM administrators, who replaced Philpott's highly respected team. The trustee mandate to fire "Philpott loyalists" also caused the controversy to spill over into the closely knit community.

The disastrous search process proved that the hierarchical plantation oligarchy that dominated both state politics and Auburn trusteeship could impose its will. But with the arrival on campus of a new generation of faculty socialized both in the new business models emerging in Silicon Valley (where bright people shared collaboratively in management decisions) and in 1960s campus politics, bosses could no longer bludgeon faculty into submission. The university senate—consisting of eighty-seven representatives, one from each department, plus vice presidents and deans, and presided over by the elected president of the general faculty—rejected a resolution welcoming Funderburk to campus. The situation went downhill from there.

A few months into his tenure, executive vice president Rex Rainer resigned, citing conflicts with Funderburk over finances and enrollment policies. Rainer later split with Fob James as well, becoming one of the governor's severest critics.

After the president called for "loyal team players," the general faculty passed a resolution of "extreme displeasure" at being excluded from involvement in university policy. On February 9, 1982, the senate released a strongly negative faculty evaluation of Funderburk's performance. Two days later a resolution expressing confidence in the president failed by a vote of 455 to 416 (I spoke against the resolution). Eight days later the trustees "fully" endorsed Funderburk. Three months afterward, vice presidents Grady Cox and Taylor

Littleton, highly respected Auburn administrators, both with Auburn under-graduate backgrounds, resigned, triggering yet another university senate in-quiry. Headed by a music professor who had initially supported Funderburk, this report criticized the president's leadership style as "dogmatic, intimidat-ing, manipulative," and "not highly principled." Funderburk responded that "he served at the pleasure of the board" of trustees and would not resign. Fun-derburk issued a press release stating that Cox was incompetent and Little-ton disloyal. On November 4, a phenomenal 72 percent of faculty voted no-confidence in the president after a two-hour debate. (I spoke in favor of the no-confidence resolution.) The final vote, 752-253 with 38 abstentions, re-mains the single largest faculty referendum on a president's performance in university history. Shortly thereafter, thirteen of seventeen deans and vice presi-dents supported the faculty vote in a nine-hour secret meeting with the trust-ees (most had already written private letters to Funderburk expressing their sentiments). The student senate, which earlier had supported Funderburk, voted 33-1 on February 14 to ask for his resignation. A student petition signed by more than two thousand students also asked him to resign. So did Alumni Director Buck Bradberry who had earlier pled with faculty to support the president. The statewide council of faculty senate presidents joined the chorus. T-shirts emblazoned with the logo "Hanly Please . . ." sprouted on campus like mushrooms. Signs placed over urinals around campus read "Flush the Hanly."

Funderburk—buoyed by resolutions of support from trustees, agricultural commodity groups, many alumni, Montgomery business leaders, Governor James, and others—boasted that he had raised more than half the $62 million goal in AU's fund drive and refused to budge. The Alabama Farmers Federa-tion (ALFA) circulated pro-Funderburk petitions at its insurance offices state-wide. The faculty attempted to elect history alumna Leah Atkins (author of a secret report on the president done at the governor's request) president of the alumni association. We lost by a vote of 55 to 33. Gerald Johnson of political science despaired of further resolutions and proposed establishment of a le-gal defense committee to secure funding in order to pursue legal resolution of some issues and to protect faculty and administrators, as well as to publi-cize what was happening at the university. Funderburk's interim academic vice president (by 1983 virtually all university administrators were "interim," a pat-tern that would soon extend to most presidents as well) warned Johnson that a member of the trustee executive committee considered the resolution to be "a declaration of war." Trustees proposed a compromise, creating a chancellor to run day-to-day operations in Auburn while Funderburk moved to AUM to handle alumni and legislative affairs. Another proposal floated by Funderburk called for the establishment of an Auburn University system headed by a chancellor and managed by CEOs at Auburn and AUM. This proposal collapsed when he insisted that the president's mansion in Auburn be reserved for the chancellor (him). This led to a university senate resolution censuring Funderburk, calling trustees "derelict" for not firing him, establishing a legal defense committee, and proposing a no-confidence vote in the trustees. Four days later the *Plainsman* called for Funderburk's resignation. After years of silence, Harry Philpott warned of irreparable harm to the university if the conflict continued. I resigned as department head on February 7, 1983, the third in line behind heads of mathematics and political science, partly because of escalating attacks on the department. Auburn churches and campus ministers officially voted to pray for an end to the controversy. Although the state house earlier had refused a request to investigate unrest at Auburn, the senate voted to do so on February 22.

Meanwhile, the controversy had taken over the state's newspapers, which carried daily reports and filled their opinion sections with editorial columns and letters to the editors about the conflict. *Time* magazine devoted its entire education page to "Choosing Up Sides at Auburn."

So far as my life was concerned, the controversy entirely consumed three years. One of my closest friends, John Kuykendall—chair of the Religion Department and a gentle man of unshakeable integrity who would shortly become president of Davidson College where he became the polar-opposite of Funderburk in inclusiveness and success—served as faculty president when the conflict began. My old friend from graduate school days Gordon Bond succeeded John Kuykendall during the worst days of the controversy. An equally gifted faculty leader, Curt Peterson from the College of Agriculture, followed Gordon, and Gerald Johnson followed Peterson. Contrary to widely circulated claims that wild-eyed 1960s radicals had taken over Auburn, these men were thoughtful, restrained, courageous leaders. In fact, the faculty was overwhelmingly conservative. That John, Gordon, Curt, and Gerald were able to mobilize an entire faculty that generally detested campus politics, says much about all of them as well as the sorry state of the trustees and the Funderburk administration.

The issues were the same ones that had caused me to leave Samford and that brought more than a thousand faculty to that historic debate on November 2, 1982: belief in shared governance; rejection of micromanagement by people who consistently demonstrated their incompetence to lead; the contempt that some trustees expressed toward faculty; the plantation mentality of presidents and trustees; and, most notably, rejection of the Chinese proverb that "men fear guns and love gold." During nearly three decades at Auburn, I met thousands of students, faculty, alumni, and even a few trustees who could neither be bullied nor bought. That is the reason I did not join the exodus of excellent faculty out of Auburn, and the reason, in the end, that I had no regrets about remaining.

Over the short term, however, I spent many sleepless nights, lost some friends, and attended too many meetings where my stomach churned and my blood pressure soared. I am convinced that many of my friends died prematurely because of what they experienced. Others lost administrative positions in which they had performed with exceptional skill, integrity, and dedication. Still others read published attacks on themselves and even their families—attacks that were as malicious as they were false. The personal scars from those days are real and remain.

Also contrary to the impression statewide that I was the major wirepuller during a chaotic quarter century of strife at Auburn, I never served a single day in the senate nor held any elected office whatsoever. I did meet constantly with dissident faculty leaders and department heads to plan strategy, but I was a private in a fine army, not an officer.

Nevertheless, Funderburk retaliated against me in several ways. After Ed Williamson's term as Hollifield Professor of Southern History expired in 1982, Funderburk refused to honor an earlier agreement to appoint me to the chair. I filed a formal grievance with the AAUP over the matter.

Next, Funderburk launched a full-scale war against the history department. Since Gordon Bond had become the public face of the controversy and I had spoken in favor of several no-confidence resolutions, the president launched attacks on Bond, me, and the department. Carefully researched letters drafted in the president's office were sent to alumni, who signed them and sent them to newspapers over their own names. Gordon discovered this when a secretary secretly began sending him copies of the correspondence. So far as I know, Gordon carried the name of Auburn's own courageous Deep Throat to the grave. At least I had advance notice of what was coming. One letter, for instance, trashed the department for ranking forty-third among history departments in a national survey. I fired off a rebuttal.

When Funderburk had arrived on campus, he had appointed a priorities and planning committee (which contained no historian) to determine departments whose graduate programs merited "the highest priority for development and resource allocation." History was one of fifteen departments selected. For a chronically underfunded department with only six telephones, even making the national list (not all doctoral history programs did) constituted a triumph. Although I knew we had miles to go to be competitive, I also knew this was equally true of all but a handful of Auburn departments and programs. Indeed, in the twenty-seven years between 1975 and 2001, five history faculty were selected by their peers as Distinguished Graduate Lecturers, the highest scholarly recognition afforded by our peers at Auburn. No other department had more than four. So I returned to my lapsed practice of writing newspapers, this time in defense of my faculty from attacks originating in the president's office. I defended Gordon's class load, citing the size of his classes (more than two hundred), his spectacular student evaluations, and his teaching awards. I turned the department's newsletter into an apologetic for the faculty and a summary of the conflict for alumni. I was buoyed by their support as well as by unanimous backing from the faculty and graduate students. Perhaps some timid souls wished I had kept a lower profile rather than jeopardize their careers. But if they did, they never told me their fears.

Meanwhile, I maintained my sanity in a variety of ways. At lunchtime three days a week a friend in the Forestry School, Dean Gjerstad, joined me in taking out frustrations on the handball courts. Other days I played basketball with faculty or on a First Baptist Church city league team. A theological dinner-discussion group, which consisted of the religion faculty and a number of campus and town ministers and their wives, doubled as group therapy sessions. My family's church, led by neutral John Jeffers, though sharply divided between pro-Funderburk professors in agriculture and anti-Funderburk arts and sciences folks, nonetheless loved and ministered to all of us.

In hope of helping others, I even penned "Flynt's Theory of Conflict Management":

Focus on what is most important; keep your dignity and never engage in activity that you deplore in your opponent; but don't be afraid to engage intelligently and actively in any ethical, responsible activity to win against your opponents on behalf of what is best for your cause; in other words, be shrewd, disciplined, and well-organized; build a network of like-minded friends and associates and spend lots of time with them sharing your feelings, frustrations, anger, and outrage; this bonding is important to their morale as well as your own; exercise (no joke, this is imperative for your good mental health when you are under stress);

be prepared to walk away; no cause or institution can be saved by one person; no matter how much you love an institution, there are times when the best action you can perform for it and yourself is to leave.

On this last point, I tried to follow my own advice. During 1983, I believed that either Hanly Funderburk or Wayne Flynt was going to leave Auburn. I was so desperate to depart that I even applied for jobs in administration. I made the final cut for the dean of arts and sciences at the University of Richmond and as dean of social and behavioral sciences at UAB.

The Richmond search reminded me of why I did not want to be an administrator at any cost. The provost conducted the interview, which began with an insulting prologue. The University of Richmond is not like Samford, he informed me. It has more students from New York than Virginia, more Catholics than Baptists. Would I feel comfortable having faculty over for cocktails in my home? That was the wrong approach for recruiting me. I responded that the university seemed to have an identity problem, that I did not serve alcohol in my home, and that he might want to look elsewhere for a dean. It was a brief interview, and he took my advice.

On the other hand, James Woodward, an engineer and provost at UAB, was as solicitous as his search committee was diverse and persuasive. I really warmed to UAB despite the low status of the college I would lead. My interviews with department heads, faculty, and community leaders went well. Following an impeccably professional search process, Woodward offered me the job. By this time, Funderburk had resigned, interim president Wilford (Wil) Bailey had urged me to reconsider my resignation, and I was confused about what to do. Woodward deepened my confusion by handing me a piece of paper and asking me to write on it what it would take to make me a dean at UAB. Flabbergasted by the request, I bought time by asking for a day or two to talk with Dartie. He agreed.

I returned home to tell her of our good fortune. She—who had made our sons' clothes, cut our hair, coasted down hills in our VW to save gas, clipped grocery coupons—would surely reinforce my inclination to take the job and live the good life. Not exactly. She engaged me in a life-changing process of value clarification. After I finished explaining that the piece of paper was blank, and I believed UAB would grant any reasonable figure I wrote down, she asked: if Auburn offered you the same salary to return to the classroom, would you become dean or return to teaching? After initial bewilderment at the question,

I replied that I would return to the classroom in a New York minute. Then it seems, she added, that the only issue remaining is money. And I thought you told our Sunday school class that life is about more than money.

I turned down the UAB deanship. I told Auburn interim president Wil Bailey that I would resume the headship for one year in order to help heal the wounds of the Funderburk years. Then I was returning permanently to the classroom.

Funderburk resigned on February 26, 1983, after it became obvious that Governor George Wallace and newly appointed trustees Jim Tatum of Huntsville and Bobby Lowder of Montgomery would cast the deciding votes to fire him. Highly respected retiring veterinary professor Wil Bailey, a prominent sixty-two-year-old Church of Christ layman of impeccable integrity and a longtime Philpott friend, hurried to cancel his first Social Security check after agreeing to serve as interim president.

Trustee Bob Harris, who had chaired the presidential search committee and held out to the end against Funderburk, requested reappointment to the board in order to ensure that the next search would be conducted better than the previous one. Wallace refused, apparently influenced by ALFA ally, prominent Wallace loyalist, and Auburn trustee Red Bamberg.

Before he left the board, Harris warned prophetically that though the wounds would eventually heal, "it will likely be beyond the lifetime of a good many of us." Jim Tatum, his replacement, agreed: "I'm not sure it could necessarily be resolved by Funderburk leaving. I don't know if we wouldn't have the same problem with another president."

They were both correct. Funderburk's departure did not end the problems because they were embedded in history and systems, not in personalities and administrations. He protested after his firing that he had only done what trustees asked of him. There is lots of evidence that he told the truth. Many influential people, agricultural commodity groups, and alumni believed his policies were correct. And Governor James, as well as powerful trustees, laid out a clear agenda for him from the beginning.

As AU faculty leaders Kuykendall, Bond, and Peterson tried to explain the events to Birmingham's Young Men's Business Club, a university was not a business. To seek truth and educate people required controversial speculation. They also mentioned Funderburk's refusal to process my professorship because I criticized his leadership and the search process. Such pettiness merely infuriated the faculty. The system was broken, they explained. An article in the *Bir-*

mingham News on February 13 explained one way it was broken by listing each trustee's campaign contributions to governors James and Wallace. The paper also noted that Bobby Lowder's Montgomery radio station won a contract to broadcast Auburn football games after he served on the search committee that hired head football coach Pat Dye. Lowder denied the implication, claiming that he had actually lost money on football broadcasts. The paper also noted that the Lowder family had been political and business power brokers in Montgomery. Ed Lowder had settled out of court in 1978 when Alabama attorney general Bill Baxley accused him of illegal loan and real estate transactions between Farm Bureau companies and his family real estate firm. Although Farm Bureau officials made no public comment about the case, their private animosity toward Ed Lowder and his son, Bobby, would percolate in the recesses of gubernatorial and trustee politics for three decades.

Nonetheless, when Funderburk resigned, I wrote Lowder, thanking him for his role in bringing the turmoil to an end and his commitment to conduct a national search for a new president. I also thanked my childhood friend Bill Baxley for holding up the reappointment of Red Bamberg, whose ties to ALFA made him a singularly biased trustee.

My state senator and fellow church member Ted Little tried to fix the system. He introduced bills in the legislature to change the selection process for trustees. The governor would appoint three candidates from six names recommended by the alumni association and three others from six nominated by the state senate. Two decades and many conflicts later, a constitutional amendment enacted a form of Ted's plan.

As for me, I both suffered and prospered from the Funderburk years. As my literary friend Tom Vaughan, dean of veterinary medicine, wrote, quoting Polonius's advice to his son, Laertes, "Beware of entrance to a quarrel, But being in, bear it, That the opposed may beware of thee." I think it is fair to say that subsequent presidents followed Shakespeare's advice toward all of us. The conflict made me tougher, harder, and meaner. I could use the toughness, but I regretted the hardness and meanness.

My colleagues selected me for the Faculty Achievement Award in the Humanities, which was awarded days after Funderburk resigned. The event turned into more love fest than academic occasion. My affection for them, and I believe their affection for me, was sealed in the Funderburk years. In the words Shakespeare put on the tongue of the English king Henry V before victory over the French on Saint Crispin's Day, "He that outlives this day, and comes safe home, Will stand a tiptoe when this day is named. . . . We few, we happy few, we band of brothers; For he today that sheds his blood with me Shall be my brother."

I know the epitaph sounds fit only for brave soldiers. But our war had been as lethal professionally as Henry's, the psychic bloodshed every bit as painful, the wounds as slow to heal. The blows we suffered were aimed mainly by alumni armed with public ridicule, misrepresentation, and vindictiveness. One alumnus wrote me: "I ask you at once [*sic*] resignation also as a teacher at Auburn and for you at once [*sic*] leave Alabama. . . . You are a disruptive [*sic*] and not needed and resented. . . . It is none of your or [*sic*] faculty's business who is president of Auburn. . . . You are [*sic*] detriment to Auburn and [*sic*] state of Alabama." In case I missed his point, the writer signed himself "Resentful." It seemed superfluous also that "Resentful" identified himself as a 1943 business graduate since there was no danger I would have confused him for an English major.

I answered the letter, as I did all the others. I entered the battle, I wrote, to prevent Auburn from becoming a second-rate technical college. I did not hate the school. In fact, my son David was a freshman aerospace engineering student there. Not willing to yield ground to the spurious "love it or leave it" demand, I intended to stay and fight. If he wished to see Auburn become the laughingstock of higher education in America, that was certainly the direction in which it was headed; but not with my help. In the spirit of the Auburn creed, I concluded, "I am sincerely yours, not resentful of you." The Bible calls a letter like that pouring ashes on one's enemy. The resolve of my reply, following a brief season of tranquility, would be sorely tested again.

• six •

"Sweet Auburn, Loveliest Village of the Plain"

Three years of stress had left my nerves jangled, my body exhausted, my spirit depressed. In December 1983, nine months after it all ended, I wrote former Samford student Carolyn Johnston: "After the epic, Wagnerian battles of the Funderburk era, the solitude of Hyde Park [where I had just spent part of a summer at the FDR Archives completing research for a new book] was a tonic for the soul." If family and faith had carried me safely through the storm, return to full-time teaching, research, and writing immersed me in the tranquil waters I loved.

Teaching

Teaching remained the life-giving elixir that nourished my career. Research and writing wore me out. Controversy sometimes twisted my spirit into shapes I neither recognized nor liked. So for years I survived at Auburn on the daily narcotic of classroom ritual. I walked into the room, exchanged pleasantries with early-arriving students, wrote a detailed outline on the board, and discussed the human odyssey. In graduate seminars, I assigned reading pretty much the way George Petrie had a century earlier, then conducted a Socratic dialogue, asking questions about the topic, challenging students' answers, occasionally filling in gaps in their knowledge, and listening to their analysis of the reading. Over four decades of teaching, I moved away from the lecture approach I had learned at Howard and FSU to a more discussion-oriented format, though I was never willing to allow a class to become the academic equivalent of a radio talk show where opinion trumped information. I carefully structured each seminar session, remembering the cynical conclusion of one Harvard law student that the Socratic method was used primarily by lazy law professors who hadn't bothered to prepare for their classes.

From the beginning of my teaching career at FSU, in the spring of 1965, I prepared notes for class. But I spent time before each class carefully reviewing the notes so that I could lecture largely note-free except for statistical data. Although I had good intentions about rewriting my notes periodically, I usually compromised by elaborate updates and revisions of the originals until no one but I could have read them.

I used outlines to teach students how to organize their note-taking and exam-preparation. When students having trouble on tests came by the office, I asked them to bring their notes. Sometimes the problem was lack of study. Most times it was how they studied. They tried to memorize the material rather than learn it, and I presented too much information each class session for that method to work unless a student possessed total recall.

As I explained to generations of students, they could think of history as an oak tree in full summer foliage, the trunk obscured by thousands of leaves. Or they could think of that sturdy tree in wintertime, where nothing hid the fundamental elements that made it an oak. The transitory leaves represented facts, but the trunk and limbs constituted the substance of history. Most students scored poorly on exams not because they knew too little about the leaves but because they did not understand the frame to which the leaves were attached. My outline was the frame. Don't learn any fact, I admonished, that is not connected to a more important system of life. Hundreds of facts are less important than a handful of patterns. This analogy seemed to help serious students.

Learning to write posed similar problems. As I patiently explained to students terrified by writing assignments, good writing is like good sport. A few athletes are born with amazing physical capacity. Most are not. They excel because of discipline, hard work, repetition, and good coaching. Good coaches spot problems, critique performance, and suggest ways to improve technique. That was my job.

Although I did not teach English or reduce grades for technical mistakes, I marked each paper not only for obvious grammatical errors but also for sloppy, uninspired writing: use of "however," "therefore," and "moreover" as lazy transitions from one idea to another; chronic use of passive verb forms in historical writing; boring introductions. I admonished students to read introductory paragraphs in *Reader's Digest* to understand ways to hook readers. I urged graduate students to jettison long historiographical descriptions (discussions of historians' disagreements with one another) after completing their dissertations if they intended their books to reach an audience beyond professional colleagues.

I also learned quickly that the quality of student writing often depended on how interested they were in the subject. Students gravitated to what they liked. And part of the centrality of history to all academic disciplines was that everything has a past: engineering, agriculture, psychology, medicine, business, mathematics, pharmacy, sport, even universities. Over the decades, I noticed that women seemed inclined to write about women, athletes about athletes, blacks about African Americans, religious students about religion or spirituality. I tried to know students well enough to suggest possibilities consistent with their interests.

I also conceded the obvious. Until the 1980s Auburn used the quarter system of four three-month sessions. This calendar helped students obtain internships or speed through boring classes, but it stifled humanities students who needed time for research, reflection, writing, and revision (which virtually never occurred under the quarter system, so that I always received frantic, last-minute first drafts of papers). The quality of research papers was so bad compared to students on the four-month Samford calendar that at first I thought Auburn undergraduates must be appallingly unprepared for college, though that was certainly not true of their examinations. As I began to understand the problem, I changed assignments, requiring students to write ten-page analytical essays that required neither primary sources nor footnotes. The exercise revealed their analytical, organizational, and writing abilities as well as a traditional research paper did, but it allowed some time for reflection and revision.

So successful did that exercise prove that I continued it even when Auburn joined nearly all other universities by adopting the semester system. In my freshman honors classes, I required students to select a pandemic of their choosing (the Irish potato famine, 1918–1919 swine flu pandemic, HIV-AIDs) and write a ten-page essay about it.

In my senior level New South class I offered students six categories of novels: poor whites; race; religion; women; community/family; politics. For each topic I included a list of novels. The race topic, for instance, included works by Shirley Ann Grau (*The Keepers of the House*), Harper Lee (*To Kill a Mockingbird*), William Styron (*The Confessions of Nat Turner*), Ralph Ellison (*In-*

visible Man), Will Campbell (*Brother to a Dragonfly*), Alice Walker (*The Color Purple*), and Zora Neale Hurston (*Their Eyes Were Watching God*). Students had to place the novel in historical context, provide a brief biographical sketch of the author, and summarize the work. I then divided the students into topical groups and invited them to our home for discussion. They summarized their papers, after which I asked questions. Dartie rewarded their efforts with home-made fudge brownies. But the greater reward for many of them was their first encounter with William Faulkner, Robert Penn Warren, Eudora Welty, Flannery O'Connor, Ralph Ellison, or some other award-winning southern writer. From my point of view, how could students fully appreciate the New South without understanding one of America's greatest intellectual stirrings, the southern literary renaissance? This exercise proved to be my most successful writing assignment, even for students who were also required to write a fully documented research paper in the class.

These students represented the rich diversity of Alabama much more fully than Samford students. AU had few National Merit Finalists, and those few tended to major in engineering, premed, or science. Unlike the history department at Samford, which attracted a high percentage of the university's brightest students, our best classes often consisted of freshman honors sections and topical courses where top students from all disciplines strayed over to our domain in order to study their favorite topic or learn with a beloved professor.

Like the university they attended, Auburn students often outperformed expectations. By and large, they worked hard, did what I asked of them, were polite, civil, mannerly, thoughtful, and a pleasure to teach. The best of them succeeded in a variety of careers: law, historic preservation, aerospace engineering, art, business, the military, journalism, and politics.

Many days during the darkest times at Auburn, I walked into classes filled with such students, shut the door, looked at them, and pondered why I was there. I was there for them. That thought allowed me to shut campus politics out of my mind. Today, I thought to myself, I am not a Samford man, an FSU man, or part of the Auburn family. I am a teacher. I know I can make these students better-informed people and more successful in their careers. Forget all the rest. I am not their father, brother, friend, lover, or coach. I am a professional teacher, So, Wayne, *teach*!

By and large, they reciprocated my hard work and affection. My student evaluations reflected that. Students and colleagues selected me for teaching awards and the 1992–93 Algernon Sydney Sullivan Award "in recognition of characteristics of heart, mind, and conduct as shown by a spirit of love and helpfulness to others." The aerospace engineering program conducted exit interviews with graduating seniors, asking them if any professor outside their department had made a major contribution to their education. I was pleased to be named. A law student at the University of Florida wrote my dean that any time she had needed to talk, I had listened and cared. Such letters constituted my fondest teaching memories.

At Auburn, graduate students replaced undergraduates within the innermost circle of my student relationships. We bonded in ways similar to my Samford undergraduates. Dartie and I invited them to our house for dinner each year, where we could talk informally, get to know their spouses, talk about their interior lives, and cultivate them as friends rather than students. Not long after I arrived at Auburn, faculty and grad students began playing volleyball or softball every Sunday afternoon. I particularly relished those sun-filled afternoons when academic protocol largely disappeared.

By the mid-1980s when I returned full time to the classroom, my list of graduate advisees had grown to unreasonable numbers, at one time reaching eighteen. I had trouble refusing an applicant who came to Auburn in my field. But the responsibilities of a major professor were arduous, particularly if the professor did not screen students for intellectual skill or writing ability, neither of which I was willing to do. I barely scored high enough on the Graduate Record Exam to be admitted to graduate school because of my woeful performance in math. What right did I have to deny others the opportunity that had been given me?

Far from discouraging applicants, I tried to share my excitement with them. I wrote one UAB graduate who later became one of my most successful students: "I believe teaching is one of the most challenging professions in America and also one of the most invigorating. I love the interaction with students, especially those who think they do not like history. I can't recall any time in my life when I did not like history . . . and remain as fascinated with it now as I was then. It both informs us about who we are as people and where we came from and suggests to us agenda for preservation and change that are respectful of our traditions."

During my years at Auburn, I directed twenty-three doctoral dissertations, with others still under way after my retirement (though I warned laggards that I did not intend to be reading drafts of dissertations in my eighties). They came from states across America as well as from China and Russia. A third were female and one was African American. They were straight and gay, liberal and conservative, Democrat and Republican, religious and secular. Reflecting the wide-ranging interests of their major professor, their topics crossed all fields of southern history: biography, labor, politics, agriculture, business history, women, poor whites, Reconstruction, African Americans, Appalachian-Ozark identity, and religion. They now teach at colleges and universities across the South and border states. Some left teaching for ministerial and archival careers. They have authored more than twenty books and two can claim half a dozen to their credit. Add to that figure books written by my Samford undergraduates, master's students, and doctoral students on whose committees I served, and the total comes closer to fifty. Although I have an entire section of bookcases reserved for their scholarly production, I am equally proud of the students who have published nothing but have taught well and served as exemplary role models for thousands of students. I taught more than six thousand students during my career, but I feel an extended influence over tens of thousands of others through my students. To say I am proud of them would be an understatement.

During the 1980s Auburn published a slick-cover folio titled "Commitment to Teaching" that extolled the university's primary objective. It spotlighted nineteen Auburn professors, including me. Interviewers asked each of us to describe our philosophy of teaching. The editor appropriately titled my interview "Sharing Excitement of Discovery." Facts alone don't add up to history, I explained. At the core of all teaching is the goal of helping students learn how to think for themselves. Professors should not try to clone themselves through their students. Human existence becomes richer when we learn to think rather than merely to exist.

My most important contribution to the dialogue consisted of discussion of the synergy between research, writing, and teaching. I described the excitement of returning from an archives full of new ideas and information that called traditional wisdom into question, and the electric moment when I walked into a class or seminar to share what I had learned. My mental universe, like the cosmos I read about as a teenager, really was constantly expanding. I often changed my mind about the best way to learn and teach. And history was never about the dead past: "History helps people develop a worldview, a sense of responsibility for who they are. Every historian needs to feel that society would be poorer without us." Upon rereading that interview nearly a quarter century later, I was relieved that I had not changed my mind about my philosophy of teaching.

When I walked out of a classroom for the final time, I did so having learned two important lessons in forty years of teaching. Students should follow their hearts when choosing a major or career path. Life is too short to be miserable doing something we hate even if we earn piles of money doing it. No one knows what the "hot" professions will be anyway. In the mid-1980s, electrical and aerospace engineering ranked first and second among lucrative career fields. But with the end of the Cold War and the decline in defense spending, hundreds of thousands of unemployed aerospace engineers lived in California alone. Some of them, I'll wager, could have been harried, overworked, underpaid, but euphorically happy teachers. I obtained the other piece of wisdom from all those frustrated, unhappy students who seemed to change majors as often as they did their clothes. Nothing they learned was wasted unless they chose to make it so.

My Auburn Family

I suppose Auburn people identify with different versions of the AU family. For many, family means football. For others, timber, cattle, or row crops form the rallying place. The life of the mind unites my Auburn family.

Any number of people from my clan would illustrate the point. But one stands out because he never let acquiring a degree interfere with his education. Nor did he waste any of his learning. Wesley (Wes) Baker grew up only a few miles from my mother's home on Sweeny Hollow Road. His father was a book collector who bequeathed Wes a love of books. After three years studying Latin at Erwin High School, he arrived at Auburn in 1988 with intellectual curiosity rare for the times. Like George Petrie before him, the classics shaped his universe.

Wes majored in history, but that was more formality than a statement of professional aspiration or intellectual priority. From historians Donna Bohanan, Joe Harrison, and Frank Owsley Jr., he learned to "see around the American narrative" to a "peace-loving Jeffersonian tradition that snaked its way through the South." Mary Kuntz and Dorothy DiOrio in foreign languages spurred his imagination in Latin and French. English professors Ward Allen, Madison Jones, and Taylor Littleton satisfied his quest for the precision, beauty, and timelessness of Shakespeare, Virgil, and modern literature. Allen welcomed him into the rarified atmosphere of the Gildersleeve Society (Basil L. Gildersleeve was the greatest southern classicist), which met at the professor's home. Students and professors read the Roman poet Virgil, whose epic poem *The Aeneid* described what classical Rome considered sacred.

Historians Will and Ariel Durant insisted that "every schoolboy knows the story of the *Aeneid,*" but the Durants' students were not mine. Few Auburn schoolboys had heard of Virgil or his poem. Yet Virgil's poetry anticipated their world, elaborating piety and impiety, the tensions between the gods and the independent spheres of humans, meditating upon war and peace, national honor and betrayal, hubris and humility, strong and conforming women.

As Wes described it, Auburn was not a "citified" university nor yet obsessed with commerce and making money, so reading Virgil seemed neither quaint to him nor irrelevant. The Vanderbilt Agrarians (three of whom were Petrie's students) survived there in the persons of Ward Allen and Madison Jones. As the Agrarians had hoped, leisure, ruralism, a slow-paced life, relationships, religion, and a strong sense of community still motivated many faculty, who welcomed like-minded students into their homes and intellectual worlds. To them, education had less to do with acquiring a marketable skill than with obtaining an education. Wes's Auburn family represented a community of the mind that invited students to enter as deeply into it as they wanted to go. The differences between this Auburn family and that of dominant trustee Bobby Lowder could not have been greater.

After graduation in 1993, Wes married an equally gifted woman he met in a language class and set out on his career. That career used none of the specific skills he learned but wasted none of them either. He spent years learning book-binding, apprenticing with English masters and reading widely. He acquired antique tools and a master craftsman's mentality. Extreme attention to detail and mastery of period binding styles characterized his work. From an eleventh-century burial book to *Newton's Principia,* he used original materials and tools to restore books.

Wes's worldwide clientele celebrate his skills. One New York rare book dealer considers him one of the finest dozen bookbinders in the world, the practitioner of a craft so specialized and difficult that virtually no one enters it any more. It may be true that Wes Baker lives in a modest house a few blocks from the equally simple house where I grew up on Michael Lane in Anniston. It also seems certain that he will not prosper in the way that money managers and corporate CEOs will. But all that seems to matter not at all to a truly educated man.

Religion

Auburn First Baptist Church was in many ways an extension of the university. For most of the history of the village, it was the only Baptist church. Faculty, students, and administrators of that denomination all attended. President Harry Philpott preached from time to time and once remarked that if judged by students' denominational preference, Auburn was the largest Baptist university in the world. The first president of the land grant college, I. T. Tichenor, was also a Baptist clergyman and church member. President Spright Dowell, who could not reconcile Baptist ethical sensibilities with the excesses of football, received loyal support from his congregation.

As part of this long and proud tradition, I agreed to teach the college Sunday school class, continuing work I had done for a decade at Vestavia Hills Baptist church. Dartie and I also participated in the "family friends" program, adopting students each year who came to our home for dinner and conversation. They represented many states, backgrounds, and theological perspectives. We welcomed them as spiritual sons and daughters and have rejoiced at their progress through the decades.

The church staff was highly professional. Our family benefited from wonderful music programs led by our gifted choir master and composer-in-residence Dale Peterson, who became the state's dean of church musicians during his long tenure at the church. Dartie often commented that the music was of such quality that members could experience fulfilling worship through that medium alone.

John Jeffers nearly matched Peterson's tenure, pastoring the church for twenty-seven years. A man of uncommon wisdom, widely read and unyielding in his commitment to traditional Baptist history and theology, he became a national leader of moderate Baptists in late twentieth-century battles with fundamentalists. Although both our sons would leave the denomination like so many other Baptist young people during the 1980s and 1990s, they retained the deepest respect for John. They also studied the Bible from members such as Charlotte Ward, a physics professor at the university, League of Women Voters activist, and theistic evolutionist, who did not bequeath her pupils a sorry theological legacy of choosing between God or gorillas.

A fringe benefit of church membership for our family was that many of the battles we had fought earlier over race and gender had already been resolved by the Auburn congregation. Thanks to John Jeffers's deft leadership, the church had accepted black visitors during the 1960s. In 1968 he had preached the annual keynote sermon at the state Baptist convention. Selecting a text from the prophet Amos, he had described the failure of churches to respond positively to racial change. Sin, he argued, could be corporate as well as personal, and churches often ignored the kind of social justice that Amos proclaimed. The prophetic sermon may have cost John the convention presidency that year. Though nominated, he finished a distant fourth among four nominees. By the end of his pastorate, church membership included African Americans, Ethiopians, Nigerians, mixed race families, Asian Americans, and a vibrant international ministry. Dartie found fulfillment teaching English as a second language that brought many internationals into our church.

That world vision extended to our entire congregation, leading to annual mission trips to Honduras and Brazil, as well as individual trips to many other countries. Dartie accompanied a delegation of church women to train female leaders in Alaskan Baptist churches. Sean, Dartie, and I traveled with another group to construct a second floor on a Baptist church in Oviedo, Spain.

First Baptist also engaged in numerous social ministries: the Shelter for Battered Women; Habitat for Humanity; Water-for-Malawi (a youth-led effort to build wells in one of Africa's poorest countries); the Child Care Foundation (providing health insurance for low-income children); Community Market (Lee County's food pantry); financial support for the Alabama Poverty Project, Alabama Arise, Sowing Seeds of Hope (a thirty-year antipoverty effort in Perry County); and many other ministries. Perhaps most boldly, one of our members, Gerald Johnson, began a statewide effort to persuade churches voluntarily to contribute an amount to public schools equal to their property tax abatement as a charitable institution. Churches had just mobilized to defeat a statewide lottery that would have funded early childhood education for poor children and college scholarships, so Gerald led our church to contribute annually to Auburn public schools. For all the antilottery trumpeting from pastors that there were better ways to fund these worthy education objectives, only a handful of the state's ten thousand churches followed our example.

Strong female leadership in all phases of church life had resulted in the election of Leland Cooper as the church's first female deacon in 1974. Miss Cooper had become a legend as founder of Auburn University's Baptist Student Union, church historian, and longtime Training Union director. As the years passed, dozens of women served ably as deacons, and by end-of-century half or more of our ordained staff were females.

All of these initiatives came at a price. Some left the church over each of these changes in policy. But as in our Vestavia Hills church, others joined precisely because of our courageous engagement with biblical justice. The Auburn community slowly changed from strongly Democratic to rabidly Republican, and most members of the church probably voted Republican in presidential elections. But their commitment to justice, whether defined by private charity or systemic change, defined our congregation.

For my part, I found many places of service: Royal Ambassador leader; Church Training director; deacon; trustee; a member of three pulpit committees to select pastors. Following years of teaching college students, my hair turned gray enough to earn promotion to a class closer to my own age. The Pilgrim's Sunday school class enrolled all ages (though most members were retirement age or close to it), both men and women, Africans, African Americans, mixed race couples, and a spectrum of political ideologies from libertarian to liberal, and theological beliefs from conservative to modernist. The class gradually grew to more than a hundred members and became my favorite church activity. Bright, articulate, engaged members challenged me to study the Bible as I had not since my Howard College days. Their freedom to disagree, criticize, and appropriate biblical truth for themselves was an affirmation of the finest historic Baptist principles. Their restraint and mutual forbearance became a constant reminder that in the age of Red and Blue America—when churches, coffee shops, and neighborhoods polarize around ideology—a few places of sanctuary remain where people of goodwill could love and respect each other despite their differences. After I retired in 2005, our decision to remain in Auburn resulted mainly from our affection for First Baptist Church.

Beyond the world of the church, I participated in a national religious dialogue both through my Baptist denominational life and my research/writing/lecturing. When asked to do so, I led student discussions at the Baptist Student Union, though as the state denomination moved sharply right, invitations to speak ceased. I preached at least once or twice a year in churches to which we had belonged such as Parker Memorial and Vestavia Hills, as well as for churches where former students or friends pastored. I served as historian for the Tuskegee Lee Baptist Association and as chairman of both the Alabama Baptist and Southern Baptist Historical commissions. I also participated in the state convention's 1989 race relations celebration. Through various university lecture series, I invited distinguished Baptist historians to Auburn, including Edward Gaustad (expert on early American religious history), Bill Leonard (dean of Wake Forest University divinity school), and a Norwegian Baptist historian who specialized in the German Anabaptists. I helped locate and preserve Baptist historical records from such diverse leaders as liberal Charlie Bell and conservative rural church leader J. W. Lester.

By the late 1970s I had become a partisan in the battle for control of the Southern Baptist Convention (SBC). The conflict involved complex issues of personality, politics, theology, and sociology. At its root it involved conservative insurgents who believed they had been marginalized and ignored and who were suddenly mobilized by 1960s–70s culture-war debates about abortion and women's roles.

My personal religious convictions stood midway between liberalism, which struck me as too optimistic about the human condition, and conservatism/ fundamentalism, which was too intolerant, mean-spirited, judgmental, and rigid. To the degree that any theological category fit me, neoorthodoxy still came closest. But I preferred traditional Baptist doctrine: soul liberty (every person's right to a relationship with God unfettered by the state); priesthood of the believer (no need for priest, bishop, or pope to explain God, the Bible, or church doctrine to me); separation of church and state (no reason for the church to impose its principles on the state nor the state to inhibit religious practice); the autonomy of each church (congregations could voluntarily associate with like-minded churches but were free to follow their own collective conscience in such matters as ordination of women and rejection of man-made [and they were always MAN-made] creeds). I found the Bible entirely sufficient for faith and practice, even if Baptists quarreled endlessly about what the Book said and meant. (I could figure it out myself and join with anyone who generally agreed with me or believed our differences didn't matter as much as our points of agreement.)

As the denomination grew increasingly creedalistic, I grew increasingly alienated. In 1981 one of two fundamentalist Alabama representatives on the powerful SBC Committee on Boards, which made all committee assignments, renominated me to the SBC Historical Commission with a backhanded compliment: "We were not satisfied with his answer doctrinally" but reappointed him anyway "because there is not a better historian in Alabama." Besides, he continued, the Historical Commission did not "have many employees." I responded with a letter to the *Alabama Baptist* which said, in part: "Believing that this was still the Alabama Baptist Convention, I did not realize I was answerable doctrinally to Rev. Wallen. When did this change occur? In addition to approving doctrine, does Rev. Wallen also excommunicate 'heretics?'"

Denominational friends retired, lost their jobs, or left Baptist seminaries for other teaching jobs. Arthur Walker, one of my former Samford colleagues, was forced out as director of the SBC Education Commission, and my friend, James M. Dunn, had to retire as executive director of the Baptist Joint Committee on Public Affairs. Walter "Buddy" Shurden, Leon McBeth, and Bill Leonard left their seminaries. As a result, I became more active in the controversy, attending as a "messenger" (delegate) ever more contentious SBC national conventions in Atlanta, Saint Louis, Los Angeles, and San Antonio, where combatants sometimes numbered thirty thousand to forty thousand. I wrote Baptist historian Leon McBeth my assessment of convention politics in 1981: "The issue before us is less doctrine than power," and "Flynts, like Baptists, react to challenges by getting mad, not by ducking for cover." To a former Samford student, I wrote about the same time: "Actually, I feel rather sorry for the new Fundamentalists. On one hand they welcome the disintegration of society as one of the final signs of the apocalypse; on the other they organize furiously to halt the disintegration of social institutions and save American society. But their intolerance and dogmatism is doing the church and Christianity more harm than good, so I feel obliged to fight them." That last sentence became less true with every passing year and spiritual casualty, until finally I left Southern Baptists completely, quite content to leave fundamentalists in charge of a declining denomination (in 1950 the SBC baptized one new convert for every nineteen members; by 2008 it baptized one for every forty-seven members). I became a Baptist living in the South who affiliated with the moderate Cooperative Baptist Fellowship and identified with the ecumenical and biracial New Baptist Covenant organized by former president Jimmy Carter, whose widely distributed 2009 essay chronicled his own disaffection with the SBC.

I wrote a friend in Huntsville in 1991 trying to explain my own denominational metamorphosis: "I treasure my heritage in the Baptist church and all things it taught me about ethical relations between people, responsibility for the poor and powerless, the responsibility to take charge of my own life, a tradition of the priesthood of the believer.... But... I find the church has changed more than I have. I find myself increasingly uncomfortable in a denomination that denigrates women, moves more toward authoritarianism, and ignores social injustice."

As the new religious right coalesced, I engaged its adherents in frequent debates. I helped organize an amicus brief of Alabama clergymen and academics opposing supreme court judge Roy Moore's location of a five-thousand-pound piece of granite containing the Ten Commandments in the state supreme court building. I also participated in a story for ABC's national news magazine *20/20* with Barbara Walters, explaining that the main point of the First Amendment to the Constitution was to protect minority viewpoints from the tyranny of an arrogant, overreaching majority. Judge Moore seemed to operate in a moral universe of absolutes, where his opinions on homosexual rights had no room for ambiguity and where every issue was either black or white. His arrogance made him scary in a democracy.

A torrent of mail informed me that Moore's interpretation of the Constitution should take precedence over federal courts. An Auburn alumnus working for the University of Alabama in Huntsville wrote that my comments about Judge Moore and the Ten Commandments were "typical of fuzzy-headed academics.... Auburn needs to appreciate its roots, tradition, and alumni a bit further before allowing such a statement . . . from one of its own." An equally unhappy North Carolinian who saw my comments on Fox News complained about "children" studying with professors who held "a 'wishy-washy' attitude about truth." A furious viewer from Houston hoped I wasn't born "in the great state of Alabama" because I was "a disgrace and you are the one that is scary! P.S. You wouldn't last long in Texas! We like real men here." Another unhappy Alabamian mainly posed questions in the form of a flawed Socratic dialogue: "Do you have any beliefs? Does God exist? Is the 1st Amendment really there? Is the 14th Amendment really there? Did God create the heaven and the earth? Do the taxpayers of Alabama pay your salary?" I answered "yes" to all questions, then inquired how they were relevant to the five-thousand-pound chunk of granite that was rapidly taking on all the aspects of idolatry criticized in the book of Exodus. He dismissed my response but wished me "good luck as you embark on another semester's voyage into the gray liberal arts."

Even the hearing-impaired weighed in. One irate listener to "talk radio" misunderstood my plea for better understanding of a society that offered us a "world of grays" to be a plea for a "world of gays" and condemned my obvious homosexual agenda. I should not have been surprised by this. Dad had warned me about my "mushy-mouth" pronunciation. Not many years later I achieved political revenge. I voted for former Baptist Sunday school teacher Bob Riley in the Republican gubernatorial primary where he drubbed Roy Moore by a margin of more than two to one.

My debate with antiabortion extremists generated even greater rage. Asked to speak to a small group of prochoice medical students at UAB, I encountered instead an incredibly bellicose and large audience of antiabortion future doctors. Despite my research demonstrating that antiabortion theology did not flourish in southern evangelical thought until the culture wars of the 1960s (the first editorial on abortion did not appear in the *Alabama Baptist* until the 1970s, and that one approved abortion in most circumstances), the antiabortion students turned the session into a public pillorying. The only thing missing was a scarlet *A* carved on my forehead.

As usual in such debates I tried to define terms. As Alabama's woeful treatment of poor children made clear (the state ranked near the top in child poverty rates at more than one in five, had an infant mortality rate higher than some developing countries, and perpetuated perhaps the nation's most unfair and regressive tax system), my antagonists could hardly claim to be prolife. They were actually pro-fetus. Once born in Alabama, it was every baby for herself. The crowd turned even surlier at that, quoting verse after verse from the Bible to prove that Christians had always opposed abortion. I ended my part of the conversation by hoping that no one with a pregnant wife, daughter, or mother whose fetus was profoundly damaged or whose life or health was threatened in birth, would be unfortunate enough to have one of them as attending physician.

My own position on abortion occupied precisely that gray middle ground so widely condemned by my critics. Abortions occur too frequently. Adoption could reduce the number. So could better sex education and wider use of contraception. But state-mandated compulsion went too far. Are we sure we know best how a poor or mentally unbalanced mother will care for a new baby? Or whether a healthy mother with four children already can manage a profoundly handicapped child? Isn't it presumptuous for those of us who will not bear the consequences for such a decision to determine what those who will bear the consequences should do?

If experimentation with embryonic stem cells seems iniquitous to a Christian, might that person set a strong moral example by simply refusing treatment based on such immoral experimentation? If they descend into the horrors of Alzheimer's or suffer paralyzing spinal cord injuries, such rejectionism would speak much more profoundly to society than compelling their views on people who do not share their theology. Martyrdom seems so much more ennobling when we choose it for ourselves rather than impose it on others.

These sentiments kicked my hate mail into the stratosphere. A local Lee County minister accused me of advocating "killing . . . unborn babies." Denying that I had ever "advocated abortion," I replied that it was always a tragedy, though sometimes "a necessary one." I presumed the minister agreed and that he would support his wife's decision to abort a fetus if the decision were necessary to save her life. But perhaps not. If other self-identified antiabortion ministers in Lee County would follow his courageous example and adopt a special needs baby, I conceded, we could considerably reduce the number of chronically rejected adoptable children statewide. Or they could help poor families care for children that a mother had refused to abort.

I should have known better than to expect rational debate about irrational emotions. A Prattville activist began an acrid correspondence in 1990 by accusing me of supporting the "murder of unborn babies for economic reasons," assured me that life begins at conception (this apparently was a priori knowledge available to the writer and should end all dispute), and concluded that I seemed to consider abortion merely an alternative form of birth control. To make sure I understood his arguments, he followed his letter with a phone call to ask if I was "intellectually or morally incapable of understanding why murdering unborn children because they are inconvenient is a critical issue to the prolife movement."

Responding that I believed there was no such procedure as a "good abortion," I added that some abortions certainly were "morally defensible"—to save the life of a mother, in cases of rape or incest, where the health of a mother made it impossible for her to care for a child—a position according to current polling data that was held by more than half of all Alabamians. Although I did not consider abortion a form of birth control, I found his charge revealing because the use of IUDs, which keep fertilized eggs (hence "life") from attaching to the womb, by his definition constituted a form of abortion. Was this form of artificial birth control permissible or should it also be prohibited? "I am perfectly prepared to face Christ with my view as I am sure you are also," I answered another of his questions. "At that point we will both discover how well we have lived out our respective discipleship."

For a while I foolishly continued to answer his letters. Denying that I was intellectually and morally incapable of understanding the issues, I added that neither was I "arrogant, intolerant, or determined to impose my ethical views on others by way of restrictive legislation." I also cited obvious areas of need where he could redirect his zeal for life: the state ranked fortieth of fifty states in aid to mothers with dependent children (a maximum benefit of $124 a month for a mother with two children); a fifth of the population had no health insurance; 35,000 children lived without insurance because their parents earned more than $1,600 a year, Alabama's Medicaid eligibility threshold at the time. Why was it, I asked, that year after year at the Alabama Baptist State Convention, messengers passed resolutions about abortion but never managed to pass one about any of these other matters? Why did evangelicals see so clearly the imperative to criminalize abortions without ever comprehending the immorality of an unjust tax system? I finally ended the abrasive correspondence by writing: "I could wish your Christian commitment to social justice, tolerance of other Christian views, and fairness matched your commitment to the antiabortion movement."

As I argued in my parallel scholarly career, Baptists held many views about all of these issues. When my interrogator checked my facts with an official of the Alabama Baptist State Convention (ABSC), he learned that no association or convention had ever addressed such issues. And he was shocked when the official defended me as a loyal and committed Baptist. Furthermore, the convention selected me to author its sesquicentennial history and named me Alabama Baptist Distinguished Historian in 1999. That same year the Whitsitt Baptist Heritage Society invited me to present its keynote address. The Baptist History and Heritage Society awarded me its Officer's Award for service and in 2009 favored me as a speaker for the four hundredth anniversary of Baptists worldwide. In 2007 the national news journal *Baptist Today* awarded me its Judson-Rice Award for "leadership with integrity."

I was also appointed to the heritage committee of the Baptist World Alliance, where I spoke to international meetings at Wake Forest University and Baptist International Seminary in Prague, Czech Republic. Dartie and I also attended Baptist World Alliance meetings in Spain and the centennial meeting in Birmingham, England. Anytime we were in England, we attended Bloomsbury Central Baptist Church, founded in the mid-nineteenth century in London; a wonderful congregation deeply engaged in social justice ministries.

From my earliest days, I never believed that Baptists possessed exclusive knowledge about the kingdom of God or had some reserved space in heaven. Hence, I worked with ecumenical groups that oftentimes were more receptive to my ideas than were Baptists. Although even the ABSC finally endorsed tax reform (along with the Episcopal diocese, North and South Alabama Methodist conferences, and the Presbyterians USA), I spoke at Unitarian, Methodist, Presbyterian, and Episcopal churches, black and white, as often as in churches of my own denomination. I had a particularly warm relationship with Auburn Presbyterian church, which launched a Loaves and Fishes Meal Program for poor, sick, and elderly residents, and I served for many years on the board of Presbyterian Community Ministries, which provided low-interest housing rehabilitation loans and emergency financial assistance to poor people. In 1999 I spoke to the Diocesan Convention of the Episcopal church about child poverty and on southern religion at Auburn's Holy Trinity Church. I also advised the Catholic diocese on a pastoral letter dealing with poverty in Alabama.

Of course, I inhabited not just the world of evangelicalism, but also the secular professional world of a state university. These conflicting venues required careful attention because they spoke different languages, followed different protocols, and were based on different assumptions. My public prayers at banquets in Alabama (nationally such "blessings" were generally banned from professional meetings lest they offend someone) recognized an audience quite different from my church. Hence, I wrote generic though heartfelt prayers (my wife, taking more literally Jesus's admonition to enter into a closet and pray in secret, refused to pray in public at all) for blessings at historical meetings such as one prayed in 1978: "Father, we thank you for sharing with us the spirit of inquiry. May we use that spirit with integrity, with the aim to both understand and mend the brokenness of man and society. Deliver us from shabby, self-serving, and petty academic jealousies so that we not only may serve history but also that we may serve you and humanity." So great is the peril of inserting God into the public square that references to "father" and "man" stirred controversy, even spreading into liberal Baptist churches. But I did not desist. I figured if I could offend antiabortionists and secularists, I might as well continue to pray the way I believed and offend feminist Baptists.

These debates reminded me of medieval disputes over how many angels could dance on the head of a pin—interesting abstraction but pointless debate. To feminist charges that there is no parallel because gendered references to God constitute a serious theological issue for women, it is worth noting that in the long-forgotten Middle Ages the dimensions of angels and their roles in human existence were equally weighty theological concerns. Only in retrospect after nearly ten centuries does the debate seem irrelevant. And we do have the precedent of Jesus using the term "father."

More importantly, many friends could not comprehend my continuing self-identification as a Baptist when my ideology seemed incompatible with that identity. I tried tactfully to explain the limitations of their stereotypes. I reminded them that some of Barack Obama's most loyal supporters were southern black Baptists, theologically among the most conservative Americans. Yes, they sometimes implied, but you are white, as if I should know better.

As I was answering questions one evening at a Church of Christ forum in Birmingham, a woman misunderstood me to say that I asked students in my office if they had accepted "Christ as their Lord and Savior." If so, she thought the question inappropriate at a state university. In my response, I clarified what I had said, adding that I thought the question would have been inappropriate even at Samford, where it might have embarrassed or even threatened the student in a situation where I controlled grades. At Auburn, the question would be presumptuous and probably unconstitutional as well. What I did at Auburn was to include religion as an appropriate historical element in all human experience. If, as a result of such a discussion, a student came by my office to talk, I would explain the role of religion in all cultures (Taoism, Buddhism, Hinduism, Shinto, Islam, Judaism, Christianity, animism) as fairly as I could without bias for or against any of them. But if a student asked specifically about my personal faith, I answered the question as honestly as I could and explained that I taught a Sunday school class that was a more appropriate venue for exploring these issues. If they came, I made sure it did not affect their grade by a device I always used. I folded back the title page of exam books so I never knew whose test I was reading until I determined a final grade.

Family and Friends

Within our family, I seemed to draw most of the attention. As I viewed family, that was too bad. In more ways than I could count, Dartie was the core from which all else emanated. Her sacrifice for me and the boys limited her own options. Her quiet service to our church and community reverberated in ways that few others knew about. Her independence of thought and fashion became legendary. And her mastery of thrift store shopping became a high art.

In 1993 I had the privilege of serving as Eudora Welty Scholar of Southern Studies at Millsaps College in Jackson, Mississippi. In addition to leaving behind religious and academic controversies for a semester, teaching two classes of gifted young people, and meeting wonderful faculty colleagues, Dartie and I had the good fortune to spend time with Welty, whose fiction we had long admired, and with her biographer, Suzanne Marrs. Both women were exceptional people. By that point in her life, Welty was crippled by arthritis and could barely rise from her chair without help. Stacks of books covered the floor except for a narrow aisle that gave her access to other rooms. She nonetheless maintained her indomitable spirit and a progressive ideology wholly incompatible with Mississippi politics.

One evening during dinner at Welty's favorite restaurant, the hostess could barely contain her excitement at seating the famous author. Finally overcome with admiration, she barged into our conversation. Already exhausted by the physical exertions of the evening, Welty nevertheless engaged in a pleasant conversation, demonstrating her legendary warmth and thoughtfulness toward hometown folk. I could not help but contrast the arthritic pain at the periphery of her existence with the existential joy at the center of her life.

That is a perfect description of my marriage. People saw, heard, and read me, the external edge of our family, and assumed that was the entire reality.

The pain of my public life obscured the tranquility, beauty, and good humor of its core, which Dartie occupied. She had her own exterior life as president of Baptist Woman's Missionary Union, teacher of English as a second language, coordinator of Loaves and Fishes for our Sunday school class, deacon, participant in Auburn's recorder music group, chief architect/supervisor/chef/repair person of our house, and mentor for our sons.

Beyond this domestic sphere, she helped me with reader's theater presentations, becoming the voice of poor white women or suffragist Pattie Ruffner Jacobs. She played the mountain dulcimer for my classes to demonstrate southern musical traditions and coauthored an annotated bibliography of southern poor whites. Though always a private person who fled public attention, she was up to the task anytime the spotlight caught her in its beam. My main domestic chores were growing roses, tending the grounds, and catching the main course for fish-fries. She took care of the rest.

Meanwhile our sons flourished. David excelled in math, science, and technology, without any genetic reinforcement from his parents so far as I know. He played soccer for Auburn High School, coached a team of nine- and ten-year-olds, commanded Auburn High School's (AHS) JROTC detachment, forged a loyal band of friends who feasted on Dartie's calzones every Friday night, then played Dungeons and Dragons until the wee hours of the morning. He and his friends became fanatical Auburn football and Atlanta Braves baseball fans, allowing me to accompany them to games. He attended Auburn on an air force scholarship, majoring in aerospace engineering. He also took enough history to enroll briefly in graduate school after his commissioning and while awaiting his pilot's slot, and wrote sufficiently well to publish one of his seminar papers.

Sean had as many female friends as David did male buddies and may still hold the distinction of being the only guy to take two dates to the same dance. He also served as executive officer in the AHS JROTC program and led its rifle team as a varsity letterman. But his interests inclined toward art and writing rather than science and mathematics. He cared nothing about football, baseball, or basketball. He won a leadership scholarship to Samford, where he majored in history and English, minored in folklore, studied in Spain, Russia, and England, served as a columnist and editor for the Samford *Crimson,* and made us proud parents. He and David shared a love for archaeology, though David preferred ancient Greece and Sean, Native America. As a second career after the air force, David also became an artist/software designer. Dartie and I were not objective, but we firmly believed that we had the finest two sons in America. If so, that was largely their mother's doing.

Our family spent many happy days at a condo at Gulf Shores Plantation on Alabama's Gulf Coast that we bought in 1985. Located midway between the tawdry resort town of Gulf Shores and historic Fort Morgan, Gulf Shores Plantation is neither in Gulf Shores nor a plantation. Policywise, it is located midway between the greed of single-generation real estate developers and multigenerational environmentalists.

As a boy, I was more attracted to mountains than beaches. Perhaps my aversion resulted from childhood vacations to Florida. We always left around three or four in the morning, a tribute both to the discomfort of summer travel in the Deep South before air-conditioned cars and Dad's agricultural legacy of having the mule harnessed by sunup. I also stayed in the sun too long the first day on the beach and invariably spent a miserable week in pain from sunburn. Gulf Coast beaches are like a good dose of sin: it's fun in the beginning but hell in the aftermath.

The boys' school terms and the necessity to rent our condo for revenue during summer months forced most of our vacations into December, before "snowbirds" arrived from the frozen Midwest, when restaurants were nearly empty, sunsets were stunning, and the Blue Angels precision flying team from nearby Pensacola Naval Air Station practiced aerobatics up and down the coast. Huge sand dunes furnished the boys places to explore. A family of foxes found sanctuary on the grounds along with endangered beach mice. A cantankerous alligator took up residence in a pond, where visiting "snowbirds" from the North fed him all winter. When they departed for Michigan, Missouri, or Wisconsin in March, he could not understand the cessation of snacks and began chasing joggers.

Walking the beach in December solitude without meeting a living soul for a mile in either direction became a living sermon text for me and the finest place for meditation to be found. In time the snake of modernity invaded our Eden. Tall houses crept across the dunes. A golf course replaced the savannah. Huge gas platforms rose out of the Gulf. Oil soiled our beaches. Worried condo officials hauled off the alligator and fox to extermination. Even the sea seemed prisoner to human invasion.

Yet my very presence on the beach gave evidence of my complicity in this violation, my willingness to own the condo even if it was behind the dune line, my desire that I, and no one else, should own a piece of nature. Nonetheless, as the Blue Angels dodged and looped and rolled above me, I marveled at one of mankind's greatest achievements. And looking out over the pounding surf and seemingly endless ocean, I witnessed one of nature's greatest vistas. Walking among the flotsam and debris that increasingly cluttered this idyllic world—

rusted metal chairs, worn-out tires, the engine cowling from a crashed World War II airplane, used condoms, seagulls and terns hobbling on one foot, the other lost to a net or other human hazards—I observed humanity at its worst, senseless and oblivious to the glorious environment all around, living life as if we have a right to consume all that exists before we die.

During our rare summer vacations at the condo, the beach became the state's finest sociological laboratory. Teenage boys gawked at nearly naked teenage girls. Men with gargantuan beer bellies announced their favorite football team on their T-shirts or caps, while their families polluted the solitude with appropriately named boom boxes, barking out rap, rock, or honky-tonk. Demurely dressed elderly couples strolled hand in hand, offering the comfort of companionship as a substitute for the teenage urgency of sex. Some micro-strollers early in the morning stared at the sand while gathering shells, driftwood, and sand dollars. Macro-strollers stared out at the sea, watching dolphins cavorting in the water, lurking shark fins, or seagulls diving for their prey. This world close-by emptied my mind of history as thoroughly as had my stroll across Saint James's Park in London.

After our sons departed for college, Dartie and I traveled abroad nearly every year. Mostly, we visited London in December, where we overdosed on theater (sometimes five or six shows in a week or ten days). We made our first trip to China with the boys in 1982, and we returned to Asia many times to lecture and vacation.

Many of our trips abroad coincided with meetings of the European Southern Studies Forum. Born out of mutual interest in bringing together the foremost European specialists in southern studies with leading American historians, the venues alternated between the South and Europe. Dartie and I attended gatherings of scholars at Cambridge University, the University of Vienna, and the Roosevelt Study Center in Middleburg, Netherlands, where I presented papers about southern religion, poor whites, and literature. I keynoted the meeting at the University of South Carolina, dealing with southern folkways battered by clashes between tradition and modernity. Other lectureships followed at Queens University in Belfast, Northern Ireland, and at the universities of Sussex and Hull in the UK.

Our circle of friends expanded as we came to know the world's leading southern writers and historians: Walter Edgar (University of South Carolina), C. Vann Woodward (Yale), Dale and John Shelton Reed (University of North Carolina), Brian Kelly (Queens University), Dan and Jane Carter (Emory), Tjebbe Westendorp (University of Leiden), John White (University of

Hull), Waldemar Zacharasiewicz (University of Vienna), Tony Badger (Cambridge), Hugh Trevor Roper (University of Essex), and Peter Parish (University of London), for whom I wrote articles in *Reader's Guide to American History.* Badger, Zacharasiewicz, and Westendorp visited us in Auburn. European insights expanded my own view of southern culture, and I trust that I helped enlarge their vision as well.

So often were we in Europe that we learned of the 9/11 terrorist attacks in the tiny Atlantic village of Port Magee, Ireland. The outpouring of sympathy was overwhelming. More than one hundred Irish nationals died in the September 11 attacks, and the bonds of Irish American affection stretched back to the diaspora of the nineteenth century. On Friday after the attack, all of Ireland came to a stop. All banks, government offices, and schools closed. Even the pubs and grocery stores sat dark and empty. All traffic stopped for a minute of national mourning. How ironic, I thought, that Ireland mourned our dead more faithfully than we did in America, where many businesses remained open. We continued our journey to Queens University in Belfast, where screaming sirens and gunfire interrupted news reports about terrorist attacks in America. As much as Europeans sympathized with us, they also welcomed us into their world, where violence and terrorism were common occurrences.

In addition to lectures around the world, Dartie often joined me on lecture tours in the States. Perhaps our most memorable was a weeklong cruise on the iconic 1920s paddlewheel steamboat *Delta Queen,* complete with calliope, from Birmingham to Nashville on the Warrior, Tombigbee, Tennessee, and Cumberland rivers. Following my two lectures, we rocked in a swing on the bow, watched the natural beauty of the Deep South's flora and fauna pass by, munched exquisite food, or danced to the music of a band playing our favorite 1930s and 1940s music.

Back home in our tiny patch of the globe, friendships became ever more precious. In our church and at the university, we had friends beyond counting.

Reporters and journalists bothered me from time to time but mainly earned my respect. They welcomed my opinion columns and helped make me a better writer by their example and by their editing. I respected their craft, admired their tenacity in tracking down stories, and applauded their style.

My activism had the downside of controversy and the upside of friendships with some of the most notable Alabamians of the twentieth century: writer and political activist Scottie Smith (daughter of Scott and Zelda Fitzgerald); illustrator/publisher Barbara Beecher and her radical poet husband, John; storyteller Kathryn Tucker Windham; short story writer Mary Ward Brown;

novelist Nelle Harper Lee (for whom our granddaughter is named); political and civil rights activists Charles Dobbins, Charlie Bell, Virginia Durr, Fred Gray, and a host of others. I managed to get along with most college presidents in Alabama other than my own. Even some politicians seemed to like me: Governors Albert Brewer and James Folsom Jr., congressmen Ben Erdreich, Carl Elliott, John Buchanan, and Glen Browder; legislators Pete Turnham, Dutch Higginbotham, Bradley Byrne, Ted Little, and Paul Demarco, to name a few on both sides of the aisle.

My friends at the University of Alabama Press—Malcolm MacDonald, Nicole Mitchell, Dan Ross, Elizabeth May, and others—taught me much about the publishing industry and carefully edited, designed, and marketed my books. But our friendship went beyond the perfunctory or professional. I really liked them as people.

Every controversy seemed to cost me a relationship but replace it with another, as if the moral arc of the universe automatically added while it subtracted. I grieved over old friends lost and rejoiced at new friends gained. Anyway, if we choose our causes based on the cost in friendship or family, we do precisely what Christ taught his disciples not to do. Of his disciples, he said, here are your brothers and sisters, here is your father and mother, here is your new family forged in righteousness. Luckily for me, most of my family and old friends hung with me even when they neither understood what I did nor approved of my ideas or methods. For that I am grateful. As for the friends I lost, I suppose that is the price we all must pay for trying to live with some degree of commitment, consistency, and integrity.

seven

"Where My Possessions Lie"

Writing about Ordinary People

Nancy Nolan, her husband, and their three sons lived in Dale County early in the twentieth century. Like most Alabama farmers of both races, they tenant-farmed someone else's land. Nolan's husband died when their oldest son was only nine. For five years, she and the boys clung desperately to a patch of cotton land, clawing a hard living from sandy soil.

The battle proved uneven. Poor soil, boll weevils, and slim crops won, and Nolan uprooted her three boys to Eufaula where she found work in Cowikee Cotton Mill. The oldest boy, now fourteen, joined her in the mill. She praised mill owner Donald Comer as a fair man who treated workers decently. As one of Nolan's friends explained after Comer bought the mill: "It used to be we were just factory folk or 'lint heads.' Now we are 'mill operatives' and we hold our heads high. All work is honorable, you know, and we are proud of ours."

Whether the workers were called lint heads or mill operatives, the grim financial reality of poor white existence forced a second son into the whirling lint and cacophonous noise of the factory. But the mother and two older brothers protected the third son from mill life. He was studious and academically gifted. At night, after his school let out and his brothers returned from their twelve-hour shifts, he taught them to read and write.

Why Write Books?

The Federal Writers' Project (FWP) employee who interviewed Nancy Nolan during the mid-1930s for the American Life Histories project left the family's story unfinished. As with all the other incomplete narratives I recorded in *Poor but Proud,* I longed to know the rest of their story. What happened to the boys? Did anyone survive the maelstrom of the Great Depression?

An incident four years later answered my questions. Following nearly every speech I made after *Poor but Proud* was published in 1989, someone would tarry behind as I signed books, waiting patiently to gain my undivided attention. After a large auditorium at Eufaula High School emptied following an education reform town meeting, two elderly men approached me. One was dressed in a fashionable suit. The other had on overalls. The fashionable one introduced himself, but I did not immediately recognize his name. He elaborated, "You wrote about our family in *Poor but Proud.* Our mother was Nancy Nolan." For a long time that evening, he told me the story of her children.

He had left Eufaula for college in the 1940s, earned a Ph.D. in psychology, and practiced in Boston. His brother in overalls, who hardly spoke that evening, worked in the mill so his younger brother could complete his education, and finally left the mill himself to operate a service station in Eufaula, where he had remained all his life. As the younger brother told their story of survival, sacrifice, and success, I thought how grand it was to be a historian of ordinary people, to provide them a niche in America's story, to remind us all that history is far more inclusive than we once believed. Best of all, as a historian of recent America, I oftentimes did hear the rest of the story.

That event in Eufaula became the model for so many conversations that I finally lost count of the stories and forgot many of the details. Some were specific, about people I had mentioned in the book. Others were generic, from people whose lives paralleled the ones I wrote about.

Some communicated with me in long, introspective letters. Margaret Johnston MacKnight lived in Auburn but had grown up the daughter of a teacher in Skyline Farms in Jackson County. She had danced in the Resettlement Administration community's square dance group, which had performed for Eleanor Roosevelt on the White House lawn.

Irma Cruise wrote that *Poor but Proud* told the story of "my people." She grew up in Hackneyville in Tallapoosa county, picking cotton side by side with African Americans and reading schoolbooks by firelight and kerosene lamps. After moving to Birmingham when her father went to work as a coal miner for Tennessee Coal, Iron, and Railroad Company (TCI), her family was caught up in a strike at Corona Mine Camp. She remembered soldiers sitting by her teachers at school, their guns resting on the teachers' desks. At night, the mine families turned out their lights for fear of being shot.

John K. Love of Oneonta, descended from Appalachian hill country folks like mine, had known my uncles and aunts and was the best friend of my cousin Charles Flynt. His mother was one of my dad's first girlfriends. But his letter was more than a trip down nostalgia's lane. He had a point to make:

> I wish this book was required reading for every high school [student] in Alabama, especially those who are unable to get a college education. I worked for [Walmart] stores as an assistant manager until I retired two years ago. I became so disgusted with the way large companies treat the working poor in this state. If people could only see how racism and fear of losing one's job is the weapon used to exploit them, maybe they could bring about meaningful change. Your book provides several possible explanations as to why so many hourly workers are willing to endure exploitation and even defend a company that routinely takes advantage of them. Many hourly paid working people believe they are powerless, but that to join a union is somehow un-American, un-Christian and pro-Communist.

A cousin and filmmaker in Berkeley, California, described himself as descended from "shoeless Baptists" and found *Poor but Proud* to be a "remarkable journey into the very bedrock of my ancestral homeland in the hills and hollows of north Alabama. As I read through your description of the early socioeconomic fabric of that region, I . . . view a vast tableau of that specific community of ours as it must have existed when it shaped the lives of so many of my people." He understood better why one ancestor remained a sharecropper in Alabama, another uprooted his family for the iron foundries of Birmingham, yet another went to work for a railroad, and a fourth migrated west to Texas. He rejoiced to learn that they had not gone quietly into the night but had rallied around a "fierce class-consciousness" born of a "sense of self-respect." "Prior to this," he wrote, "I had no information that any of our own 'lowly and unlearned' were inclined to offer any resistance, effective or otherwise, to their economic 'betters.'"

Howell Raines used the book extensively in a June 1990 *New York Times Magazine* article that won a Pulitzer Prize in journalism. Alan Neely used the book as a text in World Human Need and the Christian Response, a course he taught at Princeton Theological Seminary.

Dixie's Forgotten People, the sister book to *Poor but Proud,* explored poor whites regionwide and touched the same nerves, though from a wider geographical perspective. In an introduction to the 2004 revision of the book, I recalled that I had wanted to reach laypeople, especially those who were poverty's survivors, "who would resonate to the narrative, and who would be willing to claim the world they came from." I did not write for historians steeped in regression analysis, protracted economic theories about the origins of farm tenancy, or complicated class-conflict theory. Writing an extended essay about southern white poverty, I had concentrated on five dimensions of poor white existence. Poverty had no single explanation; it owed much to economic exploitation as well as to poor personal choices (that explanation pleased no one, because the poor often sought external villains to blame, and the rich blamed poverty on the mistakes of the poor). Nonetheless, class conflicts often shaped the story. I refused to depict the poor as hapless victims of a fate they could not avoid; they were, in fact, historical agents who found ways to assert their will amid the most oppressive conditions. I also insisted that we carefully rethink the term "culture of poverty," because their crafts, music, folklore, storytelling, and religion were rich and enduring, if often ridiculed by mainstream society. White poverty also differed from one subregion (Appalachia) to another (cotton belt). Finally, I wrote that reformers and government agencies, well-meaning as they are, had difficulty understanding poor whites, treating them with respect, dealing with their racism, or understanding their resistance to programs designed for their benefit. Although two and a half decades had passed since the book appeared, nothing had been written by historians to change my mind on these critical issues.

Reaction to the book ran the gamut from applause to criticism. Not long after it appeared, legendary Appalachian writer and activist Harry Caudle wrote me, disputing the origins of Appalachian people. On the other hand, Charles G. Hamilton of Aberdeen, Mississippi, a native of Appalachia, Kentucky, and graduate of famed Berea College, wrote that the book had provided "the finest understanding of Appalachians and related Southerners."

My liberal friend Virginia Durr wrote after reading the book: "It had so much of interest to me in it, and while it did not explain the southern poor white vote for their worst enemies, it did certainly give a sympathetic impression of them." She agreed that poor whites "have been taken advantage of and kept ignorant and been exploited, and it is not just sheer natural stupidity that has caused them to be poor and ignorant." I had managed, she wrote, to point out "their essential dignity and self-reliance."

Every time we talked, she raised the same question: why did poor whites identify with their white upper-class exploiters instead of their poor black fellow sufferers? We talked endlessly about class and caste and which counted most in southern history, how in some times (depressions) and situations (labor strife and strikes), class counted more than race, causing poor people to work together. Other times (the civil rights era) race trumped class, and resentful poor whites concluded that black progress must come at their expense, threatening their precarious toehold on the flimsy rungs of economic security. Poor people climbed the ladder of success not by toppling those on the top who fought fiercely to remain there, but by stomping back those beneath them who were trying to rise from the bottom. She never understood why this was so; perhaps I did not completely understand myself despite reading many books on the subject.

As the editor of a section of the *Encyclopedia of Southern Culture* dealing with class relationships, I invited some of the best minds I knew to address the problem. They came no closer to unraveling the riddle posed by Virginia. Unable to explain fully what I encountered in my research, I took satisfaction in a different phenomenon: the gratification of ordinary people when someone accurately told their story. Monroe J. Powell, the son of a poor white woman from north Alabama whose photograph appeared in *Dixie's Forgotten People,* wrote in 1984 to tell me that before his mother died she had seen her photograph, read her story, and been proud.

Her photograph resulted from a Samford University project supervised by Jim Brown, my friend and fishing companion, who slowly morphed from Russian historian into scholar of Appalachian culture and folkways. A group of our best students claimed one of the first National Endowment for the Humanities Youth Grants. It funded a multicounty study of surviving folk craftsmen and -women (white-oak basketmakers, blacksmiths, quilters, herb doctors, midwives). Their oral histories and student Mark Gooch's riveting black-and-white photographs (including the one of Mrs. Powell) enriched the book.

I have always felt sorry for writers whose work cannot engage human consciousness at the deepest levels of existence. Who am I? Why am I alive? Does my life make any difference to anyone? Why do such terrible things happen to me? Read my favorite book—Job's memoir (or biography) in the Hebrew Bible—engage the human drama recorded there, then try to convince me that books make no difference in people's lives.

There is, of course, countervailing wisdom. About the same time someone composed the travails of Job, the writer of Ecclesiastes admonished: "Of making many books there is no end; and much study is a weariness of the flesh."

And a contemporary Babylonian tablet complained that conditions were deplorable, youth were corrupt, women were shameless, and everyone wanted to write a book.

Some books engage the human spirit. Others do not. However else my books may have failed, I tried to make sure they engaged significant issues: lust for power, hubris, greed, injustice, endurance, survival, faith held, faith lost, faith recovered. The enduring desire to write one's own story is rooted in multiple democratic assumptions. Anyone and everyone can write or talk, though some do it better than others. Ordinary lives count for something. Perhaps their very ordinariness inspires us. The Japanese American son of a soldier who fought in Italy during World War II mused to a friend of mine about the extraordinary capacity of ordinary people in periods of extreme crisis. He concluded that what was humbling and empowering about his father and his comrades was the possibility that "whatever it was in them might be in us all."

Few expressed the vulgarized version of the democratic urge to tell our stories better than demagogic Georgia governor Eugene Talmadge, who visited the University of Georgia in 1935 and shocked university officials by announcing his plan to close the Henry W. Grady School of Journalism. In addition to persistent newspaper criticism of him, he offered another explanation for his action: "Writers are born, not made. I have never seen any worthwhile products of this school. As for myself, I can write anywhere and even with telephone bells ringing." Talmadge never provided evidence for his literary ability, which is fairly important if one seeks to record his own version of reality.

Likewise, Talmadge's modern Alabama counterpart Fob James took umbrage at my description of his first gubernatorial term as a failure. He told a reporter that all he needed to do was declare himself an "eminent historian" and he could write a book. No doubt he could do so without even that self-designation because some of my favorite histories bear the names of authors without formal training in history: Shelby Foote's *The Civil War;* Barbara Tuchman's *Stilwell and the American Experience in China;* Douglas Southall Freeman's *R. E. Lee;* Carl Sandburg's *Abraham Lincoln.* No academic credentials are known that guarantee wisdom to the mind, passion to the tongue, or eloquence to the pen.

Talmadge was partly right though. For some, writing is a gift. For others, it is a hard-earned skill like that of white-oak basketmaking, which looks easy when someone else does it but is dauntingly difficult when you try it yourself. The muse did not light on my shoulder at birth. I had to wrestle the blithe spirit into submission, as Jacob wrestled with God. The struggle could only be explained by the compulsion. I had stories that must not die for lack of telling.

My first two biographies could charitably be called "workmanlike." Boring and overwritten might be appropriate synonyms. T. Harry Williams, Pulitzer Prize–winning historian and general editor of the Southern Biography Series, which published my study of Governor Sidney Catts, continued the writing education that Bill Rogers had begun at Florida State.

Ed Harrell, my longtime suitemate at Auburn, recruited me to write the next book, *Dixie's Forgotten People,* for a series on "minorities in America," which he and a coeditor were launching for Indiana University Press. His guidelines—a book of two hundred pages directed toward a general audience—forced me to write in an entirely new way and for a different audience.

My next three books for commercial publishers—all begun and written during the tumultuous Funderburk years—required shortcuts because of the time-strapped demands of my administrative career. *Southern Poor Whites: A Selected Annotated Bibliography of Published Sources* was the ultimate scholars' book, listing and briefly summarizing three hundred pages of published scholarship about poor whites.

All of my books owed much to Dartie. She was not only a skilled editor but also an absolutely honest critic. She would read a passage, then ask me, "What exactly do you mean by that sentence?" "It's obvious what I mean," I often replied impatiently. "Tell me then," she admonished. So I would explain. "Fine! I understand that. But that is not what you wrote." Arguments ensued. Feelings were hurt. She would quit reading and go do something else. I would pick up the manuscript, read it over and over, hunt her up, apologize, and admit she was correct.

For the annotated bibliography, she functioned as research assistant as well as editor. With my time consumed by strategy meetings regarding the university's woes, I stole her away from her recorder group, mountain dulcimer, and wildflowers. She trekked to the library day after day, sitting at the computer, checking out topical references to poor whites, and affixing the call letters of books in the Ralph Draughon Library. In the afternoon after work and at spare moments during the day, I read the sources and briefly summarized each.

The Montgomery Chamber of Commerce bore responsibility for my fourth book, *Montgomery: An Illustrated History.* The book was one in a series conceived by Windsor Publications and funded by local civic boosters whose businesses were included at the end of each book. Entering the well-paying project naively, I had a grand time researching the city. As rich in history as it was rigid in social distinctions, Montgomery was a place into which one was either born or never really fit. No Alabama city (and few comparably sized American ones) furnished so amazing a cast of characters: Jefferson Davis, William L. Yancey, Tallulah Bankhead, Zelda Sayre and Scott Fitzgerald, their daughter Scottie, Sara Haardt Mencken, Senator Lister Hill, Governor Bibb Graves and his wife, Dixie, Virginia and Clifford Durr, E. D. Nixon, Rosa Parks, Ralph D. Abernathy, Martin Luther King Jr., Fred Gray, Grover Hall, Hank Williams, and a supporting cast of thousands.

I had anticipated some disagreement over my treatment of the civil rights movement, but by 1980 the city fathers (the mothers hardly mattered in Montgomery despite the city's rich legacy of obstreperous and independent-minded women) had come to terms with its racial history. My problem with the chamber arose on a more arcane matter rooted in my early career as a labor historian. Mere mention of the words "organized labor" made Alabama businessmen nervous. Many interviews passed before I discovered that the chamber had actually split over strategies for economic development. The Men of Montgomery represented a younger group of boosters organized in the early 1950s during civil rights upheaval and economic stagnation. So anxious were they to attract industry and create jobs that they refused to honor the chamber's venerable tradition against recruiting unionized plants. So opposed was the chamber to unions, that economic recruitment split the business community (a harbinger of what would happen to the Business Council of Alabama [BCA] half a century later because of differences over tax and education reform).

Beyond this blip, research about Alabama's capital proceeded smoothly and helped maintain my sanity during the Funderburk years. John Engelhardt Scott Jr., descendant of one of the city's founders, opened his phenomenal photographic archive to me. Interviews with Mabel Haardt, Will Hill Tankersley, black residents J. T. Alexander, B. Y. Farris, and George Pool, among others, allowed me to construct the racially complex, separate worlds of the city.

Best of all was the friendship that Dartie and I began with Frances (Scottie) Fitzgerald Smith, daughter of Scott and Zelda. She not only welcomed us into her life and told us enthralling stories about her parents but also introduced us to her social circle of female iconoclasts (self-proclaimed Women of the World and abbreviated WOW! They even wrote a theme song: "We're all in our places, with bright shiny faces," but you'd never guess what's on our minds). Dartie and I spent a fascinating evening with them, and I relished being the token male admitted to their sacred space. The book sold out its original five thousand press run within weeks and went into a second printing.

So successful was the Montgomery book that Windsor asked me to write a sequel about Alabama enterprise sponsored by BCA. In time, some in the powerful business alliance would develop misgivings about me, partly based on my strong disagreement with the state's century-long economic development strategy. But at the time we had a good relationship. I collaborated with my former student and friend Marlene Rikard, who used her training as an economic historian to provide excellent sketches of sponsoring companies. My brother-in-law, geologist Everett Smith, to whom I dedicated the book, was a fount of information on Alabama minerals, water, and geology. The book's stunning color photographs also introduced readers to one of the state's finest photographers, Chip Cooper. Mike Thomason, photographic archivist at the University of South Alabama, hunted down rare historic images and took some fine ones of his own.

Although the book never sold as well as its predecessor, it made sufficient impact to bring Windsor calling again about other projects. I recommended former students and friends for the work because I had unintentionally begun a new phase of my writing career. I had followed Booker T. Washington's admonition to put down my bucket where I was. After my first four books devoted to Florida politics and southern poor whites, I drifted into exploration of my own natural terrain. This, I slowly, discovered, was "where my possessions lie," to borrow lyrics from a great old hymn, and I might as well write about *those* possessions as any on earth.

What is local and immediate, those forces that most directly form and shape us, ancestors who cast powerful shadows over us, sometimes get lost in the rage to explain the larger world. That is the way William Faulkner perceived reality. He could locate all that really mattered in fictional Yoknapatawpha County, Mississippi.

That is also the way Alabama artist William Christenberry viewed the world. With his own tools and materials, he photographed, sculpted, and painted his beloved Black Belt. He believed you could find every race, class, and condition of humanity down home in Sprott, Akron, or Stewart in his native Hale County.

Nelle Harper Lee envisioned the human drama similarly. She never longed for anything more than to be the "Jane Austen of south Alabama," which was both to aspire to much and to locate aspiration in a confined locale. She bril-

liantly explored the complex social, racial, and class relationships of a small
town that could have been in Austria, Australia, Argentina, or Alabama. Only
the details differed. If I was provincial in casting my bucket down into Alabama's cool, deep waters, at least I traveled in good company.

All seven of my books after 1981 dealt with the state. One dealt with poverty, one with the state's economy, one with Montgomery, two with religion,
and two more with aspects of life in the twentieth century. My preference for
Alabama mainly represented the irresistible attraction of community in an at-
omistic world disintegrating before my very eyes. For all their parochialism
and backwardness, Alabamians understand who and where they are. Less inclined than other Americans to leave the vicinity of their birth, they simply
endured, to use Faulkner's evocative expression. One novelist observed that
in modern America, "only the South is a place. North, east, and west are just
directions." Frances Mayes, south Georgia author of *Under the Tuscan Sun,*
added that "Southerners have a gene, as yet undetected in the DNA spirals,
that causes them to believe that place is fate. Where you are is who you are.
The further inside you the place moves, the more your identity is intertwined
with it. Never casual, the choice of place is the choice of something you crave."
She must have been thinking of me when she wrote those words. The novelist/
poet Robert Penn Warren might also have had me in mind when he observed
that "a fish never thinks about water until he's out of it."

My rage to explain the South in general and Alabama in particular took me
on a visit one day to Davis-Kidd Bookstore, Nashville's largest independent
bookseller. With no apparent regard for either alphabetization or subject con-
vergence, the bookshop arrangement puzzled me until I noticed the books on
opposite sides facing an aisle. "Local interest" dominated one side, featuring
categories such as "southern fiction" and "southern studies." As if to provide
alternative reading for those newly arrived from faraway places who despaired
of the unfathomable local natives, the opposite shelves were devoted to "as-
trology," "women's studies," and "addiction."

Writing Southern Religion

Religion fit perfectly into local interests and southern studies. It might even
wander over into a form of addiction. For decades I argued with secular European colleagues that their scholarship about Dixie was impeccable, insightful,
and compelling save for one failing. Most of them had no clue about southern
religion, white or black, and thus simply ignored the subject. Though I would

study religion carefully as an academic, its DNA was registered deep in my soul before I read a line.

Danger lurks anytime historians write about aspects of existence that are both personal and existential. The more remote and impersonal our subjects, the more objective our narrative. But there is another side to this debate. What we know instinctively or by long personal experience provides us insider status. Southern religion is one subject that doesn't have to be explained to me.

I have always marveled at how difficult the subject seems to be for academics. Perhaps the problem is rooted in historic divisions between rational and emotional spheres of life. But even that does not account fully for the schizophrenia of the academy when it comes to the subject. If a cultural anthropologist studies primitive people on a remote South Pacific island, she accepts the islanders for who they are and what they believe. If women do not cover their breasts, the scholar feels no compulsion to encourage them to do so. Nor does she prejudge religions such as animism or idol worship.

Should the same scholar find herself in a remote African American rural community in the middle of Alabama's Black Belt confronted by a population with high rates of teenage pregnancy, obesity, domestic violence, or emotional Christianity, the anthropologist would analyze the people in whole, not in part. Their visceral, conservative religion might even contribute positively to their sense of self-worth, community, place, and identity, the scholar might conclude.

Unfortunately, there is a tendency for some scholars—when confronted with a racist, working-class, homophobic, religious-right, white community— to launch a campaign of political and cultural reeducation of these backward, benighted, and primitive folk. Seldom is the primary academic goal simply to accept all people on their own terms, as different from us but nonetheless worthy of thoughtful analysis and understanding, without judgment concerning the inferiority of their wisdom compared to our own.

Analysis of American religion became more complicated with the spread of Pentecostal and fundamentalism in the Midwest, Rocky Mountain states, and California. The South presently is only marginally different from the rest of the nation in most indices of religious belief. As early as 1990, a poll found small variations between national religious opinions and Deep South views on the same subjects. Belief in God stood at 84 percent nationally and 81 percent in South Central states (Alabama, Mississippi, Tennessee, Kentucky). Even in the notoriously unchurched Pacific Northwest, 81 percent of adults believed in God. The six most religious urban areas in America, judged by rates of church membership, were Provo, Utah; LaCrosse, Wisconsin; Waco, Texas; and three mainly Catholic towns in southern Louisiana. Even the South's religious politics became confused in 2008 when Chicagoan Barack Obama outpolled white Arkansas Southern Baptist minister Mike Huckabee nearly two to one in party primaries across the Bible Belt.

If anthropologists, sociologists, and political scientists are confused about religious identity, it comes as no surprise that southern novelists didn't do much better. Catholic novelists, especially, offered biting sarcasm along with perceptive insight. Birmingham native Walker Percy's novel *Lancelot* has Lance Lamar—scion of a distinguished family, famous college football halfback, Rhodes scholar, and disenchanted liberal lawyer—announce, "Christ, if heaven is full of Southern Baptists, I'd rather rot in hell with Saladin and Achilles."

Flannery O'Connor, on the other hand, recognized that southern religion was "extremely fluid" and offered "enough variety to give the novelist the widest range of possibilities imaginable." In the South, even the poor read and knew the Bible, connecting them to the "universal and the holy." Asked about her predilection to write about bizarre religious figures, she answered famously: "Whenever I am asked why southern writers particularly have a penchant for writing about freaks, I say it is because we are still able to recognize one. To be able to recognize a freak, you have to have some conception of the whole man, and in the South the conception of the whole man is still, in the main, theological. . . . I think it is safe to say that while the South is hardly Christ-centered, it is most certainly Christ-haunted." Elsewhere she explained her grotesque religious characters this way: "I have found that anything that comes out of the South is going to be called grotesque by the Northern reader, unless it is grotesque, in which case it is going to be called realistic."

Writers from Harper Lee to Eudora Welty, Rick Bragg, and Nanci Kincaid stumbled over evangelicalism. Lee and Welty grew up Methodist in Alabama and Mississippi, where Baptists suffocated minds like kudzu did the landscape. Lee pokes fun at Primitive Baptists who denigrate women. Welty describes (in *The Optimist's Daughter*) the emotional excesses of one rural family: "You can't curb a Baptist. Let them in and you can't keep 'em down. . . . When the whole bunch of Chisoms got to going in concert, I thought the only safe way to get through the business alive was not say a word, just sit still as a mouse."

Nanci Kincaid (*Crossing Blood*) describes how Lucy Conyers decided that "church is the place where God and women get together to try and do something about the men in this world. It's where women go to get talked into loving men for spiritual reasons, since after a while they run out of any other reasons to do it. God is there to keep women hoping for miracles." Vacation Bible school in Tallahassee taught Lucy Christian cheers for Parent's Night. Sashaying around with crepe paper and pom-poms, Lucy chanted: "Jesus, Jesus, He's our man. If He can't do it, nobody can."

In his memoir *All Over but the Shoutin'*, Rick Bragg described the comfort his poor-white mother derived from both television evangelists and the small Baptist church she attended. TV preachers "peddled promises, and offered hope to people who had none." But they always linked the hope to donations of money. Of the little church, he wrote: "As so many Sundays flew by, there among those good people who treated me like a member of the family, the warm decent people who found a pure joy inside the walls of that church, I learned that you can't just come to have Dinner-on-the-Ground. . . . You can't just see the show. You have to give something in trade."

It is also easy to exaggerate religious literacy in the South. Once, while shopping for books in a Birmingham thrift store, I found nothing of interest on the shelves marked "classics." I wandered over to the "religion" section and found two Faulkner novels combined into a single "religious" book: *Requiem for a Nun* and *Sanctuary.* I suppose the titles fit the section, though the content surely did not.

As such evidence of confusion accumulated, I discovered another life's work, describing southern religion to believers and nonbelievers alike, who seemed equally confounded by the subject. Much of my writing about southern Christianity appeared in the form of articles in scholarly journals. More than a dozen others appeared as chapters in books, most notably "A Special Feeling of Closeness: Mt. Hebron Baptist Church, Leeds, Alabama." This essay about a small fundamentalist rural church once pastored both by my father-in-law and by a speaker at Communist rallies probed the complexities of southern evangelicalism. The essay, published in a study of American congregationalism by the University of Chicago Press, may have been my most ambitious effort to educate the scholarly profession to the richness of the subject.

In an essay titled "A Pilgrim's Progress through Southern Christianity" (in *Autobiographical Reflections on Southern Religious History*), I joined pioneers in the field to describe my personal encounter with southern religious history. I wrote this essay for a non-Baptist, academic audience. I directed other essays toward fellow Baptists, all designed to demonstrate the wide diversity within our denomination. Many of these articles appeared in *Baptist History and Heritage,* the denomination's historical journal. Others appeared in more academic international publications such as *Studies in Baptist History and Thought.*

In addition, I lectured constantly about southern religious diversity, sometimes in Baptist churches, other times at Baptist colleges and universities, or at international Baptist studies symposia. I also served on the Baptist Heritage and Identity Commission of the Baptist World Alliance.

During the 1990s I wrote two books about very different aspects of southern evangelicalism. One explored the lives of forty-seven Baptist, Methodist, and Presbyterian missionaries who served in China between 1850 and 1950. In addition to theology and missiology, this book allowed me to probe gender issues and the process of cultural adaptation.

The other book, *Alabama Baptists,* presented four decades of research and six decades of living the faith. I tried to set the context of the book broadly in southern and Christian history, to pay careful attention to class, gender, and race, to explore especially the experiences of bivocational ministers, and once again to suggest the wide range of theological, political, and social thought encompassed in the denomination. Without repudiating historical depictions of white Baptist conservatism, I did document dissenting viewpoints. This research stimulated academic debate at numerous symposia on southern religion in venues as different as Birmingham-Southern College, Florida State University, Baylor University, Queens University in Belfast, Northern Ireland, and Hong Kong Baptist University, among others.

I also participated for many years in the American Religion Colloquium organized by religion scholar Charles Lippy at the University of Tennessee, Chattanooga. We rotated the annual meeting around the Deep South in order to involve as wide an interdisciplinary circle of religion scholars and graduate students as possible.

After Ed Harrell joined me on the Auburn history faculty in 1990, we directed many doctoral dissertations in the field of southern religion, and our department became a leader in the subject. Many universities had a single scholar of the field; few had two located in a history department; and only a handful matched the quality and quantity of our graduate students. For many years, we provided the largest number of participants in the regional American Religion Colloquium.

As interest in religion grew, Nicole Mitchell, director of the University of Alabama Press, asked me to edit a new series for the press on religion in American culture. I suggested adding to the project Ed Harrell and Edith Blumhofer, a Pentecostal historian at the University of Chicago and Wheaton College. During more than a decade, the series published two dozen books, which substantially expanded knowledge of American religion. In fact, by the beginning of the twenty-first century, religion had become one of the hottest subfields of southern history, producing third- and fourth-generation scholars.

I trace my academic interest in the subject to the late 1960s and 1970s while teaching at Samford, which made me an early second-generation participant. As so often happens in the life of historians, two lines intersected, one personal, the other professional. As Baptist theological battles intensified, Wallace (Wally) Henley (who at the time covered religion for the *Birmingham News*) summoned a group of fellow "liberals" to a meeting of "Southern Baptist Paranoids United" to "take a stab at genuine Koinonia and talk about concerns in Baptist life—especially in the Alabama Baptist State Convention." The effort obviously didn't work. Shortly after our meeting, Wally left for Washington, D.C., to join the Nixon administration. Following the Watergate scandal, he returned disillusioned but wiser, moved toward the charismatic fringe of Baptists, then left to pastor a church in Texas.

A few years later, in 1978, my former Samford colleague W. T. Edwards and I conducted a workshop for Episcopal clergy on southern religion, emphasizing the complex mixture of social gospel, liturgical, fundamentalist, neoorthodox, conservative, liberal, revivalistic, charismatic, and Pentecostal elements, black and white, which had shaped and were reshaping Christianity in the region.

By then I was lecturing at places such as Lee College, a Church of God school in Cleveland, Tennessee, as well as at University of the South, an Episcopal school in Sewanee, just up the interstate west of Cleveland. To the east of Cleveland, I also spoke numerous times at mainstream Baptist Carson-Newman College. It would be hard to imagine three more different religious colleges, all located in eastern Tennessee. Yet all could make a legitimate claim to represent authentic southern religion.

Such realizations prompted me to contact the first generation who had pioneered the field of southern religious history, men such as Rufus Spain (Baylor), Ed Harrell (UAB), Donald Mathews (University of North Carolina Chapel Hill), and Sam Hill (University of Florida). As early as 1972 I wrote Mathews of my determination to analyze religion from the sociological perspective of the rural poor. Don encouraged me to "provide a new perspective on not only the past but also the present. I suspect the first barrier to breach is the prejudice of historians who think all study of groups who identify themselves in religious terms is 'church' history." He identified one of the chief problems of the new religious history, the assumption that such topics properly belong in theological seminaries or church history programs in divinity schools or university religion departments. Asserting the legitimacy of such study for doctoral-granting history departments would be a long, tough battle. Mathews's encouraging response expanded my correspondence. I wrote historian H. Shelton Smith at Duke University about my interests in the social ideology of southern Protestants, especially about socialism, tenant farming, and organized labor. Half a decade after my letters to Mathews and Smith, I wrote David Mathews, president of the University of Alabama, congratulating him on an article he had published suggesting that southern evangelical responses to late nineteenth-century naturalism (especially Darwinism) were more complex than historians had realized. I believed, based on my research, that this complexity extended well into the twentieth century. In 1981 I wrote Sam Hill of my intention to write a book about the social gospel in the South. Sam thanked me for helping him understand how "diverse, unpredictable, and rich the southern religious tradition is."

By the late 1970s and 1980s, I was writing furiously about these subjects myself and was actively encouraging others (including Paul Harvey, a graduate student at California Berkeley; J. Lawrence Brasher, a doctoral student at Duke; and my former Samford student Andrew Manis, at Southern Baptist Seminary). All would produce influential books about southern religion as part of a third generation of excellent scholarship.

I also was able to interact with a broader academic community. When the executive director of Rural America began planning a program on rural people organizing for social change sponsored by the National Endowment for the Humanities, I responded critically to his proposal because he omitted religion, "one of the most significant aspects of rural organization" and "a powerful force in rural American life."

I concluded my career focusing on the same subject. I titled my presidential address to the 2004 Southern Historical Association in Memphis, "Religion for the Blues: Evangelicalism, Poor Whites, and the Great Depression." In many ways, the paper distilled four decades of thought about religion. Many poor white, bivocational preachers rationalized the Bible in terms of their class interests as tenant farmers, coal miners, or textile workers, criticizing the New Deal from the left, for doing too little to help the poor.

Rewards for the Ordeal

I suppose some writers wake up every morning and rush to their computer, eager to begin a new day's creative work. I never had that experience. I always loved research, which could be done in bits and pieces of days, augmented by occasional archival orgies that began when the doors opened and ended when they closed. Twelve-hour days with a brief snack break became my routine when on the road. But the variety of materials handled, the fascinating documents discovered, the eureka moments when months of confusion melted away in an hour of discovery, made me feel like an early nineteenth-century explorer for gold in a remote northeast Alabama creek. One substantial nugget made up for a month of exhausting labor.

Writing was something else again. Words are ornery little beasts. They are quite content just to lie there on my note cards and not be disturbed. I had to grab them by their vowels and consonants, rearrange them, organize them, analyze them, and force some sense into them. Though a speedy typist (a skill I had learned during high school days when I feared my future was behind a clerk's desk), I never felt comfortable composing on a machine. Computers suited me no better. So I settled down at my desk after breakfast with fountain pen and legal pad, wrote until noon, took a quick lunch break, returned to my writing until supper, and when really inspired, wrote steadily until midnight or later. Twelve-hour days were not uncommon; eight-hour days were typical; and I could maintain this schedule for months on end. Every day was exhausting, the cumulative impact enervating; but my excitement was palpable and the accumulating stacks of legal pads, exhilarating.

I wrote initial drafts fast, spending the first full day reading through my research notes (I preferred three-by-five cards, which I could shuffle in and out of outlines, wherever they fit best). The cards also disciplined my note-taking to critical information and insights. The cards arranged topically or chronologically fell into natural patterns that constituted an outline.

This was the hardest day. Once I knew where I was going, the words seemed to pour down like a springtime thundershower. On a good day, I completed between twenty-five and fifty pages. But it was impossible to write both fast and well. First drafts were a mess. My goal was to give my typist the tenth draft of a chapter, which usually underwent several more revisions when she returned it. During my nearly three decades at Auburn, I inflicted considerable grief on Wickham Henkels, Laura Katz, Laura Hill, and Peggy Mason. All of them could have translated hieroglyphics once they retired from my service. My productivity resulted partly from being part of a fine team.

Next, I turned the manuscript over to Dartie, my most unsparing critic. Fierce debates and one bruised ego later, I had incorporated most of her revisions. Later still, my writer son, Sean, assumed editorial duties and performed just as admirably.

During the first half of my career, I had to steal hours for research and writing from other duties. But for the last decade and a half, Auburn president James Martin liberated me and greatly enhanced my productivity. In 1990, as I weighed a position at the University of Florida, Dr. Martin took me to lunch and offered me one of the Distinguished University Professorships he was creating to retain faculty who might otherwise leave Auburn. He asked if I wanted to continue teaching. If so, what portion should be research/writing and how much teaching? The prospect of giving up the classroom was unthinkable. But I also coveted uninterrupted days to study, read, visit archives, lecture around the world, and write. He agreed to my suggestion that I teach winter-spring and engage in other activities during summer-fall. Of course, responsibilities for doctoral students recognized no time or season and were unrelenting. Nonetheless, I felt as though I had been transported into heaven. This, I thought, is absolutely the best job in the university. Administrators made higher salaries, but I would wager none were so happy as I. In time, some faculty (at least some of those who never received such appointments) criticized the program, which led to its demise. But it served precisely the function for which Martin had designed it. I entered my most productive scholarly years. And I never applied for another job.

In addition to sparking considerable debate about southern poverty, religion, and all things Alabama, my writing brought tangible rewards. Book sales exceeded fifty thousand copies. My biography of Duncan Fletcher won the Rembert Patrick prize for best book in Florida history and an Award of Merit from the American Association of State and Local History. An article on Baptist transitions from rural to urban America earned the Norman W. Cox prize. The Mississippi Council of Christian Social Action selected *Dixie's Forgotten People* book of the year. *Poor but Proud* won a half dozen awards, my favorite being the Lillian Smith Award for Nonfiction by the Southern Regional Council. I shared this coveted prize, the oldest regional book award in the South, with many of my heroes, heroines, and friends: George B. Tindall, Dan Carter, Paul Gaston, Robert Coles, C. Vann Woodward, Harry Ashmore, Will Campbell, my former student, Andy Manis, as well as fiction writers Albert Murray, Ernest Gaines, Cormac McCarthy, Pat Conroy, Eudora Welty, Alice Walker, and Peter Taylor. My cousin Claude Duncan, who worked for the Children's Defense Fund in Washington, D.C., at the time, gave a memorable party in my honor, where I met and talked with Marian Wright Edelman, as well as reporters Mary McCrory, Hodding Carter, and John Cochran. I also signed books for Jesse Jackson and Ted Kennedy.

In 2002 the University of Alabama journalism department named me recipient of the Clarence Cason Writing Award, which is one of my treasured prizes. It was named for a journalism professor whose book, *90° in the Shade,* I introduced in a reprint edition. The author was so conflicted over his mild criticism of the state that he committed suicide just as his book appeared.

The other books won prizes as well, raising the prospect of a serious ego trip. Dartie took care of that temptation single-handedly. Vowing that her main purpose on earth was to keep me humble, she deserved a Ph.D. for her efforts, reminding me that except for writing books and making speeches, I was pretty well useless.

We are all many persons rather than a single entity. We are sons and daughters, parents, friends, spouses; Sunday school teachers, volunteers at food banks and thrift shops; youth soccer, baseball, and football coaches. Because of that, no single category such as teacher or writer identifies us accurately. We give highest credence to whichever category we most value. For me, that was never "writer," so as the awards came and went, I nailed them to a wall in a room no one ever saw or stacked them in a closet.

To remind me how fleeting and relative fame is, I treasure a story that Scottish schoolteacher/writer Bernard McCafferty told during an interview with BBC about his new book of short stories *Walking the Dog.* He related how he had been overwhelmed by all the attention and "meet the author" gatherings across the United Kingdom until he returned to his hometown. It was the only such affair that no one attended. His feelings were hurt until a friend told him: "Aye, Bernard, there was no point in coming to a meet the author reception. We already know you." So it was when I returned to Auburn, where I was just another church member, Sunday school teacher, club member, basketball and football fan, someone who shopped at the grocery and hardware stores, went to the doctor, visited the hospital, and lived out my life far from the madding crowd.

Out of town was another matter. Invitations to lecture poured in as each new book appeared, and I relished every one of them. Most writers I know tend to be retiring, shy, or private persons who are as uncomfortable talking about their subjects as they are at ease writing about them. They communicate brilliantly in one medium but hardly at all in the other. I was spared that dilemma both by my talkative Flynt ancestors and my training in persuasive speaking. So I was never happier than when on a book or lecture tour.

The venues carried Dartie and me across America and the world: Brooklyn Public Library; the South Dakota Historical Society; Rice and Baylor universities in Texas; the University of North Carolina, Chapel Hill, and Western Carolina University; Georgia College and State University; the Edward Akin lectures at Mississippi College; the David Duke lectures at William Jewell College in Missouri; the Carlyle Marney lectures at Carson-Newman College; the President's Distinguished Scholar Lecture at Palm Beach Atlantic University; the Catherine Prescott Lecture for the Florida Historical Society, among many others. As Visiting Scholar in History at the University Center of Georgia, I lectured at Georgia Tech, Clark University, Georgia State, and the University of Georgia.

One of my favorite lectureships involved a gathering of old friends at College of Wooster in Ohio. Longtime labor historian, ASLH member, and Tennessee Valley native James Hodges put together a conference in 1981 looking at history from the bottom up. Labor historian Herbert Gutman of City University of New York, social historians James Jones of the University of Houston, and Natalie Zemon Davis of Princeton, shared the podium. It was one of the early national conferences devoted entirely to working-class history, and participants had a chance both to learn from each other and to make our pleas for a more inclusive history.

Although I often traveled out of state to speak, most of my lectures occurred in Alabama. I presented the Draughon Lectures in State and Local History at venues across Alabama. I conducted workshops for eleventh grade schoolteachers on ways to integrate Alabama historical moments into the required U.S. history course. I frequently lectured for the Theatre of the Mind series at the Alabama Shakespeare Festival in Montgomery and at the Alabama Writers' Symposium in Monroeville.

In addition to frequent lectures for the Southern Studies group in Europe, my longtime interest in Asia and book on China missionaries landed us at Hong Kong Baptist University in the fall of 1992. I lectured for old friend Jerry Barrett, who served the university as provost, and my former Samford student Barton Starr, who was a professor of history at the school. I also had a chance to lecture about American politics to the second largest American Studies program in the People's Republic of China at the University of Sichuan in Chengdu.

In all, we traveled abroad twenty-five times during my years on the Auburn faculty, mostly to speak or conduct research. Those trips were critical to my scholarship. Not only did they afford me a chance to share my research, but I also learned as much as I taught. This generation of scholars in Europe and Asia used new academic technology and their own rapidly expanding prosperity to access our primary documents and think about America in ways unimpeded by nationalism. It helps to see America as others see us rather than as we perceive ourselves.

Another aspect of my scholarship involved the media. Because I had always liked print journalists and television producers, I became a resource person worldwide for nearly any story involving Alabama, religion, or the South. I spoke several times to the Alabama Press Association and at the Southern Journalists Roundtable. Reporters called from the *New York Times, Wall Street Journal, Economist, Christian Science Monitor, Mother Jones, Arizona Republican, Washington Post, Los Angeles Times, USA Today, Newsweek, Time,* most Alabama and southern papers, plus C-Span, ESPN, CNN, ABC, CBS, as well as interviews in the *India Express,* the *Hindu,* and *Frontline* in Madras, India.

Filmmakers also came calling. I served as consultant for dozens of documentary films and some productions of southern fiction: *Roses of Crimson,* a film about the 1926 Rose Bowl game (many Auburn fans were perplexed and some even angry at my glorification of the 1925 Crimson Tide team); films about James Earl Ray, Virginia Durr, "Big Jim" Folsom, Will Campbell, and women preachers; Alabama regionalism and highways; *We Dare Defend Our Rights* for the Center for Civic Education; a film on how teachers use *To Kill a Mockingbird* in their classrooms; a Jack Bass series called the American South Comes of Age; and *Scottsboro: An American Tragedy,* which was the runner-up for an Academy Award for documentary films. My most exotic project was an interview with Finnish television for a special on the changing American South. I also consulted on the filming of a Helen Norris short story, "Cracker Man."

Quite a different use of my research and writing involved expert testimony in court cases. I testified for the defense in *Bolden v. City of Mobile,* a Supreme Court case that altered American politics by striking down Mobile's at-large electoral districts and replacing them with single-unit districts more favorable to blacks and Republicans. As I predicted at the time, this decision both broadened and polarized democracy and was partly responsible for the rise of Red and Blue America. The case also established a new legal consideration, the historical intent of local and state political decisions.

Participation in all these stemmed directly from my research, writing, and speaking. Both the writing and lecturing also institutionalized my professional relationships. My closest circle of historian friends belonged to the Southern Historical Association (SHA). With more than five thousand members worldwide, SHA enrolled nearly everyone who earned their livelihood studying the

South, plus many from other professions who simply relished any aspect of Dixie. From my first SHA Convention in November 1964, I missed only one meeting (while in Hong Kong) during the following half century. I served on nearly every SHA committee, wrote grants on behalf of its oral history project, presented numerous papers and chaired sessions, even began coordinating meetings (with David Colburn at the University of Florida) for department chairs of southern research universities.

In time, SHA meetings took on a social significance equal to their academic importance. It was the only time I saw many of my professional friends and former students. The civility, kindness, high regard for both meaningful tradition and cautious change, serious conversations, respect for graduate students and younger colleagues, and lack of political correctness at SHA meetings contrasted with the stridency, ideological agendas, and impersonalism of the larger historical organizations to which I belonged.

Within the state, the Alabama Association of Historians (AAH) and the Alabama Historical Association (AHA) served a similar purpose. The AAH enrolled any person (K–12 teacher, writer, archivist, professor, genealogist) with a professional career involving history. The AHA included mainly college professors and ordinary citizens who loved the state's history.

Regrettably, many colleagues at the state's research universities did not participate in either organization. I could never understand this. In terms of their scholarship, it reinforced a tendency to speak in jargon, write for each other, and ignore the literate, delightful lay audience. My colleagues were the poorer for this dismissive attitude, but so was the public. I learned much not only from scholarly friends who participated in these organizations, but also by listening to papers by so-called amateurs.

I paid my professional dues by serving as president or chairman of more than a half dozen such groups (the AAH, AHA, Alabama Historical Commission, Southern Baptist Historical Commission, Alabama Baptist Historical Society, as well as the SHA). My year as SHA president (2004) was the culmination of my career. Because we were scheduled to meet in Memphis for our seventieth anniversary, I organized the meeting around the fiftieth anniversary theme of the Brown decision and the conflicted 1955 SHA meeting in the same city. My friend John Hope Franklin—Harvard Ph.D., one of the kindest, most civil, and most courageous people in the profession, and the dean of African American historians—had been invited in 1955 to participate on a panel with William Faulkner, Tom Clark (University of Kentucky historian), and a distinguished journalist. When the Peabody Hotel, headquarters for the meeting, refused to allow him to register, Franklin declined to attend. Benjamin Mays, president of Morehouse College in Atlanta, reluctantly agreed to take his place on the panel.

My focus for the meeting was change and continuity in race relations. I raised money to fund a luncheon in honor of history teachers at historically black colleges and universities. I invited John Hope as guest of honor. We celebrated his ninetieth birthday with a huge party in his honor, including his favorite coconut cake, and the hotel put him up free in its presidential suite. He joked that in 1955 racism kept him out of the historic hotel and in 2004 hospitality kept him in because the suite was so large he couldn't find his way out. Officials presented him a key to the city and invited him to speak to its movers and shakers.

The ironies of the meeting were overwhelming: Memphis in 1954–55 and 2004; staid historians treated to the music of Florence, Alabama, natives W. C. Handy (father of the blues) and Sam Phillips (founder of Sun Recording Studio, which first fused black and white musical traditions in the persons of Jerry Lee Lewis, Elvis Presley, and B. B. King); the place where M. L. King Jr. was assassinated by a poor white petty criminal from southern Illinois.

Almost no one realized the finest irony of all. Only one other resident Alabamian had been elected president of the SHA. University of Alabama professor A. B. Moore, descendent of Black Belt planters, had served as the second president. He was a Petrie student and Auburn graduate. He also authored *History of Alabama* in 1934, the very year the SHA first met. That text entombed two generations of Alabamians in the steel coils of history and tradition. Not until W. W. Rogers, his Auburn classmate David Ward, Leah Atkins, and I— all with ties of one kind or another to Petrie and Auburn—wrote *Alabama: The History of a Deep South State* forty years later and a decade before my SHA presidential year, did the state have an alternative text about its past.

Moore's book did not occupy the same racial universe as ours. Of slavery, he wrote: in the treatment of slaves, "leniency and kindness prevailed;" "it was well-nigh impossible to manage a large body of ignorant slaves according to the lofty ideals of plantation life"; "ungrateful, indeed, was the slave who did not revere his 'Old Missus'"; "the Negroes were a fun-making and fun-loving people, and they had many opportunities for merriment"; "the masses of slaves seemed contented and carefree, and were sentimentally attached to their masters and the plantations"; "they seemed to forget all the toils and sufferings of slavery in their admiration of the magnificence of the plantation built by their labors and their bondage." The four of us concluded four decades later that someone apparently had failed to tell the slaves all these things, for most fled the plantation as soon as they had the chance.

Moore's treatment of Reconstruction, Populism, the 1901 Constitution (of its disfranchisement provisions he wrote: "by the elimination of the ignorant Negro vote, which was a source of much corruption, the constitution contributed a great deal to the improvement of elections in Alabama"), and most other subjects also belonged to the mythology of the plantation regime that produced his generation of historians. Every time the four of us spoke about our book at meetings across the state, the ghosts of that generation stalked us like the spirits that haunted poor Macbeth. And many of those spirits embodied nasty physical bodies.

The theme I chose for my 2004 presidential year—racial change during the years between 1954 and 2004—might not have been obvious to the younger scholars present. But for those of us who had lived through those years, the walls of Babylon seemed still to vibrate from some great subterranean historical upheaval. How proud I was to be a partner in the shaking and a chronicler of the collapse.

To Go or Stay?

In a perfect world, academic mobility would rest on many accomplishments rather than one. Great universities would seek out skilled teachers and faculty accomplished at outreach as energetically as they do prolific scholar-writers. Alas, the world is not perfect. Until it becomes so, those who publish academic articles and books possess mobility; no one else does unless they are willing to leave the classroom for administration. And even those jobs usually require a substantial scholarly résumé.

Through the years, many schools invited me to apply. Committees for endowed chairs or university professorships at Samford, the University of Alabama, the University of Tennessee, the University of North Carolina–Charlotte, and elsewhere inquired. Perhaps because I hated the very thought of it, I seemed an even better prospect for administration. Over the years, I was nominated for dean at the University of Richmond, UAB, Auburn (three times), Mercer, and the University of North Alabama. Auburn offered the interim provost job and Samford the permanent provost slot.

Presidential search committees contacted me on behalf of several Baptist colleges, including Wayland Baptist University, Charleston (S.C.) Southern, and Mobile College. The most intriguing nomination came from trustee friends

James Head and Gerow Hodges at Samford after President Wright retired. As much as I loved the school, I knew my limitations of interest, skills, and temper.

I was not meant to be a university president. But I did use the nominations to express my philosophy of administration. I urged Samford trustees to shift emphasis from bricks and mortar to better care of its overworked and underpaid faculty. A new president should also be deeply committed to the denomination and institutional church; be able to relate to Samford's many constituencies; be able to communicate a vision of academic excellence; be self-confident enough to recruit strong administrators who would sometimes challenge his judgment; involve faculty in governance; decentralize administration; be fair to all divisions of the school; and be committed to academic freedom. Had I been interested in the job, I have a hunch that letter would have sealed my doom.

I may not have learned much during the nearly two decades since I had arrived at Samford as a first-year teacher. But I had learned who I was, what I wanted, and what I would not do. I would teach until I retired; lecture anywhere, anytime; research until archivists turned off the lights, write until long after my wife and sons were asleep. But I would not become a university president.

• eight •

Democratizing Learning

University Outreach

During the spring of 1925 George Petrie added a new chapter to his illustrious Auburn career. Although he had lectured in the community and state frequently after returning from Johns Hopkins, in the mid-1920s he introduced his current events course to a broader audience. He began writing columns for the *Montgomery Advertiser* and offering commentary on the state's first radio station, Auburn's WAPI.

In a sense, none of his endeavors better fit a land grant university. The Morrill Act established land grant colleges in order to take agricultural knowledge to ordinary Americans. In 1887 the Hatch Act mandated agricultural research as a central function of these institutions. Nearly three decades later, the Smith-Lever Act added agricultural extension to their mission. Extension and home demonstration agents created by these laws began to communicate new discoveries directly to farmers and their families. This venture was a phenomenal success. Petrie simply applied the extension idea to the humanities, making discussion of current events in a rich historical context accessible to nonstudents in nonclassroom settings and thereby endearing himself and Auburn to a new urban audience.

Petrie's democratic assumption about learning and his innovative use of new techniques to accomplish it matched my instincts perfectly. Previously engaged in outreach at Samford (which had begun its own groundbreaking ministerial extension program in the 1940s), Auburn offered me a much larger stage on which to develop these ideas.

Talking on the Rubber Chicken Circuit

My metamorphosis occurred in three stages. The first consisted of an uncoordinated avalanche of speeches. Looking back, I can superimpose thematic order on them, although it hardly occurred to me at the time. Topics that engaged my conscience, teaching, and writing—poverty, race, politics, tax and education reform, Alabama's 1901 Constitution, the state's economy, and culture (religion, music, folkways, literature)—dominated my presentations. That motivation partly explained why I so often overextended. I felt passionately about these issues, I loved the state, and I wanted it to change for the better.

Belief in so simple a rejuvenation owed much to confidence in my ability to persuade. All those debating victories, all that graduate study of rhetorical theory and persuasion left me with exaggerated confidence in the power of ideas and argument to overcome entrenched political and economic elites. If my ideas were superior to those of my opponents, if I prepared thoroughly for each speech, if I spoke simply, if I carefully organized my arguments so audiences could remember them, if I used emotionally riveting examples, if I rooted my remarks in the familiar parables and ethics found in the Bible, then I would certainly carry the day for my way of thinking, or so I thought. It took a long time for me to realize that all those thousands I addressed were mainly members of the choir. They came to hear largely because they already believed.

Nonetheless, for years I traveled the rubber-chicken circuit, speaking to Rotary, Civitan, Exchange, and Kiwanis clubs; to women's clubs, Junior Leagues, patriotic societies, churches, synagogues; at public schools, private schools, colleges, and universities; to business audiences, school superintendents, teachers; Planned Parenthood, state agencies, councils, and task forces; to Leadership Birmingham, Wiregrass, Montgomery, and Alabama. In time, these speeches began to cohere, as in a series I did for Vulcan Materials Corporation employees on southern culture or to various leadership seminars about the state's tortured economic and political past.

Public policy disputes often drove my speaking agenda. Between January and April 1992, as the equity funding lawsuit involving education moved through state courts and dominated press coverage, I spoke seventeen times about tax and education reform. During 2000, despite Wickham Henkel's scowling troll and the large NO! she wrote on the front of my schedule book, I spoke forty-two times, mainly about the dreadful 1901 Constitution that helped impoverish one-fifth of Alabama's population.

When not speaking, I sped across the state to board meetings: as chair of the Alabama Historical Commission; as member of the state Democratic Party's Leadership Council; as a founding member of the Alabama Poverty Project and Sowing Seeds of Hope in Perry County; as board member of A+ (the education reform coalition) and Voices for Alabama's Children. Beyond Alabama, I served for six years on the Mary Reynolds Babcock Foundation Board (in Winston-Salem, North Carolina), the region's largest antipoverty philanthropy. I was also a member of the American Cancer Society's Committee for the Socioeconomically Disadvantaged. Following Petrie's precedent, I wrote dozens of op-ed columns for newspapers on the same topics. I authored forty-two columns during the 1990s alone.

This scattergun assault deflected the message and exhausted the messenger. I sometimes found myself speaking in south Alabama in the morning and the Tennessee Valley in the evening. I drove an average of thirty thousand miles a year, mostly in Alabama. By purposefully and meticulously bundling speeches, I could do three or four at a time in a single section of the state. This whirlwind of activity had to be integrated into my class schedule and arranged around reading doctoral dissertations, conducting graduate exams, and adhering to my tedious writing schedule. Though I was still writing books, I wasn't able to read many—a fatal flaw for a scholar.

Looking back over the 1990s especially, I realize that exhaustion sometimes produced churlishness and a messianic complex. In April 1991 I wrote Natalie Davis, a political scientist at Birmingham-Southern College, reform activist, and friend: "I know that sentiment in the state is slowly changing, and I know that I need to continue to make these speeches. But they take so much out of me and put so many miles on my car and body. So—sooner or later—I am going to have to share this honor with some other folks. But in the meantime, I intend to fight every battle I can."

During an interview with a *Birmingham News* reporter, I explained my advocacy of tax, education, and welfare reform as part of my responsibility as a member of the faculty at a land grant university. I functioned like an extension agent for better government. But people like Natalie Davis and I needed help. I expressed frustration with many of my university colleagues: "Get off your butt and do something. Take research and scholarship out into the life of the state."

The Auburn University Center for the Humanities

When not feeling sorry for myself or lashing out at colleagues, I found better and more productive ways to work. Not long after arriving in Auburn, Dartie and I began participating in a religious discussion group. We shared a meal together, followed by animated conversation about new theological ideas and ethics, our various denominations, visions for Auburn University and the state. John and Missy Kuykendall participated in the group. John soon emerged as faculty leader in the Funderburk mess, but Missy labored in near anonymity in continuing education. Always on the lookout for some new initiative to sponsor, she suggested coordinated humanities outreach. Two other faculty—Jerry Elijah Brown (a witty raconteur and brilliant professor of journalism) and Bert Hitchcock (a self-effacing English professor with encyclopedic knowledge of Alabama literature)—may well have suggested the idea to Missy. She sent off a grant to the Alabama Humanities Foundation, and we launched what later came to be called the Auburn University Humanities Center (also named Pebble Hill for the antebellum home where the center was housed, and later the Draughon Center for the Humanities in honor of one of the university's legendary first ladies, Caroline Draughon).

Our first project was ambitious: weekend programs in Auburn/Opelika, Eufaula, Demopolis, and Anniston, involving half a dozen faculty and numerous local participants. The Alabama Cooperative Extension Service offered its network to help identify rural and small town community leaders interested in the humanities. My fellow churchman and friend Warren McCord, associate vice president for extension, had developed an expansive vision of his division. As Alabama farms declined from 232,000 in 1940 to barely 43,000 by the mid-1980s, Warren turned his program in the direction of community and economic development. That coincided with our vision of building pride and leadership in small town Alabama. In a state where two-thirds of the counties were losing population, something had to be done to reverse this migration before nonurban Alabama became a vast wasteland.

The five of us realized that each of the state's sixty-seven counties contained something rich and unique. Famous writers, entrepreneurs, journalists, teachers, ministers, iconoclastic women, elegant plantations, centuries-old churches, enduring black schools, flourishing Jewish communities, prominent Native Americans bequeathed us a legacy that needed to be remembered and affirmed. Our task was to tell their stories, attract an audience to listen, build a sense of pride in their accomplishments, and leave behind an infrastructure capable of sustaining the initiative. Though we relied on academic experts for the initial effort, we also invited local citizens to tell stories they knew best. We were determined to turn over site-planning to local community people so they would have a cadre of cultural leaders when we departed. This transferred to them a sense of ownership of what we called the Alabama History and Heritage Festival.

We were not disappointed. Talented, energetic local folks plumbed their networks to furnish venues, organizers, speakers, and memorable southern hospitality. The outside scholars did little more than turn up at the appointed hour to speak. One of our first and best decisions was to avoid the state's large cities (Huntsville, Birmingham, Montgomery, and Mobile), convinced that these places already experienced activity-fatigue from all the cultural opportunities available to them. Conversely, well-educated, broadly read people who lived in small towns often shriveled on sterile vines, bypassed by symphonies, live theater, or community discussions about literature, music, and art. For those living in such places, whose mental universe stretched beyond Friday night football and Wednesday night prayer meeting, life could be stultifying.

We began the festival in Auburn with a statewide conference attended by community leaders. To attract a crowd, we brought to campus two fine writers with Alabama connections, journalist/novelist Lee Smith (once a reporter in Tuscaloosa) and African American writer James Haskins (a native of Demopolis). Local communities used their own connections to attract similar keynoters: humorist John E. Kelly; novelist Harper Lee; Jewish historian Jacob Koch. They also told us which of our academic resource people they wanted to use and selected appropriate topics for them.

The meetings in Auburn/Opelika, Demopolis, Eufaula, and Anniston exceeded our expectations. Hundreds of enthusiastic people of all ages, colors, and ideologies showed up. Local planners described audiences as the largest ever assembled for a serious cultural gathering. The success of these initial efforts led to creation of the Humanities Center. In subsequent years, we extended the weekend festivals to Dothan, Greensboro, Camden, Fort Payne, and elsewhere. Hundreds of people multiplied into thousands and finally tens of thousands. We left behind networks that continued such activities independent of us or at least using us only as adjuncts. More importantly, the festivals mainstreamed the message of community accomplishment and pride, black and white, into public schools. Citizens crossed racial and religious boundaries. In Dothan, many white people met in a black church for the first time in order to discuss religion in the Wiregrass. In the same town, we focused on a Jewish family department store and an award-winning but nearly forgotten Dothan novelist.

With success came challenges. Our little circle was quickly overwhelmed by demands on our time, so we broadened our resource base. After one festival in a town, we needed new themes and approaches before we returned for an encore. When Missy and John left to lead Davidson College, we also needed a full-time director for the burgeoning humanities center. As a member of the search committee, I had a perfect candidate in mind if we could persuade her to return to Auburn. Leah Rawls Atkins, the Auburn history department's first Ph.D. and my former Samford colleague, possessed ideal qualifications for the job. Nurturing, winsome, friendly, a good conversationalist, a world-champion water-skier and member of the Alabama Sports Hall of Fame, she had the longest list of personal IOUs and acquaintances of anyone I knew. If she had not taught their children to water-ski, invited them to her lake house on Lake Martin or her family cabin on the Warrior River, or done them some other favor at considerable inconvenience to herself, she probably didn't know them well. Once she invited my Royal Ambassadors from Auburn's First Baptist Church to camp on a peninsula near her lake house. She spent one afternoon giving the boys a demonstration of gold prospecting at the nearby Devil's Backbone mines, then on Saturday morning gathered them to her house for a gargantuan breakfast she had cooked. I had to explain to the boys that this was not our typical "roughing it" wilderness backpacking adventure.

Leah, who directed Samford's London program at the time, struggled over the decision. But the allure of "sweet Auburn" proved compelling, and she and her family returned to the Loveliest Village, where husband George had been a star football player and coach. Between George and Leah, no one began with a larger Auburn network. And no one worked better with local community leaders than she.

Leah was both relentless and innovative. She crisscrossed the state adding layer upon layer to her network of friends and admirers. She wrote one successful National Endowment for the Humanities grant after another. Her Reading Alabama series used the original concept of community meetings, focusing on local writers often better known nationally than locally (Truman Capote, T. S. Stribling, Shirley Ann Grau, William Bradford Huie, Kathryn Tucker Windham, Mary Ward Brown, William March, Eugene Walter, Albert Murray). Realizing that community libraries constituted the ideal venue for literary discussions, she not only called attention to a town's most valuable cultural resource but also endeared herself to a generation of small town librarians.

Somewhere in America I am certain someone matched Leah for energy, insight, and inspiration. And I imagine some statewide humanities programming served small towns as successfully as she did. Perhaps such efforts were as carefully conceived and thought-through as Auburn's. But so far as I know, the center's combination of programs, networks, scholarly alliances with local experts, and broad community participation were unrivaled. I know that Leah, Bert, Jerry, and Jay Lamar, Leah's successor, constituted one factor in my decision to remain at Auburn.

My own contribution to outreach probably received more recognition than it deserved because others were due most of the credit for our success. Nevertheless, in 1989, I received a University Extension Certificate of Merit. That same year, the Alabama Humanities Foundation (AHF) asked me to write a piece to celebrate its fifteenth anniversary, centering on the work of AHF in strengthening community life through public programming. Despite a variety of deadlines, I agreed. "Habits of the Heart in the Heart of Dixie" was my attempt to place AHF's outreach effort into broad social context.

Rural and small town migration patterns, urban complexity, and the atomization of American life threatened venerable traditions of community life. Books as divergent as *The Different Drum: Community Making and Peace* by psychiatrist M. Scott Peck and *Habits of the Heart: Individualism and Community in American Life* by Robert N. Bellah and others had placed the issue front and center on the nation's agenda.

The age of air conditioners, the disappearance of front porches, the decline of church revivals, and the vanishing court and market days were locking us into progressively smaller cubicles, rooms, offices, and other stifling spaces, largely away from one another. Folks no longer learned so easily about the needs of others. Modern society might produce less small town gossip and petty intrigue. But it most certainly contained less neighborliness and willingness to be bothered by someone else's troubles. This pulling away from community, this decreasing ability to connect meaningfully, to share important common symbols, had fractured and weakened social relationships and communal identity.

Rebuilding a sense of community is no easy matter. It first requires explaining what it means to be human. Such definitions emerge from religion, philosophy, literature, music, art, drama, speech, and history. This public re-definition requires that practitioners of the humanities occasionally take leave of their classrooms, where many of their seeds fall on the hard, sterile ground of career-building and degree-chasing anyway (or sometimes on adolescents not even that serious). We have to engage the community of adults who do not take our importance for granted. The larger community is not so much hostile to us as it is preoccupied with more urgent concerns: earning a living; nurturing families; preserving neighborhoods; coping with divorce, sickness, and death. Ordinary people do not perceive that humanists (a term they generally don't understand anyway) have much to contribute to their prosaic comings and goings, their quality of life, or the stability of the places where they live. Nor do we make much effort to persuade them of our relevance. Our efforts in AHF, Auburn's History and Heritage Festivals, Reading Alabama, and other Humanities Center programs had been but halting first steps at opening that dialogue.

Assessing Outreach

Having learned to perform outreach, we now had to measure its effectiveness. What criteria to use? Count how many people attend each activity? Monitor local follow-up programs? See if patronage increased at the library? Measure outmigration patterns to determine if fewer young people left for cities? How to evaluate the role of academic experts, assess their success at public programming, reward them for outreach posed even trickier problems. Resolving these issues became essential to recruiting a broader base of scholars and sustaining the undertaking.

Luckily, by the 1990s universities as diverse as Cornell, Oregon State, Washington, Florida, and Michigan State were well established in both outreach and assessment. Ernest L. Boyer of the Carnegie Foundation had published groundbreaking research on the subject. Though not a pioneer in the field, Auburn trailed not far behind the leaders. President Bill Muse and Vice President for Outreach David Wilson provided institutional momentum. Muse and his wife, Marlene, developed both deep affection for the state and an intense interest in solving its problems. Coming from poor and working-class families themselves, they empathized with those who would never have the opportunity to earn a degree from Auburn. David Wilson traced his origins to that same segment of Alabama society. An African American who had grown up in

the Black Belt in a modest house without running water, he had earned degrees
from several of America's finest universities. Taking learning to the people of
the Black Belt ranked high on his extension agenda.

Wilson appointed two outreach committees. Dean of liberal arts and political scientist John G. Heilman chaired the Outreach Strategic Planning Committee. Wilson asked me to chair the Committee on Assessment, probably because of my success in teaching and writing. If I endorsed a tripartite emphasis
on teaching, scholarship, and outreach, at least no one could accuse me of seeking rewards for outreach because I could not otherwise obtain them. By then
I was already a Distinguished University Professor, Auburn's highest designation alongside professors holding endowed chairs.

I had a wonderful committee of well-respected faculty (including Bert
Hitchcock) who bought into the process with high levels of energy and intel-
lect. We agreed that every university department, school, and college should
engage in structured outreach. As part of the annual negotiation of faculty assignments, the administrative director, chair, or head should explicitly define
outreach as part of his or her responsibility. Outreach did not equate to traditional categories of "extension" or "service," neither of which was well defined
or rewarded. Service had come to be viewed as an amorphous life as a responsible person: coaching youth athletic teams; church responsibilities; civic en-
gagements; and general good citizenship. Everyone qualified, so no one received credit. Not all faculty possess outreach skills, so not everyone should be
expected to become involved in it. But every unit should engage. If unequipped
for outreach at the time, the unit should recruit faculty with a clear capacity
for it.

Our definition of effective outreach consisted of six conditions:
1. establishing a substantive link between outreach and significant human needs;
2. applying faculty knowledge to these problems;
3. trying to improve the common welfare of the state's population;
4. ensuring the use of faculty expertise by the targeted audience;
5. generating new knowledge for the audiences and for the scholar's discipline; and
6. demonstrating an obvious link to the unit's mission within the university.

The committee provided sample grids describing types of scholarship, audiences, means of communication, criteria for validating success, and documentation schemes. We also provided guidelines for outreach portfolios to be used

DEMOCRATIZING LEARNING 207

in tenure and promotion decisions, as well as sample evaluation procedures for various units of the university. We particularly emphasized that successful outreach must be demonstrable both from the perspective of the audience and the scholar.

A skeptical faculty senate hotly debated our report. Faculty socialized in traditional academic systems clearly understood the criteria for scholarship: publish books and articles in professional journals; become recognized as a national or international authority; receive invitations to lecture before audiences of experts throughout the world; serve on task-forces and think tanks for one's area of expertise. Teaching expertise was more conflicted turf, raising issues about the credibility of student evaluations. But since the 1960s, faculty had grudgingly consented even to that "intrusive" measure. Assessment of outreach for purposes of tenure and promotion on a basis equal to the other two standards required serious rethinking of professional protocol.

After many months of senate debate, John Heilman (then university provost) asked if I would explain the committee's rationale of outreach assessment within the wider context of evaluating faculty performance. Knowing the source of most faculty opposition and the intricacies of tenure and promotion procedures, I focused instead on the democratic assumptions of public learning and pragmatic self-interest.

In a chronically underfunded state—where tax revenues were insufficient for K–12 schools, prisons, highways, Medicaid, public health, state parks, and other state services, and where only a small fraction of the population attended college—the public could quickly conclude that except for Auburn and Alabama football games, nothing of consequence to them occurred on campus. With so many worthy competing interests vying for resources, universities were constantly in danger of budget cuts. Put another way, outreach becomes the public face of universities, an important intersection where faculty and the noncollege population meet. A university disengaged from meaningful public outreach is a university in jeopardy. University outreach is worthy because it engages the enormous expertise of a public institution in order to solve urgent public problems. But if altruism and commitment to public service do not suffice to mobilize faculty, then self-interest should. In this public intersection, faculty can interact with ordinary Baptists, Methodists, Pentecostals, hairdressers, salesmen, clerks, librarians, schoolteachers, lawyers, stay-at-home moms, and business people. This interaction is good for the people. It is equally good for faculty by letting them meet the folks who pay part of their salaries.

That being the case, our assessment strategy had the benefit of connecting outreach to specific training, interest, and research, requiring carefully thought-out strategies and measurement of results, and encouraging publication of findings in appropriate professional journals. We did not propose that all faculty engage in outreach. But we did create a rational system for rewarding those who did.

The senate reacted with grudging acceptance. They adopted our report and launched the modern outreach era at Auburn. Subsequently, I took the same message to various academic units, including new faculty orientation. I suppose I was asked to speak so often because John Heilman and I had spent more time at conferences on university outreach and assessment than any other faculty and more time in spirited debates over how it could be implemented.

The time and energy I devoted to university outreach was a small gift to Auburn but a much larger one to the state. Although the concept did not originate with me or Auburn, we did become a national leader. Other Alabama universities soon launched their own initiatives, which increased the impact statewide.

During the 1990s, taking education to the people came to mean more at Auburn University than agricultural extension. At the same time, it mainstreamed extension employees into the broader academic culture instead of assigning them second-class status. And for me, it was the fulfillment of George Petrie's holistic vision of a people's university. Nowhere else in Alabama did the humanities play so central a role in outreach. That this initiative originated in Auburn humanities departments, which some of our trustees so thoroughly detested, was a delicious irony.

• nine •

"The Lord Is the Maker of Them All"

Black, White, and Poor in America

In the kingdom of God, either everyone is ordinary in the beginning or everyone is special, depending on how you look at it. After that, what we make of ourselves is pretty much up to us. But some people must cross higher hurdles than others. Two of the highest barriers in America are blackness and poverty. After five decades pondering which is the higher hurdle, I can't decide.

As with so many other dimensions of my evolving social consciousness, concern for the poor began by reading the Bible. In Hebrew scripture, responsibility for the poor, the oppressed, widows, orphans, the sick, imprisoned, and strangers in the land composed the second most frequently mentioned theme, behind only admonitions against idolatry: "do what is just and right!" (Jeremiah 22:3); "rich and poor have this in common: The Lord is the Maker of them all" (Proverbs 22:2); "the wretched and the poor look for water and find none . . . ; but I the Lord will give them an answer, I, the God of Israel, will not forsake them" (Isaiah 41:17). The New Testament devotes one of every sixteen verses to the same subject; the Gospels, one in ten, and Luke, one in seven; the epistle of James one in five. Jesus, in fact, taught in Matthew 25:31–46 that every believer's eternal fate depended not on *what* he believed but on *how* what he believed caused him to respond to the needs of the poor.

Some passages of scripture especially spoke to me. Perhaps because of my debate and persuasive speaking experience, one passage from Proverbs 31:8–9 haunted me: "Speak up for those who cannot speak for themselves, for the rights of all who are destitute. Speak up and judge fairly; defend the rights of the poor and needy." I returned to that passage again and again during half a century of advocating justice for the poor, as if the author of it were providing instructions for me personally.

Theology was no less an inspiration. Ideals of social justice, especially on issues of race and poverty, permeated the Howard College religion department, tempered only by the reality of white Alabama Baptist resistance to them. Though most Southern Baptists were one with their racial culture, many slipped beyond the boundaries of that society. As I read T. B. Maston's *The Bible and Race,* Will D. Campbell's *Race and the Renewal of the Church* and *Brother to a Dragonfly,* Clarence Jordan's *Cotton Patch Gospel,* I could almost feel my own racial culture loosening its grip.

Harry Emerson Fosdick, Baptist pastor of Riverside Church in New York City, anticipated my own experiences in his memoir *The Living of These Days.* Engagement with the poor and commitment to justice, he wrote, is not so much the way we live out the commands of the Bible as it is the place where we encounter God. Where the poor live is the natural habitat of God, the soiled and smelly garden where God walks in the evening to find his people and what is being done to and for them. This terrain is where we discover God at the margins of life, God of the outcasts, the poor, lame, blind, lepers, immigrants, orphans, widows.

My encounters with Baptists such as Charlie Bell, Charles Dobbins, and Will Campbell deepened my convictions and toughened my spine. Social justice for the poor permeated Bell's career. Dobbins—the son of a prophetic Alabama Baptist preacher and himself a reform journalist—wrote me in 1981, describing his lifelong struggle for racial harmony and social justice. I admired Campbell's heroic commitment to social justice during the darkest of times.

As I became more ecumenical in both sentiment and reading, I discovered a wider range of prophetic Christians. James A. Cogswell's 1975 anthology *The Church and the Rural Poor* brought together essays by some of the best Christian ethicists. Dutch theologian Conrad Boerma (*The Rich, The Poor—and the Bible*) grounded his biblicism in the concepts of the human family's solidarity, the worth of every person in the kingdom of God, and the biblical preoccupation with justice and righteousness. Jim Wallis, founder of *Sojourner* magazine and author of *The Soul of Politics,* connected the Christian imperative for justice to America's political culture. An anonymous member of the Sisters of Charity in Mexico further expanded my social understanding of poverty. She wrote simply that if "we don't help the few because we can't solve the problems of the many, will we help anyone?" When my frustrations with the size of my resources and the extent and intractability of poverty wore me down, I took comfort in her wisdom.

Beyond the reading, family and friends left their mark as well. My cousin Claude Duncan introduced me to the Children's Defense Fund, whose founder, black Baptist Marion Wright Edelman, set sail on a difficult political journey with a motto applicable to poor children everywhere: "Dear Lord be good to me. The sea is so wide and my boat is so small." Another cousin, social worker Shirley Thames, doggedly fought the good fight for justice in Alabama and introduced me to her circle of dedicated progressives. Two African American friends, Odessa Woolfolk and Sandral Hullett, educated me about the poor black community and especially their lack of health care.

Historian C. Vann Woodward influenced my understanding of poverty as a central theme of southern history. During his childhood and youth in Arkansas, Woodward imbibed a sense of righteousness from his Methodist parents, church, and college, which caused him to speak out on behalf of blacks and the poor not only in his historical writing but also in his personal conduct. Though more disenchanted with institutional religion than I was, he also drank deeply from the well of neoorthodox theology, which shaped his seminal book *The Burden of Southern History.* He described the burden of the southern past as slavery, racism, segregation, tenancy, sharecropping, exploitation of industrial workers, and endemic poverty. Though I doubt that Woodward knew Ecclesiastes 3:15–16 or remembered the passage when writing *Burden,* I thought the two verses pretty well summarized his book and indeed his entire writing career about the South: "Whatever is has already been, and what will be has been before; and God will call the past into account."

One final circle of influences moved me inexorably toward activism. Philosophy can be the enemy of social and political engagement or its inspiration. Occupying space in a speculative, meditative, reflective sphere that calls on us to examine our interior worlds and motives can hold us aloof from public confrontations. How can any cause be so simple, so clear-cut, so morally compelling as to summon us from library, classroom, or seminar to the barricades? Yet from Solon, the teacher of Socrates, to Marxist philosopher Herbert Marcuse, the summons has come. Solon expressed philosophy's charge to his student this way: "When does the ideal community exist? The ideal community exists when those who have not been injured are as indignant as those who have." William Faulkner put the matter even more simply in his novel *Intruder in the Dust:* "Some things you must always be unable to bear. Some things you must never stop refusing to bear. Injustice and outrage and dishonor and shame. No matter how young you are or how old you have got. Not for kudos and not for cash: Your picture in the paper nor money in the bank either. Just refuse to bear them." I simply refused to bear the reality that nearly one-quarter of Alabama's children and one-fifth of its people were meant to live in poverty.

Racism's Legacy

Christmastime 1992 arrived for Dartie and me in London, where we had traveled for theater, antiquarian bookstores, museums, musical concerts, Oxfam charity thrift stores, evensong, and other favorite English activities. A faculty friend at Daniel House, Samford University's London Centre, told me a story that Christmas about the priest at nearby Saint Luke's Church, where Samford students and their visiting parents sometimes attended Anglican services. While attending a party at Daniel House, the priest had asked my friend to explain a recent incident at his church. An American working in the city had become a faithful member of Saint Luke's. After some years in England, she prepared to return to the United States. At her final service, he acknowledged her active participation but incorrectly identified her as an Alabamian returning home. The woman was visibly offended and corrected the misinformation. She was *NOT* from Alabama and was *NOT* returning to live in that state. Why, the priest asked my friend, would an American be so offended by being identified with such wonderful people?

I spent half a century trying to answer that question. The simple answer is that Alabama's image is not the best thing going for it. Like nearly all mythology, the woman's perception of the state was rooted in hard historical evidence. In fact, she could have been thinking of Anniston, my hometown. When the first Greyhound bus carrying Freedom Riders rolled into the city's terminal on Mother's Day 1961, Kenneth Adams (a local gas station owner, Ku Klux Klansman, and the man who had attacked Alabama native Nat King Cole at Birmingham's Municipal Auditorium in 1956) led a mob of two hundred white thugs, swinging steel chains, iron rods, and clubs. So sure were they of support from fellow citizens that they did not even bother masking their faces. They tried to board the bus, shouting, "This is Alabama, you black bastards, come on out and integrate." When a courageous lawman on the bus blocked their way, the mob smashed windows and slashed tires. The driver finally drove away but made it only six miles before the tires went flat. A convoy of fifty cars following the crippled bus disgorged its occupants, who set about finishing their work. They threw a firebomb through a broken window, filling the bus with acrid smoke and forcing passengers into the arms of their tormentors. The beatings might have turned to murders had not state troopers intervened. Hours later a second busload of Freedom Riders fared no better.

Perhaps the woman at Saint Luke's Church had heard of my hometown, but she had certainly not heard about Parker Memorial pastors B. Locke Davis and Charlie Bell. Nor about black ministers N. Q. Reynolds, a Baptist, and his friend William B. McClain, a Methodist, who approached their white ministerial counterparts the following year to begin a racial dialogue. I doubt she knew about courageous white Presbyterian minister Phillips Noble or about Miller Sproull, a businessman and a member of First Presbyterian Church, down the hill from where I lived. Sproull would soon be elected a city commissioner. After white terrorists fired into black homes on Mother's Day Sunday 1963 (to celebrate the second anniversary of the attacks on Freedom Riders?), Noble and Sproull established a nine-person interracial commission. Negotiations began to desegregate department store restrooms and the library.

On a hot summer Sunday in 1963, the same day as the murders at the Sixteenth Street Baptist Church in Birmingham, Reynolds and McClain became the first black patrons to check out books from Carnegie Library, the source of so many happy memories for me. The library would not supply pleasant memories for them. A mob of Klansmen descended on them, beating Reynolds and McClain with clubs and chains and severely injuring Reverend Reynolds. The next day, Phillips Noble, his parishioner Miller Sproull, McClain, and a small group of blacks returned to the library.

My lawyer friend Charles Doster, who headed the library board, vowed to Reverend Reynolds that he would not turn Carnegie Library over to a mob. He recruited a small army of police to accompany Reynolds and McClain on their next visit, for which they all received death threats. Doster began speaking to civic clubs, churches, and any other group that would listen about the need for racial change.

Charles virtually camped in the library in order to keep white toughs out. On one occasion, he personally booted out a scruffy-looking older man who had no library card. The deeply offended patron turned out to be a retired army general from nearby Fort McClellan. He angrily told Doster that he had been kicked out of brothels, taverns, and bars around the world but this was the "first time I have ever been kicked out of a damned library."

William Faulkner wrote in *Requiem for a Nun* that "the South . . . was already whirling into the plunge of its precipice, not that . . . the South knew it, because the first seconds of fall always seem like soar: a weightless deliberation preliminary to a rush not downward but upward." Although Faulkner placed the scene in April 1861, it could just as easily have described events in my hometown a century later.

Race relations in Alabama had changed by the time I arrived at Auburn in 1977. Blacks not only voted, they elected a substantial minority to the state legislature. One of my black colleagues in the history department, Robert Reid, and his wife, Irene, became two of our closest friends.

Nor were the issues as simple to me as they had been in the early 1960s. Within months of my arrival in Auburn, the university's first African American student, who had been a master's candidate in our department, told a reporter for the campus newspaper that he had quit Auburn fifteen years earlier because "graduate school professors were not grading his thesis with the same objectivity they used in grading the theses of . . . white peers." I greatly respected his major professor, Edward Williamson—a native Pennsylvanian, Ph.D. from the University of Florida, longtime member of the liberal Alabama Council on Human Relations, fierce opponent of segregation, and allegedly a man who had become the subject of a thick file compiled by George Wallace's Alabama Sovereignty Commission. Ed's analysis of the situation was quite different from the student's. Unprepared for graduate school, he had been unable to cope with Ed's demanding standards.

As department head, my job was to defend my department and explain the situation publicly, based on my understanding of the facts. While praising the student's courage, I offered alternative explanations for his withdrawal: hostility from people who resented his presence on campus; the human inclination of students to rationalize their academic problems (i.e., I am floundering because: the professor dislikes me; the course is boring and unnecessary; my high school background is inadequate; the professor discriminates against blacks, women, athletes, nonathletes, males shorter than 5 feet 11 inches; your own favorite rationalization.)

This was the first of many painful incidents involving race at Auburn. Standards for graduate work often eliminated white students. It was inevitable that standards fairly applied would eliminate some black students as well. Years later, a black student in my Southern History class began to arrive well after I had started lecturing, when he came at all. He opened and closed the door loudly, paraded across the front of the room before taking a seat in the back. After several weeks of his discourteous and disruptive behavior, I asked him to remain after class.

I told him that I understood that he did not like me or the class, but I had no idea why. He explained that one day when he arrived (late) for class, he (the only black student in the class) heard me utter the "n" word. I explained that the lecture he referred to involved the racist political rhetoric of disfranchisement and lynching in the early twentieth century. In order to illustrate the origins of racial exclusion and violence against blacks, I had quoted a series of particularly vile passages from speeches by James K. Vandaman, Tom Heflin, Cole Blease, and "Cotton Ed" Smith, all white demagogues who justified apartheid and lynching. Although most students found the language as offensive as he did, I explained to them what it must have been like for African Americans to hear such words, or be warned by parents about what could happen to "sassy" blacks who "talked back" to powerful whites. How could white students understand black resentment and resistance without hearing the vulgarity and depersonalization of racist rhetoric, I asked him.

That began a conversation that continued for some time. There is more than enough to dislike about Alabama whites without doing to me what they do to you, I told him. Don't judge me until you know me. And if you want to know the context for what happens in class, attend regularly and arrive on time. Furthermore, here are some details of my life and attitudes on race which you need to know. He shared with me some equally frank examples of blatant racism that he had encountered at Auburn. With the tension now drained from our relationship, he attended class regularly and hardly ever arrived late. We got along fine; he scored well on exams and earned a decent grade in the course.

One other incident demonstrates the capacity to misunderstand reality based on separate pasts, limited knowledge, and mutual misperceptions. One day as I left a class on the second floor of Haley Center with a gaggle of graduate students in tow, we continued the discussion onto the crowded elevator. In the New South class, I had been discussing their reading, which differentiated between the first (1860s, 1870s), second (1920s), and third (post-1954) Ku Klux Klans (one of my doctoral students later disputed this too-easy periodization in a fine book). I had brought to class that day a 1920s application form for the women's auxiliary of the KKK. As our discussion continued on the elevator, I explained to the students that the application had more to do with 100 percent Americanism and conservative Christian values than racism. "Here is the application form," I said. "See for yourself."

The elevator door opened on the third floor and most undergraduates departed. My graduate students and I continued our journey to the seventh floor. The following week, one of the students appeared in my office to ask if I had read the day's *Plainsman*. "I think you should read this editorial." As I read, I didn't know whether to laugh or cry. The *Plainsman* writer, obviously an earnest young white woman with laudable intentions, explained how upset she had become while listening to a white professor on a Haley Center elevator recruit Auburn students for the Klan by denying it was racist and portraying it as a harmless, patriotic, Christian organization. My bemused graduate students chortled when I identified myself in the next issue of the *Plainsman* as the culprit in the story and described the context and historical meaning of the conversation (as well as the moral: don't jump to conclusions from fragmented conversations you overhear on elevators involving strangers you don't know). The point of these three stories is the limitless capacity for confusion, misunderstanding, and misassumptions involving any contentious subject, especially race.

All this—the conflicted black-white culture of Anniston; the potential for racial confusion based on conflicting stereotypes; the social pressures to conform to whiteness and blackness—make intelligent engagement with issues of race one of the most complex issues in American life. We hold our breaths in every conversation about race, afraid someone will misunderstand, attribute unkind motives to us, or be offended by what we say. There is no subject in America where we are more guarded, where we engage more in circumlocution or clarification ("Of course I never believed that myself, but. . . .").

My racial education began abstractly in adolescence and progressed through personal experiences during the 1960s and 1970s. Though not a civil rights historian, I had become a civil rights activist. I had wonderful tutors: Robert Reid in our department; my friend John Hope Franklin, dean of African American historians; C. Eric Lincoln, an acquaintance from the Tennessee Valley who taught religion at Duke. All three told stories of violence, insults, and discrimination. No decent white southerner could listen to them or read their stories without shame and embarrassment that we had allowed such a society to persist for so long.

Yet in all three cases, their memoirs were kind, generous, and largely without bitterness. Despite a severe beating as a boy administered by the adult white owner of a cotton gin, Lincoln wrote that he never met a fisherman, white or black, on the Tennessee River who wasn't kind to him: "And these relationships never get talked about. . . . The South that is going to matter is the South where people feel for each other."

C. Vann Woodward understood Lincoln's meaning. While participating in the Selma to Montgomery march, he watched angry, working-class, "redneck whites" standing by the road, hate glaring in their eyes. Woodward explained that he saw part of himself in their faces, as well, wanted to be different from them but not so different that he was no longer one of them. I knew exactly what he meant because of racial disagreements within my own family. I had concluded, along with Woodward, that as important as court decisions and civil rights legislation were, the ultimate divisions that separated races were barriers of the heart and could be surmounted only by people like Reid, Franklin, and Lincoln, who laid their justifiable bitterness down as a burden too heavy to bear.

Insight arrives from many directions in real life. When Donna and Virgil Starks joined my Sunday school class in 1999, they precipitated a new phase of my racial consciousness. Virgil hailed from an extended black family in the Tennessee Valley. He attended prestigious Rhodes College in Memphis, where he played football. Tragedy befell Virgil's family when his father died in his forties of a heart attack and his mother died in a wreck on the way to his graduation.

Virgil entered athletic administration after college, serving at the University of Akron, where he met and married Donna, a white Spanish teacher, and became a friend of Bill and Marlene Muse. After Bill became president of Auburn, he brought Virgil to the university as academic athletic adviser. Virgil rapidly ascended the administrative ladder to become associate athletic director for academics. Their three beautiful, bright daughters—Carolyn, Victoria, and Anastasia (Ana)—became our surrogate daughters. Their extended families of parents, godparents, biracial couples, white-black, black-white, black-black, white-white, gradually drove the constructions of race out of my consciousness, leaving behind only friendship, mutual respect, and love. We shared meals, birthdays, holidays, university committees, church, and other common identities. I baptized Victoria and sat with her parents at Children's Hospital while she awaited surgery. Donna took my Southern History class, flinching and silently weeping the day I showed photos of lynchings, punctuated by the haunting voice of Billie Holliday singing "Strange Fruit," a riveting ballad about white violence. Donna explained that she had been afraid to move to Auburn but fell in love with our church when they attended the first time and read a large sign that reversed one word and the meaning of a timeless racist warning. "We reserve the right to accept anyone!"

Virgil and I talked about white racial stereotypes of African American athletes, about white coaches who exploited black players without concern for the fact that most would never make professional teams and must acquire lifetime competency in something other than sport while in college. We talked politics and parenting, dreamed about where the girls would attend college, and speculated about how different their futures would be from the racially separate worlds in which we had grown up.

During an October 2008 visit to Seattle, I answered the phone and learned that Virgil had died suddenly of a heart attack after representing a senior black football player's family during Auburn's homecoming game because the young man had no relative to stand beside him. It was Virgil's final act of generosity in a life filled with such acts. One of the hardest moments of my life followed, standing in the pulpit of First Baptist Church and delivering a eulogy before Donna, the children, and a standing-room only sanctuary packed with equal numbers of blacks and whites. Huge black football players sat next to svelte Scandinavian swimmers, most too young to measure fully the mortality that levels the playing field for all and makes us part of a common humanity.

Social Change in America

During my lifetime, racial barriers fell at a speed I would not have considered possible in 1954. From the 1940s to the end of the 1990s, the number of black lawyers, editors, and reporters in the United States increased eighteen times, the number of black engineers thirty-three times. No black had led a major American city in 1949 and only two served in Congress. By 1995, nearly every major U.S. city had elected at least one black mayor, and more than forty African Americans held congressional seats. In 1960 fewer than 390,000 black men and women professionals or semiprofessionals held jobs in America; by 1980, there were more than 1.4 million. During the same two decades, the number of black sales and clerical workers soared from less than 400,000 to 2 million. By 1995, 7 million blacks worked in middle-class occupations.

In 2008, a moment of political epiphany for me, I cast two votes for Barack Obama. The first came in a decisive Democratic primary in which the state's black political maestro, Joe Reed, and the civil rights–era conference he founded endorsed Hillary Clinton. Obama won handily, an indication that Alabama's black voters no longer let white or black bosses tell them what to do. Obama's overwhelming general election defeat in the Deep South, especially in the traditionally white Democratic Appalachian foothills and Tennessee Valley (where John McCain's vote actually increased over George W. Bush's), demonstrated that race remained the central feature of Alabama politics. But for me, Obama's victory nationally was the vindication of American democracy and my lifetime's work. Where else in the world had voters elected a leader from a racial minority of only 12 percent, whose parents represented a biracial marriage, and whose father came from an unfamiliar and, for many Americans, reviled religion? Perhaps this tonic was too much for the Southland to stomach in one political dose, but at least three former Confederate states drank it straight down. Obviously we didn't do as effective a job of persuading fellow Alabama whites to our view. Only 10 percent of them voted for Obama in the general election. For many of them, race was not the central issue. For many others, it was.

Poverty in Black and White

Although my books concentrated on white poverty, my speeches emphasized black deprivation as well. As cofounder of the Alabama Poverty Project and Sowing Seeds of Hope, I focused more and more on the racial dimensions of the problem. In the 2000 census, 326,000 Alabama whites lived in poverty compared to 346,000 blacks. Those figures represented 11 percent of whites but 31 percent of blacks. Statewide in 2000, more than 16 percent of the state's population lived in poverty, a rate one-fifth higher than the national average.

This historic pattern had everything to do with race. After 1832 Alabama law prohibited anyone from teaching a black person to read or write. The state built no schools for them, dispatched no teachers in their direction. Following a brief Reconstruction season of hope, when taxes for education soared and black schools sprang up in the cotton fields to supply learning for eager children, the 1875 Alabama Constitution capped property taxes and sent public education into a downward spiral. The racist 1901 Constitution finished off what the 1875 document had begun. It froze property tax rates at ridiculously low levels in order to protect the wealth of planters and industrialists. This Bourbon regime preached a new gospel of economic development. It consisted of a familiar litany of class and race: recruit low wage, low skill, extractive industry; keep taxes low; contain or destroy attempts at unionism, whether by poor farmers or industrial workers; mobilize white elites and white working classes under the banner of white supremacy, thus assuring that every political conflict would be resolved by a white coalition based on caste rather than class. The details sometimes get complicated, but that's all a person really needs to know in order to understand the broad contours of Alabama politics between 1875 and 2010.

It also explains a painful pattern of quality-of-life problems the state faced as it limped into the twenty-first century.

Health: overall, 47th among the states; diabetes, 49th; high blood pressure, 49th; obesity, 49th; infant mortality, 48th; premature death, 48th; heart disease, 46th; stroke, 43rd; smoking, 42nd; cancer, 42nd

Income: $6,000 per person below the U.S. average

Economy: loss of tens of thousands of manufacturing jobs, especially in textiles; ranked 46th on the New Economy Index of high tech companies with highly educated white-collar employees

Education: ranked 47th in the percentage of people older than twenty-five with a high school diploma; low scores on the National Association of Education Progress tests; rated 48th in U.S. Chamber of Commerce ranking of educational performance; only 4 percent of four-year-olds enrolled in state-funded early childhood programs; less than half the national average of students who both enroll in and pass advanced placement high school courses

Taxes: ranked 50th of 50 states in total tax effort; property taxes by far the lowest in the nation

I doubt all this would be so if the population of Alabama had been like that of Iowa or Utah, homogeneously white. It is easier to care about people your own color. That race is the central nerve running through all aspects of Alabama life never occurred to me in 1960. By 2010 nothing else explained so well the state's conflicted history.

I thought often about the relationship between color and deprivation while lecturing about American poverty in India during 1995. When describing the decline of American agriculture and rural life in the 1930s and 1940s, the effects of technological change on the displacement of coal miners, textile and steel workers in the 1940s-1960s, and the postwar migration of poor blacks and whites to midwestern industrial states and California (which nationalized the problems of southern poverty), I constantly talked about race. Whites left for better jobs. Blacks left for better jobs and to escape American apartheid. I emphasized these issues in an interview with the publisher of *India Express*, an English language newspaper in Madras. Back in the states, I focused on the same themes in interviews with Paul Greenberg (*Arkansas Gazette*), Howell Raines (*New York Times*), a reporter for the *Washington Post,* and syndicated columnist Rheta Grimsley Johnson.

Dalit leaders (Dalits are the lower caste that Americans know as "untouchables") told me that color and caste mattered as much in India as in America. The darker the skin, the more likely the poverty. In meetings with the National Commission on Minorities in Delhi, I was amazed at how quickly a generic conversation about poverty morphed into a discussion of affirmative action.

The government reserved slots in colleges for minorities, shutting out gifted children from upper-class Brahman families. This policy resulted in brain-drain as some of the brightest students from wealthy families were forced to attend university in the UK or the United States. Often they did not return to India. Similar debates erupted among students and faculty at the Institute of Public Administration in Lucknow, a seething cauldron of ethnic and religious tension in a city divided between Hindus and Muslims. We were warned not to venture into the streets during Muslim Ramadan parades for fear of violence. We felt right at home. Just like downtown Birmingham during the 1960s.

The 1990 Legislative Prayer Luncheon

Earl Potts, executive secretary of the Alabama Baptist State Convention, read *Poor but Proud* when it first appeared in 1989. As the senior statesman of white Alabama Baptists and a friend of my father-in-law, the Rev. W. Albert Smith, Potts had come from a similarly poor background. Like Dr. Smith, Potts carried a keen moral sensitivity from his childhood. Kind, gentle, and possessed of a sense of personal decency and social justice, he hired a woman as assistant administrator of the state denomination. His daughter, Libby, became one of the firmest advocates of Baptist women in ministry. His son, David (my former handball opponent from Samford days), became president of Baptist-affiliated Judson College in Perry County, served as chair of the Alabama Poverty Project, and was a key figure in Sowing Seeds of Hope. This antipoverty initiative in Perry County became the template for the moderate Cooperative Baptist Fellowship effort to address poverty throughout the South. With so many familial connections and similar views about biblical justice, I could hardly refuse Earl's request that I speak at the Alabama Legislative Prayer Luncheon in Montgomery on February 10, 1990. I reasoned that following publication of *Poor but Proud* the luncheon afforded a perfect opportunity to insert my research and biblical perspective on poverty into public policy.

Not long before I spoke, Dr. Potts reminded me that Governor Guy Hunt, a bivocational Primitive Baptist preacher himself, was entering a hotly contested reelection campaign. He would be present, as would numerous legislators, supreme court justices, members of Hunt's cabinet, and other state officials. Though Potts imposed no restrictions on my remarks (he knew me too well to do that), he did seem concerned that I might overreach in my remarks or even appear to be partisan. Partisanship certainly did not fit the occasion because Hunt was the first Republican governor elected since Reconstruction, and Democrats had controlled both legislative houses for more than a century. Whatever blame I might heap on politicians for the sorry state of Alabama would be directed mainly at Democrats. On the other hand, Earl had furnished a platform where I could speak prophetically to power, and the speech would be widely reported by the press.

I chose a passage from the prophet Amos as a title: "Let justice roll down like waters." Putting aside my academic role for the Baptist preacher I still claimed to be, I read a text from Isaiah 41:17: "The wretched and the poor look for water and find none . . . ; but I the Lord will give them an answer, I, the God of Israel, will not forsake them." Following that scripture, I slipped back into my historian persona, summarizing Alabama's woes and devoting particular attention to the three-quarters of a million people who lived in poverty. A poor two-parent family of four began paying state taxes when their income reached $4,600 a year, the lowest threshold in America and $8,200 below the federal poverty line. Medicaid eligibility of $1,600 a year meant that even people with part-time jobs were ineligible for health insurance.

How did Alabama arrive at this sorry state? Who was responsible? I answered my own questions as tactfully as I could: "Those of you who make our laws and construct the edifice that will be the Alabama of the next century did not create the problems I have described. You inherited them. But how you handle them, whether you ignore these problems, improve conditions, or make them worse, will become your legacy. . . . Half a century from now virtually all of us in this room will have returned to the dust from which we came. We will leave behind tombstones on which loving families will inscribe kind thoughts. But God will judge us, as will history, more exactly, more justly, and with less concern for sentiment."

Concluding once again in preacher's mode, I considered God's options, which ranged from Isaiah 10:1–3 ("Shame on you! You who make unjust laws and publish burdensome decrees, depriving the poor of justice, robbing the weakest of my people of their rights, despoiling the widow and plundering the orphan. What will you do when called to account, when ruin confronts you? To whom will you flee for help and where will you leave your wealth?") to the kinder judgment of Matthew 25:34–40 ("Come, O blessed of my Father, inherit the kingdom prepared for you. . . . ; for I was hungry and you gave me food, I was thirsty and you gave me drink, I was a stranger and you welcomed me, I was naked and you clothed me. . . . Truly, I say to you, as you did it to one of the least of these my brethren, you did it to me").

When I finished reading the passages and took my seat, silence filled the hall for a long moment, as if everyone was holding his breath. Then applause began and steadily mounted, whether from agreement with my analysis or conformity with etiquette I never knew.

What I did know was Governor Hunt's fiery, extemporaneous response. Despite my best attempts to avoid partisanship, he obviously interpreted my remarks as an attack on his administration. He launched an emotional rebuttal about personal responsibility and private charity. He reminisced about the time his father caught his hand in a hay baler, and friends in the Holly Pond community of Cullman County and members of his Primitive Baptist congregation harvested crops for the family. Such community solidarity served society better than government welfare programs, he concluded. I agreed in theory. But not much of Alabama or America in 1990 was like the Holly Pond of Hunt's childhood.

The exchange between the two of us became the lead story in state papers as well as fodder for the *New York Times.* The *Birmingham Post-Herald* editorialized that Hunt "bristled at Flynt's speech." Its sister paper, the *Birmingham News,* engaged in the ultimate hyperbole, calling my address "the most important speech of the week," even more important than the hiring of Gene Stallings as the new head football coach at the University of Alabama. (I'm smart enough to know that *nothing* in Alabama is more important than that.) The *Columbus (Ga.) Ledger-Enquirer* used an entire page to publicize the speech, accompanied by a caricature of me outfitted in a medieval suit of armor, with a history book and Bible under my arm, prepared to do battle with the dragons of the old order. I could have used a real suit of armor shortly. The dean of the House of Representatives, Pete Turnham of Auburn (whose daughter had been a member of my Sunday school class) confided that the governor had asked him after the speech if I were a Marxist. Pete replied, "No, sir, he's a Baptist."

Two years later an economist newly employed by Auburn's Center for Governmental Services stopped me in Haley Center and introduced himself. Then he told me this story. He had worked for the Alabama Department of Eco-

nomic and Community Affairs (ADECA), theoretically the state's development office, though actually a highly political agency that parcels out community grants. It also compiles and analyzes economic data. The political
spin given the data is designed to make the incumbent governor look good
for reelection campaigns. By 1990 I had figured out why Alabama year after
year could lead the South in new job announcements, top the rankings in *Site
Selection* magazine, and still trail other states in job creation and state GDP.
ADECA lumped all jobs to be created by a new business into the year of the
announcement and did not subtract manufacturing jobs lost from those created. Those facts became a regular feature of my speeches. The economist, who
had worked for Hunt's ADECA director, explained that not only was I correct,
but the agency also altered data that he and other professional staff provided
in order to give it whatever political spin the governor's staff preferred. When
I began mentioning these discrepancies in my speeches, Hunt's advisers concluded that some disgruntled employee was tipping me off. The economist had
returned to his office one night and found a Hunt staffer rifling through garbage cans, trying to locate the agency's Deep Throat. My friend Luther Holt,
who held a master's degree from our department, shared a similarly bizarre
story. Luther had left his job as director of the Lee County Council of Governments to work on Governor Hunt's "Alabama Reunion" celebration designed
to showcase the state's talent, bring expatriates home, and fill hotels with tour-
ists. ADECA and the Alabama Library Association provided grants to produce
his book, which listed the state's amazing array of talent: admirals and generals
in the nation's armed forces; winners of Pulitzer and Nobel Prizes and National
Book Awards; famous athletes; CEOs of Fortune 500 companies; statesmen
and nationally prominent politicians; highly regarded physicians and scientists. I told Luther what a splendid resource this would be, how it would improve the state's image and create local pride in communities across the state.

   Alas, the book died aborning. The first arrow aimed in his direction came
from parochial political operatives who cared nothing about Alabama-born
CEOs of national stature, insisting instead that Luther concentrate on CEOs
of Alabama companies who were a prime source of political support and campaign contributions in the governor's reelection bid. But the piece I wrote for
the book sealed its fate. When Luther asked me to pen a brief introduction, I
complied even though I did not have time for the project. By my standards, the
introduction was both tame and laudatory. I emphasized that Luther's book
was a marvelous testament to the resourcefulness and persistence of a hard-

working people who excelled despite liabilities of poverty and underfunded schools.

When ADECA's political appointees read my introduction, they insisted that it be deleted because I was always negative about the state (presumably in this case, my mention of Alabama's indisputable poverty and underfunded schools). ADECA threatened to pull funding for the book unless Luther dropped my introduction. He felt compelled to apologize to me. I urged him to finish the project. People needed to know his findings, not read my introduction. I begged him not to withdraw his book, but I never saw it or heard the rest of the story (whether he withdrew the book, ADECA withheld funding, or the entire project simply fell apart).

Of course, I could not deny my negativity. To live as a morally responsible person in Alabama and not challenge injustice would have made a mockery of my faith. To speak truth to power had been the core of Judeo-Christian belief for four thousand years. So I often found myself in situations such as a May 1991 speech to Leadership Alabama on the interrelated problems of tax policy, economic development strategies, job creation, and education reform. The speech led to a spirited exchange with a prominent businessman about both my data and analysis. When I returned to my office, I checked the data in U.S. Department of Labor records, which showed Alabama trailing neighboring states and contradicting rosy projections from ADECA and the governor's office. I wrote my sparring partner that the data had been correct and that he might want to refer to the University of Alabama's Center for Business and Economic Research for verification. No doubt, I added, a historian in 2011 could make a better judgment about which one of us was correct (I won that gamble easily) but in the meantime "I have no intention of changing my message until you or someone else proves to me that vision is wrong." I heard nothing more from him.

In the final analysis, criticism did not alter my message, and the Hunt administration's attempts at retaliation were clumsy, inept, and not very threatening. Within three years, the Alabama Farmers Federation (ALFA) would show Hunt a thing or two about how to play hardball with a meddling college professor/preacher. But for the time being, I drew inspiration from Jesus and the Hebrew prophets. None of the Jewish prophets had tenure and their enemies fashioned more draconian remedies than faced me. Americans currently call those biblical methods "enhanced interrogation," and they can be lethal. Jesus made lots of people mad, and he did not fare well either. An anonymous piece of American folklore also reminded me of an important truth: "He who tells the truth must have one foot in the stirrup."

The foot in my stirrup did not carry me to Georgia or Florida, but to hamlets throughout the state. My world had suddenly dissolved into a whirlwind of speeches about poverty, economic development, tax policy, health deficiencies, and educational inadequacy. From the prayer luncheon speech in February through September 1990, I spoke constantly and still had to decline on average a speech a day. On July 12 I turned down five; the next day five more; two on July 14 (a Saturday) and two more on July 16. Audiences to which I spoke included the inaugural class of Leadership Alabama, the Alabama/Mississippi Social Work Education Conference, Alabama League of Women Voters, the Auburn Chapter of the Society of American Foresters, the Eufaula Heritage Society, Montgomery's Capital City Ladies Club, Jacksonville State University, the University of North Alabama, Birmingham-Southern College, Unitarian-Universalist Fellowship and First United Methodist Church, both in Montgomery, the *Anniston Star* editorial board, the Auburn Public Library, the annual convention of Alabama PTA, the state convention of Alabama Conservancy, Birmingham's Young Men's Business Club, the South Alabama–West Florida Conference of the Methodist Church—Methodist Women, and the Alabama Press Association. The stirrup of my Toyota Camry carried me thirty thousand miles that year, crisscrossing the state.

My speech to the Alabama Press Association was most memorable. I worked hard on the presentation, recapping the economic history of the state, locating most of its problems in the flawed 1901 Constitution and the Bourbon regime that illegally installed it, and summarizing the tragic human legacy it bequeathed Alabama. The typically cynical audience of journalists responded with a standing ovation, the first that its members could remember. I was deeply touched. Their coverage spread the debate about the issues to a wider audience. Between January and March 1992, I spoke seventeen times on tax and education reform. Dale County district judge Val McGee read a two-part opinion column I wrote for the *Montgomery Advertiser* and said the essays should be required reading for every candidate for public office in Alabama.

I was also getting under the skins of the groups I was needling. In mid-July 1990, the dean of Auburn's Forestry School called to arrange lunch with John McMillan, director of the Alabama Forestry Association and a key ALFA ally in the coalition against property tax reform. Our lunch was amicable. McMillan insisted that my estimate of the per acre annual tax on timber land (82 cents) was low; his agency estimated it at $1.01. He also maintained that property tax increases limited to timber land would not significantly affect the level of education funding. The state needed broad-based tax reform, not increases targeting a single industry. Nor could throwing more money at education solve problems in public schools. Furthermore, if property taxes on timber land increased substantially, companies would leave Alabama.

I conceded several points for the sake of argument, but noted that thirty miles from where we sat eating, Georgia timber owners paid an average of $4.50 per acre annually. Yet timber companies did not seem to have abandoned Georgia. I agreed with him about the need for broad-based tax reform. I did not wish to punish a single industry, and all land owners needed to pay their fair share of taxes, including me. But how did he know that investing more money in public schools would not solve Alabama's education woes? When had the state tried to solve problems created by two centuries of racial discrimination and poverty by equitably and adequately funding public schools? As for his argument that education reform needed to precede tax increases, I responded that they must be enacted together because Alabama Education Association opposed more accountability and ALFA and his organization opposed higher taxes.

An hour passed, and we reached no agreement on key issues. McMillan picked up my check and reached for his billfold. "Not so fast," I insisted. "I don't allow lobbyists to buy my lunch. That way there are no misunderstandings." I take him for an honest man just doing his job and do not believe he had sinister intentions. He seemed hurt by my rejection. I apologized and assured him I meant nothing personal. I wouldn't allow Paul Hubbert to buy me lunch either. We departed friends, though not of one mind.

The same day the forestry dean called to arrange lunch, the dean of Alabama social workers Eulene Hawkins called to ask me to sign a copy of *Poor but Proud* for a friend of hers, Representative Jimmy Holley of Elba. She told me that Holley had heard me speak several times and intended to make increasing state aid to families with dependent children his legislative priority. In 1990 a mother with three children received a maximum of $118 a month, a figure that had not increased in fifteen years and was the nation's lowest. I sent the book but recorded in my journal, "Perhaps all these speeches were not in vain, though I retain sufficient cynicism about Alabama's political process to doubt whether even this modest reform can pass our byzantine process. We shall see!"

I was wrong. The Speaker of the House of Representatives distributed my speech to members. By the end of May 1993, Holley had sponsored bills in three successive legislative sessions, increasing AFDC payments by 5 percent in 1990, 16 percent in 1991, and another 16 percent in 1992. Alabama no longer had the nation's lowest welfare payments for poor women and children. Holley paid me one of the finest compliments of my career by telling a reporter: "He has definitely had an influence on me. In turn, I have delivered that message to the legislature and we changed some funding."

By 1993, hardly a week passed without a call notifying me of some new group of volunteers setting out to solve a problem I had highlighted in the 1990 prayer luncheon speech: the Gift of Life Foundation; Voices for Alabama's Children; the Alabama Poverty Project. All across Alabama people of faith and justice mobilized to make Alabama a better place in which to live. Although my speech had been little more than a catalyst to mobilize and energize them, it had played its part in the reform movement.

On September 23, 1990, Governor Hunt presided at the Senior Citizens Hall of Fame ceremony where I received an award as Educator of the Year. It was obviously a painful moment for him. Smiles never came easily to the governor, but the one that day seemed especially plastic and forced. But then, I thought to myself, this is a unique experience for him. He has never awarded a plaque to a Baptist Marxist before.

Poor Health in America

Several years after *Dixie's Forgotten People* was published in 1979, I received a phone call from Monroe Lerner, a medical sociologist at Johns Hopkins University Medical School. As a member of the American Cancer Society's (ACS) newly formed National Advisory Committee on Cancer in the Socioeconomically Disadvantaged, Lerner feared that his group was off on the wrong foot. Consisting of sociologists, oncologists, and experts on Native Americans, African Americans, Hispanics, and Asian Americans, the committee's early discussions had focused on cancer and ethnicity. After reading my book, which noted that there were three times as many poor whites as blacks in America, he began to wonder if the central issue in escalated cancer rates among the poor might be economic rather than ethnic.

Dan Hoskins, the African American director of Collaborative Programs for ACS, and Harold P. Freeman, a charismatic black oncologist at Harlem Hospital and president of the American Cancer Society, asked me to speak at the next committee meeting. As I described problems in the Ozark and Appalachian regions (among them: poor diet; superstition; lack of physicians, hospitals, and health insurance; religious fatalism; rural isolation; low wage jobs), the reaction was similar to my speeches in Alabama. They were astonished that so many Anglo-Americans encountered problems characteristic of minority groups. They asked me to join the committee and enlarged its agenda to include poor whites.

I also broadened my reading to include other regions. I learned that in Philadelphia, for instance, 30 percent of the city's nine hundred thousand white residents lived in poverty, and only one inner-city hospital (Catholic Saint Mary's) still delivered babies because of the high cost of liability insurance. Saint Mary's was located in a neighborhood that was overwhelmingly white, poor, and Catholic. In the city's seventh health district, 99 percent of residents were poor, yet most were employed. Half of all whites in the district lived in families headed by single females with a child under the age of eighteen.

I learned that of the 20 percent of America's rural population living in poverty, two-thirds were non-Hispanic whites. Rates of rural poverty exceeded rates in urban areas. Furthermore, half the rural poor worked, and one-quarter of the families contained two family members who were employed, yet remained below the federal poverty line. Among poor families in America, the number one concern was paying medical bills.

This research opened the way for me to speak on the subject to ACS staff and volunteers at conferences in Cleveland, Ohio (1988), Syracuse, New York (1989), Atlanta (1989), Washington, D.C. (1989), New York City (1989), Hollings Cancer Center at Medical University of South Carolina (1996), and later at the National Institutes of Health in Washington and Johns Hopkins Medical School. The Washington meeting followed on the heels of national hearing organized by Dr. Freeman where cancer victims without insurance related tales that brought many of us to tears. As I listened to hour upon hour of testimony, the words of Martin Luther King rang in my ears: "Of all forms of injustice, inequities in health are the most shocking and inhumane."

The 1989 national hearings culminated in the now-renamed National Task Force on Cancer in the Socioeconomically Disadvantaged energetically lobbying congress for some form of national health insurance. I participated in that effort as well. Monroe Lerner wrote me that he believed the ACS was in the midst of a historic social change, one that, if successful, might spread to other voluntary health associations. Middle- and upper middle–class whites provided most ACS donations and volunteers. Yet, current levels of knowledge and therapies could not much prolong the lives of cancer patients within these socioeconomic groups. They generally ate healthful diets, exercised, obtained regular medical examinations, and had health insurance. It was among the nation's poor where we could save tens of thousands of lives each year. Whereas 60 to 65 percent of middle- and upper middle–class cancer victims survived for at least five years, only 30 percent of low-income patients reached that benchmark.

Speaking composed only part of my work for ACS. I reviewed pamphlets to ensure appropriate reading levels and construction. I provided bibliographies about poor whites for ACS staff so they could learn more. I wrote about poor whites for a series of society publications: *The Culture of Poverty* (1988); *Bridging the Gap in Health Care* (1989); *Report of the Interdepartmental Oversight Committee on Cancer Control and the Sociologically Disadvantaged* (1989); *Cancer and the Poor* (1992); *Cancer and the Disadvantaged: Renewing and Extending the Challenge* (mid-1990s). I helped organize a panel for a national meeting in Atlanta, recruiting Joe F. Smiddy Jr. of Kingsport, Tennessee; Angel Rubio of the Lucille Markey Cancer Center in Lexington, Kentucky; and Frankie Patton Rutherford of Tug River Health Clinic in West Virginia. They described Appalachian poverty and health problems. I also urged medical researchers to focus more on poverty across racial lines and less on ethnicity.

Nor did I forget my own state, which had one of the nation's highest incidences of cancer. Of the 30 million Americans without health insurance in the early 1990s, eight hundred thousand of them lived in Alabama. I worked with a group of Auburn faculty from agricultural extension, counseling, nutrition, and nursing to propose projects in rural health, education, and prevention.

My work on cancer and health care followed a now familiar pattern: research; scholarly writing to professional groups and experts in the field; popularizing that scholarship in opinion columns or manuals; speeches designed to reach ordinary people. Groups I spoke to in Alabama included the Jefferson County Medical Society, Jefferson County Association of Pediatricians, University of Alabama Rural Health Program, UAB's initiative on health care reform, Alabama Department of Public Health, and the Alabama Department of Mental Health. Pulling data together was simple, but the effect on audiences, even professional ones, was often bewilderment at the state of health care. Of the state's 67 counties in 1992, 31 had the same number or fewer physicians than a decade earlier; 30 had no obstetrician; 32 no pediatrician; 43 no psychiatrist; 15 no general surgeon; 14 no internist.

Physicians furnished me no end of anecdotes, problems, and insights. J. Robert Beshear, an obstetrician in Montgomery, was about to follow other specialists out of obstetrical practice because of astronomical liability insurance rates and growing risks of suits from poor women who typically did not see a doctor until their final trimester. But for ethical reasons he rebelled at deserting such women. The result of his caring was the Gift of Life Foundation, which offered early intervention services to poor, pregnant women across the Black Belt, along with nutrition, health, exercise, and wellness programs. Sandral Hullett, a black physician in West Alabama, established an organization that offered similar services. After I spoke to Jefferson County pediatricians, David Reynolds established the "I Take Ten" program. Only four of sixty county pediatricians took Medicaid patients at the time because payment rates were so low and poor children crowded out patients with insurance. David appealed to all pediatricians to devote at least 10 percent of their practices to poor children. A third of his colleagues agreed to do so. He even retired early so he could devote his entire practice to indigent children. He also invited me to speak to the national meeting of the American Academy of Pediatrics, where I could spread the word nationally about poor white children.

Focusing on children became the easiest way to obtain a hearing for the poor. However opposed citizens might be to tax, constitutional, or education reform, they were concerned about the welfare of children. The innocence, openness, and naïveté of poor children touched even the most cynical Alabamians, who seemed to understand instinctively what James Agee had written half a century earlier about the children of three white sharecropper families in Hale County: "In every child who is born, under no matter what circumstances, and of no matter what parents, the potentiality of the human race is born again; and in him too, once more for each of us is born our terrific responsibility toward life." I must have quoted that sentence a hundred times, and my eyes filled with tears every time because I had seen so many poor children for whom the potentiality of the human race died nearly as soon as they were born.

In a society grounded in values of fairness, equality, justice, and love for children, child welfare was the high ground from which to wage this crusade. Avarice, materialism, greed, and selfishness about one's personal property and possessions just as clearly represented the low ground. If I could not change the minds of my audiences about tax justice, child welfare, and decent schools for poor children, at least I intended to educate them about the inequities. I would challenge the hypocrisy of a Bible Belt population that treated its youngest, weakest, and least powerful people so shamelessly. If I could not change the minds of my white friends and neighbors about economic justice for poor children, I could at least load them down with guilt in this life and scare the hell out of them about God's wrath in the next (Hebrew scripture provided all the evidence I needed). I tried on every occasion to remind them that part of their affluence came at the expense of an unjust economic order that paid wages to janitors, garbage men, maids, yardmen, department and convenience store clerks, and many others that would not raise them out of poverty even if they worked full time all year long. And I made sure this was not the case with the people I hired to help my family.

In hundreds of speeches, articles, and opinion columns, I probed many aspects of child poverty. Bailey Thomson, editor of the *Mobile Register,* wrote that I was a "Baptist preacher of reform," "a modern-day Jeremiah," who traveled the state "lamenting how failed leadership and selfish interests have denied children their birthright." To help reporters convey the message, I furnished annual updates on conditions and offered handouts at every speech. One such document summarized data about children. In 1989, 12.5 million American children lived in poverty, an increase of 2.5 million since 1979. Nearly 32 percent of Alabama children were poor, ranking the state second only to Mississippi that year. One-fifth of Alabamians had no health insurance. Combining ten categories of child welfare, Alabama ranked 46th among 50 states. (By 2009, the state had fallen two places to 48th.)

Not content to wait for improvements to percolate through the legislative process given the powerful special interests that dominated it, I pursued various alternatives. As a member of the state's Children Steering Committee, I participated in the creation of Voices for Alabama's Children. Under the leadership of Linda Tilley, Voices became the chief advocate of children, and its annual "Kids Count" reports furnished compelling data for my speeches. I also wrote the introduction and conclusion to the organization's first Kids Count grant proposal in 1992.

Working with Catholic layman Al Rohling, director of Blue Cross–Blue Shield (BC-BS) Child Caring Foundation of Alabama, I spoke in venues across the state on behalf of insurance for poor children whose parents earned too much to qualify for Medicaid but could not afford health insurance. However much Alabamians opposed property tax increases, many of them opened wide their pocketbooks for this cause (whether out of guilt at Alabama's tax structure, concern for poor children, or both, I cannot say). A charitable gift of $240 provided a poor child one physical examination a year and hospitalization as needed. BC-BS matched each dollar given. I challenged my Pilgrim's Sunday school class to participate, and these wonderful Christians donated between

$1,000 and $5,000 a year for decades (which, with the BC-BS match, provided insurance for between four and twenty Lee County children each year). Every time I preached on the Bible and the poor, I mentioned the program, and numbers of churches joined ours (along with businesses, civic clubs, and individuals), providing coverage for thousands and making Alabama a national leader in providing insurance for poor children.

When Paul Hubbert, head of the Alabama Education Association and twice a candidate for governor, asked me to send him my ideas about helping the Black Belt, I sent a long memorandum dealing with tourism, education reform, and health. I proposed creating an Alabama Health Corps involving medical and nursing schools, county subsidies for malpractice insurance to attract physicians to rural counties, mobile units that could cover the poorest regions where hospitals were closing, and creation of a rural health committee to study the Black Belt's unique problems.

Faith in the Market Place

During a quarter century of activism on behalf of health reform and poor children in Alabama, I learned lots of lessons. The worst problems are embedded in systemic poverty resulting from a morally flawed constitution, regressive tax policy, the state's long history of racism, as well as from terrible personal choices by the poor themselves. Affluent people are too materialistic, greedy, and uncaring. Poor people are too uninformed, irresponsible, and fatalistic. America's health care system failed a sixth of its citizens, yet costs more than any other system in the world. In a nation where nearly 50 million residents had no health insurance in 2009 (a total that was increasing by 14,000 a day nationwide and 60,000 a year in Alabama), the poor used hospital emergency rooms for primary care, which is both the most expensive and least effective venue for health care unless a person has a life-threatening condition.

Christians could make a difference. They control most political power in Alabama and exercise it on behalf of what they perceive to be majoritarian moral concerns (opposition to abortion, embryonic stem cell research, gambling, alcohol use and sales). That they do not regard systemic problems of inadequate health care or child poverty as important as these other causes is a scandal that will in time turn the young and educated away from their pews and steeples, a phenomenon already well advanced among Southern Baptists, whose membership numbers and baptisms are already declining. As a retired Methodist minister wrote me, "Alabama is overrun with Baptists and kudzu vine, and they both have about equal effect. They look good but do nothing." That judgment was too harsh, but among white Southern Baptist churches, few did much to advance the causes of better health for the poor or systemic improvements in child welfare. I agreed with them that charity is good. But justice is better.

Nor did university faculties help much. Overwhelmingly correct on the abstract side of issues, they spent little time where the rubber hits the road, at the level of converting popular culture, building reform coalitions, or political networking. Quick to condemn the hypocrisy of evangelical churches, most of them were too preoccupied by affairs of the academy to be of much assistance in broader campaigns for justice.

On the national front, America moved closer every year to some form of national health insurance. The medical profession, like enlightened business people and educators, recognized discrepancies between care for the poor and everyone else. In 2002 I read with delight evidence that our ACS committee had indeed broadened the agenda of medical research in America. Cathy J. Bradley of Michigan State University led a study that concluded lower socio-economic status was more important than race in determining the quality of medical care for women with breast cancer. "Poor persons," she reported, "regardless of race, are likely to have undesirable cancer outcomes." That report, reflecting as it did a new paradigm in the fight against one of the world's deadliest killers, vindicated all those dozens of speeches, ACS reports, long hours of hearings and committee debates, and lengthy policy papers I had written for the ACS during two decades.

Forging New Alliances

From the late 1960s until the 1990 prayer luncheon, I considered my crusade against poverty and for greater understanding of poor whites largely academic and wholly futile. After speaking about white poverty at College of Wooster in Ohio, I asked a friend, "Have you ever tried to explain red-necks, goat-ropers, and good old boys to freshly scrubbed Ohio Presbyterians?" Within my own state I felt like a character out of Scott Fitzgerald's *The Great Gatsby*: "So we beat on, boats against the current, borne back ceaselessly into the past." I loved Alabama's past. But I did not want to drown in it.

Suddenly, after the prayer luncheon, my causes gained traction with opinion-makers. After that speech, I was surprised by how much favorable reaction came from what in earlier times I had contemptuously referred to as "Big Mules": bankers, corporate CEOs, leaders of high tech companies, architects of Alabama's new economy.

Frank Moody, chairman emeritus of AmSouth Bank in Tuscaloosa, wrote me in April 1990, commending one of my speeches. It was, he said, "a forceful, erudite, very simple presentation" of why the state trailed the nation in so many quality of life issues. "I have seen many articles and many statements written about the woes of the State of Alabama and its people, but none have been as well done and impressive as was yours." The speech he alluded to became my standard thirty-minute analysis of why Alabama's economy remained mired in basic manufacturing and was now excreting jobs at a frightful rate in all directions. It also challenged a century of economic development strategy and political boosterism.

If the state's post-Reconstruction development strategy had been wise, Alabama's per capita income in 1930 would not have ranked 45th of 48 states. In the following five decades, the ranking stood at 46th (1940, 1950) and 47th (1960, 1970, 1980). In 1986, it inched up to 43rd of 50 states, but in 1990 fell back to 44th. This minimal improvement was not the fulfillment of Bourbon dreams nor a validation of conservative Democratic visions. Of course, per capita income was only one measure of prosperity, but almost all other standards of economic vitality and quality of life were consistent with that one. Only when compared to Alabama's own inadequate past did progress seem steady. Compared to its southern neighbors (especially Georgia, Florida, North Carolina, Virginia), the state was simply treading water or falling further behind.

Nor was this debacle due to lack of natural resources, poor work ethic, lack of respect for economic elites, or failure of government to support conservative policies such as low taxes. Few states could boast more raw materials or freshwater, greater geological and ecological diversity, a more conservative white population, or more deferential workers. Alabama's economic failure was one of leadership and vision, of whites denying fundamental rights to blacks, of underfunded public schools and mediocre colleges and universities.

At first, reporters focused on my positive narrative about poor whites. Gradually, they transitioned to my critique of the state's political economy. That was a debate I welcomed and entered into aggressively. ALFA, the Forestry and Cattlemen's Associations, many extractive south Alabama industries, Christian Coalition of Alabama, Eagle Forum, the Family Research Council, many working-class whites, and white rural Alabama lined up against the message and the messenger. But the legendary Big Mules of the Birmingham District and Tennessee Valley began to desert their old allies.

Many of these new-generation entrepreneurs, especially in Birmingham, were the first to be well educated out of state, the first to assume control of family companies, and the first to emerge as political and corporate leaders in a city where nearly half the land was owned by out-of-state corporations. Aware of poor quality public schools, the paucity of museums, symphonies, fine public research universities, and other cultural amenities that were so important to high tech employees, they actively engaged in debates swirling through the 1990s. Tom Coker, head of the powerful Business Council of Alabama, told the *New York Times* that "business in Alabama has been more the problem than part of the solution." BCA chairs Frank McRight, Mike Warren, and others promoted various kinds of reforms. Some of them combined a strong Christian ethical impulse with economic pragmatism, which added moral passion to economic expediency.

This wing of the state's entrepreneurial elites founded a series of organizations designed to promote dialogue, education, spirited debate, and reformist political agendas: PARCA (Public Affairs Research Council of Alabama); Leadership Birmingham, Huntsville, Montgomery, and Alabama; A+ Education Coalition; Alabama Appleseed; Alabama Citizens for Constitutional Reform. Business and civic leaders such as Montgomery's Winton Blount III, Caroline Novak, and Mike Jenkins, Mobile attorney Frank McRight, Birmingham CEOs Bill Smith, Mike Warren, Herb Sklenar, Elmer Harris, Ted Kennedy played major roles in these and other organizations.

Suddenly, I began receiving invitations to speak to various local and state leadership organizations, write articles for *Business Alabama* magazine ("You Reap What You Sow"), huddle with power brokers, bankers, and business tycoons. Though I was cautious at first, I warmed to their sincerity and commitment of both time and money to reform causes. During the first class of Leadership Alabama in 1990–91, I bonded with many fellow class members. In fact, I could not help but consider the irony of liberal academic friends who cheered me on from the sidelines while my conservative business friends rolled up their sleeves, reached for their checkbooks, and in many cases deflected their careers to march on Montgomery and demand change. They worked easily and comfortably with progressive blacks, incorporated women in influential leadership positions, and did not hesitate to tangle with former allies like ALFA and Christian Coalition.

The Alabama Poverty Project

Entrepreneurial reform dealt mainly with politics, education reform, and leadership development. Beyond these important causes, I had other interests. My friend Wil Bailey introduced me to Gordon Chamberlain—retired Methodist minister, former staffer at Harry Emerson Fosdick's Riverside Church in NYC, and founder of the North Carolina Poverty Coalition.

Gordon's vision included engaging activist scholars across the South to study poverty, publicizing their findings, teaching undergraduates what they had learned, and mobilizing public policy in order to bring about systemic change. His book *Upon Whom We Depend: The American Poverty System* argued passionately for a living wage for all American workers. I agreed to serve on the board of directors and joined Bailey, Earl Potts, and Eulene Hawkins in forming the Alabama Poverty Project (APP) to implement Gordon's plans in our state. I helped recruit board members for the new, all-volunteer nonprofit, and the response was gratifying. We had some of the finest African American community leaders in the state as well as directors of leading antipoverty groups. I doubt that any board had a more impressive leadership cadre. Tom Corts, Samford's president, provided office space and after some years, half a sociology professor's time as director. The Mary Reynolds Babcock Foundation granted APP substantial short-term funding, and board members developed a long-term funding strategy based on a coalition of faith communities and higher education. APP's goal was to provide nonpartisan research, public education, and coordination, and to mobilize churches, colleges, and universities against poverty. I served several years as chair of the board and helped recruit the faith and higher education communities. Our board and staff drew heavily from Baptists, Catholics, Presbyterians, and Methodists, but also included Baha'i, Jews, black Pentecostals, and other faiths.

Sowing Seeds of Hope

Just as satisfying if more parochial was the creation of Sowing Seeds of Hope in Perry County. When moderate Baptists formed Cooperative Baptist Fellowship (CBF) of Alabama, Mart Gray, the organization's coordinator, asked me to suggest a signature ministry that could define our differences with Southern Baptists. I did not hesitate. We should establish a grass-roots antipoverty effort in Perry County. Once called the Baptist capital east of the Mississippi River, the county seat of Marion was, or had once been, home to many Baptist institutions: Judson College, the second oldest woman's college in the South; Howard College; the *Alabama Baptist* newspaper; and the Southern Baptist Home Mission Board. In antebellum times one of the wealthiest counties in America, Perry was by the 1990s one of the poorest hundred counties in the nation: 98 percent of public schoolchildren were eligible for free or reduced meals; some 50 percent of children were poor; 45 percent of blacks lived in poverty; median family income reached only a little more than $20,000 a year.

Yet Perry County had a proud educational tradition. In addition to the two white Baptist colleges, the South's oldest black college (Alabama State University) originated there early in Reconstruction as Lincoln School. The county's civil rights luminaries included Coretta Scott King, Juanita (Mrs. Ralph D.) Abernathy, and Jean (Mrs. Andrew) Young.

Our endeavor would be ecumenical and biracial. The county was deeply polarized racially, so for a year I met with white economic, religious, and civic leaders, while my Auburn friend Johnny Green, a black Baptist minister and Auburn University administrator, met with black leaders. In one exercise, Johnny and I asked our respective groups to list what they wanted to see happen in their county to provide better prospects for their children and grandchildren. Although the priorities differed somewhat, both lists contained the same aspirations: decent jobs; better health care; improved schools; safer communities; upgraded housing; more social outlets for children. After our separate groups completed their goal-setting, we combined them and watched their surprise as they discovered so many shared dreams. Marion mayor Ed Daniels, a retired black teacher, suggested a better name than our proposed Perry County Poverty Project. That night Sowing Seeds of Hope was born. CBF pledged a thirty-year effort in the county.

Local task forces on all the goals they had listed met and determined implementation strategies. CBF helped locate resources and expertise when requested. The key was the quality of local and CBF leadership, and we were fortunate to have CBF coordinator Mart Gray, and as a county coordinator Perry County native and nurse Frances Ford, a black woman universally respected by whites and blacks. Lots of idealistic young people from around the country served yearlong internships. Catholic students from Boston College came every spring holiday to work on projects. Mary Reynolds Babcock Foundation provided seed money, and Baptist churches from across the South sent teams that rehabilitated houses, transformed a National Guard armory into a recreation center and an old bank building into the county's first public library. During the summer of 2001 alone, Baptist churches raised $18,000 and sent 125 volunteers to construct and repair eleven houses.

The night we dedicated the new library in Uniontown, an elderly black man asked where we would be working the following year. "Here in Perry County," our intern explained. Accustomed to single year do-gooders or three-year government cycles of people who came and went for decades after the civil rights movement, he shook his head in disbelief when told we were committed to the county for a generation.

Best of all, coalition members who lived in Perry County and the groups that came to help represented the entire theological spectrum from fundamentalist to Pentecostal, from moderate to liberal, from Church of God in Christ to Catholic, from tiny churches to rich Samford University (whose pharmacy, education, and nursing programs provided critical resources to the county).

Samford, under presidents Tom Corts and Andrew Westmoreland, made me a proud alumnus with its leadership in the cause of justice in Perry County and throughout the state. As a member of the board of overseers, I wrote Tom a letter congratulating him for the School of Nursing's new program to help female migrant workers on Chandler Mountain. The Migrant Farm Workers' Project, I wrote, "is just exactly what Samford is all about . . . , that is, taking education in a compassionate way to the poorest and the least powerful among us."

I also wrote thanks to my former Samford student David Chestnut and his wife, Janet, for their forceful advocacy for the poor at conservative Briarwood Presbyterian Church. As Alfred Habeeb Professor, chairman of anesthesiology, and professor of obstetrics and gynecology at UAB, David was a consistent, conservative evangelical, whose compassion did not end with opposition to abortion but extended to other right-to-life issues (alleviation of poverty, child welfare, world peace). I will take such allies anytime in preference to liberals who talk a good game but do little more than vote correctly.

I did what I could to empower the powerless. But any single APP board member did as much or more than I did. Many ministers, priests, nuns, and rabbis had been saying the same things for decades, and they had no tenure and often had to contend with hostile congregations. Social workers, inspirational teachers in low-income schools, public health officials, all earning lots less than I did and working just as hard, labored in obscurity. Mainly, I provided them visibility, a voice, an audience, and affirmation of their work. I might receive the attention, awards, and accolades, but these ordinary warriors living extraordinary lives of courage, service, vision, and integrity were the foot soldiers of the justice movement in Alabama.

· ten ·

Reforming American Education

I had nearly finished an oral history with Lorol Roden Bowron Rucker, daughter of one of Alabama's pioneer suffragists and a matriarch of Birmingham's Highland Book Club, when she volunteered her philosophy of life. It was simple, she explained: "Save your money and educate your children." Somewhere midway through the twentieth century, Americans stopped believing in both.

I finally figured out the reason why. The two essential components of Mrs. Rucker's advice could be considered mutually exclusive. Money allocated to educating children could be redirected toward acquiring bigger houses and bass boats. Historically, many Alabamians saw no reason to educate their children anyway beyond the skills necessary to cultivate cotton, mine coal, or operate looms in a cotton mill. Furthermore, they believed that public officials wasted their hard-earned taxes. Nor did many planters and Big Mules see any value in educating the children of poor and working-class parents. They found more efficacious ways of preparing their own children for a successful life—private academies, tutors, or out-of-state boarding schools. Besides, they resented paying taxes, especially those allocated for the education of African American children. Fewer dollars paid in taxes for schools meant more money to spend on themselves. So, resistance to funding public schools adequately was never a solitary decision about education. It occupied a complicated intersection where race, tax policy, and public education met.

As that realization dawned on me, I devoted more and more writing and speech time to tax and education reform. I spoke to hundreds of audiences about these subjects, served on two gubernatorially appointed tax reform commissions, on several education commissions, as facilitator in the settlement of Alabama's equity funding lawsuit, as expert witness in three legal challenges to the 1901 Constitution, and as consultant for the State Department of Education in resolving two discrimination lawsuits.

Especially after 1972—when the legislature passed and George Wallace signed constitutional amendments sponsored by ALFA and other agricultural groups to base property taxes on the current use of land rather than its actual value and to cap property taxes—I tried to educate citizens about the effects of tax policy on education. My case study came from Mobile, where a company that built the city's largest shopping mall avoided paying nearly $100,000 in property taxes by planting pine seedlings on 104 acres adjacent to its shopping center just off Interstate 65. The Alabama Forestry Commission even gave the company a $5,182 state grant to buy and plant the seedlings. When a reporter for the *Mobile Press-Register* investigated, he found a state forester who had inspected the "forest" and reported that 80 percent of the pine trees had died due to lack of water or from pine beetle infestation. The Alabama Soil and Water Conservation Department refused to provide documents about the parcel of land, but the 104-acre plot that had been valued at $13.2 million before its reclassification as "forest land" was worth practically nothing afterward. Under "current use" tax classification, the owners paid $147.29 in property taxes in 1990. Meanwhile, Mobile County schools languished.

The Origins of the Education Reform Movement

Before my speech at Governor Hunt's prayer luncheon, he had appointed me to his tax and education reform commission, a decision, no doubt, he came to regret. Neither cause was dear to his heart, but they ranked high on the priority lists of many of his Birmingham-based Republican business allies. The Alabama Education Study Commission (it seemed to me this must be education commission 9,001, series Z in indisputably the most carefully studied subject in Alabama history) met on February 13, 1990, in the governor's conference room at the capitol. Frank McFadden chaired our commission; attorney Caldwell Marks coordinated tax and education reform; and a high-powered consultant from Pennsylvania advised us. Our charge was to develop a comprehensive education reform plan for Alabama public schools during 1990.

As we began our work, the magnitude of the problems seemed overwhelming. State government spent a large percentage of its total revenue on schools, but most local governments spent next to nothing. The state contained 130 separate school systems. (Florida, with a population four times as large as Alabama's had only 67.) Classroom teacher salaries ranked 37th among 50 states. Students attended school in 555 buildings that were more than 50 years old and in 2,200 mobile classrooms. White enrollment was steadily declining while black enrollment quickly increased. Students ranked well below national averages on standardized ACT tests, 21st of 28 states using the examination. The state high school exit exam was a joke, testing students at fifth and sixth grade levels in some subjects. Thanks to pressure from mainly African American political groups and AEA, prospective teachers were not required to take teacher exams that measured their competence in subjects where they theoretically were measuring the competence of their students. The State Department of Education spent virtually nothing on technology despite the advent of a technological age. High school graduation rates were among the nation's lowest. High rates of poverty and chronic health problems created the need for special education programs, which did not even exist in some schools and were pathetically underfunded in others. State-funded early childhood programs were just beginning and enrolled negligible numbers.

Thanks to vigorous AEA lobbying, the process of firing poor teachers, even those guilty of moral turpitude or incompetence, involved so many levels of appeal and cost so much that superintendents usually transferred them or recommended them to other systems in order to eliminate the problem and save legal costs. Early in the twenty-first century, a fifty-six-year-old female teacher convicted of raping and sodomizing a fourteen-year-old male student continued to draw her salary and supplement her pension while in a state prison awaiting final appeal.

Employers complained about the skill level of high school graduates and their inability to compete in a global economy. As a result, business leaders cautiously proposed increasing revenues in return for greater educational accountability. AEA demanded more money but resisted additional regulation and oversight.

Meanwhile, the nation's educational demographics tracked a transformed future for America. In 1986 nearly 45 percent of the workforce consisted of white males. But they constituted only 10 percent of new entrants into the labor force that year; minorities made up 50 percent and immigrants 25 percent. (The trend accelerated in the 1990s, and by 2009, 47 percent of American children under age five belonged to minority groups, as did 43 percent of those under twenty.) Minority students scored well below native-born whites on standardized tests, so Alabama's "human capital" clearly was not keeping up with its "physical capital."

As evidence of educational disaster mounted, President Ronald Reagan's education secretary assembled an eighteen-member national commission, which produced the landmark 1983 study titled *Nation at Risk*. The document was the rarest kind of government report, one that does not immediately disappear into the obscurity of a bookshelf. In harsh, stark language, *Nation at Risk* contended that no invading army could inflict worse damage on America than mediocre, failing schools were already causing. Comparing the performance of American schoolchildren in reading, math, and science to students in Japan, South Korea, Germany, and elsewhere, the nation's future looked bleak. The globalized economy rapidly developing in a "flat world" held even greater peril.

Critics of the report—mainly teachers' unions, civil rights organizations, and other liberal groups—mobilized against its conclusions. School accountability could not compensate for generational poverty, a history of racism, dysfunctional families, lack of nutrition, single-parent families, working mothers who could not supervise homework, crime, illicit drug use, or the erosive moral and social effects of American popular culture. To overcome such obstacles required massive infusions of federal money, which recent administrations had been loath to provide.

This critique struck me as more rationalization for a failing system than the plan for a reformed one. I doubted that Japanese, South Korean, Indian, and Chinese students really cared *WHY* American jobs were hemorrhaging into their countries so long as the trend continued. And long after low wages in Asia began rising, these countries maintained economic advantage because of skilled labor.

Republicans weren't the only ones to understand this. In fact, Mississippi's Democratic governor William Winter became the first state chief executive to cobble together a state education reform consensus. And he did so a year *before* publication of *Nation at Risk*. In December 1982, Winter summoned the Mississippi legislature into special session to pass House Bill 4 (HB4). This legislation became the first omnibus education reform package proposed by a governor and enacted by a legislature. In subsequent years, similar bills became the hallmarks of so-called New South governors, both Democrats and Republicans (a story told expertly by Gordon Harvey, one of my doctoral students in his book, *A Question of Justice*). HB4 became a watershed event in education reform by combining a variety of elements that appealed to different constituencies: state-supported kindergartens; accelerated reading programs; teacher salary increases; changes in school accreditation and teacher certification; establishment of lay boards of education to select state school superintendents; increases in sales, income, and property taxes to fund reforms.

Other visionary southern political leaders followed Winter's example: South Carolina governors Richard Riley and John West; Florida's Robert Graham and Ruben Askew; Tennessee's Lamar Alexander; Arkansas's Bill Clinton; North Carolina's James Hunt. Hunt also headed the Education Commission of the States and appointed a Task Force on Education for Economic Growth that included educators, business leaders, and governors. The task force carefully studied the relationship of American education to international economic competitiveness and reached conclusions similar to those described in *Nation at Risk*.

By the mid-1980s more than two hundred state-level task forces, blue ribbon commissions, and study groups (including the one on which I served) worked on these issues. The reports flooded the nation in the late 1980s and early 1990s, spreading reform rhetoric and ideas.

By 1992, between fifteen and twenty states had enacted reform programs similar to Mississippi's. The Business Roundtable, the National Alliance for Business, and the U.S. Chamber of Commerce had all climbed aboard the education reform express. At the same time, many state teachers' groups mobilized to derail the engine, attacking teacher testing, merit pay for teachers, tougher graduation requirements, nationally normed student testing, holding teachers and administrators accountable for their students' progress, allowing students to transfer out of chronically failing schools, and creation of charter schools that reduced bureaucracy, administrative oversight, and unionized teachers.

During the early 1990s, reform momentum continued to build. In 1991 Ernest L. Boyer, president of the Carnegie Foundation for the Advancement of Teaching and one of the nation's most influential educational theorists, wrote *Ready to Learn: A Mandate for the Nation*. Boyer's conclusions—healthy children perform better in school; health workers and teachers should work together to assure every child the best possible educational experience; early childhood education benefits every child; parents should be empowered to advocate for their child's interests; communities should mobilize entire neighborhoods for learning, establishing indoor and outdoor parks, libraries, museums, zoos, boys and girls clubs, sports teams, all of which educate children;

citizens should encourage stronger intergenerational connections in school—influenced the A+ Education Reform movement in Alabama. The nation's press publicized such reforms in special editions of *Newsweek* and *Fortune* magazines and at two national education summits.

Despite these efforts, consensus on school reform remained elusive. Shortly after President George Bush's 1991 announcement of America 2000, a nine-year strategy to enact reform, the education journal *Phi Delta Kappan,* summarized a litany of problems in achieving the president's goals: a child poverty rate of more than 20 percent; dysfunctional families (60 percent of the nation's children would live at least part of their lives in single-parent families); teachers needed better training and safer, more supportive work environments; school systems provided too little mentoring for young teachers and inadequate in-service training; local political fragmentation and deadlock; inadequate funding.

So many conflicting opinions confused the public. Citizens knew there was a crisis. But so many different views about the nature of the problem and possible solutions left them reeling. By the early 1990s, however, a coherent reform movement had crystallized nationally around three ideas: school-based decision-making (local, decentralized, shared decision-making as opposed to micromanagement by state departments and bureaucracies); teacher and school accountability; and tax reform.

The Equity Funding Lawsuit and A+

The same year that William Winter launched the modern education reform movement, a Catholic nun turned lawyer, Marilyn Morheuser, filed suit on behalf of poor New Jersey school districts. During her career as a nun, Sister Morheuser had taught sixteen years in Catholic high schools where she observed education problems firsthand. Reform groups in many states adopted her strategy, and over the next decade dozens filed what came to be known generically as "equity funding lawsuits."

The lawsuits argued that the quality of education, and thus the future of students and communities, varied widely because of differences in the value of property and the fairness of taxation. Some wealthy communities with huge financial resources flourished while poorer communities withered. In Alabama, for instance, the value of an acre of property in affluent Mountain Brook was many times the value of an acre in the destitute Black Belt. The glitzy Galleria Mall in Hoover provided sales tax revenue that furnished Hoover High School a football facility that rivaled the University of Alabama's and advanced courses and state-of-the-art technology in virtually everything, while Moulton, Lawrence County's seat of government, generated negligible sales tax revenue for its schools.

As a result of these inequities, Dewayne Key—the superintendent of schools in rural, mainly white Lawrence County—persuaded a local lawyer to sue Alabama public officials. Former state supreme court chief justice C. C. "Bo" Torbert agreed to become lead attorney for the plaintiffs. Two other groups—the Alabama Disability Advocacy Program and the Harper plaintiffs (black families represented by the American Civil Liberties Union) also sued. By 1991 the three groups had been consolidated into a single group of plaintiffs.

Meanwhile, Governor Hunt's education study commission, including me, drafted a package of reforms focusing on school readiness issues such as child poverty, preparation of children for first grade, parental involvement in schools, family dysfunction, low standardized test scores, poor job skills among high school graduates, and lack of local financial support. We issued our report, "Alabama Education: A Plan for Change," in March 1991, only months before the equity funding lawsuit went to trial. That such a bold reform could have won backing from so many key elements of the Hunt administration and its corporate cohort reflects the early splits in the traditional planter–Big Mule coalition that had governed Alabama for more than a century.

When the equity funding trial began during the summer of 1991, Bo Torbert asked me to serve as an expert witness. From the beginning of the trial in Circuit Judge Eugene Reese's Montgomery courtroom, I was confident of the outcome. The evidence presented by the plaintiffs was overwhelming and emotionally compelling. In poor counties such as Lawrence, cheap land, sparse development, and low taxes starved education. The county spent a little more than $3,000 per student. By contrast, the five wealthiest school systems in the state—Mountain Brook, Homewood, Hoover, Vestavia Hills, and Huntsville—spent more than $5,000 per student. At one Black Belt school, a broken sewer system discharged human waste onto the playground. Many schools had no air conditioning. One sixth grade science teacher showed students photographs of a microscope because they did not have access to a real one. No Choctaw County schools contained science laboratories, and a wheelchair-bound child had to crawl on a concrete floor for exercise because his school contained no carpeted area. Wilcox County schools had no computers for general student use. Camden Middle School contained one computer for five hundred students. More than 90 percent of teachers surveyed said they spent personal money on school supplies. Statewide, 1,473 school buses built before 1978 did not meet national safety standards.

One expert witness testified that in his extensive surveys of American schools he had never "before seen conditions as inadequate as those prevailing among some of Alabama's poorest schools." There was an eleven-year difference in the mean age of school buildings between the state's poorest and wealthiest systems; 50 percent of wealthier schools contained audiovisual production facilities compared to 17 percent of poorer schools. Nearly twice as many science labs were available to students in higher-funded schools. Wealthier schools also had better athletic facilities; larger libraries; lower teacher-student ratios; access to drama, debate, art, and music programs; foreign language classes; higher salaries for principals and teachers; more and better supplies.

I testified last. Half a century spent reading Alabama history proved invaluable during the state's cross-examination. State lawyers cited examples of underfunded school systems such as Arab and Guntersville, where standardized student scores and performance outpaced local funding per student. I replied that both systems were homogeneously white, had low rates of single-parent families and poverty, that Arab had changed from a poor Appalachian town into a spillover suburb for Huntsville's high-tech employees and Guntersville into a retirement destination. It was as easy to contrast the Black Belt and Arab as to understand Washington, D.C., and Utah. Substitute the homogeneous population of Mormon Utah for the poor black population of D.C., and even I could provide the nation's capital quality education on the cheap. Conversely, strand a quarter of the population in a system of apartheid for a century, underfund schools, and limit taxes by constitutional restrictions as we had done in Alabama, and the conditions described by plaintiffs were the result. So graphic and horrifying was testimony in the trial that when plaintiffs' attorneys cross-examined Anita Buckley Commander, the governor's education adviser, she wept at the description of conditions.

In the fall of 1991 Judge Reese issued an elegantly written 125-page decision, declaring Alabama's system of school funding to be both constitutionally inequitable and inadequate. His decision coincided with planning for a series of twenty-two town meetings sponsored by A+, an education reform organization founded by two members of the first class of Leadership Alabama, Royal Cup Coffee Company CEO Bill Smith and Montgomery civic leader Caroline Novak. Smith—a Washington and Lee and Harvard Business School graduate, cofounder of Leadership Alabama, and a key figure in establishing the Public Affairs Research Council of Alabama (PARCA) at Samford

University—used his charismatic leadership skills to forge a broad alliance of like-minded state leaders. The coalition included future state school superintendents Ed Richardson and Joe Morton, and a who's who of lawyers, educators, and business CEOs. Novak had earned an economics degree from Hollins College and served as board chair of the Montgomery Museum of Fine Arts and of Leadership Montgomery. Under the leadership of Smith and Novak and inspired by the national Business Roundtable's education reform initiative, A+ promoted the Kentucky Education Reform Act (KERA) as a model for Alabama because the states were of comparable size and wealth, thus neutralizing arguments that Alabama was too poor to afford a decent education system.

A+ profited both from the pressure of Judge Reese's decision and a 1992 tax reform commission report by Birmingham lawyer Tom Carruthers and Bo Torbert. The tax commission's proposals—broaden the tax base; lower the tax rate where possible; make the tax system less regressive; provide equitable treatment to all taxpayers; adjust earmarking downward from its current level of 90 percent of all state revenue; increase revenue by at least $119 million annually—paralleled and provided a potential funding source for A+ proposals. The internal politics of the Carruthers-Torbert report required compromise between major Alabama power brokers without which no reform could pass the legislature.

I wrote Carruthers in May 1992 expressing my opinion that a report weakened by further compromise might well short-circuit any possibility of structural change down the road. My bottom line included at least $400 million in additional revenue for schools; passing some elements of tax reform (preferably removing the sales tax on groceries); a strong accountability component. ("The biggest culprit in this story is higher education. . . . The educational appetite among colleges is so voracious that it can eat up any amount of money and still not produce quality higher education. We simply must hold to accountability in that area.")

While the tax commission drafted its final report, A+ was launching a statewide blitz crafted at a July 1992 retreat of major stakeholders and educational theorists. Reformers from South Carolina explained their successful strategy. David Hornbeck, national guru of business-oriented reformers, served as primary consultant.

David brought impeccable credentials to the retreat. With a law degree from the University of Pennsylvania, a theology degree from Union Theological Seminary in New York City, and additional education at Oxford University, he also possessed real-life experience as superintendent of Maryland public schools, the architect of KERA, and chief education adviser to the Business Roundtable, an elite group of Fortune 200 CEOs. Under his leadership in 1989, the Roundtable had adopted a ten-year plan to overhaul American education.

Hornbeck published his expansive social vision for schools in a book titled *Human Capital and America's Future: An Economic Strategy for the Nineties* (1991). His writings matched the apocalyptic vision of *Nation at Risk* but laid out a detailed remedy as well.

Following the retreat, A+ formed a state coordinating committee and planned a series of town meetings. The template did not vary. A keynote speaker laid out the issues broadly; distinguished local persons spoke next; then local education, business, civic, and PTA leaders, parents, ministers, and other volunteers presided at breakout sessions to guide discussions and record suggestions by attendees.

Bill, Caroline, and I met in Auburn in the late fall, and they asked me to keynote the rallies. They had already cleared the request with AU president Bill Muse, who released me from classroom duties from January to June 1993. Winter/spring classes started soon, and I had more than forty students enrolled in Alabama history, plus a graduate seminar, so the request was complicated and urgent. Nor was I under any illusions about Alabama political hardball. The furious reaction to my prayer luncheon speech several years earlier had provided a clear warning of what lay ahead. But I could think of no greater calling from God nor journey toward justice for poor children than systemic education and tax reform, so I agreed.

I had already developed the keynote speech for a similar community town meeting in Sylacauga in March 1992 for superintendent Joe Morton. I stressed that parents and teachers had to demand more from schools and students. Parents needed to emphasize education as much as athletics and turn off television sets. Citizens needed to demand more accountability from schools and finance education better. I compressed that message into seven minutes, practiced it enough to be smooth but did not memorize it so well as to be "canned." Then I headed off for all those places and people I had learned to love from Auburn humanities programs.

Given polls indicating that state voters considered public education their top concern, we expected respectable turnouts. But the national economic recession and resultant proration of school funds, as well as years of neglect of school buildings and equipment, had stoked the fires to red hot. Massive journalistic support and shrewd corporate advertising helped bring out the crowds. Our first rally in Tuscaloosa occurred just before a countywide school tax referendum in which the county ALFA chapter led the opposition and the Chamber of Commerce led reform forces. An overflow crowd of two thousand filled the school auditorium, then spilled out into classrooms for spirited discussion of the A+ reform draft.

The following weeks brought more of the same. In Jasper, eleven hundred turned out. In my hometown of Anniston, hundreds (including Opal Lovett, my beloved English teacher) filled the high school auditorium. Thousands more showed up in Decatur, Eufaula, Selma, Opelika, and Monroeville. In all, I delivered the keynote at eight of the twenty-two rallies, a grueling emotional and physical regimen. Statewide, some twenty-three thousand people attended town hall gatherings, an average of more than a thousand each.

Extensive media coverage multiplied the impact of the meetings. The *Mobile Press-Register* launched a comprehensive multiweek, front page series on Alabama's interlocking economic, educational, and tax problems. A team of *Birmingham News* reporters had just won a Pulitzer Prize for a similar series. Birmingham television station WVTM aired an unprecedented two-year investigative series called *Great Expectations . . . the Education Project,* funded by three Big Mule corporations: Alabama Power, AmSouth Bank, and South Central Bell. PARCA issued periodic reports on all these components, explaining how low property taxes accounted for the state's backwardness, poverty, health, and educational problems. As the state's preeminent independent public policy and research center, PARCA's director, Jim Williams, had made his organization the leading source of data, and the fact that it was housed at Samford—a conservative, private, Baptist university headed by a prominent and popular Republican president—gave the center even greater credibility.

The town meetings went extremely well in the beginning. I enjoyed sitting in breakout sessions and listening to ordinary people vigorously and passionately offer their complaints and suggestions. A mother in Anniston broke into tears as she described her battle against school bureaucrats to obtain help for her son with attention deficit disorder. Teachers complained about lack of parental involvement, physical threats against them, disruptive students, and spending a significant amount of their own inadequate salaries on essential supplies that school budgets should have provided. Business people complained about employees who possessed high school diplomas without high school level reading and math skills.

The week before our Anniston rally, Bill Smith asked me to attend a meeting in the governor's office. Governor Guy Hunt had just been found guilty of violating state ethics laws and removed from office. Lieutenant Governor James E. Folsom Jr. had replaced him and wanted to talk with us. Folsom's wife, Marsha, a public policy wonk herself with a passion for social justice, sat in on the meeting, as did the governor's political strategist. They all had watched the phenomenal turnout at A+ town meetings and recognized the media absorption with education reform. They also understood that Bill Smith and his business allies could raise millions for Folsom's forthcoming gubernatorial campaign. Folsom was a shrewd politician who knew that even moderate Democrats were an endangered species in Alabama. But if he could become the public face of the education reform movement, he could sharply erode business support for the GOP candidate.

After our discussions, in which the Folsoms expressed enthusiastic support for the A+ agenda, we huddled, hardly believing that after all these years of roaming in the wilderness of official opposition or at best being ignored, we were about to enter the promised land of official and public endorsement.

But we also recognized the perils. If Folsom absorbed the A+ plan and made it the centerpiece of his election bid, we were in danger of being co-opted on behalf of a partisan political agenda, something we had vowed not to do. Indeed, the considerable strength we had built depended on our *not* acting ideologically or as political partisans. Our support base was as strongly Republican as Democratic. Our strength was our independence, pragmatism, and support by a broad coalition of underpaid teachers, unhappy business people, and anxious parents.

Folsom promised to attend the Anniston town meeting, and we could hardly refuse him a minute to speak. He was as good as his word, enthusiastically endorsing the cause without trying to preempt its direction or leadership. He helped craft a legislative omnibus bill incorporating nearly all the elements of systemic educational and tax justice that reformers of all persuasions had sought since his father served as governor in the 1940s and 1950s.

If Anniston was the Mount of Transfiguration in our town meetings, the Decatur town hall on May 18 brought us back into the desert. The fifteen hundred who attended included the first organized opposition. Margaret Brown, president of the Morgan County chapter of Eagle Forum, distributed a flyer claiming that the real objective of A+ was to dilute family and Christian values. Alabama corporate executives endorsed the plan, she wrote, because the "profit motive of big business doesn't want thinkers."

As I moved from session to session, listening to discussions, the tone was quite different from earlier town meetings. Two or three persons in each ses-

sion raised similar questions about motives and leaders of the reform movement, about social engineering, and the real intent of outcome-based education (OBE). In their view, this was a plot by major corporations to strip parents
of their rights. Children would be socially engineered to accept homosexuality
as a normal lifestyle; the federal government would impose uniform national
graduation standards; and OBE would require seniors to endorse certain liberal beliefs or outcomes before they could graduate. School-based health programs would promote sex education, condom use, and abortion.

The level of conspiracy theory bordered on paranoia. Nor was it spontaneous. From the Decatur meeting through more than a dozen remaining town
meetings and in later public hearings, well-organized groups (Eagle Forum,
Alabama Family Alliance, Concerned Women of America, Alabama Christian Coalition) infiltrated every event, raising the same issues. What opponents portrayed as a spontaneous populist uprising by angry parents against
social engineering in public schools, was in reality a carefully orchestrated,
well-funded campaign by the now flourishing "religious right" to sabotage
education reform and wreck what they believed to be godless public schools.
One reason the education reform movement lost in many states (Pennsylvania,
Ohio, Nebraska, Iowa, West Virginia) was this blindsiding from the religious
right, with its attacks on corporate elites who considered children to be merely
"human capital." Right wing Republican women's organizations such as Eagle
Forum and Concerned Women of America added their own perverse findings.
Judy McLemore predicted that students would "have to demonstrate specific
attitudes and beliefs" as in the Soviet Union. For many fiscally conservative
CEOs, this began the first act in a long divorce from the GOP, which would
culminate fifteen years later in the 2008 presidential election of Barack Obama.
Though some religious right arguments reflected the genuine concerns of the
growing Libertarian conservative movement, most were pure fantasy born in
ignorance and paranoia.

The other notable event that evening in Decatur was a new twist in the
typical media interview after I spoke. A reporter for the local paper asked me
about the defeat two days earlier of Tuscaloosa County's school tax referendum. That morning, I had read a scorching attack on ALFA by the director of
the Tuscaloosa Chamber of Commerce, blaming it for distorting issues in the
referendum. Picking up on that theme, I suggested that ALFA's actions were
based not on what would improve life for most citizens but on its own selfish
concerns about protecting farm and timber property from equitable taxation.
I did not think this motivation made ALFA a good corporate citizen. (My view

was widely shared by the press and north Alabama CEOs, especially those involved in the education reform movement.)

On June 11, 1993, I received ALFA's reaction. President Goodwin Myrick, who liked to tell newspapers that ALFA ran the state and elected whomever it pleased, intended to play hardball. His letter began with the usual litany that I constantly criticized the state, always saw the glass as half empty rather than half full, and was "a negative prophet of doom" who seemed to attract more media attention than "an optimistic prognosticator of the future." After these charming preliminaries, Myrick got right down to business. My remarks in the *Decatur Daily* were part of my long campaign against his company. "I resent your unwarranted criticism even more . . . because as an Auburn University employee, you are either directly or indirectly using tax dollars for your campaign against ALFA." He attached a list of financial contributions ALFA had made through the years to Auburn, telling me (and President Muse, to whom he sent a copy of the letter), "you can be sure that any future contributions to Auburn will come under close scrutiny as a result of your unfounded and irresponsible criticism." His list included nearly $4.5 million, mostly for agricultural research.

The letter may have been part of a larger strategy to derail the equity funding proceedings. On May 28 Bo Torbert had called and informed me that all participants in the equity funding case wanted me to become court facilitator to reach agreement. Two days later, he met with me and asked in my role as a professor at Auburn, could I treat K–12 education fairly? Could I be fair to all parties as a member of the A+ board of directors? I assured him that my only concerns were that *all* Alabama children have equal access to a quality education and that schools provide the state a competent labor force. He asked me to withdraw as keynote speaker for the remaining A+ town meetings, which I agreed to do. Judge Reese accepted this arrangement on June 9, and the agreement was announced on the tenth.

I received Myrick's letter on the eleventh. Convinced that the correspondence was designed primarily to intimidate me, I immediately called Bobby Segall, a lawyer involved with the case, who told me to say nothing to the press. He believed Myrick's letter might be part of an orchestrated ALFA strategy to sabotage the settlement talks by disqualifying me for prejudice. I also informed Bo Torbert and Susan Russ Walker, lawyers for one of the plaintiff's groups, and sent a copy of the letter to Judge Reese and several other friends.

Then I bit my lip and said nothing when someone released a copy of the letter to the press and newspapers from across Alabama called about its possible effect on the legal proceedings. More calls came that weekend from out-side the state, including the *Atlanta Constitution, New York Times,* and *Chronicle of Higher Education,* all of which were writing stories about the ALFA-AU af-fair. I did not comment.

Larry Gerber—my history colleague, president of the faculty, and later na-tional vice president of AAUP—spoke all the words I longed to say about aca-demic freedom and free speech, which were protected by the Constitution, even in ALFA-infested Alabama. President Muse called on Monday from his vacation to assure me of his support. In his press release, Muse thanked ALFA for its long support, noted that most of its contributions actually purchased services for Alabama farmers, regretted severance of the relationship, then de-fended my right to report my research and opinions.

On the evening of June 14, Leah Atkins called to inform me that ALFA offi-cials had told the AU Alumni Association that day they were canceling their sky box at Jordan-Hare Stadium because of my comments. But she knew from her husband, George, that they had actually told Auburn officials two months ear-lier about the cancellation. What had triggered their unhappiness was Muse's refusal to appoint a vice president for agriculture (and even worse to some ALFA folks, his decision to replace that office with a VP for outreach who was also an African American).

Myrick's letter followed six months of constant harassment from Mont-gomery. My dean and FSU friend Gordon Bond had received a call in Feb-ruary from someone in a state agency inquiring about my teaching load. Since I had just begun speaking at A+ rallies and was not teaching that semester, my only "load" consisted of nineteen graduate students, which was load enough. I asked Gordon if the person inquired about anyone else's teaching load. His negative answer sent me into a rage. This was a blatant attempt by someone in the Hunt administration or legislature to stop my speeches about tax and education reform. After my outburst, Gordon and Tal Henson, acting chair of the History Department, handled the incident, sending information about my graduate students (during the 1990s, I directed one-fifth of the depart-ment's doctoral dissertations). On February 26, Henson received another call for more information, but when the person refused to identify himself, Tal re-fused the request and hung up. Shortly afterward, I received a call from a re-searcher in the Alabama Development Office (ADO) who said the agency was furious at me because of my *Washington Post* interview with Bill Booth, who quoted me as saying the state was "sucking wind" compared to our neighbor-ing states' economic development.

A few days later, on March 8, one of my former Samford students, Neal Wade, and I appeared on Alabama Public Television's news program *For the Record.* As we attached earplugs and adjusted microphones, Neal asked if I had solved my dispute with ADO? What dispute, I inquired? The one about the state's economic condition, he answered. Later, standing outside the station, Neal added: "Watch yourself. I was told not to have anything to do with you. I was told they were going to get you." Who is "they," I asked? "The director of ADO," he replied. "They have told people that they are going to have a meeting with you and President Muse and they are going to get you."

I was grateful to Neal for the warning. Later, as director of the Alabama Power–initiated Business Partnership of Alabama (which progressive corporations created because of the ineptitude of ADO and ADECA) and as ADO director himself during the Bob Riley administration, Neal and his team showed the state how economic development should be done. He supported A+ and persuasively connected economic development to quality education. We had our differences and debated each other on several occasions, but I had the highest regard for Neal and his professionalism.

Coming on the heels of six months of A+ speeches; harassment; being away from my wife, home, and teaching, Myrick's threat was the last straw. And I could not even explain what happened except to my family. On the evening I received Myrick's letter, I entrusted thoughts to my journal that I could not share with the world: "What insufferable arrogance. And how typical. I suppose after all those years of controlling the legislature and tax policy, no one should be surprised. But if he [Myrick] thinks he is going to intimidate me, he has another thought coming. My problem is to retain objectivity after such a letter and to remain fair to everyone in the court proceedings. But that is what I must do and will do."

Several days later, state newspapers began to publish editorials about Myrick's communication. As I read them, I wondered if he kept a journal, too, and if so, what must he be writing in it. For once, Myrick's arrogance had caused him to overreach. He had never intended for his letter to reach the public and now hunkered down under the furious reaction. The *Birmingham News* led off in its June 16 issue, comparing Myrick to the head of a Communist regime in Eastern Europe. The editors noted that both my comments about ALFA's historic opposition to property taxes and the consequent poor quality of public schools were entirely accurate: "Saying that someone who fights raising the lowest property taxes in the union to help some of the poorest schools in the union is not a 'good citizen' is about as debatable as saying the Pope is associated with Roman Catholicism." As for my criticizing ALFA while working at a state-supported university, the editor added: "That's right, he is. We pay him to research history and tell us the truth about it. This isn't Eastern Europe."

The *Montgomery Advertiser* weighed in next. Calling ALFA's decision to withhold funds from Auburn strictly a "dollars-and-cents issue" for them, the editor added: "Dr. Flynt's contribution in sharp contrast, is not. It is beyond price, for it is a contribution toward understanding, toward acceptance and responsibility, toward honest assessment of a failing and serious attention to correcting it."

Mitch Mendelson, a columnist for the *Birmingham Post-Herald,* called Myrick's letter "typically fascistic": "The Farmers Federation/Farm Bureau and its fellow traveler, the Alabama Forestry Association, have been long considered a fourth branch of government when it comes to writing regressive, inequitable, stacked-deck tax policy. Now ALFA is outraged when a teacher at a public university has the gall to speak the truth about ALFA's role in perpetuating Alabama's third-world school system. Wonders never cease."

The *Decatur Daily* added on June 24 that sooner or later my participation in school reform and the equity funding case would probably make everyone unhappy. But "let's allow him to bring a balance to this tug-of-war. He's in a unique position to do so. He is apolitical, articulate and willing. Not many of the breed are around and willing to take the heat. He's made a bunch of friends along the way with his outspoken views, too, because he uses history to explain the present." Other papers—the *Mobile Press-Register, Anniston Star, Huntsville Times, Auburn Bulletin, Tuscaloosa News*—wrote similar editorials.

Many of those friends the Decatur paper alluded to sent letters that raised me out of my "slough of despond." Literary friends like Kathryn Tucker Windham urged me to hold firm to my convictions. So did lawyer friends Tom Carruthers, Tom Radney, Ed M. Friend Jr., and John Casey. Casey, a lawyer in Heflin, pronounced himself a hill country redneck like me, who judged people by the enemies they made. And if ALFA hated me that much, I must be doing something right. I admitted to being a member-in-good-standing of the "Royal Order of Alabama Rednecks" and enjoyed hearing from all my "cousins." My religion professor at Samford, W. T. Edwards (among many other friends and not a few perfect strangers), wrote me that he was canceling his ALFA insurance policies because of their bullying.

I discovered that this was not the first time ALFA had tried to intimidate an Auburn man. Retired president Harry Philpott identified himself in a letter as "Grand Master of the Ancient and Honorable Order of Enemies of the

Alabama Farmers Federation" and conferred full membership upon me as well. In 1968 he had had the audacity to advocate ending all sales tax exemptions, mainly favoring farmers, and the Farmers Federation threatened to end all contributions to Auburn, though the only money they ever gave benefited themselves.

Strangers shared their opinions in letters to the editor or as copies of letters sent to ALFA. My favorite came from Montevallo schoolteacher Kathy Vogel. Though she held two degrees from the University of Alabama, she wrote ALFA that she intended to monitor ALFA contributions to Auburn because "I would like to think that some of my money goes for something I approve of, to someone who thinks, someone who produces, someone we can be proud of rather than the cast of 'Mayhem in Montgomery.'"

No doubt chastened both by canceled insurance policies and withering editorials, Myrick and ALFA lobbyist John Dorrill soon joined me on the road, though they spent their time meeting with hostile newspaper editorial boards, pleading their case and trying to "clarify" any misunderstandings that they were threatening to defund Auburn or trying to have me fired. Meanwhile, I drove back and forth to Montgomery for nearly four months, meeting with lawyers representing various plaintiffs and defendants in the equity funding remedy phase.

Although age fifty-two in June 1993, I was still full of optimism about the possibilities for change. So I plunged into the whirlwind of meetings, convinced that all the constellations had aligned perfectly for the reform and modernity that had eluded the state for so long. A+ and the education reform movement had split the conservative political coalition that had ruled Alabama since 1875. The state had a reform governor. Judge Reese and his equity funding decision had provided the judicial impetus for us. A bipartisan settlement process was emerging in the legislature. My job was to make sure, with the assistance of many others, that the reform process did not fail in the remedy negotiations.

My role as court facilitator was unusual. In fact, Bo Torbert, the architect of the plan, thought it unique. Governor Folsom agreed to suspend the state's appeal of Reese's decision to give us time to fashion a settlement on which plaintiffs and defendants could agree. As court facilitator, my powers were quite limited. I could schedule meetings, require attendance, and provide monthly reports and recommendations to Judge Reese. Beyond my formal duties, I tried to facilitate open communication between parties, coordinate with a person from the governor's newly formed education task force, utilize humor to reduce tension at meetings, deflate pompous egos, humanize the parties as much as possible, occasionally offer alternative wording or procedures when we seemed deadlocked, and above all else move the process toward resolution by our fall deadline.

Although the court had collapsed three groups of plaintiffs (ACE, ADAP, and Harper) into one plaintiff, they retained conflicting agendas and were represented by eleven different attorneys. Six attorneys represented the governor, lieutenant governor, Speaker of the House, state school superintendent, and State Board of Education. They also had conflicting agendas. Add to that the propensity of lawyers in such a setting to preen and show off, to take implacable positions until the very last moment when all hope of compromise seemed lost, and our sessions sometimes reminded me of theater of the absurd. Without a law degree myself, I had to learn from experience that much of what occurred had less to do with final outcome than with legal maneuver and drama. Think of the Talladega 500 NASCAR race, where everything that happens during the first 187 laps is prelude to the final lap. Reporter friends from the *Birmingham News* even gave me a basketball referee's shirt and whistle and told me I would need them. They were correct.

Although I liked and respected all the lawyers, some emerged as better tacticians and strategists than others. Former state supreme court chief justice Bo Torbert could be deferential and accommodating or tough as nails, as occasion demanded. His colleague Susan Russ Walker was an English major from Eckerd College, and a Rhodes scholar with a master's degree in English from the University of Virginia and a law degree from Yale. While other attorneys scrambled away from our conference room in the state education building for lunch each day, I savored a peanut butter and jelly sandwich and an hour's conversation with Susan about Eudora Welty, Flannery O'Connor, Walker Percy, William Faulkner, or some other southern writer.

Rick Meadows and a host of other lawyers tenaciously defended state officials, while Robert D. (Bobby) Segall and half a dozen additional attorneys represented ADAP and Harper plaintiffs. Of the plaintiffs' lawyers, I considered Torbert, Walker, and Segall the most effective. They knew when to be tough but also when and how to compromise in order to move the process forward. Both sides retained a stable of experts, which was easy to do given the national attention paid the case. *Education Week, Phi Delta Kappan, National Forum,* the *New York Times,* the *Atlanta Constitution,* all state newspapers and other national ones covered the proceedings.

In order to function effectively in my role as facilitator, I read box after box of scholarly articles in education journals, national studies, and consultants' reports. One of our first disputes involved the degree of openness and public access we would allow. Torbert strongly opposed public hearings and press conferences, fearing that it would drive attorneys to extreme positions and make compromise difficult. He also disliked my recommendation that we appoint a teachers' advisory panel as a way of neutralizing AEA's opposition to accountability measures. But the plaintiff he represented in the case, Lawrence County school superintendent DeWayne Key agreed with me on both issues, believing especially that hearings strengthened our case with a public that would ultimately have to approve any additional property taxes by passing an amendment to the antiquated 1901 Constitution.

We also had to counter a gathering storm of opposition from the religious right and other conservative organizations. Cathy Gassenheimer, the infinitely patient and conciliatory director of A+, repeatedly assured Eunie Smith, president of Alabama Eagle Forum, that we had no hidden agenda. After one three-hour meeting with her, Cathy agreed to prohibit assessment of values, hypnotism, and "guided imagery." Since we had never considered any of these, it was an easy concession to make.

Such assurances did nothing to allay the paranoia on the right. I received a steady stream of correspondence, all of it variations on a single form letter about outcome-based education. Hardly ever did they define the term, and in many cases it was obvious they had not a clue what it meant. OBE was an unfortunate piece of educational jargon, welcomed by the corporate community, which determined the value of education by its outcome: writing, reading, science, and math skills should reflect a twelfth-grade level of accomplishment when students graduated from high school. Unfortunately, some national educational theorists buried deep in ivy-covered towers on university campuses and wholly out of touch with American political and social reality, played into the hands of the religious right by deeming tolerance for alternative lifestyles a desired outcome of education. Think acceptance of condom distribution to protect girls from unwanted pregnancies, homosexuality, new age religion, or at least that's what Eunie and her cohort believed. One or two of the ACLU lawyers briefly mentioned such subjects, but they were quickly dismissed by the realists and pragmatists among the participants.

The fact that no reform plan that plaintiffs ever seriously discussed contained values-assessment did not reduce my mail from citizens convinced that OBE was devised by the devil. The letter-writers had been primed by Christian gurus who were either wholly ignorant or used such fears to construct megachurches full of terrified parents: "OBE has been used in several other states and has caused nothing but chaos in each one"; better to "get back to basics" and abandon "new age thought"; "as parents we feel this [OBE] is not the right reform for our children. We do not want our children taught in schools about morals and values. We need to pray and ask God for direction for our lives, but not teach them against God's Word"; "God is against homoeosexuals [*sic*], sex outside marriage, etc., these things should be taught at home [*sic*], *not* school Isaiah 54:13." I'm not sure how this writer reacted a decade later when Roy Moore wanted to post the Ten Commandments in Alabama public schools in order to teach children moral values.

In a letter to *New York Times* editor Howell Raines on October 14, after our settlement went to Judge Reese, I summarized the positions of Eagle Forum, the religious right, and AEA's Paul Hubbert, all of whom played harmonic accompaniment in ALFA's selfish symphony. I then praised Birmingham's Big Mules, the CEOs of Alabama Power, South Central Bell, Alabama Gas, Vulcan Materials, BE&K Engineering, as well as most of the banks.

During the legal negotiations, I wrote one of the nation's leading theoreticians of education reform, Robert Slavin of Johns Hopkins University. I had read with considerable interest his carefully nuanced ideas about modernizing American education. I was therefore puzzled when Eagle Forum and the religious right quoted his work as a primary source for their opposition to OBE. I sent him our preliminary agreement for his analysis. He read it and agreed that the plan's opponents had misrepresented his opinions. He favored: early childhood education as a way of leveling the playing field for poor children (opponents portrayed this as a statist attempt to steal children from their parents and subject them to Soviet-style indoctrination); tutoring programs using accelerated classmates to help slow learners (opponents ridiculed this idea as a waste of time because children should not teach children); Success for All (an early childhood education program that the right claimed indoctrinated children); school and staff development; adequate funding; student assessment; and school accountability. My release of his letter would have quieted honest critics, but Eagle Forum and its allies simply dropped Slavin from their list of sources and moved on to less-respected authorities.

I responded with an opinion column in state newspapers, dividing opponents of school reform into ideological zealots, whose real agenda seemed to be closing public schools in favor of private academies and homeschooling, and sincere-but-misguided parents confused or misled about OBE and social engineering. The state press explained complicated educational jargon and reassured citizens that the lawyers huddled in a room in Montgomery had no grand design to destroy Christian values or substitute federal bureaucrats for parents. Promotional efforts by the business community helped, and reform also won endorsements from the Alabama Bar Association and more vitally from Alabama and Auburn head football coaches.

By now I was determined to hold public hearings, if for no other reason than to let citizens have a chance to speak their minds and give our lawyers an opportunity to hear what I was reading in my correspondence. David Mathews—president and CEO of the Kettering Foundation, former president of the University of Alabama, and former U.S. secretary of education—confirmed my instincts. "Without the community-at-large or the public being more centrally engaged," he wrote me, "the key actors aren't likely to overcome their differences."

That was precisely what I was discovering. Rose Sanders, the community-activist wife of African American state senator Hank Sanders, bitterly denounced tracking and apprenticeship programs designed to provide skills to children who were not college bound. Teachers and parents split over the efficacy of reading based on phonics or whole language. Our consultants and teachers argued over the value of standardized testing and school accountability. Even some reformers believed the A+ plan was too complex and intrusive.

After scheduling public hearings for July 11, I had to extend hours from 8:00 a.m. to 9:00 p.m. to accommodate the seventy-three speakers who registered. Reporters Charles Dean and Mary Orndorff, among others, did a terrific job covering the hearings. Thanks to aggressive organizing by both sides, we had a spirited thirteen-hour debate. Reform organizations such as Voices for Alabama Children, Alabama ARISE, A+, Greater Birmingham Ministries, Alabama PTA, the State School Superintendents' Association, and others locked horns with Eagle Forum, Concerned Women of America, antireform businessmen, confused parents, and religious right zealots. Although we suffered through lots of passionate but wholly misinformed rhetoric, the process accomplished what I had hoped. It gave both sides of the debate a chance to be heard, and it informed our lawyers. The *Birmingham News* printed comments of all speakers.

During the legal proceedings, I suffered in silence as various special interest groups threatened to torpedo negotiation with their agendas, which were often as self-serving as those of AEA and ALFA. "If you gave them a billion dollars and no reform or accountability," I wrote in my journal on June 21, "they would be as happy as a pig in the sunshine." The next day we worked line-by-line from 9:00 a.m. until 5:30 p.m. through a thirty-page draft prepared by our national consultants. My head swirled as I listened to hopelessly unrealistic debate about modifying teacher tenure laws (which corporate reformers demanded and AEA fiercely opposed), the reduction of elective or appointive school boards to little more than ceremonial functions, teacher-testing laws to guarantee competency, and establishment of school-based community health centers. All these ideas had merit but were drop-dead issues for various influential groups. I confided to my journal when I finally returned home for one of my endlessly patient wife's 9:00 p.m. suppers: "All in all it was a good session but more tedious than even a university faculty meeting."

Tedium continued and tempers flared for weeks on end. On July 6, the governor's exhausted representative became offended because he wasn't consulted by one of the litigants about alternative wording of a section of the settlement draft. State Education Department folks were furious with consultant David Hornbeck's attempt to restructure their bureaucracy. Rants during the July 11 hearings did as much to infuriate the lawyers as to enlighten them. I shared their frustration but had already read all of it in my correspondence. As I wrote in my journal that night: "An ideal world for most of them [critics of reform] would be a return to a day when education served a talented white tenth, where blacks and poor whites knew their places, and where they ran America. Having presided in silence over a world of discrimination, injustice, and poverty, they would now like to craft education reform. To them, education reform means phonics, traditional values, abolishing tenure and 'teacher unions,' [and] no more taxes. . . . For people who fear that educational reform will produce programmed robots, Eagle Forum and Family Alliance folk sound very much like programmed robots to me."

On July 20 I spoke to a support group of seventy ministers in Birmingham about our reform. Given the attention the religious right now commanded, I believed the ministerial support group would be a critical balance. Based on the success of this effort, DeWayne Key expressed his growing frustration at the secrecy of our proceedings and the lack of frank discussion. Growing divisions between Harper, ADAP, and ACE plaintiffs and disputes over levels of accountability versus additional funding added to the tension.

Meanwhile, Governor Folsom's blue ribbon Educational Task Force (which included Bill Smith, Folsom's chief of staff Charlie Waldrep, black senate Democratic majority leader Michael Figures, influential Tuscaloosa senator Ryan DeGraffenreid, House Speaker Jimmy Clark, state school superintendent Wayne Teague, Neal Travis (CEO of South Central Bell), the state finance director, the executive director of the Alabama Council on Higher Education, AEA representative Nancy Worley, and Shelby County school administrator Debbie Smith developed a comprehensive reform plan called Alabama First, which incorporated most of the A+ agenda.

The task force also held public hearings, which I attended, and interacted with the litigant group through Charlie Waldrep, who served on both. Their influence was salutary, I thought, constantly reminding ideologues on the litigant group that whatever we decided, final funding solutions rested with the legislature and the public, not with us. Misunderstandings were inevitable, as when Waldrep infuriated the task force by telling them that all they could do was approve the litigant plan. In August, he reversed himself, proposing that the task force produce its own plan. This was a shrewd countermove that applied pressure on the now-deadlocked litigants. Due to Bill Smith's presence on the task force and liaison with the business community, I knew they had considerable influence with the administration and would have the governor's support for their plan.

As weeks passed, the original clear lines of authority (the litigant group would develop a remedy, the task force would write enabling legislation and determine the funding mechanism) became murky. What must have dawned on Charlie, Bill, and others by late July was that the obvious divisions, mutual lack of trust, growing animosity, and slow progress of the litigant group had shifted momentum to the task force. They had become initiators while we were now reactors.

This wake-up call galvanized the litigants and finally got them moving. At last they began to stay focused on the final resolution instead of endlessly rehashing matters that had already been decided. Bo Torbert utilized homespun stories and Rick Meadows mobilized earthy aphorisms to break deadlocks. Rick ended a particularly productive session on July 29 by telling me that I could record in my journal that evening how much I had learned from the sixteen lawyers. I quipped that would be the shortest entry in the history of my journal.

I now felt confident enough to intervene in proceedings more energetically. On the twenty-ninth, at a lunch with Waldrep, I urged him and the task force to stop referring to the Hornbeck plan or the A+ plan or the litigant plan. I liked Hornbeck and deeply respected his expertise and endless patience. But he had become a lightning rod for reform opponents. Our job was to "Alabamaize" these plans, I told Charlie, to take public criticism seriously, and incorporate at least some of it into our final document.

Our writer-in-residence, Susan Russ Walker, began drafting consensus documents, but at a Sunday meeting on August 1, some of the litigants once again insisted that they could reopen any issue already agreed to. The consultant we shared with the task force further mucked up things by proposing that the litigants stick to broad principles and let the task force fill in details. I strongly opposed this suggestion on process grounds; the more details they filled in, the greater prospect of conflict between task force and litigants. I privately opposed it also because AEA's representative on the task force seemed to object to every reform except more money.

By the time I returned home at 8:00 p.m. on Sunday evening, I was exhausted. I remember telling Dartie that if God had worked with sixteen lawyers when he was creating the cosmos, we wouldn't have an equity funding problem because there would be no universe; the lawyers would still be arguing over where to put it, how God should be held accountable for it, and how much money it needed.

On August 3–5, some ACLU lawyers nearly torpedoed everything by suggesting we leave open the possibility of dispensing condoms from school community health centers. Perhaps a logical idea to slow abortions and sexually transmitted diseases, I thought. But an absolute deal-breaker with realistic plaintiff lawyers, all the defendants, and the public. Why must we go through this day after day? Tempers flared again.

By mid-August the lawyers for special education students were making similarly ridiculous proposals. They insisted they would settle for nothing less than 750 new special education teachers. But all the colleges in the state produced fewer than 50 a year. And in our present condition, why would any special education teacher graduating from a non-Alabama college want to teach in our state? Task force member Nancy Worley further stirred the waters by insisting that proposed school councils consist exclusively of teachers rather than a mix of parents and teachers because only teachers should decide school issues.

More troubling were reports from Caroline Novak that Paul Hubbert planned to endorse a significantly smaller "reform" plan that would cost less by removing accountability provisions. He was preparing to run for governor against Folsom and intended to oppose the Alabama First Plan. Legislators backed by gambling interests stuck with Folsom's $750 million Alabama First Plan, but intended to fund it with taxes on casino gambling. I began to see the wheels coming off the reform bandwagon.

On August 23–27, I asked litigants to agree on those issues where we had reached unanimity, those where we had reached consensus but not unanimity, those on which we had neither, and their "drop-dead" ultimatums. Also, I suggested a new rule. When a litigant lost a vote, we would not revisit the issue. The litigants ignored me and returned to their bickering. I cynically concluded in my journal on August 24: "As in most public policy issues, blame is hard to establish and pretty well shared. Meanwhile, the children suffer. But then, who the hell in Alabama cares?"

The next day, I adopted new rules. When we could not reach consensus, I would determine whether litigants seriously intended to find common wording or simply continue to argue. Whenever they presented no new information, analysis, or argument, I would remove that item from the agenda, and we would move on to the next, leaving the existing, previously agreed-upon language in the document. If a litigant refused to sign the final agreement because of some item or two, so be it. The following day, August 26, brought a transformation. It became obvious on the twenty-fifth that Bo Torbert, Susan Walker, and the various defendants were going to make a separate deal, write a document, and present it to Judge Reese. Then the Harper and ADAP plaintiffs could accept it or walk away. Judge Reese called me for a conference to determine what was going on. I cleared my summary with Bo Torbert to be sure he understood my position, and he agreed that my summary of the proceedings was accurate. I then briefed Reese on our progress.

On September 10, spooked school superintendents from Homewood, Hoover, Vestavia Hills, and Mountain Brook asked to meet with me. I brought various litigants and Caroline Novak from A+ to the meeting. Suddenly they had discovered what to me had long been obvious. Our current school funding had been ruled inequitable and inadequate. If the bizarre coalition of AEA, Eagle Forum, Christian Coalition, ALFA, et al. killed the Alabama First initiative in the legislature, then instead of enlarging the size of the pie distributed in roughly equal slices to 130 school systems (thus allowing the wealthy ones to retain their local taxes while leveling the playing field for poor systems from new state taxes), we were left with only the so-called Robin Hood solution. Already used in Texas, this approach to equity simply took tax money from wealthy systems and gave it to poor ones. I knew that in Alabama such a solution would lead to the defeat of local tax referenda in wealthy systems and the flight of affluent white students to private schools. We had a frank but cordial exchange, where I clearly laid out our limited options. None of us wanted Robin Hood in Alabama, I concluded, but to avoid that calamitous result, we would all have to do our duty.

I hoped they would be able to tap down thunder from the religious right and put pressure on AEA. But those superintendents had no more influence with them than I did. Frightened by this reaction, Bo, the governor, and the pragmatists among the litigants began to argue for a general document to present Reese with new taxes but few reforms. In my journal, I vowed to give such a document to Reese if adopted, then denounce it as a sell-out of genuine school reform. Anticipating that Hubbert and the AEA would eviscerate Alabama First in the legislature, I believed that only a firm, reformist remedy agreement would survive this debacle, to be revisited perhaps in future years. Rumors of political pressure on Reese, who planned to run for the Alabama Supreme Court and might buckle on new taxes, worried me even more.

On September 30 at 6:30 p.m., four days before my fifty-third birthday, we completed a compromise remedy that contained real substance and won unanimous support from litigants and defendants. Governor Folsom, just returned from Vance, Alabama, where he had jubilantly announced that Mercedes-Benz had chosen Alabama for its first U.S. plant, presided at a meeting of the State Board of Education that was as full of raucous Alabama ARISE reformers as right-wing activists. Speakers for adoption of the reform plan read like a who's who of north Alabama's Big Mules. Among the opponents were representatives of south Alabama's extractive industries, the religious right, Eagle Forum, and AEA.

We presented our document to Reese on October 18, together with some oral objections by the Harper and ADAP plaintiffs; they were not sufficient to require public hearings, which I feared would degenerate into a circus. After the litigants left, I remained behind to express to Judge Reese my opinion that the remaining differences were not substantial and would not cause any group of litigants to file an appeal. We had done our job and done it well.

Our remedy plan contained specific language designed to address the specious claims of Christian Coalition and its allies: "Nothing in the Remedy Plan calls for, in any way, values clarification activities, or the assessment of any child's values. It is recognized that personal values are best learned by students from sources other than a public education, such as parents, churches, etc." It also guaranteed that no wealthy school system would receive less state money than in the current year. That none of this mattered in the final analysis to any group of critics confirmed what I already believed: the moral causes to which they were most committed were the status quo for Alabama teachers and their apparent perception that Jesus said the wealthy should not pay fair taxes to help the poor.

After thirty-one meetings with the litigant group between June 9 and October 18, four public hearings, six meetings with the governor's task force, five meetings with state and local school boards, and one session with CBS-TV (which ran a special on school reform in Alabama; to even begin to explore the complexities of what I had seen, the special would have been longer than *Gone with the Wind* and contained more bathroom and popcorn breaks) the ordeal ended.

The next day I caught a Delta flight to Charlotte, North Carolina, where I presented the Kelley Lectures at Davidson College and settled back into what passed for me at least as routine life. In the November special session of the legislature, Bill Smith and his allies got the package of Alabama First bills through the senate, thanks to the leadership of Mike Figures and Ryan DeGraffenreid. But after initially endorsing A+ plans at a Tuscaloosa meeting in November 1992, Paul Hubbert reneged, joining the religious right and ALFA in defeating Alabama First in the House. Had Paul released his legislative supporters, I believe Alabama First would have passed. Whether voters would have ratified it is another matter.

I had long lost respect for Paul's allies. I now struggled with his motives as well. Was he more interested in beating Folsom in the Democratic primary than passing the best hope of tax reform in our lifetime? Or was he, as he explained to me, motivated by his belief that the tax increase was too great to win public approval? Or, as his enemies claimed, was he merely a union boss opposing teacher accountability standards? Having enthusiastically supported him for governor in 1990, I switched to Folsom in 1994.

Nor was that the only change in state politics. A new generation of ALFA leaders forced Goodwin Myrick out and replaced him with a less arrogant and less bullying president. Judge Reese did not budge from his support for the remedy plan. Like his Populist forebears before him, he took his crusade for reform straight into the teeth of his enemies and lost badly in his statewide race for the supreme court. Joe Reed of AEA and the black coalition he led endorsed Reese's opponent, a betrayal characteristic of AEA politics (independent thinking was a fatal flaw for anyone wanting its support). Bo Torbert drifted into retirement. His partner, Susan Russ Walker, became a federal magistrate and (I hoped) was being groomed for a federal judgeship someday. DeWayne Key resigned as Lawrence County school superintendent, served as principal of a Church of Christ School for a while, but never deviated from his cause and finally returned to his old school position in Lawrence County. His son, Barkley, took a Ph.D. in history at the University of Florida. Like his father, he was unbending in the cause of social justice. My Jewish friend Bobby Segall led his son in the paths of righteousness as well. In 2008 Josh Segall mounted a spirited campaign for Congress in the 3rd Congressional District against the kind of conservative Republican his father had fought in 1993.

My son Sean, who had attended A+ town meetings and drunk in the heady dreams of what Alabama could become, went off to Missouri with his bride, where he served as communications director for the Missouri Partnership for Outstanding Schools. His relationship with Mel Carnahan, the reform-minded governor of Missouri, was similar to mine with Jim Folsom. Like me, Sean worked with a wonderful coalition of business and civic leaders, Republicans and Democrats, liberals and conservatives who cared mainly about the state's children, quality of life, and economic future. He used his considerable writing skills to mobilize a constituency on their behalf and worked tirelessly to overcome the very same arguments that had "spontaneously" surfaced among religious right groups in Alabama three years earlier. As in Alabama, standing in the shadows behind all these moralistic preachers of traditional virtue was the Farm Bureau. The Missouri Bureau condemned what it called "a mishmash of feel-good ideas," "outcome-based education," concerns about student self-esteem, and most notably "Carnahan's tax increase" for education. Defense of traditional values was good. But in the end traditional values seemed merely the rhetorical window-dressing for old-time American selfishness. It seems Alabama bloodlines ran strong and deep, materialist to materialist, idealist to idealist.

Snatching Victory from the Jaws of Defeat

If I sound cynical after all these years, that is mainly my journal talking. Journals are flawed in that way because they provide only a sliver of reality at a moment in time. I often asked students in my seminars how many had kept journals or diaries. Few men admitted doing so, but most women had. I asked the women when they wrote in their journals. "When I was unhappy," they usually answered. So it was with me. When I was angry, frustrated, shocked, hurt, threatened, overwhelmed, unhappy, I wrote. With lots of names and details. Someone, someday, I vowed, will know what I knew, how I felt, and will understand how it all happened, or at least my perception of how it happened. Often, that angry sliver of reality was correct. But many times, it was like instant replays at football games, an accurate rendering of the moment whose significance was wiped away by the next play. What seemed like defeat might be transformed into victory by shrewdness, persistence, better ideas, and patience. A+ proved that.

In a five-year retrospective report completed in November 1996, A+ turned introspective and self-critical. We raced too far out front of the public. Although citizens were not entirely hoodwinked by Eagle Forum, ALFA, and their allies, they were confused by reformist educational jargon such as "school-based decision making" and "outcome-based education." Our goals and objectives were disconnected, our agenda too ambitious and amorphous. Business leaders worried mainly about job skills and labor-force competence. Public concern focused on school safety, discipline, and teaching basics. Parents worried about graduation rates. Teachers fretted over increased scrutiny, standardized testing, and accountability. Many liberal reformers wanted schools to fix family dysfunction, end poverty, and provide needed nutrition and health care. We should have emphasized basics, better school discipline, and a high school diploma that meant the student possessed adequate skills to compete successfully in the job market. Schools do not improve simply by passing rules and laws. The attitudes of teachers, principals, superintendents, parents, and children have to change as well.

I derived additional meaning from the defeat. Never underestimate the capacity of otherwise upstanding citizens to distort issues on behalf of causes they consider dear. Don't assume that rational dialogue is possible with irrational people. This was as true of David Hornbeck's attempt to reason with Rose Sanders about apprenticeship programs as it was of Cathy Gassenheimer trying to work with Eunie Smith about hypnotism and meditation. True believers on the left and right see conspiracies where none exist.

Nor are there any permanent alliances. Idealistic lawyers could imperil the equity settlement one day and rescue it the next. In my daily journal, I castigated lawyers one week, then praised their courage, spirit of compromise, and tenacity the next. Our deepest human problems are rooted mainly in ignorance, fear, and misplaced priorities, not evil intentions. Even the zany ladies of Eagle Forum advocated policies with which I agreed: the need for more history and civics in classrooms; tougher academic standards at all levels; rigorous content exams for prospective teachers; brighter teachers who were better prepared by colleges of education; the need for more parental discipline and involvement.

As a result, I moved away from Manichean dualities of right-wrong, good-bad, black-white in my speeches and toward fact-based presentations with obvious conclusions. After 1993 I changed my stock education reform speech to include a new approach. Of 391 Alabama public high schools, 370 fielded football teams while only 286 offered a foreign language and fewer than 100 taught computer classes. Does that mean parents, students, educators, and the public have concluded that the economic well-being of their children in the future will depend more on high school football teams than computer and language skills? Montgomery's *Alabama Journal* saw fit to respond to that speech with an editorial, noting that my criticism of misplaced priorities came not from some "snobbish Yankee outsider," but from an Alabama teacher. "May this . . . teacher's lessons soon sink in on a dunce-capped political power structure and the populace whose potential is stifled under it."

What emerged after 1993 from our self-analysis was the Alabama Best Practices Center (a new division of A+), which avoided politics in favor of working with school systems to determine educational practices that worked and finding resources to implement them. The center highlighted schools that outperformed financial resources and tried to explain the factors that accounted for their success. A+ played a major role in selecting two reform-minded state school superintendents, Ed Richardson and Joe Morton, who redirected resources toward stricter financial and academic accountability. Their Alabama Reading Initiative was widely copied by other states after we led the nation in improving standardized test scores. Similar initiatives in math, science, and distance learning began to close the performance gap between poor and wealthy schools as well as between black and white children.

By 2009 the reform movement had generated some amazing accomplishments. George Hall Elementary school in a predominantly low-income black community in Mobile moved from being one of the lowest performing schools in the state to being one of the highest. (In 2003–4 only 12 percent of the school's fourth graders scored at the highest level on reading and math tests; by 2007–08, 80 percent did so.) Scattered across the state, other unlikely schools achieved equally impressive results. Although Alabama scores remained low by national standards, at least they followed a steady upward trajectory after 1993.

A+ also won a $13.2 million grant from the National Math and Science Initiative to increase student enrollment in advanced placement (AP) high school courses. In 2006 only 10 percent of Alabama students took such courses, and only 6 percent passed (comparable national rates were 24 percent and 15 percent). Thanks to the A+ College Ready program, Alabama schools in 2008–9 led the nation in increased student participation and performance on AP tests.

As for the equity funding lawsuit, Alabama continues to live with Judge

Reese's findings although the state supreme court struck down the settlement agreed to after so much difficult compromise in 1993. Arguing that only the legislature could appropriate money, the mainly Republican judges ruled that courts could not impose a remedy. In a 1997 ruling, the court reaffirmed Reese's decision but gave the legislature "reasonable time" to implement a solution. Legislators interpreted this phrase to mean when Jesus comes again, and ignored the court. As a result of this judicial strict construction of the 1901 Constitution, another entire generation of schoolchildren has been cheated out of their birthright, and Alabama corporations still struggle to find enough skilled workers.

In a fifteen-year retrospective of the case, the *Birmingham News* noted that on four occasions the state supreme court had upheld Judge Reese's findings. Yet in 2002 a study showed that Alabama schools with the lowest child poverty rates spent on average $1,000 per student more than those with the highest rates. Statewide, schools needed an additional $1.7 billion a year to pay for the "adequacy" Reese required in his order. If Alabama had taxed property at the same rate as our much poorer neighbor, Mississippi, we could have supplied nearly $1 billion a year of that additional revenue.

Governor Folsom tried to fix the problem in the way the supreme court had mandated and failed in the legislature. Governor Fob James appealed Reese's ruling to the state supreme court, but when it upheld the findings, he convinced the legislature to pass some accountability standards and a new formula that transferred revenue from well-funded systems such as Mountain Brook to poorer systems (just as I had warned superintendents would happen in the fall of 1993). I must confess that part of me relished the irony of Fob James playing Robin Hood, stealing from the rich and giving to the poor.

In 1998 Governor Don Siegelman proposed to solve inequity painlessly by legalizing a lottery for college Hope Scholarships and early childhood programs. Despite my reservations about legalized gambling, I voted for the lottery because I had concluded that Alabamians would never voluntarily raise property taxes for schools. Most adults had no children in school anyway, and those who did often thought their schools were just fine despite considerable evidence to the contrary.

Governor Bob Riley, whom I consider Alabama's first elected New South governor, appointed yet another education study commission, which endorsed many of the 1993 A+ reforms funded by a billion dollar property tax increase. In 2002 supreme court justices once again upheld Reese's ruling but also reaffirmed the legislative "reasonable time" provision (apparently five years to provide equitable schools was too much to expect from our unworthies in the legislature). As the *Birmingham News* editorialized: "No clock is ticking. No hammer is about to come down. No contempt charges hang over lawmakers' heads if they fail to respond." As a result, nothing got done.

Riley sent his billion dollar plan for tax justice to the people. Predictably, most elements of the coalition that had defeated Alabama First in 1993 (minus AEA now that Paul Hubbert was not running for governor, but including virtually all of Riley's own Republican Party), mobilized against his reform. It went down to a two to one drubbing at the hands of voters. Once again the Business Council of Alabama, African Americans, well-educated voters, and reformers provided the governor's strongest support. I gave him full credit for endangering his own reelection chances on behalf of what he believed to be right. But after that massive defeat, he did not try again.

Nearly 90 percent of respondents to a poll that fall said they were losing confidence in public schools. Most believed schools were important to the state's future and that Alabama was not making progress in improving education. They also believed that ground was being lost in teaching the basics, teacher dedication, student discipline and commitment, parental involvement, using tax money wisely, and community support.

The public was correct about some of their concerns. In 1998 a national study found that in seven of ten subject areas, Alabama high school teachers were less likely to be teaching subjects in which they were trained than teachers nationally. In physical sciences, 68 percent of teachers did not major or minor in the fields they taught; in life sciences and history, 56 percent had no major or minor in their primary teaching subjects.

Unwilling to abandon a just cause, or perhaps still relishing a good fight, I refused to turn the issue loose. When Susan DuBose, the State Education Department's social science coordinator, asked me to testify at the social science textbook adoption meeting in August 2004, I marveled anew at opposition arguments. Eagle Forum appeared again, this time condemning a new fourth-grade Alabama history textbook because of an illustration of a nearly naked Native American male holding up a cup that the organization's "expert" believed to be a drug, thus subliminally communicating messages of both sexual titillation and substance abuse. Other speakers condemned the revised U.S. history text (which I had used at Howard College when I was a student in the 1950s) as an example of liberal "political correctness."

The hearings inspired me to write an opinion column in which I discussed nostalgic myths about a golden age of Alabama education, when all upper middle–class whites had attended fine schools untroubled by fear of new ideas from outside the state, when white citizens chose not to see the racism and poverty that underlay so many of Alabama's education assumptions. Now they believed that all those problems could be overcome on the cheap, that education for a technical age and a global economy could be had for half the price of educating students in Connecticut, Washington, or Oregon.

After the failure of Don Siegelman's lottery referendum, I added a section to my education reform speech about the role of the Mississippi Choctaw Indian Foundation gambling money in its defeat. This reference brought a sharp rebuke from the state president of Alabama Christian Coalition (ACC), saying there was no proof to support my charge. "To our knowledge," ACC took no gambling money during the debate. He admonished me "to speak truth in love." I replied that given the ACC campaign of demagoguery and misinformation against Governor Riley's tax reform plan, I found his advice to "speak the truth in love" hypocritical. Furthermore, I found the caveat "to our knowledge" interesting in light of the organization's refusal to release a list of contributors. Shortly thereafter, Republican lobbyist Jack Abramoff confessed in a plea bargain deal that he had laundered Indian casino money through several intermediaries to Ralph Reed, then director of Christian Coalition of America, who had passed it along to ACC. As it turned out, of the $1 million ACC spent to defeat the lottery bill in Alabama, more than four-fifths had come from Choctaw casinos. That may have been the reason ACC chose not to publicize contributions. In fact so out of step was the Alabama chapter, that it soon withdrew from the national organization, which demonstrated too much concern for the poor. "As for a civilized dialogue," I wrote, "I welcome such a conversation with you. Perhaps we can have it in heaven with God listening in so you can explain your aversion to justice for the poor, your refusal to reveal your funding, your support of the nation's most regressive tax system, and your obsession with Jesus's teaching about property taxes." (Jesus said nothing about property taxes.) I'm sure that I did not change his mind. But my reply did end his patronizing sermonettes.

Between 2000 and 2004 I also worked as a consultant in two court cases that had found Alabama schools derelict in funding black schools and hiring black and female superintendents. As a result of those efforts in the *Lee v. Macon* and *Hall/Moffett* cases, both sides agreed to the remedy and the state saved millions in legal fees that could then be spent educating children. In 2009–11 I served as an expert witness in the case of *Lynch v. Alabama,* which challenged the constitutionality of Alabama's property tax system rooted as it was in racism and inequitable treatment of blacks. Though I found the entire process tedious and the seven-hour deposition exhausting, I kept thinking of my mom and dad. How much easier their lives would have been had they attended schools like my grandchildren's in Lake Forest Park, Washington, or even my sons' in Auburn. The fight was still worth the effort. And someday the arc of the moral universe would reach the justice side of the meter.

For all this effort, I received a modicum of consulting fees, a lot of spiritual satisfaction, and more awards than I deserved. When I received the *Mobile Register*'s first annual Alabamian of the Year Award in 1993, the *Alabama Journal* penned my most satisfying tribute: "What does it say about a state to have as the person making most sense about its problems a history professor instead of someone in, or with designs on, public office?" Where are the political leaders offering "incisive commentary on critical public issues that thinking Alabamians yearn for from their political leaders? When was the last time you heard a governor or an influential legislator say something like this [from Flynt's speech]: 'Failures in the state's health, education, and human services are not ordained of God. They result from selfishness, greed, stupidity, and failures of political leadership." Why shouldn't the public hear that from a Christian historian, I wondered? How else ought Christian historians live, write, and talk?

Globalizing Alabama's Problems

The awards were small compensation for the Armageddon I saw ahead. Even at our best, Alabama education reformers compared our improvements to national patterns. But out there on the European and Pacific rims, countries were not waiting on us to get our act together. American children have one of the shortest school years anywhere, 180 days compared to 195 in Europe and more than 200 in Asia. South Korean students, who will take many of the executive jobs in our Kia and Hyundai plants, spend more than a month longer in school each year than Alabama students. Over twelve years, they spend more than a year longer. American children also have one of the shortest school days, six and a half hours (a thirty-two-hour school week). In Denmark the school week lasts fifty-three hours, and in Sweden, sixty hours. Yet many American parents complain because they consider the school year too long already.

Unlike other systems, American children are out of school most of the summer as well, so they have plenty of time to forget what they learn. Studies show that the average child forgets about a month's work in most subjects and almost three months in mathematics. Pedagogues have even coined a name for the phenomenon, "summer learning loss." American children score better than Alabama kids on standardized tests, but fall far below Asian students, especially in math and science.

A 2009 study looked at the economic gap resulting from American educational underachievement. During the 1950s and 1960s, when the United States dominated the world in K–12 and higher education, America also dominated the global economy. During the 1970s and 1980s, America remained dominant in both categories, but China, Japan, India, and Germany rapidly closed the gap. In the early twenty-first century, the United States was falling behind in both. In 2006 the Program for International Student Assessment of applied learning and problem-solving tested skills of fifteen-year-olds in 30 industrialized countries. U.S. students ranked 25th in math, and 24th in science, on a par with Portugal and the Slovak Republic.

If the United States had narrowed the international achievement gap and raised its ranking to that of Finland and South Korea during the fifteen years after publication of *Nation at Risk,* the gross domestic product (GDP) of the nation would have increased by an estimated $1.3 to $2.3 trillion (enough to fund universal health care in 2009 or balance that year's budget deficit). If during that same time, we had closed the gap between black/Latino and white academic performance, the GDP would have grown by between $310 and $525 billion.

Even our selfishness served only our short-term material interests. Our children and grandchildren will pay for what we saved in low taxes not only for our federal deficit. They will pay also for our neglect of the poor and all those children we have left behind. Lorol Rucker explained it all so much more simply than I did: "Save your money and educate your children."

• eleven •

Principalities and Powers

Battling for a New Constitution and a New Politics

Alabama politics is a mess, an embarrassment to ethical men and women who run for office, a disgrace to the state's people, a hog-trough of corruption where it seems that holding public office is an apprenticeship for the state penitentiary. Alabamians ridicule influence-peddling in Chicago and Illinois, when in fact those guys are pikers compared to our unworthies in Alabama. Citizens who agree on nothing else overwhelmingly affirm that they are disgusted with the state's political leadership. Amid all the hokum about "Alabama values," corruption seems to be our most persistent shared political value. Perhaps someone, somewhere once read Plato's dictum that philosopher-kings must combine public power with "virtuous knowledge," but if so, the wisdom has long been forgotten.

The problem, of course, is how to change either the pig or the pigpen. Conversion, either secular or religious, can change the nature of the pig, but Alabama politicians generally don't convert until they are indicted. Lots of reform movements have focused on changing the pen, but to no avail. Whether among Democrats or Republicans, liberals or conservatives, men or women, rural or urban, old or young, black or white, the miasma of political corruption never seems to dissipate.

That is not entirely the fault of the people who hold office. Many of them are better than the structures in which they function. In a state with some of the nation's weakest ethics laws, no restrictions on transfers of campaign contributions from one political action committee (PAC) to another, and the costliest supreme court races in the nation, elected officials take office with a large, dead, smelly, albatross slung around their necks.

All this is no new revelation. Alabama's political system failed its citizens long ago. But the ghost of Halloween did not deposit our elected officials in the middle of a pumpkin patch on October 31 to be discovered the next morning by the people. Citizens in various jurisdictions elect them. Like most American politicians, once elected, they are virtually never defeated. Many newspaper editors and political scientists complain that Alabama deserves politicians as good as its people. But in a democracy, the people either get what they want in officeholders or the least bad of several candidates.

The larger issue then is why citizens are so easily misled and ill-served by the people they elect. There are lots of answers to that question. Poor education is a good starting place. If Alabama voters demanded the right to recall politicians who betray trust, they could have it. Instead, they give credence to the red-herring rationalization of a lunatic fringe of fearmongers. I saw it happen in the A+ meetings, and the phenomenon reappeared in the battle over constitutional reform. Even to repeat the arguments (as I certainly intend to do), makes the state and its voters appear stupid. Citizens elsewhere scratch their heads, wondering why essentially decent people could be completely hornswoggled by such transparent absurdity.

Standing behind the lunatic fringe were malevolent special interests who are not taken in for a moment by the outlandish charges of the minions they so lavishly fund. For them, the issue was quite simple: how to protect their wealth from higher taxes and which buttons to push to make citizens forget their long-term interests on behalf of immediate gratification. Most of the buttons were marked "race," "religion," and "taxes."

For ordinary people, black and white, who were just moving inside the magic circle of middle-class economic security, fear of losing the first home they had ever owned or the private academy where they sent their kids to school, made them easy prey to demagogues and fearmongers with much greater wealth to protect. Despite piles of statistics showing Alabamians the lowest-taxed Americans and America the third-lowest taxed of any industrialized nation, citizens deluded themselves into believing that they were "taxed to death." As a result, to be elected in Alabama required little more than fealty to "Alabama values" (cultural religion) and "no new taxes." Voters, easily seduced by simplistic platitudes, seldom engaged substantive issues. In some sense, then, Alabamians received what they deserved—low taxes, poor schools, a ravished environment, polluted water, inferior state services, a declining future in a high-tech, globalized economy, and politicians renowned for ethical "mistakes" (the concept of sin pervaded Christian theology but was unknown as an explanation of willful political wrongdoing).

I spent my life trying to change this political culture. I contributed money, time, position papers, advice, votes, and fervent prayers on behalf of dozens of friends and acquaintances: U.S. senators John Sparkman, Lister Hill, and Donald Stewart (my high school debate partner); senatorial candidates Natalie Davis and William J. (Bill) Cabaniss; congressmen John H. Buchanan Jr., Ben Erdreich, Bill Flynt Nichols (a distant cousin), and Glen Browder; congressional candidates Ted Little, Bill Fuller, Joe Turnham, and Josh Segall; governors Albert Brewer, Fob James (before I learned better), Jim Folsom Jr., Don Siegelman (another hard lesson for me), and Bob Riley; gubernatorial candidates George McMillan, Bill Baxley (my childhood friend in Dothan), Ann Bedsole, Paul Hubbert (before I switched candidates), and Lenora Pate; legislators/candidates Ted Little, Carolyn Ellis, Pete Turnham, Jack Venable, Chriss Doss, Susan Pace Hamill; judges/candidates Sonny Hornsby, John Denson, Bill English, Sandra H. Ross, Patsy Moore (my cousin), Sue Bell Cobb, and Gorman Houston; candidate for state treasurer Stephen Foster Black, and secretary of state Jim Bennett. Among my heroes in the legislature were Nelson Starkey, Mac Parsons, Mac Gipson, Lister Hill Proctor, John Knight, Tom Radney, Howard Hawk, Jimmy Holley, Mary Stephens Zoghby, Mike and Vivian Figures. Party affiliation, race, gender made no difference to me. Of the 48 names on my list, 36 were Democrats, 12 Republicans; 39 were men, 9 were women; there were 44 whites and 4 blacks.

Despite my lack of party loyalty, Joe Turnham, chair of the state Democratic Party, appointed me senior adviser to the Alabama Democratic Policy Council. In that capacity, I helped party leaders position Democrats in a centrist role that was inclusive of all voters and affirmed Judeo-Christian values of justice and fairness to all.

A constant in all this political activity was my energetic support of tax, education, and constitutional reform. Inside one of my numerous files on tax reform at the Samford University Archives is a Post-it that contains my mantra:

education is cheaper than ignorance. To make education better required more money. To provide more money equitably required raising property taxes. To raise property taxes required a new constitution. Republican governor Bob Riley tried to equalize taxes and provide better schools in 2003 within the provisions of the 1901 Constitution. Faced with economic recession and sharp proration of state education budgets, Riley forged a bipartisan reform coalition and persuaded the legislature to pass an amendment to the constitution that raised taxes on the wealthiest Alabamians while leaving low-income and most middle-class people paying the same property taxes or even less. Under provisions of the constitution, which he entrusted the legislature to modernize, the amendment required ratification in a statewide election. The old enemies of modernization and reform distorted provisions of the complicated amendment.

CEO Mike Warren, chairman of the Campaign for Alabama as it was called, asked me to serve on the board of the proamendment campaign, and I agreed to do so. Unfortunately, meetings occurred when I was in class and could not attend. Otherwise, I would have warned that the Big Mules who were raising money on behalf of reform had spent multimillions of dollars for a century convincing state voters that taxes were too high and educational deficiencies couldn't be fixed by throwing money at them. To undo in six months what these interests had successfully promulgated for a century would call for a miracle beyond their budget or my prayers.

Nonetheless, I agreed to organize Lee County on behalf of the reform campaign. Fortunately, our Republican state representative Mike Hubbard (who was Riley's floor leader in the House) was one of the few members of the governor's own party who supported his reform. Mike provided critical assistance in our GOP-leaning county. I put together a steering committee of twenty-nine members—black and white, liberal and conservative, Democrats and Republicans, men and women. It was a who's who of the county's religious, business, civic, education, and political leadership. My friend Rev. Clifford Jones, pastor of Greater Peace Baptist Church in Opelika and one of the most respected African Americans in the county, taped a passionate television message aimed at working-class voters. Auburn University and public school leaders mobilized teachers and PTA members. Republican members of the committee effectively countered misinformation and inaccuracies about the tax provisions.

I have never been prouder to live in Lee County than on the November morning when election returns poured in. Although Amendment One was drubbed statewide 66 to 33 percent, we carried the city of Auburn 70 to 30 percent and Lee County by a 55 to 45 percent margin. I took comfort in my simple theology: God doesn't hold me accountable for the decisions of Alabama, only for those places where my personal influence can make a difference.

Constitutional Reform

At the core of the problem facing Amendment One was the process required to enact it. The 1901 Constitution limited property taxes to 6.5 mills, though local governments could levy sales taxes without a public vote. Most state constitutions make no mention of tax policy, leaving the matter to statutory law.

Tax policy was only one of many problems embedded in the deeply flawed document. The constitution contained blatantly racist provisions despite federal court rulings striking them down. It was antimodern, prohibiting state funding for internal improvements such as roads and airports, economic development boards, or tax incentives to attract new industry. All these normal functions of modern government required constitutional amendments. The constitution denied most counties and cities home rule. Legislative delegations essentially functioned as county commissions.

For educated citizens or national journalists sent down to report on the state, the situation was as absurd as it was crippling. Because county governments could not govern themselves, legislators had to spend most of their time dealing with local measures. In a typical legislative session, some 60 percent of bills introduced affected a single county or municipality. If even one legislator opposed a local bill, the constitution required a statewide vote. In order to be enacted, the amendment had to win both in the county and statewide. Constitutional amendments were necessary to allow counties to cut overgrown weeds; control animals; remove litter, junkyards, and sewage; and control noise and rattletrap vehicles. So busy were legislators in 2005 crafting such inconsequential legislation, that they had no time to pass a package of bills providing for hurricane preparation and evacuation procedures for the Gulf Coast. Though unable to protect Mobile residents from hurricanes, legislators did find time to set the terms of temporary probate judges in the county, raise the sheriff's salary, and authorize the sale of beer containing up to 14.9 percent alcohol. Establishment of a foreign trade zone in Prichard (Mobile county), one of the state's poorest towns, was sent to a statewide referendum by the opposition of a single legislator, where the amendment failed statewide by 0.32 percent (though it passed in the only county that would have been affected by a margin of 59 to 41 percent). Of the 795 amendments passed by 2007, 70 percent were applicable to a single county. Some 2 percent regulated local bingo games. Potential for national embarrassment abounds. In 2004 Alabama voters narrowly defeated an amendment that would have removed segregation-era language from the constitution due to a last-minute campaign led by the Ten Commandments judge Roy Moore and the Christian Coalition.

Many of the amendments favored powerful special interests. The state's sales tax manual contained three hundred pages of sales tax exemptions, most favoring farmers. Drivers pay taxes on fuel for automobiles and trucks; fuel for motorized farm equipment is exempt. Baby formula is taxed; formula to feed baby cows is not. Food for the elderly is taxed; chicken feed is not. Nor is fertilizer, livestock feed, chicken litter, or twine and stakes used in growing tomatoes.

Protecting special interests is a wordy business. By the beginning of the twenty-first century, Alabama's constitution contained more than 300,000 words, forty times more than the U.S. Constitution and twelve times as many as the average state constitution. I ran some simple mathematical computations for speeches on the constitution. Between 1901 and 1974 voters added 326 amendments in 73 years (an average of 4½ per year). In the 20 years from 1974 to 1994, they passed 246 more (12⅓ per year). From 1994 to 2000, they ratified 134 (22⅓ per year). From 2001 to 2006, the average reached 25 a year. At that rate the constitution will soon take up an entire shelf in a bookcase.

The history of the document is an even worse story than its size. Of the 155 delegates to the 1901 Constitutional Convention, all were white males; 141 were regular Democrats, seven were Populists, six Republicans, and a single independent Democrat. Most delegates had passed age forty, and 108 were either lawyers or bankers. It is hard to imagine a less representative assemblage of Alabamians in 1901, when more than half the population were female, nearly half were black, nearly all farmed for a living, and most were young.

The delegates' primary agenda was to disfranchise black and poor white males, limit property taxes, and strip local governments of their power. Convention president and corporate attorney John Knox of Anniston expressed his intentions clearly in his opening address: "A thousand years' schooling in the theory and practice of sound government ought to make the Anglo-Saxon more skilled in its error principle, for it must be remembered that, in comparison, it was only yesterday that the negro left the barbaric shores of Africa."

The document drafted by delegates exuded racism, classism, and autocracy, quite the opposite of the democratic 1819 Constitution that gave birth to the state.

The November 1901 ratification battle featured some of the most racist arguments in state history. The Democratic Party logo for the campaign frankly announced the central issue: "White supremacy, honest elections and the new constitution, one and inseparable." Outside of twelve predominantly black counties, African Americans overwhelmingly opposed ratification, as did many ordinary white men. Statewide the referendum failed by a vote of 72,000 to 76,000 outside those twelve counties. But in those counties, blacks overwhelmingly voted to deny themselves the right to vote, if the returns are to be believed. Lowndes County, for instance, contained 5,600 registered black men and 1,080 registered whites. But the ratification vote recorded 5,326 in favor of the new constitution and black disfranchisement, and only 338 opposed. Such fraudulent returns enacted the new constitution by a vote statewide of 109,000 to 82,000. So obvious was the fraud that Booker T. Washington twice sponsored legal challenges all the way to the U.S. Supreme Court. Both failed before a court whose racial views were not much different from those of white Alabama voters.

The plantation regime did not rest with enacting disfranchisement, restricting home rule and government-funded internal improvements, or imposing legal segregation. The constitution also capped property taxes against the threat of some future neo-Reconstruction or Populist assault. All this I knew not only from my own research but from reading the book on Alabama constitutions written by Malcolm McMillan, my predecessor as head of Auburn's history department. Malcolm laid the issues before his readers in minute, exhausting detail.

Actually, I had known all this from the day we drove our battered and nearly expired 1959 Buick into Birmingham on that hot August day in 1965. Barely three months later, I sent my first letter to a state legislator, imploring my new senator to pass an amendment requiring the state legislature to reapportion itself (the constitution required it every ten years, but legislators refused to enforce their own law). My enthusiastic support for Governor Albert Brewer was due in part to his endorsement of constitutional reform. On October 4, 1995, I celebrated my fifty-fifth birthday by delivering the keynote address to a state Constitutional Reform Convention in Montgomery.

Like so many of my reform efforts, this one was largely personal. It took historian/journalist Bailey Thomson to provide legs and muscle to the campaign. Ironically, Bailey had the pedigree to be an authentic planter. His father farmed a thousand acres of prime cotton bottom land next to the Tombigbee River. But his mother was a devout Methodist with a keen sense of justice. Bailey worked for newspapers in Louisiana, Florida, and Alabama before completing his Ph.D. in communications history. In 1995 he began teaching at the University of Alabama. That same year he was a Pulitzer Prize finalist for a series in the *Mobile Press-Register,* linking Alabama's problems to the 1901 Constitution.

I devoted research, writing, and speaking to the cause. Bailey literally gave his life for it, dying of a heart attack in November 2003 while building a statewide organization, Alabama Citizens for Constitutional Reform (ACCR). I am convinced that without the organizational genius of this quiet, mild-mannered man the movement would have died with him. Combining the gifts of a skilled journalist, a widely read historian, and an Alabamian passionate about justice, Bailey conceived of long-term grassroots organizing not unlike the civil rights movement. He launched his dream at a well-planned constitutional reform rally in Tuscaloosa on April 7, 2000. When I saw the old-fashioned revival tent where we met, smelled the free hot dogs, heard the bluegrass music, and saw the size of the crowd, I knew the right man was at the helm. He had allied with Johnnie R. Aycock, an Auburn graduate and president of the West Alabama Chamber of Commerce, who yet again connected me to the new corporate reform wing of the state's business community.

Bailey also recruited a bipartisan, five-star slate of leaders: former Democratic governor Albert Brewer; former Republican congressman Jack Edwards; Barbara Larson, executive director of Leadership Alabama; Sam Jones, then-chair of the Mobile County Commission and later mayor of the port city; Odessa Woolfolk, former director of urban studies at UAB and director of Birmingham's Civil Rights Institute; Brandt Ayers, progressive publisher of the *Anniston Star;* Cordell Wynn, former president of Stillman College; Tom Corts, president of Samford University; supreme court justice Gorman Houston; Secretary of State Jim Bennett. That group included an impressive representation of Republicans and blacks.

Bailey asked me to make the keynote address on the origins of the constitution and the ways in which it had shaped the state for the worse. A version of this fifteen-minute presentation became my standard speech on the subject, which I titled "Alabama's Shame: The 1901 Constitution." I focused on three elements of the document: the antidemocratic nature of the state's governing compact; its racist assumptions; and the way it stacked the deck against ordinary people, especially by its suffrage and tax provisions. Press coverage was thorough and enthusiastic. In fact, Bailey followed the Tuscaloosa rally with a seven-day series on the constitution published in the *Mobile Register,* which won him a Distinguished Writing Award from the American Association of Newspaper Editors. The *Birmingham News* launched a series as well.

Bailey announced the creation of ACCR at the April rally, with Tom Corts as president and me on the board of directors. Tom appointed me chair of a committee to draft the organization's statement of principles and scheduled a statewide speaking tour with stops in Mobile, Tuscaloosa, Huntsville, Auburn, Opelika, Tuskegee, Eufaula, and Alexander City. ACCR bought and reconditioned a yellow school bus for the statewide tour. It was a worn-out, run-down bus, which was perfect for a campaign to replace a worn-out, run-down constitution. The tour culminated on April 4, 2001, at a rally on the capitol steps in Montgomery.

Bailey also organized college courses on the constitution. I had long devoted a lecture to the subject in my Alabama history classes and was intrigued by student reaction. Without regard to gender, race, political affiliation, or ideology, they were incredulous about the origins and provisions of the document. Most expressed amazement that the anachronistic constitution still governed the state.

Momentum increased as groups passed resolutions calling for a new constitution. A petition begun in Huntsville attracted seventy thousand signatures. More than five hundred Holt High School students rallied at the capitol. Jim Bennett and Sally Creel formed the Citizen's Commission on Constitutional Reform. Bailey Thomson edited *A Century of Controversy,* a book of essays about the constitution (my essay traced the implementation and effects of the document). The University of Alabama law review published my Tuscaloosa keynote address. ACCR also provided a panel of experts to answer questions on a statewide satellite linkup.

From the outset of the movement, we believed that constitutional reform had as much to do with ethics and religion as with politics and economics. To drive home that point, we focused on the racism, inequitable tax system, and political corruption that had resulted in the 1901 ratification. We published a broadside titled "Constitutional Reform Education Campaign from a Christian Perspective." I even wrote an ACCR blessing to be said before banquets and luncheons, though the prayer pretty well confirmed Dartie's belief that public prayers are usually intended to persuade other people rather than God.

Our cause began to gain traction, as revealed by public opinion polls. We profited, of course, from widespread cynicism about the relationship of special interests to legislators. Asked who controlled Alabama government, 40 percent of respondents in one poll answered special interests, 30 percent the governor, and 20 percent the legislature. Only 8 percent believed the people governed the state. That belief helped unify voters around a statewide constitutional convention. Of all reform options available, that one would be the most difficult for special interests to dominate, which is why they opposed it so fiercely. Letting legislators revise the document was the least preferable option. In the century after 1901, the legislature had plenty of opportunities to rewrite the document. Legislators had succeeded in that one hundred years in rewriting one section, the judicial article, and that by a single vote.

Citizens favored our approach. Capital Research, the most accurate state polling group, established a benchmark in May 2000, when 75 percent of the state's registered voters thought the state needed a new constitution. Most also preferred a constitutional convention of elected or independently (not by public officials) appointed delegates. A *Mobile Register* poll set the pro–new constitution figure at 57 percent, still a solid majority, with 51 percent favoring the convention method of rewriting. Another Capital Research poll in 2004 revealed that citizens trusted an elected convention over a legislative rewrite by a nearly two to one margin. In 2005 a statewide survey showed that only 19 percent of registered voters believed Alabama's constitution was adequate to meet state needs. More than six in ten wanted a convention to rewrite the document. An overwhelming majority of legislators also told a *Huntsville Times* reporter that the state needed a new constitution, but while in session they stonewalled every bill that tried to accomplish that end. They disingenuously blamed special interests for blocking bills authorizing a vote by the people, when they, in fact, were recipients of special interest campaign contributions and were the ones who refused to report such bills out of committee.

Reformers began to suggest other strategies. As early as 2000, I received letters despairing of Alabama solving its own problems (authors of the correspondence could cite many precedents: the refusal to enfranchise women; abolish the poll tax, literacy tests, or segregation; establish humane treatment for the mentally ill or equitable education funding; and a dozen other issues). The state's past did not augur well for prophetic leadership from the legislature. So the letters advised recourse to federal courts. Some suggested that voters simply vote down every amendment passed by the legislature until it authorized a constitutional convention.

As public opinion tilted toward a convention, legislators and their keepers grew increasingly anxious. When Governor Don Siegelman switched from apathy to enthusiastic support for a convention during his reelection campaign in 2002, it set the stage for an interesting gubernatorial debate with challenger Bob Riley, who preferred a gubernatorially appointed commission and legislative rewrite. State newspapers overwhelmingly favored a convention, as did progressive Republican legislators such as Mac Gipson of Prattville.

Democratic state senator Roger Bedford asked me to meet with him in the fall of 2000 to discuss strategy for reform. In our meeting, he introduced a stable of bright constitutional lawyers (one was an Auburn graduate and Rhodes scholar) who lobbied me to endorse either a legislative rewrite for voter approval or appointment of a blue-ribbon constitutional reform commission of the state's most respected statesmen to draft a new document. Senator Bedford feared an elected constitutional convention run amok. Although I recognized such a possibility, the idea that two hundred or so ordinary citizens could craft a new constitution worse than the one that governed us seemed farfetched. I also relished the way that even the idea of a people's constitutional convention spread terror through the offices of AEA, ALFA, the Forestry Association, Alabama Christian Coalition, and Eagle Forum. An opportunity for the people to write a constitution! An idea that Alabamians celebrated in Iraq and Afghanistan but that sparked dismay among political elites in Montgomery!

Legislators, determined to block a citizens' convention no matter how many people wanted it, began to spin historic arguments as specious as they were familiar. The real goal of reformers was to increase property taxes (our real goal was to eliminate constitutional tax provisions and move tax authority where it was in most states, in statutory law controlled by people through legislators they elected). A constitutional convention opened the possibility of control by zany, one-issue zealots (as if that hadn't already happened in the legislature). Special interests such as AEA, Christian Coalition, ALFA, and others would dominate the election (a constitutional convention could not bestow more power on special interests than they already possessed). There was no public clamor for a citizen's convention, and legislators had received no "significant constituent contact" regarding the matter. (That was a bad argument that resulted in many calls and letters, including one from my son Sean to his Republican senator Jack Biddle; Biddle had told a reporter that not one constituent had contacted him, which elicited Sean's one-sentence letter to the *Birmingham News*: "Jack, we need a new constitution.") Furthermore, our unworthies down in Montgomery had made a practice of passing wretched laws at the behest of special interests without a "single constituent contact." So perhaps the real issue was not ACCR's incapacity to overload their mail or telephone systems but our lack of funds to buy their votes through an intricate maze of legislative corridors, back rooms, and PACs where *money* represented the ultimate "*significant* constituent contact."

I received further confirmation that we were making progress when Alabama's lunatic fringe reappeared as it had in the education reform debate. If men are from Mars and women are from Venus, Sandra Lane Smith and her Alabama Association for Judeo-Christian Values came from the far side of Pluto. The real object of ACCR, she insisted, was to remove God from the preamble of the constitution. Furthermore, reformers advocated a "radical, anti-family" agenda as proven by their intention to replace the words "all men are created equal" with "all men and women are created equal." Another goal of ACCR, she argued with perfect seriousness, was to realign Alabama's borders in order to pave the way for a United Nation's takeover of the state. (With all the problems in Africa, Latin America, and the Middle East, I was unclear why the UN would want to add Alabama to its list of dependent states.) Another subtle plot she discovered was our plan to make it easier to remove supreme court chief justice Roy Moore from office. (Actually that was one of the few existing problems that the constitution handled quite well by providing a panel of retired and special judges who removed Moore for refusing to enforce federal court rulings because, he argued, Alabama's constitution took precedence over the U.S. Constitution.) Vowing against all historical evidence and reason that Alabama had "the strongest constitution in the U.S." (something not even her Republican allies claimed), Smith lumped together the weirdest coalition that ever filled an empty head: AEA, trial lawyers, the AFL-CIO, and the Business Council of Alabama. The bill by Republican representative Mac Gipson to which she referred guaranteed all those special interests representation in a constitutional convention, along with ALFA, a fact she conveniently failed to mention. Perhaps her omission of ALFA from the malevolent coalition resulted from the fact that the corporation was the largest contributor to Smith's PAC, ironically named Value PAC (in this case, ALFA seemed to get ample if quirky *value* from Ms. Smith).

To state newspaper editors, Smith sounded identical to ALFA, and they pronounced her ideas "farfetched" and "absurd." Her argument that God ordained Alabama's 1901 Constitution even inspired a wonderful cartoon depicting a vengeful and obviously perturbed deity desperately trying to find one of his refilled plague-jars (locusts, floods, fire, other pestilence). A voice offstage implores him to check the constitution "plague-jar" under the sink.

The *Anniston Star* editorial staff's account of Smith's visit with them was my favorite. According to Smith, the entire reform movement was hatched in the UN as part of its piecemeal attack on the United States, the state of Alabama, and Calhoun County. Governor Don Siegelman was the plot's chief agent in the state. Smith cited as her authority for this unique revelation one Archibald E. Roberts of Fort Collins, Colorado. (It was heartening to discover that not all wackos live in Alabama.) Roberts's newsletter, Smith revealed, described the plans of "regional revolutionaries" who "seek to dissolve governments, merge sovereign states into ten Standard Federal Regions, transfer state power to central authority in Washington, administer the affairs of U.S. citizens through a network of appointed agents." If only she had known of my subversive Marxist past in Cuba, or the way I was stuffed with fine Cuban cigars and churros before being smuggled into Florida and then Alabama, it would have sealed her argument.

The entire episode reminded me of my dentist in Birmingham during the late 1960s, who filled his office with John Birch Society literature condemning the use of fluoride in drinking water. Whether this scheme resulted more from ideology or avarice, I never discovered. Three decades later, I think of him unkindly every time my Auburn dentist caps another tooth or does another root canal. Remaining quiet in the presence of an ALFA-funded advocate like Smith would have been easier for me had this entire unflattering episode not appeared in a half page article in the February 25, 2002, issue of the *New York Times*. But that is the price people pay when they allow such a person to speak for them.

The Federal Coda

Although I was moved to tears when ACCR presented me the 2008 Bailey Thomson Award for my generation-long work for constitutional reform, I grew increasingly restive with the pace of change. Infinitely patient Bailey would have reassured me. But in his absence, I saw a public becoming better informed and a legislature digging in its heels. In the 2009 legislative session, the House Elections Committee claimed to have a majority in favor of reporting a bill authorizing a statewide referendum on a constitutional convention. But the required votes never materialized, and the issue was once again postponed.

Concluding that despite pious platitudes, our unworthies would never relinquish the levers of power until forced to do so, I agreed to serve as expert witness in two federal court challenges to the 1901 Constitution. If Alabama legislators must forever shirk their responsibilities to what even they agree is necessary for decent government, our best recourse (as at so many times in the past) is the judiciary. *Price v. King* challenged the legitimacy of the 1901 Constitution based on the clearly fraudulent ratification vote in November 1901. *Lynch v. Alabama* sought to have tax provisions of the document struck down as racist and discriminatory.

How ironic, I thought, as I was deposed in the Lynch case, that lawyers and citizens so devoted to states' rights never seem to get it. If states exercise rights, they are accountable to the people and should act justly and fairly. When they fail this most elemental measure of democracy, they forfeit their states' rights. Many of the same conservative leaders who demanded more teacher accountability during the battle over school reform fell strangely silent at our demand for accountability in the levying of taxes or in their fair and just distribution. The philosophical premise of lawyers representing the state in the Lynch case seemed to be that in a democracy, if a majority of white people don't want to pay taxes, they have every right to starve education, withhold vital health care, perpetuate inhumane prisons and mental hospitals, and deny fundamental human rights (or in short, to refuse to be accountable to all citizens). By the standard of governing Alabama based on what a white majority preferred, segregation would have lasted half a century longer than it did.

In the formative days of the American nation, patriot John Adams wrote his beloved wife, Abigail, that "a new constitution must begin in the minds and hearts of the people." Had Adams lived in Alabama, he would have known that what gestates in the hearts of the people often perishes in the back corridors of the state house. And justice, when born at all, is usually midwifed by the federal bench.

• twelve •

In the Eye of the Storm

Auburn University, 1989–2000

Living in Alabama even for a brief time leaves impressions, sometimes good, other times not so good. One of my favorite novelists, Ralph Ellison, spent only a few years at Tuskegee University. But the Tuskegee machine's accommodations and compromises, which Ellison interpreted as hypocrisy and betrayal, imprinted his fiction for a lifetime. Tuskegee formed the backdrop for *Invisible Man,* one of the finest American novels of the twentieth century. Ellison penned a paragraph that is as appropriate a summation of my three decades at Auburn University as of his three years at Tuskegee:

> Well, now I've been trying to look through myself, and there's a risk in it. I was never more hated than when I tried to be honest. Or when . . . I've tried to articulate exactly what I felt to be the truth. No one was satisfied, not even I. On the other hand, I've never been more loved and appreciated than when I tried to "justify" and affirm someone's mistaken beliefs; or when I've tried to give my friends the incorrect, absurd answers they wished to hear. In my presence they could talk and agree with themselves, the world nailed down, and they loved it. They received a feeling of security. But here was the rub: Too often, in order to justify them, I had to take myself by the throat and choke myself until my eyes

bulged and my tongue hung out and wagged like the door of an empty house in a high wind. Oh yes, it made them happy and it made me sick. So, I became ill of affirmation, of saying "yes."

The temptation for those who loved Auburn was to justify and affirm mistaken beliefs while choking themselves until their tongues hung out.

I worked for many wonderful Auburn administrators who impressed me with their integrity, their courage, and their dedication to the school they loved. I watched those men and women resign offices they treasured, rather than surrender their honor or compromise their sense of duty. I understood their affection. Like many of them, I bought in completely to the outreach mission of the university. I applauded my department's primary commitment to teaching undergraduates. I liked most of the undergraduate students I taught. I proudly watched my graduate students' careers and lives unfold and recorded in my mind how nearly every one of them enriched the world by their presence. I relished speaking with alumni who loved their alma mater sufficiently to be critical of it when necessary, as a loving parent corrects a wayward child. I bonded with a courageous faculty that would not retreat into classroom, laboratory, library, or archive when ignorant or malicious forces threatened the integrity of their university.

Auburn was always a good place. In times of crisis, it was often a great place in the willingness of its people to remain and fight rather than to despair and leave. Alas, like all fragile human institutions, it was also a deeply flawed place. A place so beloved deserves to have its story told honestly, without justification or rationalization, and that is the way I intend to tell it. My version is just that and no more. Other people have other versions, and they can relate their own accounts as they please.

Bobby and Me

My tenure at Auburn paralleled Bobby Lowder's slow but steady ascendency to control of the university, culminating in his takeover of the board of trustees in 1999–2000. Lowder was a control freak, obsessed with football, shrewd and manipulative, politically astute, and willing to spend whatever it took from his vast fortune to win a national football championship and control the board.

In his single-minded purpose and tactics, Lowder reminded me of the zealots who took over the Southern Baptist Convention in 1979. Baptists became besmirched by such tactics and the fierce reaction to them. The strategy they used to take over the denomination fragmented institutions, alienated fellow believers, and ushered in a phase of national scrutiny, withering criticism, and decline. Auburn followed a similar trajectory. As with Southern Baptists, there were legitimate areas of disagreement open to alternative interpretation within the battle for Auburn's soul. Were Bobby Lowder writing this memoir, he would offer a different view of nearly every issue.

One irony of the decades-long conflict was the battle to the death between two of my least favorite corporations, Bobby Lowder's Colonial Bank and Goodwin Myrick's ALFA (Alabama Farmers Federation, formerly the Farm Bureau). My interviews with three influential ALFA leaders revealed that the source of their animosity toward Bobby Lowder dated from his father's leadership of the company. They believed that Ed Lowder's two-decades-long tenure as CEO resulted in a suit filed against him by Attorney General Bill Baxley (charges later dismissed). According to them, he was forced to resign by ALFA's board, which included Emory Cunningham, who would later clash with Bobby over control of Auburn's board of trustees. As one former ALFA executive told me: "One thing about the Lowders [Ed and Bobby]. Anything they are associated with they are determined to control."

In 2001, during one skirmish in a long war, I received a letter from a former history major turned salesman who had worked for Colonial Bank. The letter was highly critical of me and history teachers in general who, he believed, worked very little, slacked on their responsibilities to students, and couldn't survive in a world of "true capitalism." But his embittered evaluation of me was piddling compared to his indictment of Lowder: "I worked for Bobby Lowder and know him to be an evil ego-maniac. He pictures himself as a wise man that knows what is best for everyone. He also looks at himself as a great salesman—the actual fact is that he could not give away prostitutes on a troop train."

Of course, ego, attention to detail, and the willingness to make hard decisions can be assets. They assisted Lowder in building Colonial Bank into one of the nation's fifty largest financial institutions. Bobby's siblings, obviously not afflicted with his compulsions, are widely respected as honorable, successful businessmen, public-spirited and philanthropic. But obsessive devotion to a cause can be perilous ground strewn with land mines.

ALFA was not innocent of such obsessions itself. So embittered at Ed Lowder were its leaders, past and present, that some sought to block naming Auburn's business building in his honor, contending that son Bobby did not contribute the required funds for the building's maintenance. When Bobby Lowder forged an alliance with senate majority leader Lowell Barron to push through the banker's slate of Auburn trustees, ALFA hired a private detective to collect dirt on Barron. The battle continued through various gubernatorial proxies, with ALFA funding Republican Fob James's campaigns and Lowder bankrolling Democrats Jim Folsom Jr. and Don Siegelman.

Actually, my relationship with Lowder began amicably enough. He had been a fan of Hanly Funderburk initially, but when the situation at Auburn became untenable, Lowder was instrumental in removing Funderburk as president. I observed over time that sacking former allies when they were no longer useful to him was a Lowder tendency. I wrote Lowder, praising his role in Funderburk's resignation. I suggested that if he exercised the same care in searching for a new Auburn president as he had in acquiring Pat Dye as head football coach—a truly national search; no requirement that the leader be an Auburn graduate—the university would be well served.

Although the subsequent presidential selection process produced an Auburn graduate from the College of Agriculture, James (Jim) Martin, I did not disparage the result. Gerald Johnson, university senate president and church friend, served on the search committee, certified its professionalism, and assured me of Martin's positive résumé as president of the University of Arkansas. When many faculty leaders later criticized Martin for his eminent scholars initiative and the construction of a hotel and conference center, I investigated similar programs he had begun at Arkansas and defended them to faculty critics.

On the other hand, I began to receive troubling reports from other sources about Lowder and trustee protocol. None was more reliable than Wil Bailey, who had rescued the university from disintegration during his brief interim presidency. A rigidly ethical Church of Christ layman and cofounder of the Alabama Poverty Project, Wil often traveled with me to APP board meetings. Wil's stories stoked my suspicions about Lowder and the shadowy booster world that operated on the fringes of Auburn athletics. Lowder, he told me numerous times, preferred a secretive management style. He hated reporters, newspapers, publicity of any kind, good or bad. He made no public comments, operating within a cloistered world of secret meetings and private communication.

When Bailey agreed to accept the interim presidency, he had insisted on certain conditions. The response to some of them reflected the vindictive small-mindedness that would plague the university for two decades. Bailey, for instance, insisted, over the objections of some trustees, that Taylor Littleton return to the administration as "academic adviser to the president." They reluctantly agreed but refused to allow him to occupy his former academic vice president's office in Samford Hall. Another condition was the termination of non-public meetings where trustees had made all important decisions. (Public trustee meetings merely certified the clandestine agreements.) These must stop, Bailey insisted, and trustees agreed to his terms.

At the very first trustee meeting after Bailey became president, they reneged, conducting university business in secret as usual. Wil listened with growing anger until they finished. Then he announced that when they adjourned to the public meeting that followed, his first act would be to resign as president, followed by an explanation of their earlier agreement and prompt reversal. Agitated trustees talked him out of resigning and vowed not to repeat their offense. He agreed to remain in office so long as they kept their word.

Before many weeks passed, a trustee appeared in his office on another inappropriate mission. Bailey listened impatiently, then responded: "See that nameplate on my desk? It will take me less than a minute to pick up it and my other possessions and walk out the door." The trustee apologized and intruded no more. Later still, the president got wind of a Savannah football booster offering a prized football recruit prohibited financial incentives to sign with Auburn. Bailey called Coach Dye, explained the situation, and warned that if the player signed with Auburn, Bailey would not enroll him.

Despite such accounts and differences of personality and leadership style, the core of my dispute with Lowder consisted of substantive disagreements about the nature of the university. The banker and College of Business graduate told another trustee he should compare salaries of history, English, and other liberal arts graduates to business graduates in order to determine the value of various academic majors. In an era (1980–2005) when business school enrollment exploded and a master's of business administration (MBA) seemed the path to America's nirvana of wealth and power, bankers and financial services firms grew rich on derivatives, subprime loans, and other risky financial practices that in time would bring down America's financial system. But at the time, risk-taking bankers such as Lowder were the nation's new icons. Lowder's wealth soared along with his bank's profits, until the value of his Colonial stock alone approached $200 million. In America, such prosperity commanded attention. And when such prosperity was devoted to a single cause—funding political campaigns, acquiring quiescent friends, buying political influence, or taking over a university—people listened.

Certain disaffected Auburn constituencies were especially inclined to pay attention: alienated football fans who believed presidents such as Harry Philpott and Wil Bailey meddled too much with what should be an entrepreneurial, unfettered football program where money purchased the best play-ers; agricultural commodity groups unhappy with presidents who reorganized their college and even appointed a black man in charge of university outreach; alumni and even some faculty and administrators who believed professional schools received too few resources during an era of booming enrollment; older alumni who attended Auburn during an era when half of all Alabamians lived in rural areas and farmed (not until 1960 did most state residents live in towns or cities of twenty-five hundred or more) and who concluded that the univer-sity had lost interest in them.

Lowder laid out his arguments about the university's purpose in a January 1992 letter published in the *Chronicle of Higher Education*. Selecting Clemson University as his ideal of land grant education (a curious choice because Clem-son was not considered nationally to be among elite Morrill Act land grant uni-versities such as Cornell, Pennsylvania State, Michigan State, Massachusetts Institute of Technology, Georgia, and the University of Florida), he criticized his alma mater for deviating from its original purpose. Land grant colleges had contributed significantly to science, he wrote, while adding practical courses in business, veterinary medicine, medicine, pharmacy, architecture, and engi-neering. Emphasizing the early tensions within Alabama Polytechnic Institute, as Auburn University was then called, he noted that several presidents, notably William Leroy Broun (who was also a former president of the American Asso-ciation of Land Grant Colleges and Universities), had insisted that education devoted to culture alone did not fit a person for the "active duties of life."

Lowder wrote that teaching was Auburn's fundamental mission (I agreed with him on that). Research supported teaching (once again, we concurred). Extension (outreach) promoted a "better quality of life" for all Alabama citi-zens (thus far, we were three for three). Then Lowder disclosed his real agenda. Not everyone at Auburn shared his vision. Some wished to see Auburn "com-pete academically with Vanderbilt or Emory rather than serve the traditional land grant functions that Auburn has historically undertaken. The mission of Auburn University is really what is at issue." As two decades of debate made clear, his mission was to deemphasize liberal arts, strengthen professional schools, and win an NCAA football championship at any cost.

In light of subsequent meddling by some trustees with academic standards, their demand for a change in policy that allowed students with failed grades to retake courses, and pressure placed on a faculty member at Auburn Uni-versity Montgomery (AUM) to change a failing grade, faculty understand-ably became suspicious of Lowder's rejection of Vanderbilt and Emory as role models. Could it be that Lowder's real concern was that Emory had no foot-ball team and Vanderbilt's was the worst in the Southeastern Conference? Per-haps Lowder's preference for Clemson had nothing to do with historic land grant missions and everything to do with the admission of marginally qualified blue-chip football players. It certainly had nothing to do with Vanderbilt and Emory's academic reputations. *U.S. News & World Report* in September 2009 ranked the two schools tied for seventeenth among America's best national universities, with Clemson in sixty-first place and Auburn ranked eighty-eighth. Over the next few years, as Lowder's control of the board of trustees increased, so did the number of partial qualifiers who signed football scholar-ships but could not attend without prep school or junior college remediation. Auburn and the University of Alabama led the Southeastern Conference in signing players who could not qualify under ever more stringent NCAA aca-demic standards. Trustee meddling in internal academic standards paralleled the trend of admitting skilled football players.

Putting the best interpretation possible on the position taken by Lowder and other football-crazed trustees, the issue was democratic access for even the most marginally qualified applicants, regardless of athletic participation. Those of us who were more cynical concluded that the heart of the struggle involved finding ways around NCAA rules and our attempts to improve what were, by other research university standards, Auburn's low admission require-ments.

This debate raged for a quarter century and is not yet resolved. In 1992, I was appointed to a university committee on Auburn's scope and mission, which had grown out of the spat over Lowder's letter to the *Chronicle*. My chief con-tribution to the committee's charge—in addition to suggesting that one way to save money would be to eliminate agricultural extension programs that were redundant or operated in counties that had virtually no farmers—was care-ful research in university records back to Auburn's origins as a land grant uni-versity.

Unlike some Morrill Act schools, Auburn had existed for more than a de-cade before its incarnation as an agricultural and technical college. Its classical curriculum was typical of the Methodist denomination that had chartered the college: Latin, Greek, philosophy, theology, history, literature, mathematics, sciences. These disciplines were considered quite sufficient to prepare gradu-ates for the "active duties of life," whatever they may have been.

I. T. Tichenor, the first president of the land grant university, merged the college's historic and new identities. In his second annual report (July 30, 1873), he complained that "men of letters" who composed the faculty had little interest in "agricultural pursuits." These "nurses or guardians" of the college's traditions threatened to strangle or starve it to death. But farmers prejudiced against "book farming" posed an equally serious threat.

In his third report (1874–75), Tichenor reasserted his fear of attacks from opposite directions. The school's mission, he told trustees, was to teach agriculture, mechanical arts, and military tactics "without excluding other scientific and classical studies." Indeed, the college's six professors included professors of mathematics, languages, natural sciences, and moral philosophy. Only two of the six taught applied subjects such as agriculture and engineering. Such a curriculum would not make a student wealthy or famous, Tichenor philosophized, as would traditional curricula of law and medicine (the nineteenth-century equivalents of business schools?). But it would serve the needs of Alabama's ordinary people and supply a graduate ways to "benefit his countrymen." Those advocating this new concept of education as service to humanity must be content to be misunderstood, "sustained by the consciousness that its purposes are right, its ends are pure, its methods wise, and its ultimate triumph assured."

By hiring George W. Petrie a few years later to teach Latin and history, Auburn validated Tichenor's vision and cemented the school's place in land grant history. It was Petrie's vision of Auburn, more than president Broun's (whom Lowder quoted) or Tichenor's (whom I referenced) that shaped Auburn.

A summary of my research found its way into the final draft of our mission statement. By citing only Broun's conclusion in his letter to the *Chronicle*, Lowder had distorted the university's history and made it appear overly simplistic. Whatever our conflicting interpretations of Auburn's history, a battle had begun in those years that would continue to reverberate into the twenty-first century. Although I disagreed with Lowder's reading of Auburn traditions, I was not entirely unsympathetic to his demand that resources be reallocated from declining enrollment programs so long as the procedures were uniform and fairly administered. Although most liberal arts professors believed this was a malicious strategy aimed at them, I believed it would benefit underfunded core curricula courses in our college largely at the expense of declining programs in agriculture. Problem was none of us believed trustees would implement a strategy of strengthening the liberal arts core at the expense of agricultural programs no matter the extent of enrollment shifts.

In the winter 1992 issue of the *Auburn Circle* literary magazine, editors juxtaposed Lowder's letter next to an interview with me as polar opposites in this debate. However one defined Auburn's mission, I wondered why some trustees would not aspire to putting the university's academic programs in the top ten nationally (or even seventeenth, like Vanderbilt's and Emory's). That certainly was their goal in football. Could anyone imagine a press release from athletic director David Housel congratulating the football team for ranking eighty-eighth in the final NCAA football poll? Then why congratulate the university for ranking eighty-eighth or even sixty-first academically? It was revealing, I added, that Lowder cited Clemson University as a model for us, a school without doctoral programs in most of the humanities and social sciences, but with a strong football tradition, instead of land grant universities such as Florida and Georgia, which had both. By then, I had served on a civil engineering departmental self-study where one executive of a top-ten American engineering construction firm praised Auburn engineers for their values, work ethic, technical knowledge, reliability, and civic-mindedness, but criticized their lack of breadth beyond engineering and especially their poor communication skills. I also chided Lowder for refusing to come on campus and debate physicist Eugene Clothiaux, who was chair of the university senate, about the issues raised in his letter. Lowder had said he would debate the issues, but when invited to do so, he had declined.

When my comments reached wider circulation in the *Atlanta Constitution,* I received new "fan" mail. A "pissed-off reader in or around Atlanta" (and self-described devoted Auburn fan) wrote that I was "an ass, an oaf, a dullard, a simple butt, a knave, an academic incubus, an incorrigible scapegrace, a carousing scalawag, or merely an elitist air-headed bastard." That torrent of opprobrium tumbled out of only the first line of seven paragraphs. The second paragraph did not advance any arguments but did demonstrate the author's mastery of invective: "Attempts like yours to redefine what a university is are unspeakably ugly to me. Your incessant querulousness; indeed your booger-eating, bed-wetting, hand-wringing dirge cries for a social justice [*sic*] but really only pees on the fiery enthusiasm of the children seeking enlightenment."

Such critics, largely quiescent since the Funderburk days, reappeared from the dark crevices where they had taken refuge. Some nationally prominent Auburn scholars needed only one such letter before circulating CVs and leaving for other schools. Most Auburn faculty were like me; they had sufficient scar tissue from earlier years, had bonded so tightly with colleagues and students, and cared enough about the school to dismiss such incivility as unrepresentative of true Auburn people.

By 1996 I began to understand that Lowder's campaign was much more complex and political than I had realized. In September I received a flyer called "The Auburn Alert." It attacked Republican U.S. senatorial candidate Jeff Sessions of Mobile who, during his term as Alabama attorney general, had issued a ruling allowing Governor Fob James to "take over the board." (Actually Sessions had ruled that Lowder could not remain on the board after his term expired despite the fact that his crony, senate majority leader Lowell Barron, had blocked confirmation of a replacement.) Even worse, according to the flyer, Lowder's proposed replacement was vice president of ALFA. The flyer quoted Birmingham lawyer and former AU football player Gusty Yearout criticizing Sessions's ruling, pretty much sealing the deal for many AU football partisans. The flyer hinted that Sessions had sold his opinion for thousands of dollars in campaign contributions from ALFA. Years later, when Republican attorney general Troy King ruled in Lowder's favor in another suit that allowed the banker to extend his trustee term, there was no comparable outcry of injustice from Yearout and others despite King's admission that he had received a $10,000 campaign contribution from Lowder. King returned the contribution in order to avoid the "appearance of impropriety."

The James Martin Administration

Although I got along well with president Jim Martin personally and thought him generally a successful president, most of my faculty colleagues disagreed. Several issues troubled them. Many senate insiders and former administrators believed he caved in to the trustees (a conclusion I reached only much later and after considerable research). Faculty criticism of the hotel and conference center, the eminent scholars program, and Martin's emphasis on research, further weakened him. On all three matters, I sided with Martin. I wrote him on June 4, 1990, that superior teaching usually went hand in hand with original research. Auburn must maintain a dual reward system that did not punish one priority in order to benefit the other.

Ironically, it was Martin's eminent scholars program that brought him down. During the 1988–89 academic year, I served on a search committee, chaired by former vice president Taylor Littleton, to fill the newly established Goodwin-Philpott Eminent Scholar chair in religion. J. W. Goodwin, an Auburn alumnus and wealthy Birmingham businessman, had already contributed millions to the university's music program. He added an additional million to honor his old friend Harry Philpott, whose religion degree from Yale, support of the Religion Department, and refusal to name Shug Jordan athletic director, were all so inimical to Lowder's vision of the university. Rumors circulated that Goodwin had been Ed Lowder's business partner until they had a falling out.

The Religion Department was small, though its leadership under Rollin Armour, John Kuykendall, James (Jim) Dawsey, and Richard Penaskovic had made it respected on campus. Our pool of candidates was limited, and I had some misgivings about all of them, including our final choice, Vincentian priest and theologian Charles E. Curran. Though an orthodox Catholic on some issues, he was a controversial liberal on others, including abortion, birth control, and homosexuality. Furthermore, whereas his faculty predecessors Armour, Kuykendall, and Dawsey were Baptist, Presbyterian, and Methodist, respectively, all of whom appealed to our overwhelmingly Protestant students, we had few Catholic students, nor had the state many Catholic residents. Nonetheless, Curran was clearly the best qualified candidate, author of an impressive list of books, and the only theologian ever to head the three leading professional societies in his discipline. After a quarter century on the faculty, he had been forced out of Catholic University for what many Catholics regarded as heretical views. For the next two years, he had served on the faculty of the University of Southern California.

Curran had some reservations about coming to Auburn, which was serving yet another term of AAUP censorship for violations of academic freedom. Also, the town had few Catholics and only one congregation that sponsored student ministries run by Vincentian Fathers. But they approved his candidacy, and in early April, liberal arts dean Mary Richards and Ron Henry, academic vice president, offered Curran the lucrative and prestigious Philpott chair with a promise of tenure. Philpott and Henry called him to urge acceptance. Martin announced that Curran's "extensive experience in the areas of religious ethics and moral theology make him a true eminent scholar and we think his teaching at Auburn will be of benefit to our students."

Then on April 16, Richards called Curran to report a bump in the proceedings. Martin had developed doubts about granting him tenure. Martin gave no reason for his refusal, explaining only that anyone who had the information he had would have made the same decision. Curran replied that any Catholic priest who had taught for a quarter century at Catholic University had been vetted thoroughly and had nothing to hide. Henry sent Curran's credentials to the tenure and promotion committee, which recommended tenure. Martin rejected their proposal, instead granting him a temporary, one-year, untenured appointment to an endowed chair, undoubtedly one of the strangest eminent scholar appointments in U.S. higher education. Curran, who had already with-drawn from two other searches, had no choice but to accept. Those of us on the search committee strenuously objected to Martin's action but to no avail.

Curran came to Auburn and kept his peace, knowing that more controversy would only complicate his job search. Insiders furnished more details about the affair, which Curran later confirmed in his memoir *Loyal Dissent*. Accord-ing to speculation, Archbishop Oscar Lipscomb of Mobile had expressed res-ervations about him to a Catholic trustee, who raised the issue in the secret April 7 trustee meeting. Some other trustees chimed in. One later commented that he did not understand all the commotion about tenure anyway. He had never heard of Curran, and "if Auburn is being hurt by this decision, it's only among a small portion of the academic community. Auburn is not, and I don't ever want it to be, a Harvard. Auburn is intended to educate the middle-class group of people in the South." Curran speculated that Lowder, who disliked both Philpott and Goodwin and thought Auburn had no business with a Re-ligion Department anyway, reinforced the general inclination of the board. Martin, in no mood to buck the board anytime but especially on this matter, caved in.

Martin vociferously rejected this interpretation of events, insisting that he alone made the decision to deny tenure after learning more about Curran. Later, he admitted that he had never contacted Curran's references, who in-cluded three university presidents. Someone leaked the story to the *Atlanta Constitution,* and my correspondent from Powder Springs had a new target for his venom. In a September 17, 1990, editorial, the Georgia newspaper roasted Auburn. To one trustee's announcement that the university had no desire to be like Harvard, the paper editorialized that Deep South states were so ad-dicted to football that they had not produced a rival even to the University of Texas or North Carolina, much less to Harvard. How could a public university fail to rise above a sectarian theological dispute, the editor wondered: "So Au-burn will keep its reputation for modest intellectual endeavor. And the South's middle class, apparently, will be satisfied with an academic mediocrity that its representatives say is good enough for it. The South continues to hobble for-ward. Put one foot forward, shoot the other; put one foot forward, shoot the other again."

Trustees rushed to their own defense, denying any role in the affair. Some did admit to being upset about the possibility of controversy surrounding Cur-ran. I suppose controversies swirling around them for three decades were em-barrassment enough for one university to bear. As much as Martin and the trustees tried to wish Curran away, the incident involved larger and more important issues. The October 1990 faculty senate meeting appointed political scientist Michael Urban to chair a committee charged with investigating the affair. His committee concluded that Martin had not followed proper hiring procedures, refused to provide reasons for denying tenure, and violated tenure guidelines. Martin defended his actions at the November faculty meeting but still refused any explanation. The AU Senate gave him a disquieting historic deadline of December 7 to reply or face censure. On January 15, 1991, the university senate voted to censure him, 48–39. Auburn's AAUP chapter filed further charges against the administration for denial of academic freedom, leading to yet another national denunciation to add to our long list of such penalties by various agencies.

Meanwhile, unbeknownst to the faculty, Martin was cornering me in his office, demanding that I become interim provost to replace Ron Henry, who had resigned over the affair. Dean Mary Richards had quit as well. The fiery, diminutive dean, our first woman in the post, walked across campus with me shortly before her resignation, ranting about Martin's subservience to the trustees. Pausing suddenly, she raised her tiny little finger and raged: "See my little finger! I have more bone in that one finger than Martin has in his whole body." I declined the offer.

Despite my normal propensity to rush into controversies—especially since I had served on the search committee that brought Curran to Auburn and felt so strongly about the two main issues (trustee meddling in issues inappropriate to their sphere according to accreditation guidelines; academic freedom to research and publish one's opinions, however controversial they might be)— I demurred this time. In retrospect, I can't say that I'm proud of that decision. Part of my reluctance was due to my friendship with Martin and the positive accomplishments I believed he had made. Partly, my hesitancy resulted from a conversation my colleague Ed Harrell had had with Martin (they were long-time friends from their University of Arkansas days). Ed insisted the issues were not as clear-cut as the faculty and I believed, and Martin continued to insist privately that he alone had made the tenure decision about Curran. Trustees had not pressured him.

To say the affair crippled Auburn at a critical time is an understatement. The university was struggling to get off AAUP censure. Now that was impossible. Martin's eminent scholars program held out the possibility of recruiting a number of world-class scholars. Many of those announcements now resulted in as small a pool of candidates as we had in our Religion search. We also lost two excellent administrators in Richards and Henry. Shortly afterward, Michael Urban and other promising scholars announced that they had had enough of Auburn and left for other universities. Within months, President Martin retired and joined the exodus.

The William Muse Administration

I must begin my account of the Muse years (1991–2000) with full disclosure. Bill and Marlene became my dear friends. Marlene served with great passion on the Alabama Poverty Project board with me. Both supported racial and economic justice statewide and within the Auburn community. This became a source of backstage ridicule by both Lowell Barron and Lowder, who (according to sources I interviewed) characterized them as "starry-eyed, liberal do-gooders" and "short-termers" whom the trustees would soon run off.

As a historian striving for objectivity even toward friends, I know Bill and Marlene made mistakes. Bill became so solicitous of the faculty that he sometimes hesitated to make hard decisions to reduce, eliminate, or combine weak programs. Even some of his early allies on the board of trustees (notably, Representative Jack Venable and School Superintendent Ed Richardson) finally abandoned him because they said he would not make tough choices or at least waited too long to do so. Perhaps the critics were too harsh. In the end, Bill eliminated one hundred programs with low enrollment. His decision to merge journalism and communications, under pressure from Lowder, angered some of his most devoted faculty supporters.

Marlene was a strong, opinionated woman transposed into a society accustomed to quiet, social, noncontroversial, largely ceremonial, first ladies. Some trustees took an immediate dislike to her. They viewed her as too meddlesome, liberal, and outspoken. She, like Bill, cultivated a fiercely loyal circle of faculty friends, intensifying the sense among some trustees that the first family was bonding so well with faculty that it might not only end faculty-administrative conflict but turn into an old-fashioned love-fest. They seemed to prefer presidents who fought incessantly with faculty. Perhaps some of them even delighted in periodic AAUP censure. Such action certified they were not giving in to the faculty "union."

Because I had played no role in the presidential search, I walked across campus with Ed Harrell to the trustee meeting on a cold December morning in 1991 filled with anxiety. After a decade of disastrous presidential searches, I didn't feel confident about Auburn's prospects this time either. Faculty were angry at being kept in the dark about the process. When we arrived, Ed and I barely found seats in the packed room. As three television cameras filmed the event for statewide broadcast, Bill Muse briefly described his life. A native Mississippian born in the Delta, he had six male siblings. His father ran a saw-mill and ribbon-cane syrup mill, managed a farm, and in 1936 "surrendered" to preach, serving as a bivocational minister. Bill had excelled sufficiently in baseball to earn a scholarship to a small regional university where he became an outstanding student and leading member of Tau Kappa Epsilon (TKE) so-cial fraternity. Like me, he profited from a National Defense Education Act fellowship. He earned an MBA and a Ph.D. in business at the University of Ar-kansas, writing his dissertation on the financial management of social frater-nities in the United States.

This launched his career as a national officer and ultimately president of TKE. He entered academic administration at Georgia Tech, then moved steadily higher at Ohio University, Appalachian State, University of Nebraska at Omaha, Texas A&M, and finally as president of the University of Akron. His back-ground seemed well suited to Auburn, despite the fact that he had no Auburn degrees. He was a Deep South man from the Mississippi Delta, came from a farm background, had strong social fraternity connections, and loved sports.

Therefore I was surprised when the trustee meeting took a strange twist. Bill had been assured by board chairman Mike McCartney that the meet-ing was a formality. He had the job. Negotiations on salary and other matters had been completed. After an hour of comments, he and Marlene were led from the room to await his formal election as president. While they waited impatiently, quite a show took place in the conference room. Lowder moved to table the motion to elect Muse Auburn's fifteenth president. He asked for more time to consider the appointment. According to other trustees, he had supported another candidate and believed a delay would embarrass Muse and cause him to withdraw. Lowder was surprised when one of his board allies, Jim Tatum of Huntsville, either became confused and voted the wrong way, or—as I believe—simply stood his ground because he believed Bill was the best choice for the school. By a five to four vote, Lowder's motion failed. The trustees then unanimously chose Bill president. While they waited an hour with growing anxiety in a small room down the hall from where their fate was being de-cided, Marlene expressed serious reservations about the process and thought they ought to "get out of here."

As we left the tumultuous meeting, Ed Harrell (the world's leading authority on Pentecostalism) turned to me and said: "You know, Wayne, I'd bet anything that Muse's father was a Pentecostal preacher." Ed was right. He had preached for poor white and black Church of God congregations throughout the Delta, earning criticism from white planters.

Within months, Bill probably agreed with Marlene's reservations about his decision. Auburn was about to suffer some of the harshest NCAA penalties in football history for flagrant rule violations during the Pat Dye era. A Kappa Alpha (KA) Old South parade in Auburn nearly turned violent when thousands of blacks and whites alternatively booed and cheered Confederate-attired fraternity boys as they rode their horses down College Street. A black man snatched a Confederate battle flag from an onlooker and set it afire. Legislators and many Auburn alumni freaked out over Muse's support of a courageous decision by President Martin, granting a charter to the Auburn Gay and Lesbian Alliance (AGLA). He also had to deal with AAUP censure, a desegregation lawsuit, and proration of education budgets during the 1991–92 recession.

Bill handled every crisis with patience and skill. Using his TKE background and national fraternal network, he invited KA officers to his conference room, where Herb White, his talented director of public relations (who had risen phoenixlike from incineration by the Funderburk crowd) presented the fraternity boys with a collage of negative state and national press clippings about their parade. Muse challenged them to rise above their fraternity loyalties and do what was best for Auburn. Despite fierce objections from neo-Confederates (who had the advantage of parading without serving under fire at Gettysburg or Atlanta) and many fraternity alums, Auburn KA students acted more wisely than their elders, voting to discontinue the annual Old South parade. Bill also appointed an assistant to the president for minority advancement and developed strategies to increase black enrollment. He worked successfully with predominantly black Alabama A&M University to resolve the higher education desegregation lawsuit. Muse not only withstood legislative and public pressure to deny AGLA a charter, he wrote an opinion column in state newspapers, calling for tolerance and respect for the rights of people different from ourselves. Our students, I might add, reacted more maturely on this issue than many of their elders in the state legislature.

On matters of academic freedom and AAUP censure, the president worked with university senate chairs Barry Burkhart and Larry Gerber to put new policies in place to end such conflicts. More importantly to me, when his first test occurred (ALFA's letter threatening to end contributions to the university unless I ceased criticizing the organization), Muse did not hesitate to defend my rights both to free speech and academic freedom. He also fulfilled a longtime

effort by Auburn faculty to acquire a Phi Beta Kappa chapter, the most prestigious American academic honor society, which certified the high quality of
the liberal arts curricula.

To deal with recurring proration and short-funding of higher education,
Bill did something previously unheard of. He forged a cooperative relationship
with University of Alabama chancellors Phil Austin and Tom Meredith to create the Higher Education Partnership of Alabama (HEPA). The organization
lobbied the legislature and developed a coordinated strategy for funding four-
year state colleges and universities.

In order to address the issues debated long distance by Lowder and me in
our 1992 exchange about Auburn's history and mission, Muse in July 1992 appointed the 21st Century Commission. Consisting of administrators, faculty,
students, alumni, and a few trustees, the commission conducted wide-ranging
studies and conversations with all Auburn constituencies, meeting seventeen
times between 1992 and 1997. During my brief season of hope for Auburn, I
deluded myself into believing that we could really resolve the university's internal conflicts and unite the Auburn family.

Within months of Muse's selection as president, I was impressed with the
man. In fact, on Christmas eve 1991, I wrote my trustee friend and newspaper
publisher Jack Venable that after a decade of turmoil, I was ready for a stable,
depoliticized climate:

> Had it not been for the faculty's demand for integrity within the university, I fear
> that in recent years a primary consideration for hiring would have been one's po-
> litical or family connections, and promotion and tenure would have depended
> as much upon political contributions as your teaching and research competence.
>
> I care very much for Auburn and hope to spend the most productive years of
> my career here. Like most faculty, I long for tranquility and stability. I don't care
> to spend time on faculty governance. And when the university is well run and
> competently administered, faculty are generally content to teach their classes,
> meet with students, conduct research, publish it for the benefit of their col-
> leagues and the public, and leave administration to administrators. But when
> conditions descend to the levels reached by Auburn during the 1980s . . . , the
> inevitable result seems to be an adversarial relationship within the university,
> with all the anguish, turmoil, and collective embarrassment that brings.
>
> It is in this perennial season of hope that I pray for a new beginning for Au-
> burn University. I pray for an atmosphere of mutual trust, cooperation, and pro-

fessionalism, which will allow Auburn to take its place among the nation's finest universities.

Bill and I bonded, especially after the ALFA affair. I was asked to represent the faculty speaking at his May 29, 1992, inauguration. My remarks that day were candid and frank, as befitted the university's recent history. They were also passionately sincere in summarizing my conception of what Auburn ought to be. If Lowder's letter in the *Chronicle of Higher Education* constituted his best brief statement of what Auburn was all about, my brief remarks that day were my best rejoinder:

Greetings, President Muse! And good luck!

In greeting a new president on behalf of the faculty, I plead your indulgence. No one can speak for twelve hundred opinionated, often cantankerous individuals. All strong faculties of all fine universities would resent the arrogance of anyone presuming to represent their sentiments. So with that proviso I offer our collective welcome to a new president, beginning a new era, and in that greeting I want to share with you my vision as a representative of many similar but not identical visions. . . .

I want us to work together.

I am sick to death of controversy and division. I would like to see leadership from the president, and I would like to see forbearance, patience, and understanding from the faculty. If a person makes ten important decisions a day, that person will make more mistakes than if the person makes ten important decisions a year. The faculty wishes for fewer mistakes. The president hopes for more understanding. I hope we both get what we are hoping for.

I would like to see our young people dream dreams and our old people see visions. Of one thing I am certain. We will have lots of problems: There will be tight budgets, curricula problems, turf fights (and I don't mean between zoysia and Bermuda), and battles over which segments of this university are the most important.

So we need to raise our collective sights: What is our vision of this university a hundred years from now? What must we do during our watch to make sure that this institution is bequeathed to coming generations in a stronger and better state than we found it? If all we do is focus on our liabilities, if we accept the notion that Alabama will never fund a great university, then we reconcile ourselves, our students, our alumni, and ultimately, our state, to mediocrity. That may be the way things are presently. But there is at least one faculty member (and I sus-pect there are hundreds of us) who will not for a minute accept such a destiny.

Think what miraculous change thousands of alumni, faculty, and students might accomplish over a generation, were they committed to having this uni-versity achieve all that is within its potential. . . .

And finally, we greet you, President Muse, as a university. We are part of a whole. And no part counts for more than another in the function of this insti-tution.

Deep in my soul, I believe that we must learn about the past in order to sur-vive the present and cope with the future. But I also believe in the unity of all knowledge and the application of that knowledge to the wholeness of the hu-man race. Does the past make any sense to people in Africa who are starving after years of drought? Do I have more to offer such people than my colleagues in fisheries and agronomy or in poultry sciences? In a world that has been radi-cally altered by technology, what arrogance it is to consign engineers to the role of tinkerers in technical colleges. Improvements in asphalt technology can re-duce what it costs to repair highways, thus releasing funds from that purpose for urgent health care needs.

Yet I also know that in this land of great abundance people live lives of quiet desperation. A full belly and a huge bank account, flourishing agriculture, and a bountiful economy can leave a famine of the spirit, a hunger better addressed by poets, artists, philosophers, and theologians than by engineers and farmers.

Within the university—despite our warring separate spheres—we believe (or at least at our best we do) that there is a oneness to the human spirit which we address in hundreds of complex ways. But all those ways assume that our role is to find new and better methods of meeting the challenges of our times. The faculty desires to enrich the human experience and pass the accumulated wis-dom of the ages forward in a centuries' old ritual of learning that has never been matched for its efficacy, no matter how poorly or unethically we may sometimes have performed our task.

It is in this spirit of mutual respect, commitment, and pride that this faculty greets you. Though many in number and opinion, we are fiercely united in our devotion to the life of the mind, and to a spirit of unhindered inquiry, in the edu-cation of new generations. As such we welcome you to our enterprise, we pledge our loyal support and our concerned criticism, as each is warranted. We urge you to inspire, lead, and invigorate us even as we pledge to assist, advise, and sup-port you.

In March 1997 the 21st Century Commission presented its recommendations to the trustees, including new mission and vision statements, goals for teaching, research, outreach, and enrollment, as well as financial plans to achieve all this. Muse presented our report. Lowder, who had been expelled from the board for eighteen months by Governor Fob James, had obtained a favorable state supreme court ruling and was back on the board. He demanded to know how the university would fund its existing programs with limited money. Muse, Financial Vice President Don Large, and Provost Paul Parks responded with a five-year financial plan that called for modest tuition increases and eliminating academic programs that were not viable according to Alabama Commission of Higher Education (ACHE) standards. These savings could be reallocated each year to "peaks of excellence" programs designated by the university. Given Lowder's agenda, I was pretty sure none of those "peaks" would arise from our college. Lowder expressed his opinion that the plan did not go "far enough" and Lowell Barron opposed tuition increases to fund it. Trustees refused to act on the plan.

Lowder, as was his habit, asked Muse to come see him at Colonial Bank headquarters in Montgomery. (Bill believed that mandating a private meeting in this venue was Lowder's attempt to intimidate him.) When the president arrived, Lowder reiterated his objections to our committee report and the administration's financial plan to achieve it. He claimed Auburn tried to do too much, had too many programs, and must eliminate more. He suggested that Muse "step aside" and let the trustees take the heat for cuts. A lesser man would have welcomed that prospect, knowing as he did the depth of faculty contempt for many of the trustees in the first place. But Muse also knew trustee usurpation of his presidential duties and peremptory dismantling of departments and programs (no doubt based on the assumptions contained in Lowder's article in the *Chronicle*) would be ruinous to the university and would create a firestorm.

The 1998 "Roles" Commission

Muse believed the key event in his troubled presidency occurred in 1995, when Lowder's twelve-year trustee term expired. New governor Fob James decided not to reappoint his nemesis. However, the state constitution allowed a trustee to retain his seat until the senate confirmed a replacement appointed by the governor. James, as was his habit, dallied with other matters while Lowder lined up Democratic majority leader Lowell Barron to block James's appointee.

When the governor finally nominated Phil Richardson, an ALFA vice president, the trustee battle became a blood feud between Lowder/Barron/Colonial Bank and James/Richardson/ALFA. As usual, the ham-handed James lost.

The governor did win the first round in their long sparring match. In a typical fit of pique, James decided to preside at a trustee meeting (technically, governors chaired the board of trustees, though in fact they rarely attended). He arrived with two state patrolmen in tow and announced that he was removing Lowder and James Tatum from the board under terms of a legal opinion rendered by Republican attorney general Jeff Sessions. The two state troopers watched while Lowder and Tatum walked out of the room. The governor added insult to injury by mockingly searching under a table several times while loudly wondering where Lowder had gone. It was all grand theater for evening-news broadcasts. Lowder was not amused. And he would soon mobilize his fortune, making certain James was the next man out the door. Three years later, with Lowder his largest contributor, Siegelman drubbed the hapless incumbent and installed a full slate of Lowder cronies on the Auburn board.

During Lowder's eighteen-month absence, the board functioned as a rational, supportive governing agency. Governor James asked each trustee what he thought of Muse, and every response was positive. Trustees even persuaded Muse to turn down a prestigious presidency at the University of Minnesota, praising his leadership, and boosting his salary. But after winning a five to four supreme court decision overruling Sessions's opinion, Lowder returned to the board in 1997 with a vengeance. Upon regaining his trustee seat, one of Lowder's first acts was rejecting the 21st Century Commission report. Muse and the trustees established yet another study group, this one named the Commission on the Role of the University in the 21st Century (Role Commission). Unlike the earlier commission, which consisted mainly of administrators, faculty, students, and alumni, this one contained five trustees and five Muse appointees. The president appointed administrators Paul Parks and William (Bill) Walker, an AUM administrator, and two faculty (senate president Glen Howze from agriculture and myself).

Yes, I know the adage: "Fool me once, shame on you! Fool me twice, shame on me!" I was stupid to accept. The intrusive presence of five trustees (including Lowder) was a flaming red banner of danger. But I still inhabited the naive realm of hope. At Bill's request, I had cochaired the Auburn Family Campaign, part of a massive new fund-raising effort. Athletic director David Housel, librarian Yvonne Kozlowski, and I were in charge of the effort on campus. We pledged 1 percent of our salaries for three years. I sent one of my usual upbeat letters to faculty, asking them to contribute sacrificially to the campaign, for which I was vociferously criticized by many of my colleagues. Despite substantial faculty opposition, our committee raised more than $2 million from Auburn administrators, faculty, and staff, a remarkable statement of loyalty to the school. But persistent rumors circulated that those of us who pledged 1 percent of our incomes gave a higher percentage than some trustees. Whether that was true or merely the result of anger and cynicism, I never learned.

During these years, I spoke frequently on behalf of Auburn. I addressed alumni clubs in Oneonta and Childersburg, which specifically requested that I come and talk about academics at Auburn. (Most alumni chapters didn't bother with faculty, inviting only football coaches; sadly, that's all many active alumni cared to hear about.) Muse and UA chancellor Meredith also asked me to speak in Montgomery, representing the state's four-year faculties to explain to legislators and business leaders the effect of budget cuts on higher education (which, ironically, Governor James levied in order to move the state toward greater equity in K–12 funding as required by Judge Gene Reese). I also spoke to parents of incoming Auburn freshmen at Camp War Eagle, an innovative summer orientation program begun by Muse. By the end of 1997, I had invested so much energy in the Muse administration that there was no turning back, no way to disengage without guilt that I had betrayed both Bill and my colleagues. So, forward I marched into the jaws of hell.

At our initial Role Commission meeting, I offered two motions. One was to adopt *Robert's Rules of Order* as a parliamentary guide for our meetings. From years of using this familiar guide and watching how Southern Baptist Convention officials had maintained order using it in tumultuous meetings, I believed it would neutralize the power of trustees. Second, I nominated Lowder as chairman. Knowing how he hated publicity, I understood that he would be furious at me. However, knowing also how he coveted power, I thought he might rise to the bait. He did not. That decision was predetermined. Bill Walker and State School Superintendent Ed Richardson were elected cochairs.

During months of deliberations, Glenn Howze and I joked about the way Richardson and Walker postured and maneuvered to become Muse's successor. We even made informal wagers on which one would prevail. One influential CEO confided to me that Richardson was told early in the process that Muse would be fired, and trustees would appoint him interim president. Another well-placed administrator told me that trustee Paul Spina believed he had been promised the job.

Before our first public meeting, trustee members of the commission insisted that our sessions be private. Howze and I, plus two of the administrators, absolutely rejected secret sessions. Glenn and I planned to resign and publicly denounce the whole process if the five trustees and Walker forced through such a procedure. Fortunately, both AU and AUM faculties loudly denounced secrecy as well. That tore away Lowder's cover.

Muse responded to trustee demands for programmatic cuts by appointing a study group that established criteria for eliminating programs. The senate appointed a shadow committee to monitor the process. We held open sessions with angry faculty, the campus AAUP chapter, alumni groups, and others.

Once the ax fell, I received calls at home from outraged parents and alumni. I asked them how much money they had given to the program they considered so vital to the university. Long pause. "Nothing" came the typical reply. "Well, that's part of the problem with small programs, isn't it," I responded.

The one hundred programs eliminated were mostly marginal. The merger of nursing programs at AU and AUM under a dean based in Montgomery did not please some of the local medical community, but both programs were relatively new and had weak alumni groups. Our public hearing raised more hackles from aviation management folks, especially airline pilots and airport managers, who didn't want their program moved to the College of Business. Muse expended all his considerable capital with faculty on behalf of the downsizing, fearing more draconian measures if the trustees usurped the process.

He did reject the trustee decision to eliminate the Ph.D. program in economics. Although controversial because of its association with the Ludwig von Mises Institute and the free-market school of economics, the department maintained rigorous standards, generated respected scholarship, and attracted competent graduate students. Furthermore, it met all ACHE viability standards. Muse believed the trustee decision to abolish the program resulted from an internal board squabble between Lowder and the department's chief advocate among trustees, John Denson. Denson—a highly respected Opelika lawyer, Republican, friend of governor Fob James, fervent advocate of free-market economics, and bitter enemy of Lowder—also believed that Lowder's determination to kill the department's doctoral program resulted from spite. I'm not so sure. Economics—like history, chemistry, physics, zoology, psychology, literature, foreign languages—is a "hard" rather than an "applied" subject. It is entirely possible that Lowder's myopia rather than his spite was to blame. At any rate, a majority of trustees ignored Muse's recommendation and terminated the doctoral program

The commission finished its divisive work in November. The glare of sunshine was the faculty's strongest ally. Unwilling to reveal their real agenda—to strengthen professional programs at the expense of liberal arts and economics and to fire Muse—the trustee cadre floundered over procedural issues and winced under angry alumni protests about downsizing their favorite area. Meanwhile, Muse's administration worked with the senate task force on restructuring. We received more than six hundred letters and many oral presentations from students, faculty, and alumni defending programs, which was one of the best consequences of the public debate. Had trustees won the secrecy they desired, there would have been no such input but rather the cannibalism of robust liberal arts programs and a blood bath.

In addition to programmatic mergers, cuts, and terminations, the commission designated seven "peaks of excellence" for additional funding. Though many departments that believed they should have received such designation complained when their applications were denied, at least the process seemed open and democratic (although one persistent rumor claimed the history department was near the top of the list but Muse left it off his recommendation because he knew the trustees would reject the choice). An administrator chaired the Priorities Committee but faculty provided a majority of members.

I interpreted my role on the commission in terms of Sun Tzu's *The Art of War*. When outnumbered and outgunned, retreat and fight a defensive action. Keep damage to a minimum. Don't launch frontal assaults until you command superior forces. Keep your forces intact, build strength, and wait for a more propitious moment.

In the final analysis, the peaks of excellence chosen were relatively new or developing areas. None but fisheries made the various academic lists of the nation's best. Although lots of Auburn folks believed the university was adequately funded and provided high-quality graduate programs, our strengths were really strong undergraduate education and successful outreach. Years of campus turmoil and salaries well below regional and national averages (except, of course, for football coaches, whose salaries ranked among the highest in the nation), had drained the university of many of its best scholars and hindered the hiring of "five-star recruits" (to use a football analogy).

University of North Carolina scholar John Shelton Reed has developed a simple, commonsense instrument for rating universities that is better than more esoteric ones I have studied. A university's real reputation for academic quality is what Americans believe it to be. Eliminate opinions of people who reside in the state where the school is located and anyone who attended the university. Ask anyone else what they think of the school, and that constitutes the university's reputation. By that measurement, lots of Americans had heard about sports at Auburn and knew them to be good, though with a whiff of scandal. Beyond that, few even knew what state Auburn was in or identified any outstanding academic programs with it.

Peer evaluations by knowledgeable American scholars, ratings by the *Chronicle of Higher Education,* or professional academic disciplines provided similar results. During Role Commission proceedings, even the *Birmingham News* contended that for a variety of reasons (precarious and chronic underfunding, too many colleges, and duplicate programs) university graduate programs in Alabama "lack quality." As evidence, editors cited a study listing the top doctoral programs (excluding medicine) in the South. North Carolina claimed thirty-seven, Virginia fourteen, Georgia nine, Florida four, Alabama none.

Although that made our peaks of excellence a plausible strategy to raise the university's academic visibility, I was more concerned about strengthening what we already possessed. In one of our early commission meetings, I presented a position paper outlining five central components of Auburn that must be improved. First came the core curriculum. This addressed business CEO complaints that Auburn students knew lots about technical details of their jobs but little about the larger world in which they worked. Nor were their communication skills impressive. I wrote (to the obvious discomfort of Lowder) that majors in banking, finance, and computer engineering might well furnish less important life skills to successful twenty-first-century entrepreneurs than courses in Chinese, Hindi, or Japanese civilization. In a society where most people changed professions five times in a lifetime, what type of education provided life skills anyway? The capacity to understand human society as a whole and not its fractured parts was the most important knowledge taken from a college education.

Other objectives also rated high on my list. Specific preprofessional education (premedicine, prelaw, pre–veterinary medicine) provided an imperative platform for successful specialized careers. Graduate programs were not only important to state and national economies, they kept instructional costs down by providing an inexpensive supply of teaching assistants and instructors. Skill acquisition mattered because of the number of one-of-a-kind state university programs at Auburn (fisheries, archival training, architecture, poultry sciences, pharmacy). Finally, outreach—the Rural Studio, Cooperative Extension, engineering's distance learning, and the Center for the Arts and Humanities—provided critical services in nonacademic settings.

The result of our wrenching public hearings and internal debates over the quality and future of university programs left the commission deeply divided. Ed Richardson's report to the board of trustees on September 4 ratcheted-up the tension another notch. Typically blunt, Ed referred to the "reluctant participation" of the faculty and administration after stages of "opposition and resistance," which hindered the progress of the commission. "Such attitudes," he added, "could only occur in an environment in which little leadership had been exercised," an obvious backhanded slap at Muse. He denied that Lowder was "trying to take over Auburn University" or that he himself had presidential ambitions. Ed's presentation was a consensus view of the five trustees no doubt, but hardly representative of the ten-person commission. Furthermore, these were Ed's conclusions before we had met the first time.

Two weeks later the commission met on the AUM campus. Both Glenn and I had prepared responses to Richardson's charges. Two days earlier, on September 16, I had met with Muse and former senate president Barry Burkhart. Muse, in a particularly forlorn mood after Richardson's public scolding, warned me that "Lowder is vindictive," that I should watch myself, and that he would not remain at Auburn if Don Siegelman were elected governor. (Rumors already abounded about Lowder's huge contributions to Siegelman in his race against Fob James.)

Glenn responded to Richardson's attack before the entire commission and reporters on September 18, defending Muse and the faculty. He traced the university's administrative problems to the James administration's diversion of funding from higher education to K–12. This lost revenue had required skillful planning with faculty and staff to avoid layoffs and other draconian measures. Trustees had supported Muse's policies until the supreme court placed Lowder back on the board. Only after Lowder's return did trustees who had praised Muse the year before begin to accuse him of inefficiency.

I followed Glenn's statement with a recitation of my version of Auburn's problems. I emphasized that the commission process had begun with two flawed premises: Auburn's problems originated in low faculty morale resulting from noncompetitive salaries; the current administration inefficiently managed the university. I presented my own perception of what had gone wrong, focusing on internal and external problems. The chief interior problem was an academic culture that resisted change. When faculty legitimately complained about administrative-driven reorganization, they offered no alternative scheme for eliminating underperforming departments, majors, or programs. The faculty was not entirely to blame, because trustees publicly announced that certain low-ranking programs dear to them were central to Auburn's land grant mission and therefore would not be reduced or eliminated regardless of inefficiencies. That had taken the wind out of prioritizing. But the faculty must put in place an ongoing process to measure performance and reallocate resources if we wanted to avoid trustee meddling.

Externally, the trustee process was the university's major problem. Since the early 1980s, trustee-faculty interaction had been confrontational and adversarial. If conditions did not change in a hurry, I predicted that "the three-year conflict of the 1980s will be telescoped into a matter of months. The current faculty has fewer Auburn connections, is more mobile, and has fewer senior leaders . . . , and conflicts will escalate to confrontation much more quickly. No matter who 'wins' such a battle, the 'loser' will be Auburn University." Faculty perceived trustees as "patronizing" and "paternalistic." Faculty could be "brittle, unreasoning, hard-headed and turf-oriented," I admitted. But even in that irascible mode, they were "also the heart and soul of the university." Better both sides adopt attitudes of mutual respect and cooperation. Trustees should begin meeting regularly with small groups of faculty, not just senate leaders, for frank conversations.

Furthermore, the trustee selection process had become dangerously politicized. Selection as an Auburn trustee had long depended on support of the current governor, and though that system had produced some fine trustees, it was fundamentally flawed. As for misplaced priorities, some trustees seemed to have misplaced quite a few themselves. Witness their obsession with top-ten national rankings in football and their preference for Clemson as an academic model for Auburn. They claimed the university had financial problems. Yet a Huntsville newspaper alleged that a coach fired years earlier still drew $110,000 a year and that Auburn had paid $1.5 million to failed coaches during the 1990s alone. Why not apply market forces to football? When a coach did not achieve success, his fate should be the same as a nontenured faculty member who failed: loss of job. No buy-outs, jobs as presidential advisers or fund-raisers, hidden perks or benefits. Unlimited trustee terms were absurd at a university with so many gifted, devoted alumni as Auburn. Trustee terms of twelve years, followed by multiple reappointments, delivered the university into the hands of an oligarchy.

With both sides now fully deployed, we only had to wait for the heavy artillery to arrive in order to commence combat. The trustees' strategy consisted of threats, firings, intimidations, and naming Walker and Richardson as presidents. Ours consisted of the Southern Association of Colleges and Secondary Schools (SACS). As soon as the commission meeting ended, Mary Orndorff, who covered education for the *Birmingham News* and had written about my education work since we had first met during the equity funding lawsuit, walked up to me and asked: "Were your remarks directed at Mr. Lowder?" "No," I responded. "The problem is the system, not a person. I would say the same thing if it applied to a personal friend like [trustee] Emory Cunningham or [former trustee] Morris Savage."

Trustee Paul Spina followed Mary, chiding me for a personal attack on Lowder. I denied the charge and reaffirmed that the trustee system was the problem. Lowder was next. He termed my remarks a "public, personal attack on me," adding "I do not appreciate it." His eyes flashed and his mouth twitched with fury as he spoke. On the return trip to Auburn with Barry Burkhart and Yvonne Kozlowski, I shared with them Spina and Lowder's comments. Both expressed concern about possible retaliation, though I slept well that evening.

Three days later, on the twenty-first, Burkhart, Muse, and I met again to talk about implementation of commission recommendations. Muse, in a defiant mood, pledged that he would not recommend any policy that would harm the long-term future of the university regardless of the board's actions. Barry warned that Muse could not afford to lose faculty support, which was both his best protection from trustees and a barrier against potentially his worst enemy, the faculty (recalling images of the Funderburk and Martin administrations, where presidents did what they believed trustees wanted only to lose their presidencies anyway because of faculty revolt).

Muse reiterated what he had told us earlier about a potential Siegelman victory six weeks hence. If Don won the governorship, he would replace pro-Muse trustees Emory Cunningham, Bessie Mae Holloway, and John Denson with a pro-Lowder slate. In that eventuality, Bill vowed to seek another presidency. He ended the meeting by looking straight at me and repeating his earlier warning, "Lowder is extremely vindictive." I did not sleep so well that night.

Bobby's Revenge

I didn't have to wait. Muse had warned me repeatedly to beware of Lowder. So I was not surprised in January 2000 when liberal arts dean John Heilman sat down with me after the dean's office closed one afternoon and warned that at a trustee meeting Lowder had asked if there was a term limit on appointments of Distinguished University Professors or a review process for them once appointed. Trustees asked Muse to investigate the matter. Although the trustees mentioned no specific person, Muse told Heilman that he believed the inquiry was aimed at me. John asked me to provide whatever documentation I had about the appointment.

In addition to a copy of my appointment letter from President Martin, which mentioned neither term limits nor review process, I included a university procedural description of "University Professor," which included a paragraph that read: "The rank of University Professor shall be carried by incumbents until resignation or retirement from the University, subject to the normal standard of continuous high performance. The rank is conferred by, and can be altered by, the President of the University alone." I also called Dick Jaeger, Malcolm Crocker, and David Lewis, all colleagues with the same appointments. Jaeger, Crocker, and I had been appointed at the same time, Lewis several years later. Neither of my friends in engineering had received appointments that mentioned term limits. David's initial letter had mentioned a specific term, which he had rejected. A follow-up letter to him deleted that provision, and he agreed to the appointment. In all our cases, we had remained productive scholars, could have left for other places, but took ourselves off the market because we liked Auburn and were satisfied with the professorships. For the university to renege on a permanent appointment now would be tantamount to breaking our contracts.

I passed all this information along to Heilman together with the absolute certainty of legal action against the university if it violated our contractual agreements. Although I knew the inquiry was aimed at me, I also knew the trustees would never single me out because my research, publication record, teaching, outreach, departmental evaluations, and a pile of national, state, and professional awards deprived them of any legal grounds for a negative review (unless, of course, compatibility with trustees had become the basis for job retention at Auburn). Thus, if trustees wished to get rid of me, they would have to limit the terms of all professors who had received University Professor appointments. Such action would have ensured a class action lawsuit, which given our appointment letters and the nature of contract law, we were certain to win.

I heard nothing more of the matter. But over lunch with Muse on August 17, 2000, the president once again warned of Lowder's vindictiveness. By now I felt my father's rage seeping through every pore of my skin. Or perhaps it was the more distant fury of my ancestors on the English-Scottish Borders, archers at Agincourt, knights at Towton, or Confederates at Gettysburg.

Muse's problems were worse than mine. Some of his key administrators understood the implications of a Siegelman victory in the governor's race as clearly as Muse did and were already switching sides. Several high-ranking officials who regularly interacted with trustees believed Lowder had secured control of the board and rushed to ingratiate themselves with him. Ultimate pragmatists and survivors in the game of university politics, they would prosper under future administrations. Trustee John Denson also confided that as the Lowder faction gained confidence in Siegelman's election and their unchecked power, secret trustee sessions featured more and more jokes about liberal arts.

At the November university senate meeting, a resolution dealing with the issues I had raised in my September speech passed overwhelmingly. It criticized trustee "micromanagement" and asked Governor-elect Siegelman to reform the way Auburn trustees were selected. It proposed a one-term limit among other changes. Meanwhile I wrote journalist friends and business leaders, detailing what was happening at Auburn, emphasizing that the problems preceded Muse. I explained in a letter to Stan Tiner, editorial page editor of the *Mobile Press-Register* and a relative newcomer to the state, the convoluted history of trustee politics and micromanagement. As early as 1986, the Academic Standards and Retention Committee had recommended toughening the university's admission standards. Not only had a majority of trustees rejected the report, they had transferred such issues to a committee headed by Lowder. Allegedly, an internal university study leaked to the trustees had revealed that the effect of the new standards on scholarship athletes would have been disastrous.

I also outlined the board's alleged conflicts of interest. Trustee Jim Tatum's wife became a member of the Colonial Bank board, allegedly without recommendation of the local bank. Jimmy Samford's office was in the Colonial Bank building, where he performed legal work for Lowder. Paul Spina allegedly moved to a new house in order to reside in a district with an open trustee seat and, according to some newspaper reports (which he denied), had received loans from Colonial Bank. Mike McCartney of Gadsden owned a construction company that allegedly received Colonial Bank loans. Rumors claimed that Richardson had been promised the presidency (I added that "only time can test that rumor"). And, of course, Barron's interrelated links to Lowder were long-standing. I mentioned Lowder's political contributions (though reporters had a hard time tracing them through a labyrinth of transfers from one PAC to another). The most obvious pattern was that neither party nor political ideology counted for much. Only control of Auburn mattered. Stan's enterprising reporters could verify or refute all these allegations if they worked at it.

I wrote Elmer Harris, an Auburn alumnus and CEO of Alabama Power Company, a similar letter in November. Although I was sure Emory Cunningham had already briefed him about the university's agony, I wanted to be sure. I reiterated that the central issue was structural, "not solely personal." Recalling "Red" Bamberg's disastrous tenure as a trustee (punctuated by his boast about how many times he had flunked English at Auburn), which lasted for nearly half a century, I suggested that there must be a better way to run a university.

My grievance with Lowder, however, was deeply philosophical. His vision of the university was that of a center of applied learning in agriculture, business, and engineering, with liberal arts serving a service role. Since I was not an "Auburn man," had no degrees from the school, and was nearing retirement, this new design for the university's future meant nothing to me personally. But I believed that it would diminish the value of all degrees, including my son's, who had majored in aerospace engineering but was then a Microsoft designer because he had received an education at Auburn rather than a technical skill. I did not want to see Lowder turn the university into a glorified technical college.

My short-term prognosis included the trustees firing Muse and bringing in a sycophant to do their bidding, which would spark a faculty revolt and return us to the days of the barricades under Funderburk. As cochair of Governor-elect Siegelman's transition team, Harris should use his influence to head off this catastrophe. Elmer tried. He failed. And all I predicted in that letter came true in spades.

• thirteen •

"Ever to Conquer, Never to Yield"

Inside the Auburn Tigers, 1977–2005

Two stories capture the contradictions of football in Alabama, both what is conquered and what is yielded. Following the intersectional game between Auburn and Syracuse in October 2002, Bud Poliquin, sportswriter for the *Syracuse Post-Standard,* rhapsodized about his visit to Jordan-Hare Stadium. Attending a game in Auburn, he wrote, was like "going to Mass in Rome." The environment was "equal parts Woodstock, Mardi Gras, New Year's Eve, and Madonna's last wedding." He interviewed an Auburn fan who missed his wife's birthday in order to cheer on his alma mater. One orange-and-blue devotee emailed that "country, God, and college football are usually our top three passions, but not always in that order." Syracuse's athletic director conceded he was envious of the environment (eighty-four thousand howling fans, long lines of RVs on the road for miles outside of town): "When you talk about the epitome of what the college football experience is all about . . . that's it. Auburn is the epitome." Poliquin ended his story: "Believe me on this. Please. I have descended into college football's Grand Canyon. I have stood in its Alps. I have gazed at its ocean sunset. I have attended a game at Jordan-Hare Stadium in Auburn, Alabama. And I've been changed forever."

There was another side to the story that Poliquin obviously didn't follow in upstate New York. A year after his paean of praise to Auburn football, a resident of Pinson (my mother's hometown), upset over the University of Ala-bama's double overtime loss to Arkansas, held a gun to his son's head and pulled the trigger shortly after the game ended. Miraculously, the bullet nar-rowly missed the twenty-year-old man's head. The son acknowledged that he probably had chosen an inopportune time to ask his dad for a car. One could conclude from these stories that football is a state-sponsored religion in Ala-bama. Bobby Lowder, Pat Dye, Terry Bowden, Tommy Tuberville, David Hou-sel, Wayne Hall, Brother Oliver, and a great crowd of companions would prob-ably respond in chorus that it may be more important than that.

"Fearless and True"

Dad made an Auburn football fan out of me in the same way he bequeathed me a temper and a sense of family honor: by constant, consistent example. From his first 4-H Club meeting at Auburn as a teenager, he had adored the school. All those football games he had attended with my uncles, lubricated with strong doses of alcohol, sealed the deal. Having never set foot in a class-room on campus, he had adopted Auburn football as my absent sibling.

Like Dad, I grew up with my favorite team and player. Auburn University won its first national football championship, in 1957, and that team contained my teenage hero, Lloyd Nix. Nix was a knuckleball-throwing left-handed quar-terback from the tiny village of Kansas in west Alabama who graduated from equally insignificant Carbon Hill High School in coal country. Before the 1957 season, he had run the ball a total of thirty times and thrown one pass as a third-string quarterback at Auburn. He seemed destined to graduate on time but contribute little to the football team. But Nix had dreams of something bigger.

His opportunity arrived when two more-talented players pushed their sta-tus as campus celebrities over the brink. Following a pattern of cutting class and violating team rules, the gifted starting quarterback broke into a girls' dorm, got drunk, and raised hell one time too many. Coach Shug Jordan kicked both players off the team and vowed to go with his cautious, smart, disciplined, third-stringer. He told the team that adversity drew men together, that they could win without a flashy quarterback. With two dazzling halfbacks and a smash-mouth fullback—Billy "Ace" Atkins, who was renowned for his block-ing, running, punting, and placekicking—plus some of the nation's finest line-men, the team had only the weakness at quarterback. Pundits picked Tennes-see to win the SEC crown that year because of reservations about Nix. After an undefeated season, including a 40–0 win over archrival Alabama, the Tigers beat out Ohio State and Michigan State in the final Associated Press poll for the mythical national championship.

In 1958 Nix led the team to a 9-0-1 season, and I had the pleasure of sitting with my dad and uncles at Legion Field to watch what I still consider the greatest defensive effort in football history. Auburn held the Tennessee Volunteers to minus yardage for the game, while Nix worked his methodical magic in a low-scoring victory. Auburn's twenty-four-game unbeaten streak did not end until Nix departed for dental school and Tennessee won the 1959 season opener in Knoxville.

There is life beyond football. Nix opened a dental practice in Decatur. Billy Atkins, the most valuable player on the 1957 team, played pro ball in the American Football League, married, and had a son whom he christened with his nickname. Ace Atkins starred as a defensive end on Terry Bowden's undefeated 1993 team. But he prefers to be known as a successful journalist and crime novelist. All these men were wonderful Auburn football players. But the sport did not define them. They not only earned football championships, they received an education. How appropriate! Auburn was, after all, a university.

One of my first acts upon arriving at Auburn in 1977 was to purchase season football tickets. I have bought them every year since, attending games with Dad, Dartie, David, or my equally rabid daughters-in-law and grandson. I not only attend nearly every home game, I have traveled with my father or sons to Oxford, Baton Rouge, Knoxville, Lexington, Orlando, Atlanta, and New Orleans to watch the Tigers play SEC and bowl games.

I didn't teach many football players, but the ones I did have in class were first-rate men. Not one failed, and that was not the result of any preferential grading either. They earned their As, Bs, and Cs the old-fashioned way. They worked hard. I have no patience with negative faculty stereotypes of "dumb jocks." Lloyd Nix, Johnny Green, Gregg Carr, Ace Atkins, and Pat Nix, among many others, are fine, successful people who pushed themselves hard and probably succeeded beyond their athletic skill level.

Despite all that boosterism, I must admit that football was not even my favorite sport. I endured the games of fall in order to immerse myself in the contests of winter. Although Auburn failed to record a winning percentage during many basketball seasons, I was there for nearly every game, shouting myself so hoarse that I sometimes had to apologize to my Sunday school class after a particularly competitive Saturday game because I could not be heard the next morning. After reinstitution of the SEC basketball tournament format in 1979,

I organized a group of faculty and church friends to attend every tournament except one, plus some NCAA regionals when we were invited to participate in "March Madness." I may have seen more Auburn basketball games during the past thirty-three years than any other person. I may even have violated some obscure NCAA rule by having my two favorite players, Greg Turner and Mark Cahill, over for supper so Sean, who sometimes attended games with me, could meet them. Neither started for the Tigers, but both were excellent students and fine men who are a credit to Auburn. If Sean had sports heroes (he did not), I wanted them to be like Greg or Mark.

I occasionally attended baseball games and track meets as well to watch my students perform. And I never understood why the Auburn family relished football so much more than swimming, which Auburn dominated at both NCAA and Olympic levels. When twenty-seven Tiger athletes, representing ten countries, performed in the 2008 Olympics, not one was a football player. Between 1984 and 2008, AU athletes won fourteen gold medals (almost all in swimming or track and field), more than most countries could boast. I finally made my peace with the fact that Auburnites were football fans rather than sports fans and just enjoyed the incredible talent available to me nine months a year on campus. Except for football, AU sports were easy tickets to acquire in order to watch some of the greatest athletes in the world.

The fact that I was a miserable failure as an athlete—too slow, too short, too weak—did not keep me from having the soul of a Charles Barkley. I loved the game, whatever it was, and I loved the Auburn Tigers. But my affection was not without condition. Like fan George Petrie before me, I believed in "good, clean sport." Unfortunately, much of American sport descended into an ethical quagmire in the late twentieth century.

Rather than single out sport excesses, I prefer to view them as a metaphor for American society. As *Sports Illustrated* writer Gary Smith has noted: "Sports, having somehow become the medium through which Americans derive their strongest sense of community, has become the state where all the great moral issues have to be played out, often rough and ugly, right alongside the games." No one understood the metaphor better than two Auburn faculty members, Wil Bailey and Taylor Littleton. Large-animal veterinarian and Shakespeare scholar, respectively, Bailey and Littleton loved sports. But like me, they worried about the way sport excess corrupted universities. As a former chair of the NCAA, Bailey was an idealist with firm connections to the real world. Together the two men wrote a splendid book about the pathology of America's dual university culture (scholar-athletes) titled *Athletics and Academe: An Anatomy of Abuses and a Prescription for Reform.*

They did not interview presidents at Auburn or Alabama, so as tempting as it is to substitute familiar names to presidential quotations found in the book, that would be a mistake. My point is that the scandals, abuses, booster corruption, and trustee micromanagement on behalf of athletics that I am about to describe are not unique to Auburn. They proceed from misplaced priorities, huge financial considerations, situational ethics, and the belief that only by cheating can a university successfully compete. Besides, to use the ultimate adolescent rationalization, "everyone does it."

Some of Bailey and Littleton's most poignant and revealing interviews with anonymous presidents, almost all of whose universities had major sports programs, say it all:

> Let me tell you this: every university president has to contend with the tendency of the institution to live a life comparable to that of the society it's a part of. But the point is, it shouldn't be that way. I mean the university should always be the book by which we pull the standard up, not respond to it. What we've seen, for example, in this deteriorating relationship between athletics and the institution itself in terms of academic and behavioral standards is probably the most visible reflection of what has to be described as a serious ailment.

> Most of our trustees serve on major corporation boards and they understand their role; they're interested in broad policy matters. They want to know important things, of course, but they would be shocked, insulted, if I asked them to become involved in an athletic policy decision.

> [The faculty] attitude and that of the students too, when it's another school, "Well—we always knew those people were outlaws." But when it happens at their school, they're generally ashamed, embarrassed, like we all are—and that's the way it should be.

> The ideal situation is to not have your board mucking around in athletics. The only way that you are going to stop that from happening is to be willing to put your job on the line. If you ever compromise on that, if you ever open the door and allow them to get involved in athletics, then they are likely to drive the whole program crazy. So it has to be a very clear understanding that as long as you are the president, board members are not allowed to mess around in athletics.

What you often have is more assistant football coaches recruiting thirty football players a year than you have admissions officers recruiting an entire student body. This disproportion is a very serious matter because the money and the opulence in the athletic program disconnects it from the rest of the university. Cheating, outright corruption—these are of course the worst abuses and everyone agrees with that. But these subtle abuses of disproportion are insidious, aren't usually disclosed, and they first cost you faculty support, but students are not far behind in noticing this division too.

Even in the best-run universities, there are always serious deferred maintenance problems in classrooms and laboratories, but not in the athletic plant of those programs with big revenues. The programs, that is, that are clean, wouldn't think of cheating. But they say, "We've got to be competitive in our weight room and the concourse to the stadium and everything else," so they spend a lot of money to make the athletic plant magnificent. By comparison you've got a faculty group doing vital medical research in little cubbyholes carved out of hallways; still, you've got a great weight room. I understand now the big thing is how many square feet your weight room has.

I think that we just basically are saying that there's one thing in America important enough to set up separate rules for—the only thing important enough to society to really exempt you from many of the requirements of the university, and that's athletics. And don't think that our students don't see this. They accept it, don't challenge it, and carry that perception away with them into later life.

When I'm asked to speak to fraternity groups I tell them that if their organizations don't serve the academic purposes of the university, they might as well be sponsored by the local filling stations. *Everything* the university sponsors ought to be involved with the education of students, with learning—the learning that will shape their careers and the kind of lives they will lead. Now athletics can gain new friends for you, keep the alumni coming and all that—be great entertainment, but unless they contribute to this kind of learning, to our central mission, their games shouldn't be sponsored by the University of ——.

Some chief executive officers are just going to have to lose their jobs. It's easy for me to say because I'm not going to be one of them at this point; but I've been recruited during this past year by two major Division I institutions and it was clear to me that athletics problems were going to be an issue. I believe that these things can't be handled diplomatically. In the end the chief officer has to say, "Look, friends, there's a way we're not going to run this place. I'm not looking for trouble, but I'm telling you I want to meet my responsibilities and I can't meet them in the way you guys are operating. Now you can either have me as your president or you can get somebody else." Why some presidents seem reluctant to lose their jobs over athletics, I don't know. No one in higher education thinks any less of them for that.

I ought to take time every night to bow down and give thanks for the integrity of the people I'm privileged to work with here. All the potential for scandal and these rock-solid people just bend over backward. If you've had any experience at all in being responsible for a major athletic program, you can never sleep like a baby—as long as the enterprise is connected with all this money and you've got thousands of people who are boosters, you've got all the potential for a disaster.

It's frightening to recognize that these sports have become so financially a part of America that they have created the impression that a major role of a university is to entertain its alumni and supporters. And I mean not just to entertain but to entertain at a certain level. And this tremendous fix the public has on sports leads to the pressure to recruit.

Sometimes you've just got to be very direct, and I've said to my AD, "If there's a booster who sort of likes to hang around and talk to the players and you're worried about him, introduce me because I've got something to say." And I tell him that he does not have enough money, if he gave it all to the university, to pay for the damage and embarrassment he would cause by committing an act that would get us into serious trouble.

It's not just alumni, there's also this group around the program all the time who are wealthy and their lives seem to be so barren, empty, without meaning, and they try to get their kicks from being around a successful athletic program. They just love this identification with the coach and the players; there's a kind of re-flected glow for them.

Auburn afforded many examples of misplaced priorities. When football coach Tommy Tuberville came to Auburn, he commanded a salary of between $750,000 and $900,000 a year, depending on performance bonuses. He managed 130 student-athletes and 9 assistant coaches. He earned nearly four times the salary of William Muse, who oversaw 23,000 students, 1,200 faculty, and thousands of staff. Tuberville's salary was eight times the average salary of an Auburn faculty member, whose success or failure at preparing students would significantly affect forever the quality of their lives.

As for tainted degrees, that 1957 national championship team that "Ace" Atkins led, won only one of two national polls because the NCAA had penalized
Auburn for recruiting violations. One poll would not rank a team on probation. Nor was the team allowed to play in a bowl game. The next undefeated,
untied team, in 1993, on which Ace Atkins the son played was not eligible for a
chance at the national championship that it earned on the playing field because
of similar violations. In all, Auburn was the third most penalized university in
NCAA history, with seven major infractions, and the SEC was the second most
penalized conference. At least equipment and facilities for the 1957 team prepared them adequately for a championship season because Auburn boosters
would have it no other way. Many engineering students who graduated that
year were not so lucky. Two engineering departments lost their accreditation
because supervising agencies deemed their facilities and equipment inadequate. The Auburn family had tolerated that.

"Fight on, You Orange and Blue"

When writing *Alabama in the Twentieth Century,* I struggled over where to locate my discussion of football. Should it be included in the chapter on sports,
education, politics, religion, culture, or economics? So many choices and so
much to tell. The NCAA naively considers football to be a part of collegiate
education. The organization obfuscates many issues about how sports should
be regulated. But on one, its guidelines are clear. Article 6, dealing with "institutional control," specifies that an institution's "Chief Executive Officer has ultimate responsibility and final authority for the conduct of the intercollegiate
athletics program and the actions of any board in control of that program." If
the university created an athletics advisory board, a majority of members must
be administrators, faculty, and staff. In numerous conversations I had with
Bill Muse, he sincerely believed that he was in charge of the athletic program
while president of Auburn. My interviews do not support his assumption. Nor
does the history of the school. Nor does the private testimony of many Auburn
sports figures, administrators, and observers.

As far back into the past as the 1920s, Spright Dowell was fired because influential football boosters did not approve of his management of the program
or his even-handed discipline of players. After Governor James appointed Shug
Jordan to the board of trustees, one of Jordan's first statements in May 1979
was a call for trustees to stop "rubber-stamping" presidential proposals and

become more assertive in managing the school. Trustee board vice chair R. C. "Red" Bamberg agreed with Jordan. Though neither trustee specifically mentioned football, that was certainly the subtext, as numerous letters from football boosters made clear. "Turn the football program over to the coaches," was the common theme of these letters. Problem was control by coaches invited corruption and scandal. In a conversation with my labor historian friend Jim Hodges at the College of Wooster in Ohio, he told me that he decided to quit the football team and transfer from Auburn to Vanderbilt when he discovered that some players were being paid.

Rumors began to circulate within SEC football circles that in the late 1980s Auburn was once again paying players. Pat Raines, an offensive lineman at Montgomery's Sidney Lanier High School, told a reporter for the *Anniston Star* that he was ready to sign an Auburn scholarship when an assistant coach from another school told him: "You know, they pay their players at Auburn. How will you feel when you're down at the goal line and you make your block, and the guy on the other side of the line who's making more money than you misses his?" Raines signed with Alabama instead. Such stories infuriated Auburn folk, who vigorously denied the charges. That is until Eric Ramsey turned on his tape recorder.

Ramsey signed a scholarship out of Homewood High School in 1986 despite hearing rumors that coaches emphasized football more than academics and treated certain players better than others. Quickly disillusioned at Auburn, he also discovered that some players were receiving payoffs from a pot of money provided by boosters. Though not a star, he found a way to cut himself in on the action.

Bill "Corky" Frost—a Lilburn, Georgia, contractor, fanatical Auburn football supporter, and close friend of Auburn head coach and athletic director Pat Dye—became his sugar daddy. When Ramsey first charged the program with offenses, coaches (unaware of Ramsey's tape recordings) vigorously denied the charges. One of my former Auburn students, Blair Robertson, then a reporter for the *Montgomery Advertiser,* heard the tapes and quoted them in stories that won him the 1991 Green Eyeshade Award for journalism. Ramsey's attorney, Donald Watkins, later released the tapes to the *Birmingham News,* which published some of them on October 20, 1991. On one tape Frost blasts player performance against Alabama, complaining, "As much money as I've put into Auburn football . . ." he had a right to expect more from the team. Frost had his own way of contributing to the program, as the transcripts revealed.

Ramsey: What about the bonus [money] you paid last year? Are you going to
    cut me out?

Frost: No sir! That's still good.

Ramsey: That's cool.

Frost: You'll get your bonus from me [$500 for touchdowns, $200 for intercep-
    tions, $100 for each "big hit"] . . . with the meat [stocking Ramsey's freezer
    with steak every month or two]. But I don't want to ever hear about it. It
    would hurt Auburn.

Ramsey: You won't.

Frost: Don't ever hurt Auburn. Auburn is a great place and I love it. I'll be your
    friend until the day I die. Auburn's been mighty good to you whether you re-
    alize it or not.

In a late 1989 taped phone call, Ramsey asked Frost for help with a late car
payment:

Frost: When is your next payment?

Ramsey: April 1st.

Frost: Send me your April 1st coupon through the mail. I'll take the pressure off
    until you get it sold. Keep trying to sell it, but don't give it away.

Ramsey: I've already got sixteen hundred, but I need twelve hundred to go with
    it [in order to trade cars].

Frost: Rather than sending you one hundred a month, you would rather me send
    you twelve hundred?

Ramsey: Yes.

Frost: It'll be [a few days] before I can do it. But I'll just go ahead and send you
    twelve hundred.

In another conversation, Ramsey asked Frost to pay his car insurance.

Frost: Have you seen [recruiting coordinator Frank] Young?

Ramsey: Yes, but I paid my rent with that. He wouldn't give me no extra.

Ramsey alleged that Young gave him $300 a month for rent, and Frost provided
his family a $500 Christmas present.

    As the scandal widened, CBS television's *60 Minutes* aired the Ramsey tapes,
featuring incriminating interviews with assistant coach Larry Blakeney, Pat
Dye, and boosters. According to Ramsey, Dye sent him to Lowder's Colonial

Bank, where a $9,000 loan awaited him. In the early stages of the exposé, I questioned Ramsey's motives and defended Dye. I told one reporter, "I think Dye has been smeared and, to some degree, without any evidence thus far. I am pretty objective about this whole process, and I have yet to see any evidence that Dye has run a crooked, corrupt, exploitative program. If there's evidence there, I would like to see it." Boy, was I naive. It took nearly ten years of investigating and a mountain of evidence to convince me. Now I am convinced.

Auburn fans generally were not. When Blair Robertson and the *Montgomery Advertiser* first broke the story, Dye heaped invective on the paper during his radio show. In the wake of that attack, some Auburn fans retaliated against the paper's newsboys. An Auburn trustee reportedly ended his participation in a local charity sponsored by the paper.

In the midst of all this controversy, an NCAA investigation, and serious budget problems, Bill Muse accepted the Auburn presidency. In retrospect, he conceded that he did not do a good job of investigating the school. But once on the job, he acted quickly to establish clear lines of authority based on NCAA guidelines concerning institutional control. He asked Dye to step down as athletic director (confirming Philpott's earlier decision not to allow Jordan both jobs for fear of just such a scandal as befell Dye). If the football coach is also the AD, who scrutinizes the coach? Muse also hired one of America's most respected athletic administrators, Mike Lude. He strengthened the academic support system to provide athletes closer oversight and better counseling. He also pledged to accept any NCAA penalties and run the Auburn program in accordance with its regulations. One of the NCAA charges that Muse revealed in a press conference was lack of institutional control. Other charges included gifts of cash and merchandise to an athlete. An assistant coach provided cash to a player. An athlete obtained a loan in violation of NCAA rules. Two assistant coaches violated ethical conduct regulations. Two assistant coaches and the AD failed to report NCAA violations. The head coach, who had received information about extra benefits to an athlete, did not forward the information to university officials. Muse ended his press conference by quoting George Petrie's Auburn creed: "I believe in honesty and truthfulness, without which I cannot win the respect and confidence of my fellow men."

Already suspecting that the root of the problem stretched well beyond the athletic department, Muse asked trustees to reaffirm the president's authority over intercollegiate athletics. On December 17, 1991, they resolved that "the President has complete and total administrative responsibility for intercollegiate athletics programs, within general policies established by this Board of

Trustees." The resolution also deleted a section from its 1983 guidelines that allowed the trustee athletic committee (chaired by Lowder for decades) to "consider and recommend for action by the Board the employment of Athletic Director and head coaches of revenue-producing sports."

When Lude arrived on campus, he demanded that trustees put the AD on the president's cabinet and change reporting protocol so he answered directly to the president, who then reported to the board. Rumors began to circulate nearly as soon as the board passed the resolution that they were not honoring it. When Muse hired David Housel (Mr. Auburn) as AD in 1994 to replace Lude, David's first major task was hiring a new basketball coach. He quickly focused on a bright young Duke assistant coach, Mike Brey. According to reports, Brey agreed to take the job until Lowder and Lowell Barron intervened on behalf of their choice, Clemson coach Cliff Ellis.

On August 18, 1993, the NCAA found Auburn guilty of "major violations" based on thirty-six of Ramsey's recorded tapes. It levied a two-year probation (depriving the school of the chance at a national championship in the undefeated season that began only two weeks later), stripped the school of telecasts during the 1993 football season, and mandated educational programs for coaches, scholarship reductions during the years from 1993 to 1996, permanent disassociation from Auburn athletics of a former assistant coach, former administrative assistant, and two boosters, separation of AD and head coach positions, and other penalties. Dye, after a dramatic public threat that he did not intend to be made the scapegoat in the scandal, was persuaded (allegedly by Lowder) to resign. He did not starve. According to university reports, he became a million-dollar "consultant to the president."

"Fly down the Field . . ."

After a brilliant first two seasons, Coach Terry Bowden, Dye's successor, fell on hard times by Auburn standards. His record dropped to 8–4. Lowder considered that unacceptable. Worse yet, the 1998 season brought complete collapse after a number of injuries to key players. Lowder had seen enough. In an interview with Phillip Marshall, a sportswriter for the *Huntsville Times,* he announced that Bowden would be fired at the end of the season. Although Marshall did not cite Lowder as his source, David Housel confirmed to Bowden that it was Lowder. Housel told Bowden that even if he won five of his last six games, he would be fired. His only hope was if Fob James defeated Siegelman in the November gubernatorial election. Bowden called his attorney. They proposed a settlement, and Housel picked up the phone. Bowden assumed he was calling Muse. Instead, he called Lowder. Housel told him Bowden wanted to settle, and the banker told Housel to have Bowden call back after lunch. In his afternoon call, Bowden told Lowder that he understood what was happening, and he just wanted out. Lowder agreed. Sometime later that day Housel informed President Muse of the startling development.

The president, who was out of town, finally reached Bowden by phone late that night. He explained that Lowder had no authority to fire him. Under NCAA guidelines, that was a presidential prerogative. Terry asked if he could guarantee another year as head coach. Muse declined to offer that assurance. Although Muse believed Terry had decided to remain at least through the game Saturday, Terry resigned Friday, leaving the team without a head coach.

The week's chaotic events triggered a firestorm. The *Plainsman,* with its typically feisty reporting, detailed Lowder's role in the firing and even called for his resignation. This led to a fierce fight in the student government association (SGA) and on the board of student communications, which censured editor Lee Davidson by a five to four vote for biased reporting. SGA president Will Stegall, a student in the College of Business, led the attack on Davidson. Papers across the South defended Davidson and blasted the communications board. The university senate voted sixty to four to commend Davidson and her staff.

Trustee Paul Spina led the defense of Stegall. At the January 22, 1999, trustee meeting, Spina read a statement praising the SGA president who "courageously passed a resolution calling on the *Auburn Plainsman* to report actions on this campus in a fair and balanced way." But the national journalistic reaction had its effect, and the communications board amended its resolution, deleting language threatening to fire Davidson.

Controversy continued to swirl around Bowden and Lowder. Bowden's $620,000 settlement barred him from making negative or derogatory comments about the university, the athletic department, or the board of trustees. Nor were the trustees permitted to disparage him. This led to signs posted across campus for a new AU MasterCard commercial. The script had Bowden walking off the football field as an announcer intoned:

Paying off the coach's contract—$620,000.
Paying off the mortgage on coach's lake house—$850,000.
Paying off coach's cars—$40,000.
Paying off coach's daddy [FSU head coach, Bobby Bowden] for canceling
    [1999] football game—$500,000–1,000,000.
Paying new coach's salary—$700,000 annually.

Tossing your university's reputation down the pipes—priceless.

Some people money can't buy . . . but for everyone else, there's MasterCard.

From the inception of the controversy, Lowder denied that he had fired Bowden. But as *Birmingham News* sportswriter Kevin Scarbinsky wrote in his October 25 column: "The official line says that Bowden resigned of his own free will. Right. And Thelma and Louise drove off their cliff because they wanted to fly. . . . Bobby Lowder—trustee, benefactor, kingmaker, executioner—is that man behind the curtain. Woe unto the Auburn coach who pays no attention to him. Bowden's biggest sin wasn't losing games. It was losing Lowder's confidence." Assistant coach Bill (Brother) Oliver deepened the intrigue by suing Auburn, charging that he had been promised the head coaching job, that Lowder began plans to fire Bowden fifteen months earlier, and that Pat Dye played a role in the firing. He settled out of court.

On October 30, seven days after his resignation, Terry called me early in the morning. He asked if I thought he could survive if his family decided to remain in Auburn. In a long monologue, he accused the football program of serious violations, discussed his hiring, Lowder's role in the events, Muse's support, and Housel's being caught in the middle and wanting to survive. I had no idea what advice to give him, so I merely listened to his story.

Time passed, other matters intervened, and I had no further contact with Terry until April 25, 2001. That day he called to ask me to meet him at his father-in-law's farm near Loachapoka. He had important information for me. Properly cautious about what I might hear, I asked if I could bring past and current university faculty chairs with me. He agreed. The next day Barry Burkhart, Gary Mullen, and Larry Gerber joined me for an unorthodox version of "Inside the Auburn Tigers." I cannot vouch for the accuracy of everything said that day. In fact, I was able to find contradictory evidence about some of what Terry told us. But other information I uncovered substantiated the central narrative and much of the detail of what he said.

Lowder and Mike McCartney, who served as pro tem chair of the AU trustee board at the time, wanted defensive coach Wayne Hall to replace Dye after Lowder told Dye to resign. But new president Bill Muse and AD Mike Lude insisted on a broad search. Furthermore, Hall's role on Dye's staff made him a toxic candidate with the NCAA. One name that surfaced was the overachieving, frenetic, rapid-fire-speaking head coach of Division I-A Samford University, Terry Bowden. I knew Terry casually and had invited him to speak to our Auburn-Opelika area Samford Alumni Club. He had led my alma mater (where he had spent his early childhood sliding down the bank of the stadium while his father, Bobby, coached the Howard College Bulldogs) to its best football record since his father's era. When Dad called me in London during the 1992 Christmas season to tell me Auburn had selected Bowden as head coach, I was stunned and delighted. But I did wonder why Lowder had chosen him.

It took years to piece together the answer to that question. When Lowder's daughter, Catherine (who had taken New South history with me), graduated from Auburn in 1991, assistant football coach Wayne Hall called Bowden to suggest he hire her to coordinate recruiting visits for Samford prospects. Terry explained that his small school had no budget for such a position. Hall told him not to worry, Catherine's father would contribute the money. Terry already knew that Bobby was the power-broker of AU football and gratefully accepted the offer.

Catherine bonded with Terry and his wife, performed her duties admirably, and one day told Terry that Dye was going to be fired and her father wanted him for the job. After Dye "resigned," Terry met with Lowder, McCartney, and booster Ruel Russell in Birmingham, who bombarded him with questions. Impressed with Bowden's performance, they asked John Montgomery Sr. to recommend him officially to the search committee.

When Bowden reached the final interview, Lowder called to tell him the questions, and rehearsed him for three hours about appropriate answers. The next day, Terry wowed the committee. Immediately after the search committee meeting, Lowder called Bowden to tell him he had been selected and invited Terry and his wife to spend the night with the Lowders in Montgomery. Lowder's trustee athletic committee met the next morning to announce Bowden's appointment as head coach.

Once Bowden was selected, Lowder instructed him to retain Hall on his staff. Terry's brother, Tommy, also a holdover from Dye's staff, warned Terry that anything he wanted as head coach would have to go through Hall to Lowder. On Terry's second day as coach, Mike Lude told him not to retain Hall. When Lowder heard that, he reportedly called Lude and warned him that if Hall went, so did Muse. Terry retained Hall.

By the end of the week, Terry explained, an assistant coach had brought him a ledger, listing the names of players who were being paid, how much each received, when the money was paid, and who provided the payoffs. The pay-for-play scheme involved nine to twelve players. The players received $600 a month in cash plus $12,000 to $15,000 "signing bonuses" for the best of them. Between fifty and sixty boosters supplied $5,000 annually to an assistant coach.

Generally, they asked no questions about how the money was spent. When they did, the coach explained that every team did it, and it was the only way Auburn could compete. Bowden claimed that names in the ledger included those of three future AU trustees.

I pressed Terry about whether the trustees and other boosters knew where their money went. After a moment's hesitation, Terry answered that some knew, others did not. I also asked about the ledger. Terry responded with a farfetched story. Following his resignation, he had gone to his office to clean out his desk, but the notebook had mysteriously disappeared. Later I learned that he still had the ledger, had shown it to newspaper reporter Paul Davis, and would later show it to Owen Brown, president of the alumni association.

Terry explained that he had to decide what to do. During the NCAA investigation, rumors had circulated about widespread payoffs and alumni fundraising. But no athletes other than Ramsey had filed allegations to the NCAA (though two others had initially supported his claims). Muse had no proof, only persistent rumors. Terry believed that if he took the information to Lude or Muse, they would report it immediately to the NCAA, resulting in the death penalty for Auburn football and putting him out of a job. He could continue the pay-for-play scheme and take his chances of discovery, or he could continue the practice and phase it out as players graduated. He sought advice from his family, and decided to avoid whistle-blowing. He told the assistant coach to pay the players until they graduated, then end the system.

Terry alleged that he also confronted Lowder about the pay-for-play scheme. According to Terry, the trustee not only knew what was happening but deplored the fact that so much money rolled in that second-rate players like Ramsey had heard about it and included themselves in the deal. Furthermore, in retaliation against Alabama, which Auburn coaches believed had encouraged Ramsey's revelations, they used $30,000 of the money to support Bama player Gene Jelks, who reported violations in Alabama's program to the NCAA. Terry insisted this payoff be ended for fear Alabama boosters would retaliate against Bowden's program.

Perhaps Bowden came to wonder when his record declined after the first two spectacular years whether Lowder had been correct when he said that Auburn could not compete without the system. After 11-0, 9-0-1, and 8-4 seasons, Terry's offense continued strong but his defense declined dramatically. He blamed defensive coordinator Wayne Hall for the problem and also fretted over Hall's close association with Dye and Lowder. He believed he had gained sufficient control over the program, support from Muse, and backing from alumni, to fire Hall. In the ensuing fallout, recruiting coordinator and Hall friend Rodney Garner resigned, taking with him to Tennessee Tee Martin, a quarterback recruit from Mobile who would lead the Vols to a national championship. (Martin had earlier committed to play for Auburn.)

Firing Hall began Bowden's rupture with Lowder. Terry's failure to stay in constant contact with the trustee further exacerbated his problems. Lude demanded that communication go through him. Torn between conflicting demands, Terry tried to comply with his AD's guidelines. But when Catherine Lowder, who had come from Samford to work for him, warned that her father was miffed with Terry, he would call the trustee. Contacts between the two became less frequent after Bowden fired Hall. The team's disastrous performance during Terry's fifth year gave Lowder all the ammunition he needed to dispatch Bowden as he had Dye. No reassurance from Muse assuaged Terry's belief that Lowder had hired him and Lowder could fire him.

Bowden contradicted Muse's account of his years in Auburn, alleging that there was no institutional control of football by the president or AD, that Lowder ran the program personally and had even suggested that Terry renew pay-for-play the year before he was fired. If one believes Bowden's detailed description of events when he met with me that day at the farm, corruption in Auburn's football program during the late 1980s and early 1990s is beyond belief. Had the NCAA received the same briefing we did, I have no doubt they would have investigated, and if they had found evidence to support his claims, would have closed down Auburn's football program as they earlier had meted out the "death penalty" to Southern Methodist University. If Bowden's account is accurate, trustees exercised not only athletic power reserved for the president but also knew about and participated in massive violations of NCAA rules.

As Terry related one sickening detail after another in our April 26 meeting, I fought the urge to tell him to stop, that I didn't want to hear all this. I suppose my reaction was not unlike that of anyone who suddenly acquires horrifying information that robs them of innocence and idealism about persons and institutions they have loved and respected. The following day, I returned to the farm and spent the morning with Bowden recording his story on tape. I felt like Watergate's Deep Throat.

I need not have inflated my importance so much. After Lowder blasted Bowden in an interview with a Houston, Texas, sportswriter, Terry concluded that the trustees had violated their agreement not to say anything critical of one another. Lowder's pressure on Bowden to vacate his Auburn mansion further infuriated the ex-coach. While in Troy with his brothers and father for the annual Bowden Football Academy, he repeated some of this narrative to the *Dothan Eagle*. Within hours of Terry's interview with us on April 26, Opelika journalist Paul Davis recorded the same stories on tape. In later years, the charges surfaced on *ESPN The Magazine* and in *USA Today*. This escalation attracted widespread media interest and withering criticism of Lowder's role in the affair. Terry obviously told the same story for months to anyone who would listen.

Paul Davis wrote a detailed account of these events for the *Opelika-Auburn News* in September 2001, which he claimed derived from those who had seen my oral history. That was untrue. No one but the transcriber and I had seen it. Davis's account created a media frenzy. My son Sean reached me at a bed and breakfast in Hyde Park, New York, where Dartie and I were staying while conducting research in the FDR Presidential Library. Sean told me about Davis's story and the conflagration that had burst from it. Laura Katz, my poor administrative assistant, was being deluged by phone calls, and Sean asked me to call her immediately. When I talked with Laura, I learned that ABC Sports wanted me to appear on their Saturday night national football broadcast to discuss Terry's claims. ESPN, the Associated Press, and *USA Today* (along with dozens of other sports reporters) had called as well, seeking interviews based on Paul's story. Never was I more delighted to own neither a cell phone nor an answering machine.

If my Auburn critics were correct and my intention was to destroy Auburn football, this was surely my opportunity. All I had to do was make a phone call agreeing to appear on ABC's national stage to the adulation of all those who knew, as I did, how out of control college football had become. I had checked already with the NCAA on its statute of limitations (four years), which had expired. They would do nothing no matter what I did. Knowing that Terry's oral history (though not his interview the day before with the four of us) also carried legal restrictions, I could not reveal its contents without court orders. That left only the conversation by the five of us on April 26 to share with the world. And to what effect? As in the case of Ramsey's allegations, coaches, trustees, and boosters, would all deny Terry's charges. Unlike Ramsey, I could not use the single piece of evidence I had at the time, my tapes, unless someone subpoenaed them. I was confident that the major participants—Hall, Dye, Lowder or some other trustee—would not sue Bowden because none would risk revealing information on the tapes, disclosure of the ledger, or the contents of my journals. Little did I know that Paul Davis already had most of this incriminating information on his own tape.

I struggled with my ego and ethical standards for a long, sleepless night before calling Laura again and telling her I was not participating in any interviews. My fifteen minutes of fame (or potential infamy) evaporated that morning. My refusal spared me Ramsey's fate the day he graduated from Auburn: a cascade of jeers, boos, and catcalls, culminating in obscene gestures between Ramsey and the audience. As we prepared to leave for home, I tried to put the week's events in some kind of perspective. Seventy-two years earlier that very month Franklin Roosevelt had written thirty thousand American ministers, asking their opinion of conditions in their communities and of the new Social Security Act. During the following ninety-six days to the end of December 1935, the president had received more than eight thousand letters from preachers who registered a collective wail of anguish unparalleled in American history. They sent the president lists of "widow women" and children who were starving, the names of neighbors who had no work, money, clothes, car, or house. As we flew home, Dartie and I discussed how imbecilic it had been to worry so over football at Auburn. Perhaps, I thought to myself, some great disaster will befall America like the Great Depression or some pestilence such as the ancient Egyptians experienced to take our minds off college football and straighten out our priorities.

We were soon back in Auburn, where the chronically underfunded university now paid a long list of failed former coaches more than $2 million a year from its inadequate budget. Not many months earlier, in better days, a grateful university had reimbursed Bowden's property taxes, paid his homeowner's insurance, and given him up to $10,000 a year in landscaping expenses, this last figure nearly as much as the maid who cleaned my office made in a year. I could tell I was going to have to work hard to dredge up a serious case of grief over this cast of characters.

For many months after our April meeting with Terry at the farm, he called regularly. During each conversation, he provided additional details. When I sent Terry a copy of my chapter on sports from *Alabama in the Twentieth Century*, he phoned on January 28, 2002, to correct some errors and urge me to use stronger words (change words like "allege" to "said" or "stated"; name the assistant coach who collected booster money). I regularly warned Terry that some of his allegations seemed libelous to me. He brushed my concerns aside, assuring me that with all the documents and information he had, they would not dare sue him. Lowder, he vowed, had picked the wrong man to try to intimidate.

After months of bravado, he phoned on May 20, 2002, in a panic. I had a hunch I knew the reason why. That morning's copy of the *Birmingham News* carried a story about Bowden's comments the previous day concerning a story out of Mobile involving quarterback Tee Martin. The article linked Martin to a local woman who had helped the Tennessee Vols recruit him with various unallowable gifts. Asked for comment about the story, Terry blasted Garner (who by then had left Tennessee to become recruiting coordinator at the University of Georgia). Terry warned Georgia coach Mark Richt (who formerly had been an assistant coach for Bobby Bowden at FSU) to keep Garner in check or he would revert to his conduct in Auburn. The suggestion of cheating infuriated Garner, who held his own press conference that morning. He warned that if Bowden endangered his coaching career, he would call Bobby Lowder and Jimmy Rane and ask them to tell reporters what they knew about Terry.

Bowden asked if I was going to cite him in my book as a source for allegations of Auburn's NCAA violations. Lowder's lawyers were forcing him to sign a document denying knowledge of NCAA violations in order to obtain the $800,000 equity in his Auburn house. Henceforth, he would have to swear in public and private that he knew nothing about alleged violations. I was astonished. Hadn't he known about such threats during all those months of conversations? "They have my butt in a crack," he replied. "I've got to have that money."

I reminded him that although I would not use the oral history, that was the least of his problems. At the April 26 meeting at the farm, I was not the only person present. He had bared his soul to me, Burkhart, Mullen, and Gerber. His allegations that day were actually more incriminating and detailed than the oral history. He had mentioned Lowder and three other trustees by name. When I had offered him the chance to correct his oral history, after careful reflection, he had changed nothing of substance. When I had warned that some of his inflammatory charges might be libelous, he had brushed aside my caution.

He replied that he understood my situation, but reaffirmed that if anyone printed his charges, Lowder would just produce his signed document that he knew of no NCAA rules violations. He had recently talked with *Time* magazine, which planned to send a reporter to Auburn as early as that week to fill in details of the story. But he had called them also to renege on his agreement. If they wanted to run the story, they would have to obtain independent verification of what he had told them. I asked Terry what he was going to say when I published his allegations in my book. He thought for a minute, then said, "I will say 'no comment.'"

On May 23, I told Gerber and university faculty chair Jim Bradley about Terry's call. Paul Davis phoned the next day to ask me about my conversation with Bowden. I confirmed that I had had one but supplied no information. Paul ran a story anyway on the twenty-sixth, summarizing the conversation at the farm according to those "who had heard the tape" (he was obviously citing his own recording or accounts by one of the participants from the meeting on the twenty-sixth). Finally in a January 31, 2009, column, Paul wrote that Terry had told him everything he had told us at virtually the same time.

On May 25 my neighbor, whose husband was then academic adviser to the athletic department, innocently provided a fascinating footnote to Terry's claim of lack of institutional control. Her husband, already hobbled by coaches who ignored his tutoring program in preference for their own academic advisers, had taken spring semester grades in to coach Tommy Tuberville's office to show him how well football players had done in their classwork. Tuberville scanned the numbers, then told his secretary, "Send these to Bobby." Not give these to AD David Housel. Or "pass these along to the president." But "send these to Bobby." Was he supposed to do that, my neighbor asked. Probably not, I thought. But what a minor violation that was in Auburn's grand scheme of things.

Research during subsequent years fleshed out the story. An ALFA vice president told me he had seen another and earlier account book of payments to players. A lawyer called to say he was the one who had delivered money to Gene Jelks. Boosters had contacted him on November 5, 1991, and given him checks for Jelks, which led to the player's allegations of NCAA violations at Alabama. He had appeared numerous times before the NCAA infractions committee about the matter. He also implicated University of Alabama alumni and prominent attorneys, who allegedly threatened to ruin his legal career. Someone had shot out windows in his car and law office. He said that he had five boxes full of canceled checks from Auburn boosters that had funded Jelks's expenses. He could not understand why people who loved one school felt obliged to destroy the other. If he ever revealed this, he grieved, "they" said they would destroy him.

Meanwhile, Muse had concluded that some trustees were violating their pledge to respect NCAA guidelines against contacts with coaches. Lowder's athletic committee "had firm control of athletics and did not plan to relinquish it." The committee never "officially" met because that would require announcements of the meeting and keeping minutes, neither of which were done. Yet it met regularly off the main campus, usually in a conference room at AUM. Although some trustees on the committee often met with the AD, they did not welcome input. Muse concluded that until the appointment of Lude and Housel, Lowder had functioned as the university's de facto athletic director. Lude, accustomed to less intrusive trustees at the University of Washington, was appalled by what he observed as common practice at Auburn. Lowder approached Lude just after Muse appointed him and invited the AD to confer with him. When Lude informed Lowder that he followed both trustee and NCAA guidelines and reported only to Muse, some trustees pressured the president to "get rid" of him.

Muse wrote in his memoir that he failed to understand "the importance of athletics to many of the trustees and their desire to control its operations and the willingness on the part of the individual trustees to exercise their perceived authority." Lowder's committee essentially wanted to run the football program while others (the head coach, AD, president) took the heat and bore the consequences for trustee and booster micromanagement, including NCAA violations.

"War Eagle, Win for Auburn"

Central to my decision to retire early was the issue of institutional control of Auburn. There is sufficient evidence of football coaches and athletic department officials communicating directly with Lowder instead of Muse to question seriously who ran the university during the two decades from Jim Martin's presidency through Bill Walker's interim term. I became enmeshed publicly in the issues during the winter of 2001 when a struggle broke out over Bobby Lowder's attempt to fire Bill Muse and take control of the alumni association. David Housel (as fine an AD as any university could boast of but a man who loved Auburn too much for his own good) became involved in the power struggle. He wrote the president of the Henry County Auburn Club that the "quickest way to lose Athletic Department participation in the club program," was "to attack even once, Golda [McDaniel, Lowder's choice for alumni association president and, later, trustee], the Board, the President, or anyone associated with Auburn." David even added a love-us-or-leave-us handwritten postscript: "With Auburn facing proration, Auburn people need to be *together now* more than ever. Hope you will join us in a *positive* unifying effort."

David's letter incited another round of anger and recrimination. He should have known that Auburn alumni were independent-minded, strong-willed folk who would not submit to what they viewed as a threat. A week after his letter, the president of the Dale County Auburn Club wrote a friend of mine, canceling his scholarship donor contribution. He added in a fury: "I will no longer support the athletic department (and I believe, Bobby Lowder) with my scholarship level contributions. I support a vote of no confidence one hundred percent and . . . would ask for the resignation of Bobby Lowder." For Housel to "even suggest that we shut up and toe the line insults and enrages me."

When reporters asked interim president William Walker if he knew Housel was going to send such a letter, he denied any knowledge. Housel confirmed that he had acted on his own initiative and denied the letter violated NCAA rules regarding institutional control. I was not so sure. It made sense to me to request an NCAA investigation to determine conflicting interpretations of institutional control over athletics. So, at the March university faculty meeting, I proposed this resolution:

> Whereas former Auburn University President William Muse alleged to the Associated Press on March 6, 2001, that university trustees bypassed him "to manage athletic coaches,"
>
> And whereas such conditions appear to the faculty to constitute a serious lack of institutional control over athletics at Auburn University,
>
> Whereas actions were taken in February 2001 by the Athletics Director to deny coaches participation in AU Alumni Clubs that allowed criticism of the Trustees and such actions were taken without the approval of the University's president,
>
> Therefore, be it resolved that the university faculty formally request an investigation into all matters of direct trustee contact with the athletics program by the National Collegiate Athletics Association.

Because only a handful of faculty knew of Bowden's allegations at the time, the ensuing debate focused more on process than substance. Had they known what Paul Davis revealed in the *Opelika-Auburn News* in a series of articles two years later, I have no doubt my resolution would have passed easily. As it was, faculty voted to refer the matter to the University Athletic Committee.

Before that committee could meet, I became the favorite target of football-crazed zealots. In the sepia world of the blogosphere—where everyone has an opinion even in the absence of any information—opinion becomes truth, truth becomes fanaticism, and fanaticism forges collective identity. Once collective identity has been established, it must be enforced. Intruders, outsiders, even members insufficiently loyal to group-think, must be silenced, ridiculed, marginalized, or driven out. One effect was a new wave of hate mail. A Cullman alumnus from a family with many AU graduates wrote me:

> The Board of Trustees *does* suck, sir, but they don't approach you in terms of self-importance. You must be the biggest asshole on the Auburn campus.
>
> Your "plea" to the NCAA must be the highlight of your esteemed career. I would hope that you, in the future, would take your miserable little life and your miserable little existence and go crawl in a hole.
>
> I love Auburn University and agree changes need to be made, but your approach is so misguided that it borders on insanity. WAR EAGLE!!

One AU athletics e-chatroom voted me the "Bonehead of the Day Award," though my dad would have been furious when they awarded it to some guy named Flint. But the Auburn family is never of one mind. Another posting announced: "If all those that post on this message board could have Flynt's honesty and integrity, or better yet, if the Board had his integrity, we would not be on this board discussing this issue."

History department colleagues supported me courageously given the possibility of retaliation. They congratulated me on the "Bonehead of the Day Award," calling it a "singular honor" and urging me to "keep up the good work." One administrator privately agreed with my call for an NCAA assessment, condemning Housel's letter as the equivalent of swapping free speech for a candy bar. Since I barely knew how to turn on my computer, much less how to access a "blog," whatever that is, my only consciousness of this dispute came when critics or friends sent me printed copies. As Forrest Gump might have said, sometimes it's better to be dumb.

Meanwhile, history colleague Jim Hansen, who served on the AU Athletics Committee, urged the chair to ask former president Bill Muse to testify. Bill hedged in his March 15 interview under tough questioning by the five committee members present. Although he did not believe Auburn had violated NCAA guidelines on institutional control, he did testify that "a subset of the board was operating unofficially to provide very strong oversight over athletics, and in some ways clearly infringing upon the authority of the president." He added that he believed David Housel "understands that he is not to take any action of any consequence without consultation with that [trustee athletic] committee." He also mentioned frequent direct contacts between coaches and Lowder.

Muse's testimony confused me. He stated specifically that coaches ignored established reporting channels and went directly to Lowder. Housel had to clear actions with the trustee athletic committee. The trustee athletic committee virtually never met "officially," but met "unofficially" five or six times a year, conducted detailed athletic business normally left to the AD at other universities, and never advertised meetings or kept minutes.

AU's faculty athletic committee decided that the sum of this indictment did not equal a violation of institutional control. However, it did "request" that the trustee athletic committee meet publicly, keep minutes, and include a representative from the faculty athletic committee. The fact that the *Montgomery Advertiser* had filed a suit (later won) against trustees for violating Alabama's open meeting law reinforced this "request."

Committee chair Dennis Wilson—a member of my church and a man of unquestioned integrity—conceded that "it's a process gone awry. We've perhaps got a board that provides too much management rather than oversight— but I wouldn't call that a lack of institutional control." Perhaps not. But there is a simpler way to summarize what everyone now knew as a result of my resolution. The trustee athletic committee micromanaged the football program. Some coaches ignored the president and AD, reporting directly to Lowder. And the trustee committee violated Alabama state law. I was not the only one confused. The *Chronicle of Higher Education* headlined its account of the committee's proceedings in its May 4, 2001, issue: "Auburn Trustees Have Usurped Control of Athletics, Former President Says."

"Power of Dixeland"

A year later, President Walker sent me a certified letter asking me to turn over my oral history with Terry Bowden so he could "review carefully any information you have concerning any alleged NCAA violations." Assuming correctly that this was merely his attempt at plausible deniability in the event of future NCAA investigations and trusting him no further than I could throw Stone Mountain, I replied that I would be delighted to provide him a copy of the oral history as soon as university attorneys certified that under terms of the 1976 copyright law and absent Bowden's signed consent, I could legally do so. I heard nothing more from him and assumed his heart was not in any effort to publicize Terry's charges to another front-page national media frenzy or to the NCAA. I regretted his failure to "force" me legally to divulge the contents.

Next in the coach's football line came Tommy Tuberville. After rebuilding the program from the late 1990s debacle, Tuberville led the team to successive winning years and a number six preseason national ranking before the beginning of the 2003 season. Disaster befell the team as it struggled to a six-five record the week before the final game against Alabama. Although fans were disappointed, they generally remained loyal to Tuberville, a thoughtful man who appeared to run a clean program.

Then on November 20, President William Walker, AD David Housel, and trustees Earlon McWhorter and Byron Franklin flew on a Colonial Bank corporate jet to a secret rendezvous with University of Louisville head coach Bobby Petrino. The cadre did not follow conventional protocol, notifying neither Louisville's AD nor its president of the visit. When an angry Auburn trustee broke the story following Auburn's upset victory over Alabama the following Saturday, all hell broke loose. Fans rallied overwhelmingly behind Tuberville.

Walker began damage control immediately, claiming that he was merely making initial contacts suggested by a "search firm" he used to help find a possible replacement for Tuberville. The following week a university spokesman clarified that the "search firm" was actually "an individual working at no cost to the university." Bobby Lowder said he knew nothing about the trip, a denial met with derision by Alabama sportswriters. Even Lowder's trustee ally Paul Spina laughed: "I told Bobby, if you drive the getaway car and hold the pistol, you're involved." Trustee Jimmy Rane was not amused, commenting ominously, "Honorable men know what they should do when they embarrass themselves and the institutions they represent." I doubt that Lowder appreciated Spina's attempt at humor either. Governor Bob Riley, technically chair of the trustee board by virtue of his title, scolded the plane's passengers: "It is . . . difficult for me to understand why I, as chairman of the Auburn board, was not informed that a search process for a new head coach had begun."

Matt Hayes, writing in *Sporting News*, blistered Auburn with merciless satire:

> Just when you think [the SEC] can't possibly get more salacious and sleazy, here come Auburn president William Walker and fat-cat booster–Auburn trustee Bobby Lowder. It's the Bill and Bob Revue, live from the dirtiest village on the Plains, with school presidents lying to coaches, coaches lying to players, and players and coaches twisting in the wind.

Aubie underachieves with a 7-5 season, so puppeteer Lowder, the de facto president/athletic director/CEO by virtue of his gazillions, wants to make a change. Walker, about as potent as those sweet lemonades at Toomer's drugstore, hops on a plane at Lowder's behest with figurehead A.D. David Housel and two trustees to offer the job to . . . Petrino before informing current coach Tommy Tuberville they're unhappy with his job performance, much less that he's toast.

"The most amazing thing I've ever seen," one SEC athletic director says. "Where do they go from here?"

The solution, folks, is very simple: Fire Walker, fire Housel, fire Petrino, and pay Tuberville the $4 million settlement he's owed so he can walk, too—before he wins a lot more in punitive damages from a lawsuit. Then ban Lowder from association with the university ever again. Finally, tent the Auburn athletic department and the office of the president, fumigate and start over. There, that wasn't so bad, was it?

Somewhere on the scale of laughable to pathetic is the state of football in the state of Alabama.

One of the state's best sportswriters, the *Birmingham News*'s Kevin Scarbinsky, was less wordy:

> Let's see. The Gang of Four flew to see Petrino on a Colonial Bank plane. Auburn trustee and grand poobah Bobby Lowder is the Colonial boss.
>
> Will anyone believe Lowder didn't know they were using his plane? Will anyone believe he didn't know why they were using it?
>
> Will any Auburn officials be held accountable for this shameful affair? Will Lowder be among them?

No, as it turned out. Walker and Housel resigned, taking Rane's advice and falling on their swords. Despite criticism from Riley, Rane and Spina, fellow trustees McWhorter, Franklin, and Lowder decided to stay around for a while. No reason to act in haste when such important matters as Auburn football hang in the balance. Besides, there was unfinished business with Tuberville. It took them five years more to get him, but they managed to do it.

In 2006 the head coach spoke optimistically to Birmingham's Monday Morning Quarterback Club. He was in the middle of a six-game winning streak over the University of Alabama. With Walker and Housel gone, he announced, the "petty infighting" and "internal power struggles" had ended. The prediction of one big happy Auburn family was a tad premature. During the first week of

December 2008, at the end of another season of unfulfilled promise, Tuberville "resigned," to the surprise of Auburn's AD and president. Perhaps like Dye and Bowden before him, he had received a signal that his time was up from the CEO's office at Colonial Bank. The *Auburn Villager* believed so, writing, "The group wanting him out then [the 2003 "Jetgate" scandal] and responsible for his firing last week is headed by trustee Bobby Lowder, according to informed sources." No one in Auburn gasped in surprise at this stunning revelation.

Eddie Gran, one of Tuberville's fired coaches, later spoke reflectively about the Auburn football program: "If you could take five groups there, put them together and say, 'This is the route we're going,' it could be a dynasty. But you've got five different groups going five different ways, and the head coach having to look behind his back. For ten years. That ain't right."

Since others had taken my place in the firing line, all this could have been quite abstract to me. That is, until I sent the manuscript of my book *Alabama in the Twentieth Century,* to the University of Alabama Press in 2004. Only one of twelve chapters dealt with sports, and only a few paragraphs of that chapter dealt with Auburn football. In deference to Terry Bowden, who had not yet found a coaching job, I kept my references vague. No names. Few specifics. I expected no problems. After all, this was the University of Alabama Press. The editorial staff might chortle a bit at Auburn's woes, wince a little at my brief description of their own football scandals, but then they would do their usual professional job.

Imagine my shock when the director emailed me on July 15, 2004, saying the press had run into a problem. In subsequent phone conversations on July 20, I learned that the University of Alabama's lobbyist had been summoned to a meeting in Montgomery and warned of a likely suit over a book the press was publishing about Auburn football. The lobbyist contacted the press director, who informed him there was no such work under consideration, though my book briefly alluded to Auburn football. Assured by the lobbyist that mine must be the book, the director asked if I would mind if university attorneys read the section in question. Perhaps I should have said, "no way," and withdrawn the book. But I liked the staff, was loyal to the press, and wanted them to publish the book. After the chapter was carefully scrutinized by university counsel, I made two or three cosmetic revisions (as many about UA as AU football scandals) and prepared to leave for a meeting in London. Only days before I left, I received a call asking for yet another legal rendering.

By now I was wondering who in Montgomery commanded such attention from a UA lobbyist about Auburn football. My list wasn't long. And they were both Auburn trustees. I became my father's son again: "I am done with this! Publish the book or send it back." A university's integrity should be worth more than its annual budget, I concluded. Else, better close the school while it still had some reason to exist. A calming response from the editor lowered my blood pressure, and we worked out our differences. Some poor attorney spent the night scrutinizing my manuscript again, and we agreed on yet more inconsequential changes that did not affect the narrative's content.

The book appeared, as I predicted, to considerable reader interest and no lawsuits. As I had explained over and over, following thirty years of careful research, with an entire file drawer of findings about Auburn trustees, a huge clipping file, dozens of interviews, and various oral histories, I was fairly certain none of Auburn's trustees wanted to encounter me in a courtroom. That's where people have to take oaths, can perjure themselves by not telling the truth, and can actually be sent to jail. That's the venue where witnesses can be deposed and documents subpoenaed. That is not where Auburn trustees can be found.

I thought my troubles had ended when the book appeared. But that was before Paul Finebaum entered the scene. A former sports print journalist who graduated to syndicated talk show stardom, Paul was a shock-jock (or so others told me because I had never heard him) famous for his adversarial style and snide comments about guests after they left the studio. Though a bright, well-informed sportswriter, he mainly channeled insider information and outrageous opinions into high ratings. I also knew he considered Lowder to be the most powerful sports figure in Alabama and one of the most influential in the country. Lowder liked that, and for a time Colonial Bank sponsored his program. (Lowder used advertising as a club; when newspapers riled him, he canceled Colonial Bank advertising; when they pleased him, as Finebaum did, he rewarded them.)

So I was not surprised when Finebaum's assistant invited me onto the radio show. I politely declined. A few days later an old friend from Vestavia Hills Baptist Church, who claimed to be a friend of Paul's, called. Paul wanted me on the show, he began. Not interested, I replied. Paul thinks you are afraid to come on, he retorted. That comment was a mistake. By now I was sick of obscene Auburn fans, bullying trustees, and meddling lawyers. I could feel Dad's spirit welling in my chest once again, but I controlled my first impulse toward uncontrolled fury, breathed deeply, thought carefully, then replied: "Have you ever heard of Vance Havner, the famous Baptist evangelist back in the 1940s and 1950s?" "No," he replied. "Well," I continued, "he once told a revival congregation that in a fair fight between a skunk and a bulldog, a bulldog will win every time. But usually it just ain't worth it. I want you to tell Paul that." I do not know whether or not he passed along my message. I do know that I have not heard from representatives of Paul Finebaum again.

• fourteen •

Valhalla on the Plains

In Norse mythology, Valhalla was the great hall where the god Odin received the souls of fallen heroes who had died bravely in battle. There he treated those with torn and wounded bodies to feasts and respect. By the time Bobby Lowder and his cronies had finished their purges, Auburn was littered with wounded warriors who deserved the joy and respect of such a place.

The Way Universities Work

From years of service on the Samford University Board of Overseers and contact with the school's trustees, I learned a good deal about the way university governance systems work. At private schools such as Samford, the trustee board tends to be large, the trustees wealthy and busy. They have interests and lives beyond the university. They generally have to be persuaded to join the board, and they view their service as a gift to the school. They hire a person as president who they believe will be a strong leader and who will not need constant oversight because they are too busy to engage in the internal operation of a university. They give lots of money and advice when requested. They value the university's various constituencies but do not grovel to them.

State universities function quite differently. Their boards of trustees (BOT) tend to be smaller, more politically active, more responsive to specialized constituencies, and more meddlesome with regard to the school's internal affairs. They are more likely to intervene on behalf of hiring a friend or relative or admitting a child—their own or that of a friend, customer, or political ally. They are particularly likely to intrude into sports programs on behalf of whatever game solidifies and electrifies them or the school's fan base (basketball at Kentucky, football at most SEC schools). They are less likely to contribute large sums of money, and when they do, it is usually intended for buildings named for them or their family or to enhance the dominant sport.

Although these differences are not the sole reason that the top 20 American comprehensive universities in the *U.S. News & World Report* annual survey are all private, it is certainly a contributing factor. Not until the 2009 appearance of the University of California–Berkeley in 21st place and the University of California–Los Angeles in 24th, did a public school make the ranking. Only 16 of the top 50 academic universities were public, only 2 (Vanderbilt—which is private and tied for 17th—and the University of Florida—which tied for 47th) belonged to the SEC. Auburn ranked 88th among the 110 (tied with Clark, Drexel, Iowa State, N.C. State, Saint Louis, Tulsa, and Vermont). The University of Alabama tied for 96th. Clemson—Lowder's model for Auburn—tied for 61st.

Another common denominator of the top 20 was that less than half played Division I scholarship football and most of those were not very good (Duke, Northwestern, Rice, and Vanderbilt, plus the Ivy League schools). Only Notre Dame and Stanford excelled in both academics and football. A third of the top 20 had no football team at all. Not that this information makes any difference in Alabama. If I conducted a statewide poll consisting of only one question—would you rather Alabama and Auburn be number one in football or academics—I do not doubt the outcome. So in a sense, Lowder gave many Auburn people what they wanted, obsession with football to the detriment of academics.

Lowder's Hostile Takeover

In November 2000 Lowder emerged from his usual seclusion to answer questions from Auburn's student government association (though he still refused to debate faculty leaders). He grandiloquently titled his twenty-minute speech "The Rules of Life." Beginning with the truism that an underfunded university can't do everything, he quickly transitioned to his more controversial litany that agriculture, engineering, veterinary medicine, pharmacy, and business deserved preeminence. He criticized the *Plainsman* for distorting facts, accused journalism faculty of unduly influencing the paper, and called for limitations on press freedom (he obviously did not distinguish between the roles of journalists and public relations people in a university). When students questioned the composition of the BOT because it consisted of white businessmen, he responded that it also included lawyers. To student charges of micromanagement, Lowder replied with a perfectly straight face, "We don't just reach down and eliminate something." Of course, that is precisely what he and a majority of the trustees had done to the Economics Department, over the protest of the university's president. The new peaks of excellence reflected his priorities.

Tension between academic and trustee priorities permeated the atmosphere. Even Jack Miller, Lowder's lawyer and a new board appointee, noted at his initial meeting that he had "never seen this kind of disconnect" between trustees and faculty. That was because he had attended Duke where trustee-faculty relations followed the private university model. Had he been around Auburn for a while, he would have understood why there was such a disconnection. It resulted from trustee micromanagement and the contempt that many trustees had for faculty, well summarized by Lowell Barron's famous quip that inmates shouldn't be allowed to run prisons.

Actually, Lowder did not have to abolish programs in order to eviscerate them. Jerry Brown—an agriculture/journalism alumnus who had played such a pivotal role in humanities outreach and who loved the school no less than his fellow journalism grad David Housel—began referring to his alma mater as "Vichy Auburn" and soon departed to become dean of communications at the University of Montana. His successor as chair, Hal Foster, resigned nine months after taking the job, blasting trustees as he left. "Three influential trustees," Foster announced, had created "an atmosphere of fear and intimidation": "They ought to get down on their knees and beg God for forgiveness and then they ought to retire." He believed the recent merger of the journalism and communication departments was motivated by trustee retaliation for the *Plainsman*'s unrelenting criticism of them.

In order to implement his plans for football and university reorganization, Lowder needed to gain complete control of the university. This involved packing the board with his allies. Accomplishing that goal required picking a governor who would allow him to hand-pick trustees and a well-connected state senator who could steer his choices through the senate confirmation process. The University of Alabama had a self-perpetuating BOT that nominated its own replacements, who then stood for senate confirmation. But the governor, under terms of the 1901 Constitution, nominated Auburn trustees and served as titular chair of the board.

In 2000 angry reformers passed a constitutional amendment by a two to one statewide vote that changed the trustee selection process. The amendment (a revision of the one offered earlier by Lee County senator Ted Little) limited trustee terms to seven years and transferred nomination to a five-person committee, consisting of the governor, two representatives of the alumni association (AA), and two trustees. This transferred the battle for control of Auburn from the governor's office to the alumni association.

Lowder's ideal presidential candidate was an insecure, weak-willed man who would do the trustee's bidding without leaving Lowder's fingerprints on policy. Above all, Lowder hated public meetings, reporters, and media attention. Before the November 2000 Auburn trustee amendment passed, Lowder focused on buying governors. Lowder was the largest contributor to Don Siegelman's campaign (at least $57,000), and those of us who had followed Don's career closely assumed that Lowder would dictate the governor's nominees to the board. Lowder told him to reappoint Lowder, and three months after taking office, Don complied. Next up was the reappointment of Jimmy Samford, Lowder's lobbyist, and the nomination of Byron Franklin, former AU football player. Senate Democratic majority leader Lowell Barron, Lowder's crony, lubricated their way through confirmation as efficiently as he had blocked confirmation of Governor James's appointee to replace Lowder in 1997.

When Siegelman finally realized that turning Auburn over to Lowder jeopardized his 2002 reelection chances, he desperately tried to backtrack, criticizing his own appointments, asking one of them to resign, and admitting to the *Birmingham News* that he should have listened to "the alumni association, the students, the faculty, and the administration at Auburn." If those were the people he didn't listen to, that doesn't leave much input beyond Colonial Bank's CEO and Lowell Barron. But as Siegelman soon discovered, we influenced thousands of voters; Lowder and Barron, only a few.

Lowder did not appreciate Siegelman's last-minute conversion. By August 2002, Lowder, Colonial BancGroup, Colonial Bank, and the Colonial Bank State Political Action Committee reportedly had given $254,000 to PACs that donated $401,000 to Siegelman's Republican opponent, Bob Riley. His trustee pal, Jimmy Rane, CEO of Great Southern Wood Preserving, donated $124,000 to the same PACs, and Colonial Bank lobbyist/Auburn trustee Jimmy Samford donated $9,000 to identical PACs. (Perhaps this confluence of enthusiasm was one of the most miraculous coincidences in the history of Alabama politics, but I doubt it.)

By November 2002, when Riley defeated Siegelman by a razor-thin margin of four thousand votes, Lowder had complete control of the board. *Opelika-Auburn News* reporter Jacque Kochak reconstructed Lowder's intricate web of financial ties to fellow trustees in a meticulously researched February 2002 exposé. Earlon McWhorter, an Anniston real estate developer, took out nine loans from Colonial Bank after 1997, two of them after Siegelman appointed him to the board in 2001. Paul Spina, a Hoover developer, received four Colonial Bank loans between 1999 and 2001 while he served on the board. Trustee John Blackwell of Huntsville, also a developer, took out six loans between 1998 and 2000, all of them after being appointed to the board. Lowell Barron of Fyffe had one Colonial Bank loan, granted coincidentally while he was blocking Governor James's nominee to take Lowder's place on the board. Barron also had a financial stake in Blackwell's companies. Jimmy Rane of Abbeville served on the Colonial BancGroup board and received three loans. Jack Miller of Mobile was appointed to the board in 2000 and headed a law firm that handled Colonial Bank business for which his firm received more than $1 million as the holding company's chief counsel. He also received $41,000 in 2000 in unspecified "employment related expense," earned $77,000 as a consultant for Colonial BancGroup, and served as secretary of RFL Services, Inc., which was owned by Lowder and provided aircraft to BancGroup and its subsidiaries. Jimmy Samford lobbied for Colonial BancGroup, and, like Miller, had an office in the bank's corporate headquarters. The only female trustee, Golda McDaniel of Columbus, Mississippi, had no apparent financial connection to Lowder, but he had managed her campaign to become president of the alumni association in 2000. Don Siegelman served as chair of the board. In all, nine of fourteen trustees had some special financial relationship to Colonial Bank.

All these parties asserted their independence from the Colonial Bank CEO and cited low interest rates as the reason for their business with the bank. Whether the loans were obtained below prevailing commercial rates is unknown because banking regulations do not allow such disclosures. However, Michael Olivas—an attorney, professor, and executive director of the Institute for Higher Education Law and Government at the University of Houston Law School—called the business connections on the Auburn board "not just unusual, but extraordinary. I am not certain I have ever seen so many overlapping and intersecting business relations on one fiduciary body. I cannot ascertain if there is a conflict of interest, but there certainly is the appearance of a conflict . . . and perhaps insider dealing."

As for variety, the BOT contained one woman, a single African American, eight white business CEOs, and three white attorneys. Until 2000 they could serve any number of consecutive twelve-year terms. As for independence, individual trustees cast only seven no votes between 1999 and 2001 compared to 1,452 yes votes (a 99.52 percent unanimous board).

As an avalanche of letters to the editor made clear, Auburn people were much too smart to believe the trustees' smoke-and-mirror claims of independence. Editorial page writers introduced the outraged letters with headings such as "Lowder runs the AU show" and "Lowder reigns over Auburn." Editorial cartoonists had a field day at Lowder's expense, aided and abetted by Paul Spina's untimely characterization of his buddy as "just this li'l' ol' harmless guy who looks like Howdy Doody."

Ed Richardson, who became Auburn's interim president in 2004 (and who as a trustee would play a major role in dismissing Bill Muse), agreed with a 2004 trustee audit committee report that concluded intertwined financial relationships between trustees posed no ethical problems. Since the audit committee consisted only of trustees, two of whom admitted to such financial ties themselves, it was difficult to take their conclusion seriously. Nor, it turned out, did the Southern Association of Colleges and Secondary Schools (SACS) do so.

Because of Alabama's weak ethics laws, the report may have been technically correct. Investigations of Lowder's exclusive contract to broadcast AU football games and Colonial Bank's monopoly on credit card business concluded that the contracts passed muster. Rumors that university bonds fetching high interest rates seemed to float through the same bank came to nothing. And Lowell Barron was cleared of ethics charges despite the fact that his son's company subcontracted a half million dollars worth of building rehabilitation business while Barron headed the BOT's Property and Facilities Committee, which authorized the work. In many states, legislators are forbidden by law to serve on BOTs because of such potential conflicts of interest. Auburn's practice was as unusual as its interlocking trustee financial arrangements. Lowder intended to keep it that way. In the 2009 legislative session, Lowell Barron blocked bills to strengthen state ethics laws and introduced his own package to gut whatever powers remained to them for reasons that many Auburn people

J. D. Crowe, editorial cartoonist for the *Mobile Press-Register,* drew this spoof of the Auburn family in the persona of TV's Addams family. Identifiable characters include (*third from left*) President William Walker, (*holding the football*) Bobby Lowder, and behind Bobby, the athletic director David Housel. The frightened man in the foreground is a representative of SACS, the Southern Association of Colleges and Secondary Schools, which had just saddled Auburn with probation for trustee-meddling in academic and athletic programs and for interlocking trustee financial relationships. Courtesy J. D. Crowe, *Mobile Press-Register,* December 12, 2003.

understood all too well. The remaining independent members of the board who raised eyebrows at such procedures—Bessie Mae Holloway and Charles Glover—soon found their services no longer needed.

A brilliant insider's analysis of the BOT and its powers arrived anonymously in my mail one day. After detailing trustee micromanagement of the university, the author laid out a careful scenario of how trustee members of search committees tried to select a new provost and vice president by manipulating procedures. Of interlocking financial arrangements, my anonymous source observed: "I'm not of the mind that Lowder financially controls votes on the board. I *AM* of the mind that he ensures his way by financially controlling a governor who appointed Lowder allies, people who share his philosophy for the university, [are] weak-willed . . . , folks that Lowder knew would pose him no problems on the board."

My letter-writer reported conversations with AU students who descended on the legislature in large numbers, trying to block Siegelman and Lowder's trustee slate. A state senator told a delegation of four students: "People in my district don't care who sits on the Auburn board of trustees, but they do care whether our two-lane highway becomes a four-lane highway." When SGA president Lindsey Boney urged Republican state senator Jack Biddle to vote against the slate, the senator told him he would have to take up the matter with Bobby Lowder.

My source concluded with a sweeping indictment of the university community:

> Here's what I mean: Lowder and the "leaders" who operate like him point out that they do not "control" anyone. They are *RIGHT*. People allow themselves to be controlled. They sacrifice their own power, giving it instead to Lowder. We'd find out if Lowder, Samford, Barron, and Miller actually controlled others on the board if Auburn administrators, athletic coaches, student leaders, etc., would look him in the eye and say, "*NO.*" But that hasn't happened. People allow themselves to be directly or indirectly blackmailed. Gov. Siegelman allows campaign contributions to make him a political whore. Vice presidents who like their country club membership and six figure security don't put up a fuss. Presidents and coaches let trustees dictate who [the] defensive coordinator is. Athletics Directors let them hire basketball coaches. Student leaders who fancy themselves as more than pawns are duped by trustees (including them at the decision-making table, while never actually giving them a real voice). Faculty who fear that their programs might be cut sit in silence. Media who fear their advertising budgets might take a hit restrain coverage. Football fans who just want to win ignore it all. Well-meaning but misguided Auburn folks [who] look through orange and blue glasses just want the problem to go away. The problem is not going to "go away."

His proposed solution? Pass a new state constitution that would change the trustee selection process. Remove Barron when his term expired in 2003. Mobilize every possible Auburn group to demand the trustee selection committee select independent trustees. Get rid of Lowder's cronies as their terms expire. Then get rid of Lowder. "As for the interim president, watch him like a canary.

Scott Stantis, editorial cartoonist for the *Birmingham News,* drew many caricatures of Bobby Lowder during various Auburn controversies. In this one, he depicts Lowder as Gollum, the devious, ring-obsessed character in J. R. R. Tolkien's Lord of the Ring cycle. Courtesy Scott Stantis, *Birmingham News,* December 21, 2003.

As for the new president, raise Cain throughout the search process and then pray that he will stand up and say no the first time a trustee tries to draw up his flight plan. And do all this in the *OPEN*. Sunshine never hurt anyone."

Most of this I already knew. But what should I do with this information? After all, this was not my university. When my dear friend Auburn journalist Neil Davis called shortly before his death and told me I must do something to save Auburn, I cut him short. "*You* do something, Neil. This is *your* school. I have no degrees from here. National ridicule of Auburn does not diminish the worth of my degrees." He was hurt. Later I regretted my angry and frustrated words to one of the best men I ever knew. Perhaps as partial atonement after his death, I wrote an opinion column about Auburn's board of trustees. Some of my friends were shocked at my candor and worried about my well-being.

Auburn had a long history of political meddling and packing the BOT, I wrote. Lowder and Siegelman had merely refined the practice into high art.

With his money and his understanding of the political process and Jack Miller's power in the state Democratic Party, the banker had "become one of the shrewdest political operatives" in Alabama, attracting ('buying" might be a better word) Lowell Barron as an ally-trustee and surrounding himself with weak-willed sycophants. Whether because of his obsession with football or his determination to "recast the school according to his own inaccurate and myopic understanding of what a land grant university ought to be, Lowder used his political influence to pack the board with trustees beholden to him." I listed the financial connections on the board. I detailed Lowell Barron's financial conflicts of interest, inappropriate trustee meddling with the football program, and Lowder's attempt to take over the alumni association. I called attention to collapsing faculty morale and the exodus of some of our brightest people. Interim university president Ed Richardson answered my opinion column with one of his own with me as principal target. I did not respond. Time and history would prove which one of us was right.

Coup d'etat at the Auburn Alumni Association

I was now moonlighting as an informal pastoral counselor to a long list of wounded Auburn University friends who were on their way to other universities, other careers, or into retirement. I stood in awe of their love for Auburn, their tenacity, and their absolute refusal to bend to the new regime. And none of them had tenure.

Most of my "clients" were academic administrators or professionals from the properties and facilities division or the Auburn Alumni Association (AA). Facilities folks had to deal with Barron's chairmanship of the BOT property committee and Lowder's obsession with locating the new student center (the most important building for students whose tuition helped pay our salaries) in some place that would not interfere with traffic flow or stadium parking for football games. Alumni staff were caught between their professionalism and conscience on one side and the new administration's determination to comply with a BOT-orchestrated purge of alumni leadership on the other.

Betty DeMent, the first female AU vice president and the director of alumni affairs, would have experienced trouble no matter what her campus politics because she was a woman in a traditional man's role. Many graduates believed the alumni association existed primarily for the purpose of facilitating contact between football coaches and alumni clubs and channeling money into the program (although at Auburn that became mainly the function of a separate foundation lest too many prying eyes and inquiring minds learn what went on behind closed doors). Worse still, she had integrity. Her loyalty was to Auburn, not to the clique gaining power and authorized by state law to run the place. She also knew the convoluted history of alumni-Lowder relations. Colonial Bank had received the vanity credit card contract for many years. The AA was legally a private corporation and therefore not technically required to follow the state's open bid law. Termination of the contract in 1999 infuriated Lowder and precipitated his attempted coup d'etat. Passage in 2000 of the constitutional amendment altering trustee selection lent a sense of urgency to his cause.

To make matters worse, the *Auburn Magazine* functioned as a voice not only for Lowder's admirers but also for his detractors. As the finger of blame for closing programs in economics and other disciplines pointed more and more in his direction, letters poured in to the magazine criticizing his tightening grip over the university. The magazine dutifully published them, with the ratio of critical to defensive letters steadily increasing.

Normally I would have paid little attention because state newspaper editorial pages were now overflowing with editorials, cartoons, and letters critical of Lowder. But in this case, I had a personal stake in the outcome. Mike Jernigan, an Auburn undergraduate history major who also took a master's degree from our department, worked his way up to become editor of AU publications. He transformed a dull alumni newspaper into a sprightly, colorful, well-edited, and award-winning magazine. The ultimate Auburn sports fan, he and his wife could be seen at virtually every football and basketball game with their two daughters decked out appropriately in orange and blue cheerleader attire. To top off his bona fides as rival to David Housel as Auburn's chief fan, Mike even wrote a splendid biography of George Petrie, who began so much that Mike cherished—the history department, the Auburn creed, and Auburn football.

As tensions mounted and Lowder became ever more critical of the magazine's policy of allowing Auburn graduates to have their say, Mike Jernigan and Betty DeMent defensively created an *Auburn Magazine* advisory board, hoping in that way to protect the integrity of the publication. Members included me, plus a prestigious collection of magazine editors and publishers as well as successful journalists and writers such as Paul Hemphill and Pulitzer Prize–winning columnist Cynthia Tucker. Although my busy travel schedule often kept me away from meetings, I attended when I could and marveled at the wisdom of fellow board members and their high estimate of the quality of the magazine.

In his oral history with me, President Muse traced the origins of the final takeover of the alumni association to mounting criticism channeled through the organization. Lowder tried to stop negative letters in the magazine. (Muse noted that neither he nor Housel attempted to stifle the magazine despite numerous negative letters about them.) Lowder was equally furious at the *Plainsman* for its criticism, and the Journalism Department, which he believed prompted student journalists to investigate and criticize his actions. Of course, the AA was receiving plenty of direct criticism of Lowder, so it hardly depended on a student newspaper or letters to the alumni magazine for its growing concern about trustee meddling in university affairs. Those concerns, Muse explained, contributed to the AA board taking bids in 1999 for the vanity credit card. Colonial Bank bid but lost.

Lowder focused his fury at the outcome of that bid on Betty DeMent. It is a wonder he had time to run Colonial Bank given the amount of time he expended on taking over the AA board and sacking her. That effort culminated in an unprecedented contested election in the fall of 2000. On Thursday, October 19, before the usually routine vote by a handful of early-arriving football fans on gameday, the local paper broke a story that a group "speculated to have the backing of a powerful faction from the . . . trustees" intended to replace the slate of officers recommended by the alumni association.

Andy Hornsby, former director of the State Department of Human Resources and one of those targeted for defeat, called it a coup attempt and reacted furiously: "This is shaping up to be one of the most divisive things in the history of Auburn University" that could split alumni, drain gifts from the university, and set in force a chain of unforeseen events. His prophecy soon came true in spades.

Golda Ann McDaniel, who headed Lowder's slate for president, expressed amazement at the speculation. She complained that some alumni blamed everything that happened at Auburn on trustees. Meanwhile, behind the curtain, Lowder and his trustee friends implemented their master plan, fanning out across the state to solicit signatures on proxy ballots. Prominent football boosters and Lowder allies such as Paul Spina and Ruel Russell led the effort, according to published reports. Insider sources also reported that Lowder had launched the coup only in the last forty-eight hours before the vote in order to reduce reaction time by his opponents.

Hornsby promised a vigorous counterattack over the following two days to obtain his own proxies. Campaign tactics degenerated into what *Birmingham News* education reporter Thomas Spencer called "fax-machine sabotage and anonymous smear sheets." A story published in the *New York Times* reported that Lowder's critics claimed one of his cronies "jammed the fax machine in the alumni office with sheets printed with the Auburn battle cry, 'War Eagle,'" in order to prevent incoming proxies that favored Hornsby. A local judge summoned from his preparations to attend the secondary circus (the Auburn–Louisiana Tech homecoming football game in Jordan-Hare stadium) was asked to rule on the primary circus (the alumni vote).

That Saturday morning, Birmingham attorney Jim Pratt, who held a box full of 910 proxy votes for Golda McDaniel, argued that his votes trumped a call to adjourn without voting. He repeated the argument before Judge Jacob Walker later that afternoon, arguing that the fax machine tie-up was irrelevant. Walker declared the election invalid. Alumni association president William Porter stated the obvious. He didn't know who would win the struggle, but Auburn University was the "clear loser."

By the time of a court-ordered alumni meeting on December 1, the rival camps had reached a compromise. Lowder's faction would support the AA slate in exchange for McDaniel being allowed to name a new vice president when her term expired. Lowder's group also planned to sever athletic fundraising from AA control (and oversight), a move applauded by AD David Housel as giving the "athletic department more flexibility and freedom when contacting alumni for support for athletic priorities."

When I read David's statement, my stomach knotted. Given our meeting at the farm with Bowden, still unreported and unknown except to Paul Davis and four faculty members, I could well imagine how they would use this new "flexibility and freedom." The *New York Times* tried to make sense of the matter. Reporter Kate Zernike, who obviously couldn't decide if her story concerned football, higher education, Alabama culture, or state politics (it, of course, dealt with all four) concluded: "If, as a writer in a far colder land than this once wrote, each unhappy family is unhappy in its own way, then the Auburn family's unhappiness seems particularly Southern, tangled in byzantine politics, ancient grudges, and, above all, college football." For a Yankee, she was a quick study in Auburn politics.

As part of the compromise, alumni and development were split into separate departments after public meetings where trustees cloaked their real agenda (I believe) with red-herring complaints about the yields on Auburn endowments. Ironically, DeMent didn't control that. Investment committees of the AU Foundation and trustees decided how and where to invest university funds.

As often happened, the *Plainsman* wrote the most insightful editorial about the affair. Using metaphors of war, student editors described Lowder's careful planning, stealth attack, diversionary arguments, and ultimate objective. Most tellingly, the students asked an interesting question. If investment and scholarship policies were so flawed, why hadn't Lowder, McDaniel, and Spina (all of whom had served as president of the alumni association) changed the policies during their terms of office? Perhaps demonizing DeMent served a more devious purpose: removing her for permitting criticism of Lowder in the alumni magazine or for bidding university credit card business.

Sadly, more and more alumni included David Housel in Lowder's circle. His letter to 123 alumni clubs to cease criticism of trustees or face expulsion from athletic department participation in their activities seemed to confirm such accusations. His visit to Petrino on Lowder's jet several years later removed all doubts in many minds. I never understood why he went, and he never explained. But I continue to believe he thought he was somehow saving Auburn, however mistaken that opinion might be. Certainly no one loved the school more.

As for the trustees, I never doubted their agenda. One alumnus reported in the pages of our local paper on March 14, 2001, that following a basketball tip-off club breakfast, Lowell Barron told him that "we need to straighten out the alumni association" which published so much "garbage" in the letters to the editor section of the magazine.

As for poor Betty DeMent, her life plunged into the hell especially reserved for university employees who loved the school more than the trustees did. Her boss allegedly ordered her to instruct alumni staff to support the trustee slate in the 2000 proxy battle. She told him to send her a document and she would circulate *his* instructions. He sent nothing. Though not a dues-paying member of the alumni association himself, he threatened that after several favorable evaluations, he could not assess her positively because she had been insufficiently supportive of athletics and the trustees.

In June 2000 trustees sent eighty thousand copies of a new publication, *Auburn Update,* to alumni. Trustee chairman pro tem Jimmy Samford described it as a way to showcase positive aspects of Auburn. Trustees also hired a Birmingham public relations firm to improve the image of the BOT. It needed some sprucing up. By spring 2001 the AA asked readers of its magazine whether the board should support a vote of no-confidence in the trustees. The response was overwhelmingly affirmative.

After Muse was fired, interim president William Walker threatened to defund the alumni association, and DeMent retained a lawyer. Mike Jernigan resigned. Betty followed shortly thereafter. A major American research university renowned for its close-knit family, where trustees muscle a puppet president to defund its own alumni association? Wake me up, I thought, I must be dreaming.

The Seventh Muse

Next on Lowder's agenda was finishing off the man who rallied people such as Jernigan and DeMent to oppose one man rule at Auburn. Except for Bill Muse's courage, I would have sat out this new rage of cannibalism, where Auburn people consumed their own. But he, who, like me, held no Auburn degrees, nevertheless had developed strong affection for the place. When crowds had filled the huge conference center hall to beg him not to leave for the University of Minnesota, his voice broke and tears filled his eyes. The problem with being with the English army at Agincourt under Henry V was that under the spell of his rhetoric, the leader's cause became the cause of all. As events soon proved, I was not the only one who felt that way.

Muse's problems with trustees did not begin at the time or for the reason Lowder claimed (because Muse insisted on involving faculty in university consolidation decisions and refused to cut liberal arts programs in favor of professional schools). They dated back to that first board meeting on December 17, 1991, when Lowder barely lost a five-four vote to postpone Muse's selection and force him to withdraw. Muse's friendship with trustees Jim Tatum—the trustee who crossed Bobby up that day by voting his conscience rather than Lowder's dictate—Emory Cunningham, John Denson, Jack Venable, Charles Glover, Wayne Teague, and Bessie Mae Holloway, exacerbated the problem and caused Lowder to have them removed one by one when their terms expired. There was some value in term rotation, he mused, so long, of course, as it did not apply to him or his cohorts.

The situation worsened when Roy Saigo, who served as chancellor of the AUM campus, made a fatal blunder on a Montgomery television news program. Asked his opinion of Governor James's temporary removal of Lowder from the board, Saigo had commented that he believed the governor's appointees should be confirmed. Lowder allegedly had a representative of Colonial Bank call Saigo the next morning and inform him that he had been removed from the bank's board.

Saigo's problems with Senator Lowell Barron involved a different matter, a master's of business administration graduate student from the senator's district who complained about a failing grade she had received. She had asked the professor for permission to complete the course as independent study because she had moved to North Alabama. He agreed, specifying what she must do to complete the course. She finished none of the assignments, so he gave her an "incomplete," which in time automatically became an F. She requested the F be removed, which the professor, department head, dean, and president refused to do. Barron was outraged and charged that Saigo should have "taken care" of the problem.

Lowder and Barron lobbied other trustees to fire Saigo. Muse investigated their charges, met with faculty and administrators, and received mixed reports about the chancellor. He urged Saigo to seek a job elsewhere but resisted persistent demands from trustees to fire him. Barron finally cornered Muse at a football game (where else?) and told him if he did not dismiss Saigo, he would make sure Muse was fired. Saigo finally found another job and resigned.

Rumors of the affair leaked to a visiting SACS accreditation team evaluating AUM, raising serious concerns about trustee micromanagement and inappropriate intrusion into academic affairs. Unfortunately, Muse reassured the team that he really was in charge of Auburn, spelling out none of the details he later revealed in his memoir. The SACS team reaccredited AUM but no doubt filed away the rumors for another day.

Board interference in university operations steadily intensified. Some of Muse's own administrative staff, seeing the BOT power shift as Siegelman packed the board with Lowder choices, began to mimic coaches, responding directly to trustee inquiries without telling the president. Barron demanded that AU grading policy be changed to allow students who failed courses to retake them and expunge F grades. According to faculty on the committee during the final stage of that debate, Barron issued an ultimatum to Muse and the faculty: do it or the trustees would impose their own policy.

In late January 2001 trustees Samford and Miller (Colonial Bank's lobbyist and lawyer, respectively) came to Muse's office and informed him that they had learned he was looking for another job and asked him to resign. Muse reminded them of the contract he had signed while Lowder was temporarily off the board and promised to leave when it expired. They demanded he resign by

March 1, but promised to honor the payout provisions of his contract. At least they were consistent. If Auburn paid millions to coaches for not working, why not pay presidents not to work as well. By now, fed up completely with Auburn, I even planted a whimsical thought among some of those AU administrators who allegedly chatted with Lowder on occasion. If he really wanted to get rid of me, I would go cheaply. No multimillion dollar presidential assignment or coaching contract to pay off. Give me half a million dollars, and I'm out of here. Lowder either never learned of my generous offer or chose to ignore it. Perhaps he concluded that paying me might set a bad precedent. Think of all the other faculty who might queue up for that offer!

Not content merely to be rid of Muse, trustees found it necessary to humiliate him as well. When Muse accepted the presidency of Eastern Carolina University, he informed the board that he would remain in Auburn through July. While one protestor held up a sign begging "Let Muse leave with dignity," trustees meeting in a packed room in Foy Student Union passed a resolution removing him as president immediately and installing provost William Walker as interim president. They did not allow Muse to speak. In one of the little noticed ironies in Auburn history, SGA president Lindsey Boney (a student serving as ex-officio member of the board) spoke for the faculty (who had no ex-officio voice on the BOT), praising the university president who was not allowed to speak. When Boney finished, the audience stood and gave their departing president a thunderous ovation. Trustees at first sat in stunned silence. Then, in undoubtedly the most hypocritical act I witnessed in nearly three decades at Auburn, they slowly stood and joined in the applause. All except one, that is. In that large, packed room, Lowder remained true to his convictions. He sat alone in sullen silence.

Trustees shuffled Muse to a tiny cubicle little larger than a closet for the remaining days of his contract (perhaps to show faculty who was boss at their university). Muse then departed for North Carolina, where he shortly afterward suffered a heart attack. He believed the stress of his Auburn years contributed to his cardiac problems. David Wilson had already departed to head outreach for the University of Wisconsin system on his way to becoming president of Morgan State University in 2010.

I began a solitary and solemn meditation about what all this meant, moving slowly from cynicism to stoical resolve. Bill Muse's firing at one level was like being deported from a third world banana republic: it isn't an experience you enjoy, but neither is it the worst thing that can happen to a person. Auburn spent $5,872 per student; ECU spent $7,322. The state of Alabama couldn't decide whether college campuses were primarily dedicated to educating new generations of state leaders or merely venues for football games. But for all the stupidity, arrogance, and micromanagement by trustees, most Auburn people were wonderful, as Bill discovered. He and Marlene returned often to town, always welcomed by their many friends. As so often happens in such crises, I immediately thought of an insightful passage from southern literature that fit Auburn's situation perfectly. Jewish essayist Harry Golden, the witty editor of the *Carolina Israelite,* once wrote sardonically that no state can long prosper that drives out its prophets and exalts its fools.

The Whirlwind Cometh

The reaction from Auburn people nationwide turned what should have been my saddest hour on the Plain to one of my most satisfying. More than six hundred students, faculty, and staff staged a protest rally at Samford Hall, which ironically contained the former president's new cubicle. "Lowder A&M" T-shirts went on sale, along with lots of other satirical items. My favorite shirt offered a quick poll: Lowder was (A) "the savior of Auburn;" or (B) "a plague on the magnitude of plastic-eating fungus destroying CDs and DVDs worldwide." Auburn's AAUP chapter hosted a 5K "resignation run" on May 3, followed by a campus rally where protestors chanted "nine times No, the Board must go." (It doesn't qualify as great poetry, but it did convey the message that nine Auburn campus groups had called for trustees to resign.)

The university senate met on April 17 to consider such a vote. Our chair, biologist Jim Bradley, was fearless and less inclined to raging temper than I am. But even he had trouble controlling the emotions and rhetoric that day. Some faculty called the resignation resolution "fantasy" and "illogical." A professor from the veterinary school argued the pragmatist position that we had to work with the BOT whether we liked it or not. But she used an unfortunate analogy: "I'm not a psychologist, but I am a veterinarian. If you want to train a Rottweiler, you don't kick it in the butt repeatedly because it won't pay much attention to the training. Let's stop kicking the dog—let's back off and try to train the trustees." Ralph Mirarchi, professor of wildlife and zoology, tweaked the analogy a bit more in the direction of his specialty: "Sometimes you have to put that Rottweiler down when it's out of control." On March 14 the general faculty voted no-confidence in the BOT by a margin of 366 to 29 (93 percent to 7).

The alumni association's board of directors approved a resolution of no-confidence on March 27 by a vote of fourteen to three. Prior to the vote, the

VALHALLA ON THE PLAINS

AA board solicited advice from fifty-two thousand alumni, and more than 92 percent of the fifteen hundred respondents supported the no-confidence vote.

Sallie Owen, one of my best undergraduate students when she was a journalism major at Auburn, began a four-part series in the *Montgomery Advertiser* titled "Uprising in Auburn." She had learned her craft well. She gave all parties a chance to be heard and conducted the same in-depth research, interviews, and analysis that had made the *Plainsman* one of the most respected campus newspapers in the nation and the recipient of dozens of major journalism awards.

The *Chronicle of Higher Education* and other state and national papers covered the story in substantial detail, none of them flattering to trustees in general or Lowder in particular. Cynthia Tucker, my colleague on the *Auburn Magazine* advisory board, minced no words in a column blasting governor Siegelman and the trustees. But she directed special scorn toward Lowder: "Auburn University is suffocating under the dictatorship of a power-hungry and petty man, Alabama banker Bobby Lowder." I explained to the *Atlanta Journal-Constitution* that "what we're in for is a protracted war."

If so, we now had some significant new allies. As in the Funderburk affair, Harry Philpott, approaching the age of ninety and the end of his life, marched forth once more to the conflict. He praised Muse, condemned trustee "micromanagement" of the university, and contrasted it with the cooperative trustees with whom he had worked. Former trustee Bessie Mae Hollaway, member of the board for fifteen years until Lowder's 1999 purge, broke her silence as well. In an interview published by the *Mobile Register,* she said Muse did everything possible to please the board. As for Don Siegelman's comment that he knew of no connection between Bobby Lowder and Golda McDaniel's proxy campaign for president of the AA, Hollaway commented, "You'd have to have been in a cave not to have picked up on some of that." During one nonpublic trustee meeting, she remembered Lowell Barron berating Muse. Nor had he been gracious to her, telling the only female trustee at one private meeting that her proposals were the "dumbest ideas I have ever heard." After the meeting, she overheard Barron tell another trustee, "she's got to go." That was signal enough to Siegelman who, subsequently, did not reappoint her.

In an attempt to get Siegelman's attention, five professors—Malcolm Crocker and Richard Jaeger (University Professors of mechanical and electrical engineering), James Bradley (chair of the university senate), Judith Sheppard (chair of Auburn's AAUP chapter), and I—asked our senator, Ted Little, to arrange a meeting with the governor. Ted scheduled a half hour on May 2, 2001. Jim and Malcolm produced a well-written, candid appraisal of the importance of Auburn to the state's economic future along with a description of the political turmoil that was ripping the institution apart. We warned that trustees had violated SACS guidelines and engaged in conflicts of interest. Several trustees had threatened some faculty and senate leaders. Nine campus groups and the alumni association had voted no-confidence in the board. We asked Siegelman to cancel the presidential search. We told him morale had collapsed and many faculty intended to retire early or leave. The situation was intolerable and required reconstituting the board. Siegelman listened, joked about how many alumni he obviously had alienated, and did nothing. Two months later, Little urged him to appoint faculty to the BOT by executive order. Nearly a year later, the governor wrote Jimmy Samford, suggesting appointment of nonvoting faculty from AU and AUM to the board since students already served in that capacity. This crumb was much too small and far too late. We had warned him at the May meeting that his actions toward Auburn jeopardized his reelection chances. Most of us would soon join a movement to make that warning become reality.

At least I had the support of my colleagues. Crocker's dean told him that he was jeopardizing the College of Engineering's fund-raising efforts and warned ominously that there would be a "parting of the ways" if he continued to meddle in trustee matters. He also instructed Malcolm to alter his report to the advisory engineering council, which had criticized the board.

On July 12 Jim Hayes, Siegelman's chief of staff and a friend of mine, visited my office. Paralyzed below the waist by the cancer that would soon take his life, Jim asked a number of questions beginning with "what's going on at Auburn?" I assumed he or someone had told the governor about that 93 percent alumni vote of no-confidence, and Siegelman was finally getting the message. Because I believed Jim to be one of the most honorable men in Alabama despite his association with Siegelman, I spoke frankly. Auburn people believed the governor had sold the school to Lowder in return for the trustee's campaign contributions. Jim asked how the faculty would react to Walker as permanent president. It would be a disaster, I replied, feeling certain that this was a BOT trial balloon. Jim said that he had planned to leave my office to run the idea by Jim Bradley. But if Walker had no credibility with the faculty, there was no point in further conversations. What about continuing the search, he inquired? I warned him that the university senate had asked that the search be postponed. We had told Siegelman that in May. Jim replied that he believed consultants whom the university had hired would report on July 23 that the search should proceed.

That very week, Siegelman urged that the search be postponed because the process was so obviously "tainted." Jim Hayes resigned as his chief of staff shortly thereafter. The governor began to distance himself from Lowder. I marveled that it took Jim Hayes's resignation, three years, and ten votes of no-confidence to jar Siegelman out of his political stupor. For a governor who would soon be neck-deep in his own ethics problems, his association with the BOT was entirely consistent. The State Ethics Commission and various attorneys general stayed busy investigating allegations against Lowder and Barron. Complaints included wiretapping, extortion, and campaign contributions in exchange for selection to the board, all dismissed after further investigation. Some Auburn folk believed that Lowder's influence peddling even reached inside the ethics commission itself, where a former law partner of Colonial Bank attorney and trustee Jack Miller chaired the agency in 2001.

That same year, newspaper investigations into trustee flights on university aircraft revealed an equally troubling pattern. From March 2000 to March 2001, the university spent $17,000 on chartered flights for trustees, not including flights sponsored by the athletic department. One-sixth of those flights involved Lowell Barron, including trips from Auburn to the resort town of Gulf Shores. Within one five-day period in January 2000, Barron chartered more than $1,800 worth of trips to and from Birmingham and Auburn. A flight log for December 31, 2000, recorded that another trustee, Jack Venable, and his son flew to Orlando to watch Auburn play in the Citrus Bowl. The university, though seriously strapped for money during yet another year of state-mandated proration, defended the practice as representing only a small fraction of total flights. Barron explained that "the trustees are the governing body of the university," and "for them to be accommodated with transportation to university events I think is very proper and appropriate, especially compared to large corporations who often accommodate their officers with flights to business affairs." Perhaps his explanation merely reflected the corporate ethos favored by Lowder, but it rang hollow on a campus where whole departments were disappearing because trustees claimed the university was being financially mismanaged.

Although ethics charges against trustees came to nothing, a newspaper suit by a coalition of papers (*Montgomery Advertiser, Birmingham News, Mobile Press-Register, Anniston Star, Opelika-Auburn News,* and many others) was more successful. Based on a 1915 sunshine law that prohibited public bodies from meeting in secret or executive session, the suit struck a blow at secrecy, Lowder's most effective weapon.

Trial testimony left no doubt that Auburn had violated the law. Of eighty-two matters that trustees publicly voted on in 1999, every single one resulted in a unanimous ballot, fairly strong inferential evidence that prior consultation had occurred. Trustee Jack Venable, himself a newspaper publisher, admitted that his colleagues improperly discussed subjects behind closed doors. Even Lowell Barron conceded the point. In his deposition, former president Muse detailed matters resolved in secret meetings with a quorum of trustees present but without public notice: possible merger of Wallace State Community College in Hanceville with Auburn; use of seats in the trustee sky box at Jordan-Hare Stadium; lottery legislation; fund-raising; how the BOT was organized.

The most disingenuous defense of secrecy came from Lowder's trustee athletic committee, which never officially "met" yet met constantly. Public meetings, trustees explained, might reveal football secrets and give opposing teams an advantage. Surely Alabamians understood that winning football games trumped state law, I mused. Under cross-examination, the university admitted at least thirty-nine violations of the sunshine law between 1999 and July 2001. Lee County judge Robert Harper ruled against the university and in favor of open and honest government.

After trustees fired Muse, the university entered a stage variously described by cynics as Lowder U. or Interim University (because William Walker, the "interim" president presided over an administrative structure where the provost and six of fourteen academic deans were also "acting" or "interim" appointees). Siegelman's July 2001 advice to suspend the presidential search until some of the internal conflicts could be resolved did not sit well with Lowder, who saw his chance to install a minion who would do his will and allow him to escape being pilloried in the editorial cartoon section of newspapers.

Jack Miller, who chaired the presidential search committee, soldiered on. But the university senate refused to appoint members to the committee and voted for a one-year delay. A year later, trustees were so pleased with William Walker's performance, they proposed to remove "interim" from his title and install him as permanent president. By then he had sued SACS to block an investigation of trustee abuses, threatened to defund the alumni association, driven out AA trustee critics, presided over the elimination or merger of programs the trustees disliked, and generally served them well in every way.

He had also put me in my place. In 2003–4, I served my year as president of the Southern Historical Association. The president had to raise money for the presidential reception and other social events. In my case, that involved a luncheon I planned in honor of history professors at historically black colleges, a ninetieth birthday party honoring America's preeminent African American historian, John Hope Franklin, and a reception following my presidential address. I took most of the funds from my Distinguished University Professor account but needed more. Samford University's history department contributed generously, as did the University of Alabama Press. Auburn's history department, the alumni association, and David Wilson (VP for outreach) helped as well.

My friend Leah Atkins did some research and told President Walker that I was only the second SHA president from the state of Alabama and the first Auburn faculty member ever to be so honored. The precedent at other universities was strong and prideful presidential support, which she was sure he would want to provide as well. His response was terse and not exactly supportive: "Hell no."

Had Walker contributed and the trustees discovered that fact, it would not have enhanced his administrative ambitions at Auburn, so it was a wise decision on his part. As for me, it made no difference since the Memphis SHA could not have gone better. For administrators like DeMent, Wilson, and history chair Bill Trimble, who provided me funds, it was an act of courage. Two of them would be gone before the year ended. In fact, it may have been their final act of defiance.

Walker, who had commissioned yet another study by consultants to tell us what was wrong at Auburn (I noticed that none of the studies paid for by administrators and authorized by trustees mentioned what was wrong with them) analyzed university problems in a way eerily similar to Leslie Wright's nuggets-of-wisdom-never-followed a generation earlier:

> One way to build up the commons is by trying to develop a culture of respect for other people. Somewhere along the way, some folks associated with Auburn seem to have forgotten the notion that it is okay to disagree. It has almost gotten to the point in some cases that if you disagree, you have to be disagreeable. That is contrary to the whole notion of the academy.
>
> I think, however, where we need to do a little work is in learning how to disagree without being so disagreeable. We need to respect one another's position.

I was relieved to know that policy disagreement at Auburn carried no risk of retaliation. I hope this reassurance made Bill Muse, Betty DeMent, Mike Jernigan, Jim Bradley, and Malcolm Crocker feel lots better.

The university senate voted against removing "interim" from Walker's title on May 29, 2002, but this action really did not much matter. Shortly thereafter,

Walker returned from Louisville on board Lowder's corporate jet and discovered that Auburn's "culture of respect" no longer included him. The *Plainsman* ushered Walker off campus with Richard McVay's pledge for administrators, a clever parody of the Auburn creed:

> I believe that this is a political world, and that I can count only on who I know. Therefore, I believe in butt-kissing, shameless butt-kissing.
>
> I believe in rudimentary education, without which I cannot control a multimillion dollar football program. I must bow to the latter and patronize the former.
>
> I believe in deceit and subterfuge, without which I cannot win the position of lap dog to my superior administrators.
>
> I believe in a fat wallet, a grade-changing pen and a spirit that is not afraid of petty ethics violations, and in corporate sports that allow me to pursue my personal interests without fear of consequences.
>
> I believe in the almighty dollar, which incites fear in lesser men and pads the aforementioned wallet, bringing happiness to me.
>
> I believe in caller ID, which allows me to offer no answers to the public on my actions.
>
> I believe in having a friend in charge of the state senate, that I may not fear honest people slipping through the cracks of a nomination process.
>
> And because Auburn administrators believe in these things, and an antiquated state constitution ensures that I may continue to do them, I believe in Auburn and love it.

In January 2004 Walker's cochair of the Role Commission, State School Superintendent Ed Richardson, received the dubious distinction of becoming Auburn's eighteenth president (and the third in thirty-nine months). Though yet another "interim," he managed in a matter of months to fire the men's basketball and baseball coaches, national alumni director Betty DeMent, the university lobbyist, and the media relations chief. He vowed to abolish the existing alumni association and replace it if he concluded that the elected officers were unacceptable. Fully justifying his reputation as a bull-gone-berserk-in-a-China-shop, he vowed to whip Auburn into shape pretty much the way a principal would an elementary school. But he did have one advantage over Walker. As a former state school superintendent, Richardson understood the peril Auburn faced from a now angry SACS and a new alumni group.

Auburn Trustee Improvement PAC (ATIP)

Following the wisdom of Sun Tzu in *The Art of War,* I had concluded that our forces were now ready to move to the offense. Since early 2000 I had written privately to numerous state leaders, informing them about what was happening at Auburn: *Mobile Press-Register* editor Stan Tiner; state senators Ted Little and Hank Sanders; Governor Siegelman; attorney Tom Carruthers; Alabama Power Co. CEO Elmer Harris. A group of us had also contacted the Commission on Higher Education when it held hearings on Auburn's crisis. Some of these leaders understood the calamity befalling Auburn as well as we did but were powerless to influence the course of affairs. Others didn't care or were allies of Lowder and Miller within the state Democratic Party hierarchy. In fact, my movement from Democratic affiliation to Independent owed as much to Auburn trustee politics as to statewide party corruption. Except for the Republican Party's zany cast of characters (Roy Moore, Fob James, Goodwin Myrick, Eunie Smith, Sandra Smith) and the GOP's determination to cling desperately to the last years of the nineteenth century, I probably would have wound up in the GOP of my youth, due mainly to the negative role of Democratic-connected trustees such as Miller and Barron and the positive role of progressive Republican leadership of the tax and education reform movements.

Governor Siegelman seemed to be the slowest learner I had ever dealt with. In February 2001 he ignored my advice in yet another letter meticulously laying out the problems he had created for himself by appointing Earlon McWhorter and Golda McDaniel as trustees. Fresh from the vote-packing battle to control the alumni association, his appointment of McDaniel particularly infuriated alumni. Already serving as the AA vice president as a result of the previous year's alumni-trustee compromise, she vowed to keep her old job as she began the new one, arguing that serving as trustee and as vice president of the alumni association at the same time posed no conflicts of interest. She then announced her intention as a trustee to "bring Auburn people together."

The alumni board had other ideas, offering her the option of resignation or forcible removal, not exactly the model of unity she had in mind. Meanwhile hundreds of students boycotted classes to protest trustee appointments, and Ted Little launched a short-lived senate filibuster to block their approval. Owen Brown, Auburn alumnus and former head of Sun Microsystems, withdrew his $2 million pledge and reported that other alumni were doing the same.

During this episode, I received an anonymous letter proposing a strategy to remove Lowder and his cohorts from the board. The author of the letter, a 1956 alumnus living in Montgomery, told me his name after his wife, who worked at Auburn and feared retaliation, retired. His advice paralleled our final strategy: form a political action committee; raise money to defeat pro-Lowder incumbent legislators; create a newsletter to inform alumni about what was happening; recruit leadership from respected officers of the alumni association; act immediately while alumni were furious at the trustee appointment of McDaniel. "As for Lowder," he wrote angrily, "a cunning, conscienceless, malignant, genetic redneck—he is a perfect Snopes (*vide* Faulkner), rising to power off a huge launch from his crook father and on the stabbed backs of innumerable businessmen and other victims who are just waiting for some way to strike back." His letter was prophetic.

It also reminded me of a piece of wisdom from one of my favorite presidents, Theodore Roosevelt: "It is not the critic who counts; not the man who points out how the strong man stumbles, or where the doers of deeds could have done better. The credit belongs to the man who is actually in the arena." The persons "actually in the arena" could have been the mantra of the Auburn Trustee Improvement PAC. At a meeting at Don Logan's home on May 6, 2002, this anonymous idea sprouted wings. Don, CEO of Time-Warner/AOL, hosted a meeting of Auburn folks devoted to staging their own coup d'etat. Issues discussed included formation of a political action committee, a procedure to solicit contributions, financial goals, whether to endorse candidates publicly or merely contribute to campaigns, advertising strategy, and a host of other issues. I was flattered to be invited to join ATIP's executive committee, which included many Auburn people I most admired: Don Logan; Aaron and Brenda Green from my Sunday school class; Ed Dyas (an All-American Auburn football player and Mobile surgeon); my 1957 national championship team idol Lloyd Nix; Taylor Littleton; Herb White; Morris Savage; Bob Harris; former state school superintendent Wayne Teague; University of Florida vice president E. T. York; Richard Jaeger; Owen Brown; developer Bill Harbert; trial lawyer Jere Beasley; columnist Rheta Grimsley Johnson; Harry Philpott; and a host of others. Our fund-raising goal was $1.5 million by the 2002 election cycle. We particularly targeted Siegelman and Barron.

By 2004 ATIP polling suggested we were cultivating a rich patch of terrain. Favorable opinions of Auburn among alumni had declined by nearly 10 percent and negative views had doubled in two years. Though highly favorable about the university's academics and alumni association, a whopping 92 percent disapproved of actions by trustees and administrators. Nearly two in three believed those involved should resign or be fired. Asked who was to blame for recently announced SACS probation, 53 percent cited the BOT and 6 percent more cited trustee involvement in sports. Asked if they were satisfied with current membership of the BOT, 73 percent answered negatively (that figure had increased from 47 percent in 2002). Nearly three-fourths ranked Bobby Lowder's trustee performance as poor (56 percent) or fair (18 percent). We could win political campaigns with those numbers.

SACS and Auburn's Armageddon

The Southern Association of Colleges and Secondary Schools' investigation of Auburn paralleled Bill Walker's administration and lasted nearly three years. The time line involved many intersecting issues:

February 12, 2001: Muse is fired

April 24, 2001: a petition for investigation is filed with SACS

July 11, 2001: SACS announces a team will investigate

August 3, 2001: AU sues SACS in federal court, claiming bias against the school

January 15, 2002: a U.S. district judge rules that SACS must extend AU due process

September 3, 2002: SACS and AU agree to allow a court-ordered attorney to investigate allegations

December 18, 2002: the attorney's report largely exonerates AU but determines that the board overstepped its authority in overruling President Muse and eliminating the doctoral program in economics

January 9, 2003: a U.S. district judge orders the attorney to write a second report discussing trustee involvement in the firing of Terry Bowden and the interlocking trustee arrangements with Lowder and Colonial Bank

August 29, 2003: the attorney files a second report, which was sealed because it contained references to the financial transactions of trustees

October 15, 2003: charges surface that Lowell Barron and Jimmy Samford pressured an AUM faculty member to change student grades

October 16, 2003: AU officials fly to Washington, D.C., to discuss the accreditation situation with Secretary of Education Rod Paige, U.S. senators Richard Shelby and Jeff Sessions, and Representative Mike Rogers

November 20, 2003: Walker, Housel, Franklin, and McWhorter visit Bobby Petrino in Louisville

December 6, 2003: Walker, McWhorter, and other AU officials receive
   SACS report
December 10, 2003: public announcement that SACS has placed AU on
   probation
January 14, 2004: Governor Riley meets with Walker and suggests he
   resign
January 16, 2004: Walker resigns, urging the "Auburn family to pull to-
   gether and begin a healing process"

In 2001, just before university senate chair Bruce Gladden's term expired, the senate passed a Joint Assessment Committee resolution that had been rec- ommended by professors in the College of Business. It called for an external assessment of the board of trustees. As implemented by new senate chair Jim Bradley, the committee consisted of Andy Hornsby (former AA president and a foe of Lowder), strong faculty representatives, and Interim President Walker. After the committee decided to ask SACS to conduct the external assessment, Walker stopped attending meetings.

The case against Auburn filed on April 23, 2001, cited issues all the way back to February 1988 when trustees had approved minimum admissions and graduation standards developed by the board rather than by the university senate or president. Other items included trustee involvement in the Charles Curran affair; lack of institutional control over athletics; trustee imposition of the "grade forgiveness policy" for eliminating F grades; the politicized nomina- tion process for trustees; compromising business relationships between trust- ees; contractual conflicts involving university credit cards and campus build- ing projects; and dismissal of President Muse.

I provided some of the material, including contact information for Terry Bowden, who, I insisted, should be interviewed, and various letters anony- mously posted to me that documented inappropriate contact with Lowder in- volving athletic matters and questioned institutional control of Auburn by the president. I also included a series of questions for SACS investigators to ask Bowden based on faculty interviews and my research.

From the outset, I thought our strongest case rested on SACS criterion 14: "Business relationships between board members may compromise the inde- pendence of the board and allow the board to be controlled by a minority or [a] single member." Given reporter Jacque Kochak's article on interconnected trustee relations at Colonial Bank and unanimous trustee votes once Lowder gained control of the board, I thought this would be a no-brainer. Even William Walker signaled as much at a July 2001 university senate meeting when he announced that "I can almost assure you they [SACS] will recommend the Board of Trustees change their way of doing business."

Auburn's forty-five-page defense prepared by the president, however, conceded not a single complaint. Some of the responses were ludicrous. For example, the university report rejected the charge that Lowder had "picked" two recently appointed trustees. Governor Siegelman had privately admitted as much to Ted Little and other senators on more than one occasion. Not content to wait for its report, Walker sued SACS on behalf of the university in federal court on August 3, 2001, the first comprehensive university ever to do so. SACS noted that Auburn, among eight hundred other southern colleges and universities, had helped craft the very guidelines the school now challenged in court. The organization denied any prejudice against the administration or BOT, accused Auburn of breaching its "relationship with its peer institutions," and noted that no accrediting organization could ignore widespread media accounts of unrest at a member school.

Initially, the legal appeal seemed to favor Walker and the trustees. I met with the court-appointed attorney on September 1, 2002, in my office. We began by chatting generally about my perception of conditions at Auburn. I was surprised when he listed athletic abuses among other concerns of the court. I had assumed this complaint belonged exclusively to the NCAA. Before I proceeded further, I asked whom he legally represented, SACS or federal judge J. Owen Forrester, who had jurisdiction of the case? He presented a lengthy history of the complaints and litigation, concluding that he represented the court. I gave him numerous documents I had collected over the years, then asked if he wished to have a copy of Bowden's oral history, explaining that no one else had seen it because of my interpretation of copyright restrictions. If he represented SACS, I could not give him a copy. If he represented a federal court and requested it, I would provide it. He asked for a copy of the document. I explained the context of the interview, my misgivings about Terry's credibility given contradictions I found subsequently in his accounts. He asked for the transcript anyway. I also told him about Lowder's angry comments to me after the Montgomery session of the Role Commission and his attempt to term-limit Distinguished University Professorships. He took copious notes, and followed up by asking questions.

I wrote in my journal that evening: "I doubt . . . anything will come of this investigation." The attorney's comments suggested that he believed cosmetic BOT procedural changes had already corrected the problems specified in our indictment. "We will see what happens," I ended my entry that night. On December 9 SACS proved me wrong, finding Auburn in violation of five of the nine categories included in the original April 23 complaint. SACS placed the school's accreditation on one-year probation. The organization especially targeted interlocking trustee financial relationships through Colonial Bank and their micromanagement of the university's athletic programs.

It is uncommon for a comprehensive university to suffer such a severe penalty. According to the *Chronicle of Higher Education,* only Georgia Tech among similarly sized institutions nationwide had been placed on probation between 1997 and 2000. One national expert explained that most comprehensive universities negotiated with SACS and solved their problems internally rather than suffering penalties, "so this reflects a breakdown, it seems to me." To arrive at this "breakdown" cost Auburn $1,015,167 in legal fees, a hefty price to pay for hubris. But then as George Sarkiss had taught me as a seventeen-year-old freshman at Howard College, "Whom the gods would destroy, they first make mad with power."

Reactions to SACS probation came fast and furious. Editorial pages across the state demanded reform and provided a forum for outraged AU alumni. ATIP and alumni association officials urged Walker to resign. I wrote Governor Riley on December 4, 2003, thanking him for his leadership in the recently failed tax reform effort, then added a long paragraph explaining my perspective on the chaos at Auburn and blasting Lowder's control of the board. I explained that I had chosen early retirement in preference to working in such a repressive environment, though the issue was not my past but Auburn's future. In his February 3, 2004, reply, Riley wrote that he shared my concerns, especially in light of SACS probation. He hoped to balance membership on the board through the appointment process, which SACS had mandated as a resolution to its penalty.

That would certainly be a change. In the previous legislative session, Lowell Barron had blocked confirmation of a selection committee trustee to replace Barron himself, whose term had expired. The senator's strategy was to ensure that none of his Democratic allies attended the senate confirmations committee meeting, thus denying a quorum to confirm his replacement. Some Auburn folks never seem to learn their lessons.

Marching to Zion

Perhaps the mythical biblical dwelling place of Zion is no place at all, but a state of mind. If so, I approached that state of paradise the day I offhandedly announced to a reporter friend that I planned to retire five years earlier than I had intended in order to escape constant conflict at Auburn. He turned a passing remark into a long interview that made its way into papers across the state. My remarks were more meditation than critique. There was a time when I thought I understood the Auburn family, who it was, what it believed—and I wanted to be part of it. Over time, I became unsure whether there was one family or many. And if many, I only wanted to be part of the ATIP/university senate/faculty/*Plainsman* family, not the Lowder/Barron/Spina/booster branch.

Somewhere between George Petrie and Bobby Lowder, the Auburn creed had lost much of its meaning to me. When I saw the words on the scoreboard at Jordan-Hare Stadium—"I believe in honesty and truthfulness, without which I cannot win the respect and confidence of my fellow men"—I recalled obscene letters from Auburn fans who denounced my "honesty and truthfulness." In the end, I was simply too worn out to continue. I had expended too much emotional energy on defense to play a role in the transition to a new era that I believed was not far away. Even with the prospect of a $100,000 reward from the state's retirement system for two more years of teaching, I concluded the money wasn't worth the anguish. Never once did I regret my decision. Lowder did not go quietly into the night with me. He dug his fingernails as deeply as possible into Auburn's wounded flesh and screamed against every attempt to pry them loose.

Despite Lowder's best efforts to prevent it, change proved inexorable. After a series of independent trustees won seats during Riley's term, Jack Miller died, opening another seat held by a Lowder ally (although Miller had slowly distanced himself from his mentor and made a significant contribution to strengthening academic standards that his clique of trustees had done so much to erode). The year 2011 would be pivotal. Rane's and Lowder's terms expired, along with those of five other trustees. By the end of the year, ten of the fourteen BOT members would be new. Another Lowder ally's term will end the following year. That put a premium on the 2010 gubernatorial election.

Although Lowder's influence waned with the departure of veterans from the 1999–2001 coup, I never underestimated his shrewdness, his passion, or his obsession with Auburn. Some years ago, as his power began to slip, he approached a friend of mine whom he asked to be his "eyes and ears" on campus, reporting what was going on. My friend declined. Miller's death removed a legal genius and an influential Democratic Party power broker. The end of Barron's trustee term jeopardized Lowder's influence in the confirmation process, as did the possibility of a Republican takeover in the senate in 2010.

Selection of a strong, experienced, and self-confident new Auburn president, Jay Gogue (who had the added assets of being an Auburn graduate from the College of Agriculture and a former basketball player), strengthened the independent forces. Lowder must have choked on one of Gogue's first interviews, when the new president volunteered, "I have a really strong respect for our faculty, and that means I'm going to listen to them." That had not been the mode of operation of his two predecessors.

In addition to a new board and president, Lowder also entered a new life cycle in 2009. Reckless and questionable Colonial BancGroup policies triggered bank failure and criminal investigations. Worthless subprime loans and derivatives led to five consecutive quarterly losses of more than a billion dollars. Lowder's 7.7 million bank shares, worth $190 million at their peak, had plunged to barely $3 million by August 2009. On August 14, the bank he had founded in 1981 was taken over by the Federal Deposit Insurance Corporation, which lost $3.8 billion in the transaction, and sold to BB&T of North Carolina, which emphasized that it valued ethics, honesty, and team building in its corporate structure. Colonial's collapse was the sixth largest bank failure in American history. Months earlier, new leadership at Colonial had shown Lowder the door. Many CEO's have taken down one large institution, but few have nearly destroyed two. Lowder enters rarified corporate history.

Ironically, Lowder's three primary public criticisms of Muse were the president's incapacity to make hard financial decisions, to terminate unsuccessful programs, and to shift resources to applied learning such as business and engineering rather than theoretical subjects such as economics, philosophy, ethics, English, religion, and history. In retrospect, had Lowder known more economics, history, and ethics and less about banking, accounting, and management, he might have fared better. Risky loans and questionable Colonial Bank policies brought down his empire, so perhaps his financial judgment was not even as astute as the man he fired. At least Muse balanced his budget and saved his institution. That is more than Lowder could say. And his reputed capacity to buy politicians in 2010 was greatly diminished, though in Alabama some politicians still come cheap.

Valhalla for the Auburn Family

On September 30, 2005, as I locked the door of my office for the last time and turned in my key, I pondered the prospect of some local Valhalla, a place where people such as Neil Davis, Paul Davis, Jerry Brown, Hal Foster, Bill and

Marlene Muse, Taylor Littleton, Harry Philpott, Leah and George Atkins, Betty DeMent, Mike Jernigan, David Wilson, Bob Harris, Emory Cunningham, John Denson, Morris Savage, Gordon Bond, Jim Bradley, Larry Gerber, Gary Mullen, Barry Burkhart, and a host of other wounded people would receive their rewards. Somewhere in the other world, Odin must await them, having prepared a sumptuous banquet in their honor.

I offered one such hero a letter of admiration and encouragement as she left. The quotation with which I ended my letter came from one of my favorite Appalachian novels, Charles Frazier's *Cold Mountain*. In the book, a "goat woman"/herb doctor tells a suffering acquaintance: "That's just pain. It goes eventually. And when it's gone, there's no lasting memory. Not the worst of it anyway. It fades. Our minds aren't made to hold on to the particulars of pain the way we do bliss. It's a gift God gives us, a sign of His care for us." I hope the lines brought as much comfort to her as they have to me.

• fifteen •

Ken's Barbeque and Other Third Places

Despite years of increasing conflict at Auburn, I never became entirely unhappy at my workplace. The ratio of unhappiness to happiness certainly increased during my final five years, but there were compensations: students, research, writing, outreach, lecturing around the world. Nor did I feel sorry for myself. Few people I know are entirely happy at work. Even my father, who was loyal to Swift and Co. as few people after his generation tended to be, experienced incompetent, arrogant bosses who provoked him either to quit or transfer (which was one reason we moved so often).

Furthermore, my family remained my primary sanctuary in a strife-filled world. My wife made home a place of joy and delight. Our infrequent disagreements were mere commas in the progression of a nearly perfect marriage. I can't imagine what life would have been like without her. Our sons, now grown, had married brilliant, kind, strong-minded sisters, who bore us three incredible grandchildren. Although Seattle—where David, Kelly, Dallas, and Harper lived—was far away, planes flew there many times a day from Atlanta. Sean, Shannon, and Ambrose settled in Birmingham to our great delight. If workplace was a conflicted environment, homeplace was a uniformly happy and nurturing one.

Auburn First Baptist Church functioned as an extension of home. It was, after all, the place where the family of God gathered. For many contemporary Christians, church is merely another venue for conflict. Our congregation certainly contained opposing ideologies and contentious factions but tried hard to be open, courteous, and kind. By and large, it succeeded. In important ways—support, encouragement, intimacy, honesty, inclusiveness, love, and nurturing—the people of this congregation became a kind of family to us. The family of God sometimes, in fact, is more loving than the family of blood relatives.

Ken's Barbeque and Ivory Towers

If work and family represented the first two places in my life, Ken's Barbeque constituted an authentic third place. Barbecue is a complex culinary art never mastered by Julia Child (southerners would resent the French school of cuisine even commenting on the art of slow-cooking meat over a hickory fire). Yet Child's essays on sauces and the way they enhance flavor is not irrelevant to the discussion. Every southerner worth his or her salt (and it takes a lot to make good barbeque) guards a treasured family sauce recipe as if it were part of the family jewels. Dad made his own sauce and cooked up fine barbeque. Whether it's a pecan-enhanced sauce from the Gulf Coast, a white sauce–saturated barbecued chicken recipe from Decatur's Big Bob Gibson's Bar-B-Q (which opened in 1925 and has repeatedly won the famous Memphis barbeque blue ribbon), or Tuscaloosa's Dreamland Bar-B-Que in Tuscaloosa (black-owned and serving nothing but ribs redolent in a vinegar and tomato sauce with white bread); whether the meat is chipped, chopped, or sliced; accompanied by fries, coleslaw, dill pickles, or Brunswick stew; whatever it is and however it's served, it's barbeque and just fine. Immigrants generally have not been welcome in Alabama unless they bring automobile plants with them. But the Greek owners of Irondale's Golden Rule Barbeque are welcome anytime, any place.

Barbeque may seem like, well, just barbeque, to the uninitiated. But the marketing makes it as different as the sauces. Chuck's Barbeque in Opelika outfits its employees with T-shirts that proclaim the owner's evangelical faith: "Jesus, the Bread of Life." Nearby in Auburn, a more secular T-shirt proclaims a different message at Mike and Ed's on College Street near campus: "You can smell our butts for miles." Mobile's Brick Pit proclaims its meat to be "the best damn smoked bar-b-que in the great state of Alabama." Dreamland's more understated advertising for its ribs proclaims, "ain't nothing like 'em nowhere!"

Appropriately for a democratic state with a rich populist heritage, Alabama avoids North Carolina's fierce intramural battles over sauces, whether they be tomato or mustard-based, as well as that state's continuing debate with Texas over whether God at the moment of creation ordained pork or beef to be His barbeque preference. Alabamians like it all and pity people who cannot be more tolerant and ecumenical in their cuisine. Above all, we appreciate the democratic origins of the plate: you cannot purchase barbeque at the ballet, Broadway theaters, or the Alabama Shakespeare Festival. The best you can hope for in such effete venues is a cucumber, egg salad, or tuna sandwich, or perhaps a Caesar salad. Barbeque is the macho soul food of black and white mill and factory workers, long-distance truck drivers, cops and firemen, soldiers, sailors, and marines. It's the South's regional dish, and an expatriate has as much trouble finding satisfying barbeque in San Francisco, Portland, or Seattle as he does finding grits (which I once asked about in a downtown greasy spoon in Seattle, only to elicit the startled reply of a confused twenty-something waitress, "Wasn't Grits a 1980s rock band?").

Every true southerner has a favorite barbeque joint, though we are tolerant of other people's mistaken loyalties and may even choke down a sandwich at their favorite place rather than offend them. My favorite is Ken's Barbeque on Highway 79 in the Pinson Valley. Mother and Dad, Aunt Ina Hagood, Uncle Walter, and Aunt Louise Flynt all ate there before me, so I am a second-generation Ken's gourmet.

Everything about Ken's appeals to me. It's not fancy. In fact, in its former incarnation, the building was a gas station. Despite the inevitable kitchen fire and remodeling, the place does not attract customers by its ambience. Ten tables and a long counter with stools furnish too few places to feed everyone trying to get in. Ken Roberts and his wife opened the place in February 1970. The location was remote from large population centers then, so his clientele consisted mainly of commuters on their way to or from work. Originally, he sold only barbeque sandwiches and plates. Even now ribs are a Wednesday afterthought rather than a staple item.

Dad began selling Ken premium Swift pork butts when the restaurant opened. The owner believed the secret to good barbeque was fresh pork, so he never bought frozen meat. That meant Dad had to make special deliveries to keep him in stock. He liked to patronize his customers, so he and Mom, together with my aunts and uncles, would meet there for breakfast or lunch. Fast food restaurants offered cheaper meals, but Dad loved the two-inch-high biscuits and the fried ham. A single serving of ham was as big as a steak. Only a Jefferson County sheriff's deputy, a fifteen-year-old boy, or a University of Alabama offensive lineman could finish off a legendary double portion of ham. (The father of Andre Smith, the most famous UA offensive tackle of the past generation, worked there, which may explain the size of his three-hundred-plus-pound son). When Dartie and I ate there with Mom, I would order a single serving, which the three of us shared; then Mom took home enough to last for a week. The grits, gravy, and Royal Cup coffee provided ample foundation for obesity, heart attack, or a caffeine high, but it also satisfied a working man's yearning for a fitting start to a physically demanding day.

Lots of retirees, commuters from Blount County, truck drivers, sheriff's deputies, plumbers, and electricians came for breakfast, along with five motorcycle riders who showed up only on Saturdays. Many customers arrived decked out in Auburn or University of Alabama hats or shirts proclaiming their football loyalties. Although I sometimes drove all the way from Auburn to buy barbeque for my annual graduate student dinners, I knew I was entering hostile territory. The owners were Alabama grads or fans, as were most of the customers.

Lunch brought in the barbeque crowd. There are conflicting stories about the origins of Ken's sauce. He claimed to have originated it. Others report that he copied the ketchup-based sauce from a small barbeque joint in Tarrant City, then modified it to his taste. But the secret of his success, he believed, was neither sauce nor location. People came because he served reasonably priced fresh pork. The lunch bunch featured a wider mix of people, including lawyers, bankers, college students, and professional people stopping by to eat side by side with blue-collar folks. Conversation centered on college football and politics, seldom religion.

In 1990 Ken sold the business to his son (who soon decided the business was not for him), his daughter, Denise Gilbert, and Rick Wheeler. They kept regular hours from 6:00 a.m. to 6:00 p.m., Monday through Thursday, and stayed open an hour later on weekends. Ken's didn't open on Sunday. As Rick explained, "If you can't make a living on six days a week, you can't on seven." As for his clientele, Wheeler (a sociable man who enjoys conversations with customers), told me: "You meet people who are simple, uneducated, to really rich professional people." He particularly welcomed sheriff's deputies, whose presence was reassuring. He confided that a nearby bank had been robbed numerous times, but never Ken's.

Ken's could also function as a sociological laboratory. Denise Gilbert was an early female CEO of a small business. The restaurant's clientele began all white, as was most of the Pinson Valley. Though mostly Democrats in the 1970s, customers had turned strongly Republican before the end of century.

More and more blacks came, first in family groups or work crews, then in mixed-race groups. One day at breakfast in July 2009, I counted sixteen whites and seven blacks. Four couples in their seventies, one of them black, ate breakfast together that morning, holding hands before they began, while one prayed a fervent blessing.

The staff was as diverse as the clientele. Sylvia Ann Bolden, a black woman, retired after twenty-five years as a waitress but returned because she missed her regular customers. Most whites were courteous and kind though beneath the civil veneer of others she sensed hostility toward her. Ken, Denise, and Rick treated her fairly. When white customers didn't, she prayed that God would give her patience to be kind to people who were unkind to her: "You know, God will get you through this kind of trouble if you just ask him." When Rick needed advice on racial issues, he conferred with Ann. A white waitress, Wilma Cagle, worked at Ken's for twenty-three years before retiring. Ann and Wilma set a standard for everyone else, working side by side throughout their careers.

A white couple, Bobby and Elizabeth (Liz) Pierce, originally from Walker County coal mining families, cooked Ken's famous biscuits. They had raised a family in the Avondale textile mill community, where Bobby had plied his trade for thirty years as a Merita Bread Company baker. They moved to a house on a dirt road between Morris and Pinson after their children left home and supplemented their Social Security income by cooking thirty pans of biscuits (930) each morning at Ken's, arriving shortly after 5:00 a.m. to begin work.

Exhausted at the end of a shift, Liz would often sit with Mom, Dartie, and me to talk, pretty much wiping out the distinction between cook and customer. She had grown up poor, one of thirteen children. She and Bobby attended Liberty Baptist Church, a small rural congregation (though Bobby preferred to stay home and listen to Pentecostal evangelist Joel Osteen on television). After getting to know her, I gave Liz a copy of *Poor but Proud*. The next time we came for breakfast, she joined us for coffee and told me simply, "That was our lives you wrote about." When the Pierces retired because of advancing age and declining health, Rick and I both grieved. The biscuits never seemed as good to me after that.

Helen White lived in Palmerdale, learned her pie-making skills from her family, and perfected them on her husband and children. She delivered sixty to seventy chocolate, coconut, and lemon ice box pies a week to Ken's for more than three decades. Mom and Ina were two of her best customers, sometimes buying an entire pie to share and taking home what was left.

Whenever I felt Auburn's ivory tower blocking my view of the real world from my windowless office in Haley Center, a visit to Ken's set things right. It became one of my most important third places, where I met, observed, and talked with people quite different from my students and colleagues.

Third Places

Sociologist Ray Oldenburg's book *The Great Good Place* contends that living a rewarding life requires a person to occupy three places: workplace; home-place; and third place, where different kinds of people from all walks of life and social strata interact, experiencing and celebrating their unique identities. A third place proves particularly useful when the other two places offer a person little or no satisfaction. Dysfunctional families or schools, contentious churches or jobs deprive people of essential nurturing. My postretirement life contained lots of third places: Ken's Barbeque, where I ate and collected stories and aphorisms; the Tallapoosa River and Hatchett Creek, where I fished; Southeastern Conference basketball tournaments and Atlanta Braves baseball games, where I watched and cheered; the Tennessee Valley Old Time Fiddlers Convention (my version of Woodstock without the excesses); the Encyclopedia of Alabama, where I volunteered much of my time.

All people have ivory towers, places unique to them that obscure their view of the world. The tower may consist of traditions, prejudice, family, friends, school, job, protocol, ritual, or regimen. Whether people drive eighteen-wheelers, work as nurses, practice law, preach the Gospel, or teach in a university, towers exist in many different shapes. Towers are pervasive because they are familiar, secure, safe, and comfortable.

Academe is usually the reference point for ivory towers, conveying a sense of disengagement, the detachment of elites from ordinary people and from the real world. Although the stereotype is exaggerated and unfair in many ways, there is some basis for the mythology. Professors are preoccupied with their own work and family, with their teaching, writing, speaking, and endless meetings. Like everyone, they often hate parts of their work. If, for instance, more than a small fraction of faculty attend a session of the university senate or general faculty meeting, it is a sure sign the university is in deep trouble.

Like the mythology of all family places and workplaces, actual academic life breaks down perceived similarity or sameness. All faculty may teach, but there the commonality of their lives ends. Some Auburn faculty, for instance, loved football and winked at the sport's excesses. Others denounced sports altogether, refused to buy season tickets or even attend games if offered one for free. One told me that given what I knew about abuses, I shouldn't attend games. For her, the term "student athlete" was an oxymoron. Because I appreciated sport at the highest level as a great human achievement, sometimes accomplished by young men and women who were not likely to make As in physics, calculus, or history, I ignored her advice. Furthermore, if one loves a place, a people, and a way of life, he finally has to stop apologizing for attending games that are enormously meaningful and important to the culture. (I attended a bullfight in Spain, not because I enjoyed seeing bulls killed, but because I wanted to understand the Spanish people.) I listened to Hank Williams, the Delmore and Louvin brothers, instead of opera or atonal music because I like them better and because they are part of my culture. Towers obscure vision in different ways for different people.

I might have wished from time to time that Auburn was the University of Chicago, a top-twenty world-class university with thirty-eight Nobel prize-winners on its faculty and no football team. But then I would have had no contact with ordinary students. Above all else my workplace was authentic to southern culture, and that was fine with me.

Southern Folkways

The fare at Ken's Barbeque included stories as well as cooked pork. My interest in folklife began at my father's knee, laughing until my sides hurt at his stories and aphorisms. As I conducted research for my books on southern poor whites, the repertoire of historical research broadened. My Samford colleague Jim Brown introduced me to folk music, something unfamiliar to my family. If Mom had married her guitar-picking boyfriend instead of Dad, perhaps I would have inherited at least one musical gene. As it was, about the best we could do so far as musical tradition was concerned is tune in to the Grand Ol' Opry on radio every Saturday night. That was enough to make me a lifelong fan of the Louvin and Delmore brothers and especially of Hank Williams. I rejoiced when fellow citizens elected Williams their favorite Alabama musician in a 2008 *Birmingham News* poll. "I'm So Lonesome I Could Cry" not only contained the finest poetry I ever heard about white working-class people, it was also my favorite waltz at our Starlight Club dances. One of the bands always played it for me without having to be asked.

Rich as the South's folk music heritage is, its tradition of storytelling may be even greater. I spent many joyous hours listening to stories. Zora Neale Hurston—a Notasulga native whose family moved to Florida when she was a child—became one of the South's finest folklorists and novelists. After completing graduate work in anthropology in New York City, she wrote *Every Tongue Got to Confess* (the book's original title, *Negro Folk Tales from the Gulf,* described its subject matter more accurately). In folk cultures, she wrote, people take the "universal stuff and season it to suit themselves." Their local color added originality to ancient wisdom. Though often humorous, stories generally made a serious point. Black folklore baptized everything and everyone with laughter. Storytellers made even the Bible conform to their imaginations. Hurston crisscrossed the Gulf region—a single black woman driving her own car, packing her own gun, passing herself off as a bootlegger—offering prize money for the best stories. Her collection ranged from bawdy tales to Bible stories.

The stories I collected through the years corresponded to Hurston's pattern of laughter, regional seasoning of universal themes, and gender/class-based put-downs. One storyteller grew up in Cowikee Cotton Mill village on the wrong side of the tracks in Eufaula. Though poor themselves, the white family paid a few cents a week to hire a black woman to clean and cook for them. The two women bonded in their common misfortune. When the white woman became depressed over the declining status of her family during the Great Depression, the black cleaning lady admonished: "Don't you get depressed, honey. You just as blueblood as anybody in this town. Hold your head up so high that your behind can't touch the ground."

Another storyteller named his dog "Jesus H. Christ." There was more to his eccentricity than just irreligion. When he shouted for his dog from his front porch, neighbors thought he had joined the Pentecostals. The profane good old boys who constituted his closest circle of friends congratulated him on bodacious profanity that stopped just short of blasphemy. And his hunting buddies were delighted because they thought the name served as a totem, conferring magical power on their hunt.

Dad, who on occasion was known to drink more than he should, recognized certain dangers in the practice. While he owned my grandfather's country store on Sweeny Hollow Road, he rented it to Bobby, a Thai immigrant who did not completely understand southern folkways. During Uncle Curt's carpentry repairs on the man's house, Bobby told him that some animal had taken up residence in the attic. Curt investigated and found a family of squirrels living there. "How can I get rid of them?" the newcomer asked, "Can you shoot them for me?" Curt, whose eyesight was failing, declined but asked Ronnie Davis, a drinking buddy, to help out. Davis agreed to kill the squirrels for a six pack of beer. On the appointed day, Ronnie showed up with his weapon in hand but began drinking beer before he started shooting squirrels. After several fell victim to Davis's marksmanship, the others scattered across the attic, taking refuge behind trusses and shingles. Unfortunately, when Ronnie ran out of beer, Bobby (in a serious mistake of judgment) brought him another six pack. By the time Davis had finished the beer and the shooting, Dad described Bobby's roof as "looking like a piece of Swiss cheese."

My Auburn University colleague Jane Moore, who had one of the finest collections of stories I ever heard, told me about Jewell Bell, a friend from Dozier who was a bit slow mentally. She lived in an older house that was not completely enclosed underneath. One night a skunk crawled under the house and sprayed an odoriferous scent sufficient to wake up Jewell Bell, who sat up in bed, took a deep breath, and commenced a pitiful wail. Her mother came running to comfort her, caught a whiff of the skunk, and quickly hustled Jewell Bell out of the bedroom. When she finally quieted her daughter and explained what had happened, a relieved Jewell Bell bellowed: "Thank the Good Lord. When I woke up and smelled that smell, I thought I had done burst open."

Such stories can define southern culture in provincial ways that make it the butt of jokes. For instance, Shyam Bhurtel, a Nepalese Ph.D. from our department who was teaching at a university in his home country, won a Fulbright fellowship to return to Auburn for postdoctoral study. After landing in Atlanta, he rented a car and began driving to Auburn. On the way, an Alabama state trooper pulled him over for speeding and asked to see his driver's license. Shyam had neglected to acquire an international license, but had his Nepalese document. He showed it to the trooper, hoping it would substitute for an American license. "What is this?" the trooper inquired skeptically. "It's my driver's license from Nepal," Shyam answered. The trooper inspected it carefully, while Shyam, a charming person and wonderful conversationalist, expertly discussed Auburn football. Finally, the trooper returned his license, giving him a warning, then asked: "Nepal? Isn't that up around Sylacauga?" Shyam told the story as a putdown of provincial Alabama state troopers, whose limited knowledge of world geography couldn't even locate Nepal on the correct continent. I attributed a different meaning to the story, concluding that a good-natured trooper, not wanting to ticket an Auburn grad on his first day back in the states, was simply having some fun at Shyam's expense.

Distinguishing provincialism from grass-roots shrewdness is not always easy, but it certainly is important. The best example I know of the contest between folk wisdom, provincialism, and formal education comes from Helen Lewis, a sociologist friend who specialized in Appalachia and whose research I used in *Dixie's Forgotten People*. She summarized a series of letters to the editor that appeared in a paper in Blue Ridge, Georgia. The correspondence concerned Gorilla Haven, a three-hundred-acre sanctuary for gorillas who were aging or had become incorrigible. Fannin County was an all-white mountain redoubt of twenty thousand people a few miles from the North Carolina state line. Many of the residents were newcomers, fleeing Florida hurricanes or northern taxes. Local Appalachian folk were not overjoyed by the influx of outsiders and particularly disliked the idea of the gorillas one couple brought with them. They complained that the sanctuary lowered property values and escapees might even attack local residents. Many newcomers thought these anxieties silly. This provoked a local man to comment that he had rather have the gorillas than the Floridians. Another clever Appalachian wrote that the gorillas would be fine if they were indigenous, but unfortunately they came from somewhere else. That letter inspired a retort from a man who had been in favor of the gorillas until he read the letter but had changed his mind because of the indigenous animal argument. If all animals not indigenous to the Appalachian mountains could be banned or destroyed, then he could shoot his neighbor's yapping Pomeranian dog that kept him awake every night.

I also collected aphorisms, beginning with my father's and continuing right through meals at Ken's Barbeque. Rick Meadows, the State Department of Education lawyer during the equity funding lawsuit possessed the finest single repertoire I ever recorded (they often kept me awake, smirking and writing furiously during agonizingly boring legal discussions). Over four months of deliberations, I recorded dozens of Rick's sayings. Furious at one lawyer's insistence that we reopen an issue long resolved, Rick called his comments "about as useful as a sackful of hammers." He dismissed some consultants cited by plaintiff's lawyers as "dumb as posts." Analyzing a pork barrel proposal, he responded: "In addition to $11.6 million in obvious pork, there is a great deal more money in the budget of a porcine nature." He dismissed another suggestion as "a cocker-spaniel system, by which I mean it goes happily wagging after everything that comes along, as opposed to a Doberman, which is testy and resistant to everything." Growing agitated at one session, Rick raged, "I'm as serious as a heart attack." Describing one diminutive consultant, he confided to me, "She's not as big as a bar of lye soap after a hard day's washing." Ruralism and erudition seldom intersected in a more entertaining fashion.

The Encyclopedia of Alabama

The range of learning from folk wisdom to elite culture is precisely what I was determined to incorporate in the new online Encyclopedia of Alabama (EOA).

When Bob Stewart, director of the Alabama Humanities Foundation (AHF), cornered me one day on the steps of the capitol and asked me to become editor of an electronic online encyclopedia, I thought he had lost his mind. I was just learning how to turn on my office computer and was a confirmed neo-Luddite. At the same time, I recognized the importance of the project. The most recent Alabama encyclopedia dated to the early 1920s. The project, first proposed by the University of Alabama Press and AHF, attracted little enthusiasm from other universities. Some considered the project too parochial; others were overwhelmed by the magnitude of the task. At first, I declined as well. With Auburn in its usual turmoil, me approaching retirement in 2005, and lots of my doctoral students rushing to finish dissertations, the last thing I needed was another long-term project. But Stewart's appeal was convincing. If I didn't do it, no one would, and the project would die aborning. Whoever headed the project had to teach at a major research university with a large library where essays could be fact-checked by graduate students. The project required university support for space, staff, and technology. AHF pledged to organize a major fund-raising drive and to support a grant proposal to the National Endowment for the Humanities (NEH).

I recruited staff, who submitted an NEH planning grant; we met with leaders of the New Georgia Encyclopedia (the NGE had just been started but would soon become the nation's premier online encyclopedia); and we began to draft guidelines and assemble editorial and management boards. My first task was to recruit Jeff Jakeman, a history colleague and director of the department's acclaimed archival administration program. Jeff came on board as editor and brought Steve Murray, one of my gifted graduate students, as assistant editor. They knew computer technology about which I was entirely ignorant. On the other hand, I had one advantage over them: few people possessed a longer list of professional IOUs, knew more folks worldwide who had written about Alabama, or was better connected to foundations and progressive business people.

Jeff was a tenacious bulldog capable of making things work. Technologically sophisticated, meticulous in detail work, resolutely upbeat, he assembled a splendid staff, including my talented former editorial assistant Laura Hill. Jeff found a technology platform that worked for us and that had just gotten NGE up and running.

Although Bob had promised I wouldn't have to raise money, that became one of my primary responsibilities (and one I thoroughly detested). But Bob, Jeff, and the project itself kept me energized. My vision of the project included many components: the encyclopedia could be used for economic development and tourism by people located anywhere in the world; it could be accessed by any Alabama teacher or student by way of a computer (making out-of-date history texts a thing of the past); it allowed Alabama people and scholars of the state to tell our own story, warts and all, in order to balance bad events in state history with wonderful accomplishments; it highlighted the state's magnificent biological, ecological, and geological diversity; and it would build pride in the distinctive history of every county and community. Our campaign committee, chaired by Birmingham philanthropist Edgar Welden and Jim Hayes, my old friend from the Siegelman administration, performed wonderfully. U.S. senator Richard Shelby acquired a substantial slab of pork for us, without which the EOA probably never would have made it online. Many of my longtime friends—Mike Warren, Ed Friend Jr., Ann Bedsole, and a host of others—made substantial contributions as well.

I often claimed in speeches that EOA was the greatest collaborative intellectual venture in the state's history. Academic friends sometimes considered the statement hyperbole. I challenged them to name any academic project in state history that had brought together so wide a coalition of scholars, institutions, and funders. No one ever suggested a better choice. On our home page, we list forty-three partners, including fifteen colleges and universities, plus museums, archives, businesses, publishers, state agencies, newspapers, and other organizations. Any project that could weld together Auburn and the University of Alabama had to be special. State school superintendents Ed Richardson and Joe Morton understood the potential of the project for public schools and provided operating funds that, along with Auburn's support, assured our survival.

As editor in chief (another term for "general flunky"), I had oversight of the project, while Jeff and Steve ran day-to-day operations. I insisted on reading every one of the five hundred–plus essays until I retired after EOA's formal launch at a gala sponsored by AHF on September 15, 2008. I was extremely proud of the high level of scholarship from scholars throughout the world.

Matching author to article was the most daunting part of our job. The scholars were quite busy with their own careers, and many had to be persuaded to participate. Nevertheless, we mostly obtained the authors we wanted. My goal for EOA was simple: I wanted it to speak to and for *all* Alabamians, ordinary people as well as movers-and-shakers. I did not want it to fall victim either to elitism or the special agendas of state agencies, corporations, lawyers, or even academics. I wanted articles to be fair and balanced. I wanted EOA to be as interesting to the patrons of Ken's Barbeque and the people from whom I collected stories and aphorisms as to teachers and professors.

That meant essays on college football, Alabama NASCAR drivers, the Tal-

ladega 500, the Ken Underwood Coon Dog Memorial Graveyard in Colbert
County, Railroad Bill, Gandy Dancers, herb medicine, lane cakes, Mobile's
Mardi Gras, the Tennessee Valley Old Time Fiddlers Convention, Hank Aaron
and Hank Williams, mules, cotton, peanuts, gospel music, the Delmore and
Louvin brothers, and yes, even "Barbeque, Alabama Style." Each article was
signed by the author and corrected or revised as necessary.

We organized the nearly thousand essays into twelve subject categories: agriculture, arts and literature, business and industry, education, folklife, geography and environment, government and politics, history, peoples, religion,
science and technology, sports and recreation. I authored seven essays, representing special interests across my forty-year career: the overview essay on
Alabama; *To Kill A Mockingbird;* religion; Southern Baptists; poverty; biographies of Governor Bibb Graves and Pulitzer Prize–winning journalist Harold
Eugene Martin. It gave me immense satisfaction that so many of my former
graduate students wrote fine essays for EOA as well.

By the encyclopedia's first birthday, the site had received 1.3 million page
hits from a half million visitors from more than 180 countries, all 50 states,
more than 600 school systems, and thousands of colleges and universities. Because we could track readers and their interests, I found the weekly updates as
fascinating as the articles. When a meteorite hit a lady in the UK in June 2008,
a London paper noted that such an event had occurred only once before, in
Sylacauga, Alabama, on November 30, 1954. That week, our most frequently
visited article (1,940 hits) was Sylacauga's "Hodges Meteorite Strike," and most
of the visitors accessed our site from the UK.

When EOA broke the 1 million page barrier ten months after launch, I was
pleased at the most frequently visited fifteen articles. As I had predicted when
we began, they were a representative mixture of the state's past, focusing on
our mistakes and foibles as well as our triumphs and successes. In descending
order of frequency, the articles were the Scottsboro case, Harper Lee, segregation, letter from the Birmingham Jail, plantation architecture, agriculture,
To Kill A Mockingbird, Montgomery bus boycott, Birmingham campaign of
1963, Martin Luther King Jr., Cherokees of Alabama, modern civil rights movement, Creeks, Alabama overview article, "Bull" Connor, and Paul "Bear" Bryant. More importantly, as we trained teachers to use the site, EOA enormously
enriched the education of hundreds of thousands of Alabama children in agriculture, geology, environment, science, business, technology, sports, history,
and culture.

The *Library Journal,* America's premier library publication, recognized our efforts in April 2009 by naming EOA a "Best of Free Reference" work in the United States. It was wonderful recognition of efforts by Jeff, Pat Kaetz (our new managing editor), and the team they assembled. When I retired from the project in 2008, I knew we had created something of great value that would redefine how people throughout the world thought about Alabama and even the way we thought about ourselves. We had honestly confronted our past without letting it define our dreams for the future.

In the end, I am no more sure EOA will survive than that Alabamians will craft a modern constitution, conservatives will consider the welfare of poor children to be a right-to-life issue, evangelical Christians will support a just tax system, or race will cease to be the defining issue in Alabama politics. A person does the best he can saying his lines while on stage, then retires when he can no longer remember them. That is the way life and time work, one generation preparing the way and then moving aside for the next.

I really don't need assurance of victory for my causes or dreams in my lifetime anyway. I only need fidelity to those beliefs that define me as a person. In 1951 my favorite theologian, Reinhold Niebuhr, wrote a prayer that admonished readers to live in a different dimension of time from people who view life in other ways: "Nothing that is worth doing can be achieved in a lifetime; therefore we must be saved by hope. Nothing which is true or beautiful or good makes complete sense in any immediate context of history; therefore we must be saved by faith. Nothing we do, however virtuous, can be accomplished alone. Therefore we are saved by love."

Amen.

Acknowledgments

When writing this memoir, I probed my own memory as the primary source, supplemented by many interviews and oral histories with friends, family, and acquaintances, half a century of extensive correspondence, and an exhaustive clipping file. Not entirely convinced of the invincibility of my own memory, even augmented by a daily journal that I kept intermittently, I asked many participants in these events to read the entire manuscript or at least chapters relevant to their own experience. I thank them for extending to me the greatest gift of friendship: honest, frank, candid criticism. I followed most of their suggestions. Sometimes I trusted my journal more than their memory (though I uniformly trusted their records more than my memory). They also suggested many excellent changes in style, organization, and prose, which improved the narrative.

For the sake of common courtesy and professional honesty, I acknowledge the following friends for the kindness of reading the entire manuscript and thoughtfully criticizing it: my former Samford student and dear friend for nearly five decades Carolyn Johnston, Elie Wiesel Professor of Humanities at Eckerd College, Saint Petersburg, Florida; two of the finest interpreters of the South during the past four decades, historian James C. Cobb, Spalding Distinguished Professor, University of Georgia, and sociologist John Shelton Reed, William Rand Kenan Professor Emeritus, University of North Carolina Chapel Hill. For refreshing my memory about the education reform movement, I salute A+ Education Partnership cofounders Caroline Novak and Bill Smith, as well as the organization's longtime director Cathy Gassenheimer. For family history, I relied tremendously on my father (James Homer Flynt) and mother (Mae Ellis Moore Flynt), my aunt Lillie Mae Beason, and my cousin George Beason.

My literary craftsmanship profited not only from two of the finest fiction writers of the late twentieth century, Nelle Harper Lee and Mary Ward Brown of Monroeville and Hamburg, Alabama, respectively, but also from the deft editorial skills of my talented writer/editor son, Sean. I also thank him for constantly reassuring me that I was not as bad an absentee father as I once believed myself to be. The staff and editors of the University of Alabama Press add value to everything they publish, and this memoir is no exception.

The chapters on Auburn University received the closest and most meticulous scrutiny, partly because they are the most complex, deeply painful, and disputed parts of this memoir. Many Auburn readers tempered, corrected, and qualified my narrative: Dwayne Cox, university archivist who will soon complete the most authoritative history of Auburn University ever written; five former chairs of the university senate—Gerald Johnson, Barry Burkhart, Larry Gerber, Gary Mullen, and Jim Bradley; former academic vice president and W. Kelly Moseley Professor of Science and Humanities emeritus Taylor Littleton; trustees Bob Harris and John Denson. I especially owe all of these readers a debt too large to ever repay for their detailed critique and their willingness to return to unpleasant times and memories.

Finally, I thank Peggy Mason, my friend, unflappable typist, and hieroglyphic interpreter, who does not despair at the scribblings of fountain pen on legal pad that disputes the prevailing technological world and confirms how deeply an unreformed rebel against modernity I really am.

I realize that no memoir, nor any work of history for that matter, is flawless. When telling our own stories, we craft events to our own purposes however committed we are to accuracy and objectivity. I do not doubt that many of the people I criticize in this book would tell the story differently, and I urge them to do so. But in the final analysis, this is the way I remember my own life. I cannot say how others remember theirs. As the younger set says these days, the memoir is what it is, my story.